Communications in Computer and Information Science 2547

Series Editors

Gang Li , *School of Information Technology, Deakin University, Burwood, VIC, Australia*

Joaquim Filipe , *Polytechnic Institute of Setúbal, Setúbal, Portugal*

Zhiwei Xu, *Chinese Academy of Sciences, Beijing, China*

AF172941

Rationale

The CCIS series is devoted to the publication of proceedings of computer science conferences. Its aim is to efficiently disseminate original research results in informatics in printed and electronic form. While the focus is on publication of peer-reviewed full papers presenting mature work, inclusion of reviewed short papers reporting on work in progress is welcome, too. Besides globally relevant meetings with internationally representative program committees guaranteeing a strict peer-reviewing and paper selection process, conferences run by societies or of high regional or national relevance are also considered for publication.

Topics

The topical scope of CCIS spans the entire spectrum of informatics ranging from foundational topics in the theory of computing to information and communications science and technology and a broad variety of interdisciplinary application fields.

Information for Volume Editors and Authors

Publication in CCIS is free of charge. No royalties are paid, however, we offer registered conference participants temporary free access to the online version of the conference proceedings on SpringerLink (http://link.springer.com) by means of an http referrer from the conference website and/or a number of complimentary printed copies, as specified in the official acceptance email of the event.

CCIS proceedings can be published in time for distribution at conferences or as post-proceedings, and delivered in the form of printed books and/or electronically as USBs and/or e-content licenses for accessing proceedings at SpringerLink. Furthermore, CCIS proceedings are included in the CCIS electronic book series hosted in the SpringerLink digital library at http://link.springer.com/bookseries/7899. Conferences publishing in CCIS are allowed to use Online Conference Service (OCS) for managing the whole proceedings lifecycle (from submission and reviewing to preparing for publication) free of charge.

Publication process

The language of publication is exclusively English. Authors publishing in CCIS have to sign the Springer CCIS copyright transfer form, however, they are free to use their material published in CCIS for substantially changed, more elaborate subsequent publications elsewhere. For the preparation of the camera-ready papers/files, authors have to strictly adhere to the Springer CCIS Authors' Instructions and are strongly encouraged to use the CCIS LaTeX style files or templates.

Abstracting/Indexing

CCIS is abstracted/indexed in DBLP, Google Scholar, EI-Compendex, Mathematical Reviews, SCImago, Scopus. CCIS volumes are also submitted for the inclusion in ISI Proceedings.

How to start

To start the evaluation of your proposal for inclusion in the CCIS series, please send an e-mail to ccis@springer.com

Francisco José Domínguez Mayo ·
Luís Ferreira Pires · Edwin Seidewitz
Editors

Model-Based Software and Systems Engineering

12th International Conference, MODELSWARD 2024
Rome, Italy, February 21–23, 2024
Revised Selected Papers

 Springer

Editors
Francisco José Domínguez Mayo
University of Seville
Seville, Spain

Luís Ferreira Pires
University of Twente
Enschede, The Netherlands

Edwin Seidewitz
Model Driven Solutions
Frederick, MD, USA

ISSN 1865-0929   ISSN 1865-0937 (electronic)
Communications in Computer and Information Science
ISBN 978-3-031-96840-2   ISBN 978-3-031-96841-9 (eBook)
https://doi.org/10.1007/978-3-031-96841-9

This Springer imprint is published by the registered company Springer Nature Switzerland AG
The registered company address is: Gewerbestrasse 11, 6330 Cham, Switzerland

If disposing of this product, please recycle the paper.

Preface

The present book includes extended and revised versions of a set of selected papers from the 12th International Conference on Model-Based Software and Systems Engineering (MODELSWARD 2024), held in Rome, Italy, from 21–23 February.

The International Conference on Model-Based Software and Systems Engineering provides a platform for participants from all over the world to present research results and application experience in using model-based techniques for developing all sorts of systems. Model-based software engineering has emerged over many years as an approach for developing IT systems in which models take a central role, not only for the analysis of these systems but also for their construction. More recently, a similar approach has become increasingly widely used not only for software systems, but also for physical, cyber-physical and business systems. This model-based software and systems engineering approach relies on an increasingly rich ecosystem of techniques, languages and tools. MODELSWARD is an opportunity for researchers and practitioners alike to come together and discuss, moving this ecosystem forward.

MODELSWARD 2024 received 47 paper submissions from 22 countries, of which 7 (28%) were included in this book.

The papers were selected by the event chairs and their selection was based on a number of criteria that included the classifications and comments provided by the program committee members, the session chairs' assessment and also the program chairs' global view of all papers included in the technical program. The authors of selected papers were then invited to submit revised and extended versions of their papers having at least 30% novel material.

The papers selected to be included in this book contribute to the understanding of relevant trends of current research on Model-Based Software and Systems Engineering, including: Modeling Environments, Modeling Language Engineering, Software and Systems Engineering, Modeling Languages and Standards, Domain-Specific Modeling, Frameworks for Model-Based Development, Model Transformation, Generative Approaches, Artificial Intelligence (AI) for Modeling Support and Modeling for AI Applications.

We would like to thank all the authors for their contributions and also the reviewers who have helped to ensure the quality of this publication.

February 2024

Francisco José Domínguez Mayo
Luís Ferreira Pires
Edwin Seidewitz

Organization

Conference Chair

Edwin Seidewitz   Model Driven Solutions, USA

Program Co-chairs

Francisco José Domínguez Mayo   University of Seville, Spain
Luís Ferreira Pires   University of Twente, Netherlands

Program Committee

Achilleas Achilleos   Frederick University, Cyprus
Ludovic Apvrille   Télécom Paris, Institut Polytechnique de Paris,
                            France
Souvik Barat   Tata Consultancy Service Research, India
Ankica Barisic   Université Côte d'Azur, I3S/Inria, France
Andreas Biesdorf   Trier University of Applied Sciences/Siemens
                            AG, Germany
Antonio Brogi   Università di Pisa, Italy
Manfred Broy   Technische Universität München, Germany
Christian Bunse   Stralsund University of Applied Sciences,
                            Germany
Jan Carlson   Mälardalen University, Sweden
Yoonsik Cheon   University of Texas at El Paso, USA
Dickson Chiu   University of Hong Kong, China
Massimo Cossentino   National Research Council of Italy (CNR), Italy
Cihan Dagli   Missouri University of Science & Technology,
                            USA
Francisco Duarte   University of Minho, Portugal
Sophie Ebersold   Université Toulouse II-Le Mirail, France
Holger Eichelberger   Universität Hildesheim, Germany
Vladimir Estivill   Universitat Pompeu Fabra, Spain
Stephan Flake   S&N CQM Consulting & Services GmbH,
                            Germany
Verena Geist   Software Competence Center Hagenberg, Austria

Giovanni Giachetti   Universidad Andrés Bello, Chile
Paola Giannini   University of Piemonte Orientale, Italy
Alexander Kamkin   ISPRAS, Russian Federation
Guy Katz   Hebrew University of Jerusalem, Israel
Jun Kong   North Dakota State University, USA
Christian Kop   University of Klagenfurt, Austria
Tomaž Kosar   University of Maribor, Slovenia
Vinay Kulkarni   Tata Consultancy Services, India
Pierre Laforcade   Le Mans Université, France
Lucas Lima   Universidade Federal Rural de Pernambuco,
    Brazil
Dongxi Liu   CSIRO, Australia
Luis Llana   Universidad Complutense de Madrid, Spain
David Lorenz   Open University, Israel
Der-Chyuan Lou   Chang Gung University, Taiwan
Beatriz Marín   Universidad Politécnica de Valencia, Spain
Assaf Marron   Weizmann Institute of Science, Israel
Steve McKeever   Uppsala University, Sweden
Fredrik Milani   University of Tartu, Estonia
Dragan Milicev   University of Belgrade, Serbia
André Miralles   INRAE - National Research Institute for
    Agriculture, Food and Environment, France
Stefan Naujokat   TU Dortmund, Germany
Clémentine Nebut   LIRMM, Université de Montpellier, France
Mykola Nikitchenko   Taras Shevchenko National University of Kyiv,
    Ukraine
Olaf Owe   University of Oslo, Norway
Ian Peake   RMIT University, Australia
Branko Perisic   Singidunum University, Serbia
Dana Petcu   West University of Timisoara, Romania
Roberto Pietrantuono   Università degli Studi di Napoli Federico II, Italy
Henderik A. Proper   TU Wien, Austria
Elke Pulvermüller   Osnabrück University, Germany
Jochen Quante   Robert Bosch GmbH, Germany
Aurora Ramirez   University of Córdoba, Spain
Ana Ramos   University of Aveiro, Portugal
Gianna Reggio   Università di Genova, Italy
Yassine Rhazali   Moulay Ismail University of Meknes, Morocco
Alberto Rodrigues da Silva   IST/INESC-ID, Portugal
Colette Rolland   Université Paris 1 Panthéon-Sorbonne, France
Norsaremah Salleh   International Islamic University Malaysia,
    Malaysia

Stefan Sauer	Paderborn University, Germany
Christian Schlegel	Technische Hochschule Ulm, Germany
Jean-Guy Schneider	Monash University, Australia
Wieland Schwinger	Johannes Kepler University Linz, Austria
Anthony Simons	University of Sheffield, UK
Alin Stefanescu	University of Bucharest, Romania
Krzysztof Stencel	University of Warsaw, Poland
Arnon Sturm	Ben-Gurion University of the Negev, Israel
Andreas Tolk	MITRE Corporation, USA
Jan Tretmans	ESI (TNO) and Radboud University, Netherlands
Naoyasu Ubayashi	Waseda University, Japan
Sylvain Vauttier	Université de Montpellier, IMT Mines Alès, France
Jacques Verriet	TNO-ESI, Netherlands
Mirko Viroli	University of Bologna, Italy
Gera Weiss	Ben Gurion University of the Negev, Israel
Gereon Weiss	Fraunhofer Institute for Cognitive Systems IKS, Germany
Husnu Yenigun	Sabanci University, Turkey
Marc Zeller	Siemens AG, Germany
Kamil Zyla	Lublin University of Technology, Poland

Invited Speakers

Francis Bordeleau	École de Technologie Supérieure, Université du Québec, Canada
Jordi Cabot	Luxembourg Institute of Science and Technology, Luxembourg
Federico Ciccozzi	Mälardalen University, Sweden

Contents

Methodologies, Processes and Platforms

A Framework for Comparative Analysis of News Content: A Model-Based
Approach 3
    Bahareh Fatemi, Fazle Rabbi, Yngve Lamo, and Andreas L. Opdahl

Analyzing Side-Tracking of Developers Using Object-Centric Process
Mining 23
    Saimir Bala, Thanh Nguyen, and Jan Mendling

Enhancing Scenario-Based Modeling Using Large Language Models 43
    David Harel, Guy Katz, Assaf Marron, and Smadar Szekely

Model-Driven Development of Chatbot Microservices 69
    Adel Vahdati and Raman Ramsin

DynaTool: A Tool for Optimizing Hybrid Software Process 88
    María Cecilia Bastarrica, Luis Silvestre, Andrés Wallberg,
    and Daniel González

Modeling Languages, Tools and Architectures

Specifying, Analysing and Implementing Decision-Support System
Architectures 107
    Mert Ozkaya, Mehmet Alp Kose, and Egehan Asal

An Approach for the Comparative Evaluation of Requirements
Formalisation Approaches 132
    Shekoufeh Kolahdouz Rahimi, Kevin Lano, Sobhan Yassipour Tehrani,
    Chenghua Lin, Yiqi Liu, and Muhammad Aminu Umar

A Pluggable Type Checker for Representing Kinds of Quantities 151
    Steve McKeever

Model-Driven Engineering for Data Provenance: A Graphical W3C PROV
Modeling Tool 173
    Marcos Alves Vieira and Sergio T. Carvalho

LLM as a Code Generator in Agile Model Driven Development 198
    Ahmed R. Sadik, Sebastian Brulin, Markus Olhofer,
    Antonello Ceravola, and Frank Joublin

A Modeling Framework for Hardware-Software Systems with Machine
Learning Components 213
    Francesco Bedini, Tino Jungebloud, Ralph Maschotta,
    and Armin Zimmermann

Code Generation for Smart Contracts in Enterprise Application Integration 229
    Mailson Teles-Borges, Rafael Z. Frantz, Jose Bocanegra,
    Eldair F. Dornelles, Sandro Sawicki, Fabricia Roos-Frantz,
    Antonia M. Reina-Quintero, and Carlos Molina-Jimenez

Deploying Machine Learning for Automatic Metamodel Instance
Generation 247
    El Abbassia Deba, Karima Berramla, and Abou EL Hassene Benyamina

Author Index 269

Methodologies, Processes and Platforms

A Framework for Comparative Analysis of News Content: A Model-Based Approach

Bahareh Fatemi[1(✉)] ⓘ, Fazle Rabbi[1] ⓘ, Yngve Lamo[2] ⓘ, and Andreas L. Opdahl[1] ⓘ

[1] University of Bergen, Bergen, Norway
{bahareh.fatemi,fazle.rabbi,andreas.opdahl}@uib.no
[2] Western Norway University of Applied Sciences, Bergen, Norway
yngve.lamo@hvl.no

Abstract. In the digital age, the volume of news data available from diverse sources is vast and continually growing. On the one hand, the quantity of information can overwhelm reporters and on the other hand, news reporting is further complicated by the inherent complexities of multifaceted events that evolve over time, as well as the biases and perspectives that different reporters and media outlets bring to their coverage. Despite such challenges, journalists must report on events in a timely and ethical manner. However, there is a lack of computational methods for analyzing massive news streams in an explainable and responsible way. In this paper, we propose a content based news analysis framework based on news comparison that enables modeling various analytical tasks such as analyzing the perspectives of news publishers, monitoring the progression of news events from various perspectives, exploring the evolution patterns of events over time and analyzing news article variants and for uncovering underlying story-lines. Our approach utilizes a knowledge graph to represent key concepts in the news domain, such as events and their contextual information, across various dimensions. This facilitates a multi-dimensional and comparative analysis of news article variants. We demonstrate the practical applicability of our method through a running example. By adopting a model-based approach, our framework offers the flexibility needed to represent a broad spectrum of domain concepts.

Keywords: Category theory · Content analysis · Model-based framework · Knowledge graph · Natural language processing · Computational journalism

1 Introduction

In every human community, individuals share news to keep one another informed about significant events and developments. News plays a crucial role in this exchange of information, and journalists are tasked with the responsibility of turning facts into engaging and informative stories [21]. Good journalism is grounded in core ethical principles such as *trust and accuracy*; *independence*; *fairness and impartiality*; *humanity*; and *accountability* [2]. However, it is important to recognize that completely unbiased journalism is an ideal that is rarely achieved in practice [9,21]. The subjective nature of news reporting and the presence of bias are inherent aspects of the media landscape.

© The Author(s), under exclusive license to Springer Nature Switzerland AG 2026
F. José Domínguez Mayo et al. (Eds.): MODELSWARD 2024, CCIS 2547, pp. 3–22, 2026.
https://doi.org/10.1007/978-3-031-96841-9_1

4   B. Fatemi et al.

One of the key challenges for journalists is to account for these various perspectives and present a balanced view of events, despite the subjective nature of news. A significant challenge for journalists is to navigate these diverse perspectives and offer a balanced portrayal of events. Journalists also need to keep track of ongoing events worldwide, and carefully analyze their dynamics to inform their audience about the changing world. As global media coverage grows more abundant, journalists and researchers face the challenge of distilling complex and evolving narratives from vast amounts of data. The need to analyze event progression stems from the desire to uncover how events unfold, identify emerging trends, and understand the dynamics and causal relationships among different phases of an event. However, this task is complicated by the dynamic nature of news coverage and the vast amount of information from diverse sources. A major challenge in this process is managing and interpreting data from numerous publishers, each offering unique and sometimes conflicting narratives. This need for effective analysis extends beyond journalism to other disciplines, including sociology, history, political science, and information science, where professionals also rely on news articles for various forms of research and insight. In this paper we present a model-based framework that employs a diverse range of models to represent knowledge from news articles and uses computational methods for the analysis of news events. This paper is an extended version of our previous work [15], where the foundational concepts of a multidimensional meta-model for news content analysis were introduced. The extended framework integrates the following components:

- state-of-the-art natural language processing technique for parsing content from news articles;
- a multi dimensional meta-model allowing data to be arranged into hierarchical groups and a knowledge graph schema for structuring event related information;
- a content comparison method based on category theory;
- a logical framework for capturing the content-based dynamic patterns of events; and
- a statistical analysis method for analyzing news article variants.

We utilize knowledge graphs to represent news events, incorporating key information such as the source article, publication date, involved persons, involved countries. To enhance the clarity and consistency of our representations, we also annotate news events using IPTC (International Press Telecommunications Council) Media Topics and store it as an important dimension. IPTC is a global standardization organization that provides metadata standards for the news industry. The hierarchical structure of IPTC Media Topics enables the extraction of news events across various levels of abstraction. By combining different attributes and relationships of news events along with the domain ontology in IPTC Media Topics, the framework allows users to extract different views of news events from a knowledge graph.

The framework integrates a computational model based on category theory which allows us to analyze news events at a higher abstraction level, for example, to compare and categorize events and to analyze flow of progression of events. We present novel application areas of category theory for analyzing events stored in a knowledge graph and how they progress.

In Sect. 2, we present a method for extracting structured information about news events from news articles using large language models (LLMs). We present a running example while describing the proposed method. In Sect. 3, we present our model-based framework for content analysis. In Sect. 4, we provide a discussion about the proposed method and provide a comparison with existing works.

2 Harvesting News Events Knowledge Graph with a Pre-trained LLMs

Harvesting news events into a knowledge graph is an important topic that has been investigated in several projects to support various tasks within the news domain. Opdahl et al. [14] provide a comprehensive review on the use of semantic knowledge graphs in news production, distribution, and consumption, highlighting their potential to integrate heterogeneous information across the news industry. The Global Database of Events, Language, and Tone (GDELT) is a Google-sponsored project that monitors news media from all over the world and provides a real-time update of events in every 15 min [3]. Rospocher et al. present a method to automatically build Event-Centric Knowledge Graphs from news articles using NLP techniques, such as Entity Linking and Semantic Role Labeling [16]. Liu et al. introduce a domain-specific knowledge graph called the "news graph" that incorporates collaborative relations between entities and topic context information for news recommendations [13]. Berven et al. study the harvesting of news events into a knowledge graph by presenting a knowledge graph platform for newsrooms [5]. They propose an event detection technique that identifies potentially newsworthy events from clusters of news items according to named entities, topics, and location.

To structure the information about news events we propose to use a dimensional meta-model (Fig. 1 top) which allows storing events with contexts along various dimensions in a hierarchical model. The lower section of Fig. 1 illustrates a knowledge graph schema designed to structure events and their contextual information, including the event's location, involved countries, and entities. This knowledge graph is further enriched with IPTC Media Topics, enabling access to hierarchical information through the *:HAS_PARENT* relationships. A Neo4j graph database has been used to store news events and their relationships with other entities. The information model is centered around *Event* which also allows us to preserve the epistemic view of individual publishers. For example, if two publishers publish 2 news articles about a certain event, we will be storing 2 instances of $Event$ (along with their contextual information) in our knowledge graph.

In our proposed technique, we take input from GDELT every 15 min. The input includes web addresses to news article texts. These articles are parsed for analysis using pre-trained large language models (LLMs). Specifically, we use GPT-3.5 Turbo to extract information from the news articles and harvest news event related information. LLMs have shown their effectiveness in annotating natural language text based on predefined ontologies[20]. In our previous study we explored the effectiveness of GPT language model in the classification of news articles in IPTC news ontology [8]. Particularly GPT 3.5 Turbo model in zero-shot setting was 82% and 61% successful respectively in first and second level classification of news articles according to IPTC ontology. We explored two prompting strategies namely **simultaneous classification** in

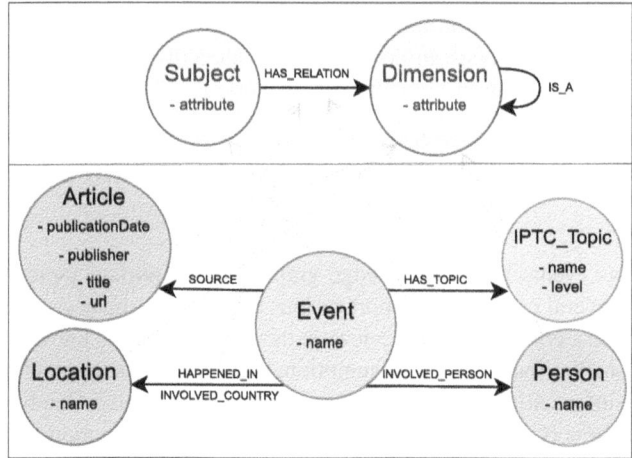

Fig. 1. Dimensional meta-model (top) and Knowledge Graph Schema (bottom) for structuring event related information.

which we provided the model with the entire ontology and tasked it with the simultaneous classification of a news article into one of the Level-1 categories and its corresponding Level-2 subcategories, and **hierarchical classification** in which we initially provided the model with Level-1 categories and requested it to classify the news article accordingly. After determining the Level-1 category, we provided the corresponding subcategories belonging to the chosen category and tasked the model with classifying the news article into a specific subcategory. The experiments showed that in the hierarchical approach some issues related to misclassification and hallucination was effectively resolved or mitigated. Although by fine-tuning GPT model they can perform more effectively, for this study we relying on their ability to annotate data according to IPTC news codes in zero-shot setting.

Figure 2 illustrates the general structure of the prompts we have used to extract structured information from news article texts.

The proposed method in this paper is demonstrated with a running example which includes a knowledge graph of news events about $Niger$ and $Gabon$ extracted from the news articles published by 6 media outlets (*aljazeera.com, theguardian.com, reuters.com, independent.co.uk, nytimes.com, and washingtontimes.com*) from July 28th to September 2nd 2023. The knowledge graph consists of news events in $Niger$ and $Gabon$ about two coups that took place during the above-mentioned period.

3   Model-Based Framework for Content Analysis

We propose a novel model-based framework for news content analysis that incorporates techniques for multidimensional comparative analysis. This framework enables the examination of different perspectives on news content, capturing temporal event patterns, and analyzing the progression of events at various levels of abstraction. It allows the user to select an appropriate dimension and abstraction level. For instance, a user might be interested in comparing the perspectives of different publishers over

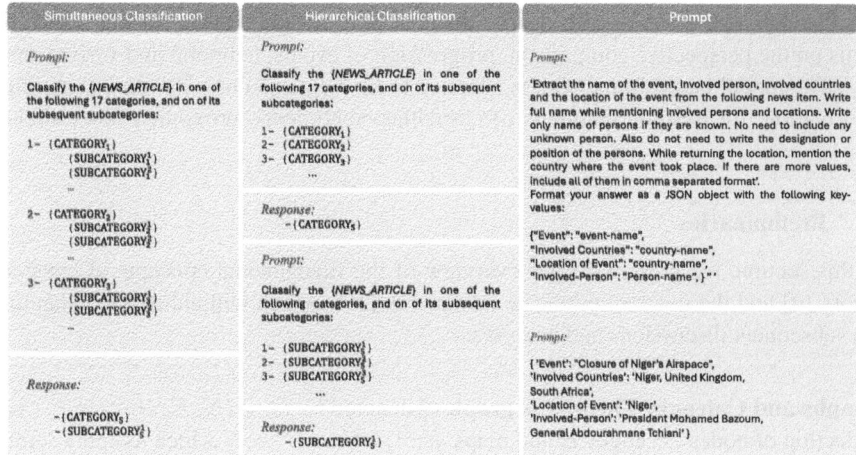

Fig. 2. Prompts for extracting event related information [8, 15].

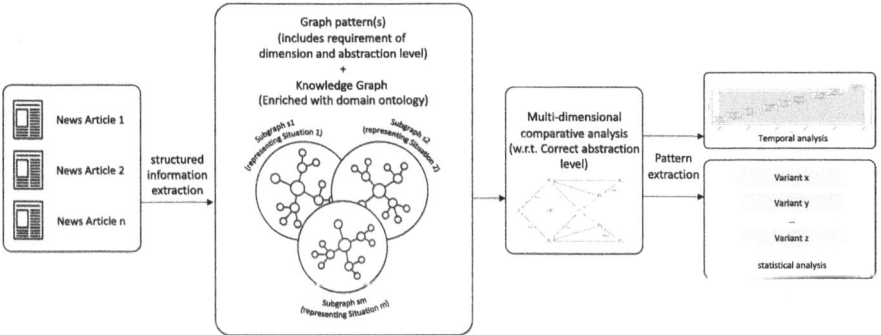

Fig. 3. Model-based framework for multi dimensional comparative analysis of news contents.

a certain period of time or the progression of events at a certain level of abstraction. The knowledge graph incorporates events and their contextual information across various hierarchically organized dimensions. For instance, the *IPTC* Media topic ontology structures topic names in a hierarchy, where the highest level of abstraction (level 1) includes 17 media topic names. This hierarchical organization allows for the selection of dimensions and abstraction levels to extract information from the knowledge graph, which is then used for comparative analysis. The results of this analysis are utilized to identify patterns of variants. We propose a semi-automated approach to variant analysis, involving human input to enhance the process. Figure 3 illustrates the model-based framework which employs models for representing computational methods for the analysis of news events. Graph patterns are used to specify search criteria. We propose to use categorial operations to perform comparative analysis over the search results (i.e., subgraphs). Category theory allows us to deal with abstract structures and relationships between them. It allows us to study the news content from high levels of abstraction and thereby enables us to gain deeper insights into media contents. In this paper we focus on the perspective comparison, progression of events, temporal and variant analysis. The model-based framework is adaptive to new dimensions with more contextual information, for example numbers of casualties, sentiments, proximity, news angles, etc.

3.1 Preliminaries

In this section, we present a brief overview of the fundamental concepts of category theory [4] and the diagram predicate framework [19], which will aid in understanding the subsequent discussions and analyses.

Graphs and Category Theory. A **graph** G denoted by $G = (N, E, src^G, trg^G)$ is a collection of nodes N, edges E and maps $src^G, trg^G : E \rightarrow N$ which assign a source and a target node to each edge E. A **graph homomorphism** $\varphi : G \rightarrow H$ is a pair of maps $\varphi_N : N_G \rightarrow N_H$ and $\varphi_E : E_G \rightarrow E_H$ that preserves the sources and targets:

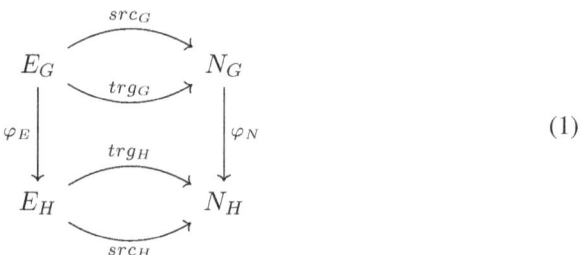

$$(1)$$

A **category** C is a structure in which the following elements participate: a set of objects, denoted as $A, B, C \cdots$, a set of morphisms, denoted as $f, g, h, \cdots$, and a relation that associates to each morphism a pair of objects, which is denoted as $f : A \rightarrow B$, where A and B represent the domain and co-domain of the morphism f, respectively. The composition of the morphisms is written as $g \circ f$ and has two properties

1. Associativity: If $f : A \rightarrow B, g : B \rightarrow C$, and $h : C \rightarrow D$ then $h \circ (g \circ f) = (h \circ g) \circ f$,
2. Identity: For every object X, there exists an identity morphism $1_X : X \rightarrow X$, such that for every morphism $f : A \rightarrow B$, we have $1_B \circ f = f = f \circ 1_A$

The **category graph** has graphs as objects and its morphisms are graph homomorphism [17, 19].

In category theory, a maximal **pullback** object A (see Diagram 2) is a construction that captures the common elements and relationships between objects B and C in a category, and a minimal **pushout** D is the result of gluing two objects along a common sub-object [6]:

$$
\begin{array}{ccc}
A & \xrightarrow{f} & B \\
{\scriptstyle g}\downarrow & & \downarrow{\scriptstyle g'} \\
C & \xrightarrow{f'} & D
\end{array}
\qquad (2)
$$

Table 1. A sample signature $\Sigma_1 = (\Pi^{\Sigma_1}, \alpha^{\Sigma_1})$ used for conflict modelling.

Name ($P \in \Pi^{\Sigma_1}$)	Arity ($\alpha^{\Sigma_1}(P)$)	Semantic Interpretation ($[\![P]\!]$)
[IPTC_Topic]	$E \xrightarrow{f} I$	$\exists e \in E, (\|f(e)\| \geq 0)$
[Location]	$E \xrightarrow{g} C$	$\exists e \in E, (\|g(e)\| \geq 0)$
[Person]	$E \xrightarrow{h} P$	$\exists e \in E, (\|h(e)\| \geq 0)$

Table 2. The atomic constraints from Table 1 and their graph homomorphisms.

Name ($P \in \Pi^{\Sigma_1}$)	Arity ($\alpha^{\Sigma_1}(P)$)	$\delta(\alpha^{\Sigma_1}(P))$
[IPTC_TOPIC]	$E \xrightarrow{f} I$	$Event \xrightarrow{\text{HAS\_Topic}} IPTC\_Topic$
[Location]	$E \xrightarrow{g} C$	$Event \xrightarrow{\text{HAPPENED\_IN}} Country$
[Person]	$E \xrightarrow{h} P$	$Event \xrightarrow{\text{INVOLVED\_PERSON}} Person$

The pullback object can be seen as a generalized intersection of two objects over a common third object, while a pushout can be seen as a disjoint union (where the common part is preserved) of them.

Diagram Predicate Framework (DPF). DPF [19] is a meta-modeling framework founded on the mathematical principles of category theory and graph theory. It offers a graphical notation for defining models and their interrelationships, making it an effective tool for representing complex systems and concepts. DPF enables the specification of models across various levels of abstraction and facilitates the definition of structure and constraints through the use of predicates. These predicates can be applied to a model or a segment of a model to delineate properties or conditions that the model must fulfill.

The relationship between knowledge graphs and the DPF lies in their shared use of graph-based representations to model complex systems and their interconnections. Knowledge graphs map entities and their relationships using nodes and edges, but DPF takes this a step further by introducing constraints and predicates that enforce logical consistency. Both frameworks provide hierarchical modeling and abstraction, breaking down intricate concepts into manageable layers of detail. DPF's predicates add a semantic layer similar to ontologies in knowledge graphs, setting rules and properties that validate the model. Moreover, with its roots in category theory, DPF can bring a solid mathematical foundation to the expressive nature of knowledge graphs.

In DPF, a model or specification $G = (S, C^G : \Sigma)$ comprises an underlying graph S along with a set of constraints C^G, which are defined by a predicate signature $\Sigma = (\Pi^\Sigma, \alpha^\Sigma)$. A predicate signature encompasses a collection of predicates, each of which has a name and an arity (also referred to as a shape graph). A constraint involves a predicate from the signature in conjunction with the sub-graph of the model's base graph that is impacted by the constraint. The semantics of a predicate is the set of all graphs that satisfy the predicate denoted as $[\![P]\!]$, called its set of valid instances. Table 1 shows three predicates defined on the model in Fig. 1. In Sect. 3.4, we will apply these predicates to our temporal pattern analyses.

3.2 Perspective Comparison

Understanding news coverage requires more than just knowing what events occurred; it involves analyzing how different sources report on these events. Perspective comparison is a crucial aspect of news analysis because it uncovers the varied ways in which different publishers interpret, emphasize, and present information about the same events.

In this section, we present a method for perspective comparison that leverages the knowledge graph to analyze how various publishers report on events. In our proposed method, we compare the perspectives across various dimensions of these events. For instance, we examine the types of events that were reported by different publishers during a specific time period while they were covering a particular event and its subsequent development.

To effectively compare the perspectives of different publishers on the same news events, we propose leveraging category theory operations, particularly pullbacks and commutative diagrams. This approach enables a structured and formal analysis of how different sources report on the same events and helps identify commonalities and differences in their reporting. Figure 4 gives an overview of the proposed method for perspective analysis. All news article-related information is represented as a graph database, denoted as I. It contains comprehensive information about news events, including details such as event locations, event types, and involved countries and individuals.

To compare the perspectives of different publishers, we represent their individual reports as subgraphs of I. Specifically, S_1 and S_2 in the figure represent the reports from two different publishers. These subgraphs can be computed by querying the graph database using Cypher queries [1], which extract fragments of the graph that correspond to the local perspectives of the publishers. For example, if we are interested in comparing how two publishers cover the same event, we can extract subgraphs that contain the media topics and event details reported by each publisher. The objective is to analyze the extent to which the media topics used by the two publishers align or differ in their coverage of specific events.

The pullback object C in Fig. 4 which is computed from the following two morphisms: $S_1 \xrightarrow{m_1} I$ and $S_2 \xrightarrow{m_2} I$ is central to our method for perspective comparison. It captures the information about the events from the perspectives of both S_1 and S_2. From the pullback object, we can figure out the perspectives of different publishers as shown in Fig. 4 by object D_1 and D_2.

Here the proposed method is illustrated through a running example. The focus is on computing and comparing the perspectives of two publishers regarding their news stories covering events in *Niger* from July 28th to September 2nd. While the pullback object can be computed programmatically using general-purpose programming languages (e.g., Python with the Neo4j library), this paper demonstrates how a Cypher query can be employed to perform this computation. Cypher queries are utilized to extract relevant data from the Neo4j graph database. Cypher, a query language for graph databases, allows queries to be expressed as graph patterns involving variables. These queries retrieve specific subgraphs from the entire graph database that represent

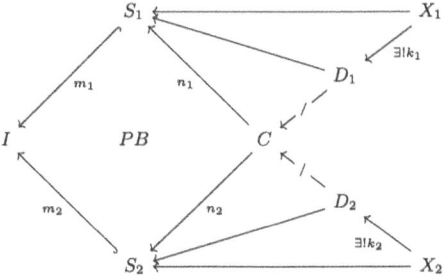

Fig. 4. Pullback object (C) computes the commonality between S_1 and S_2; D_1 and D_2 objects are used to compute the dissimilarities between S_1 and S_2 [15].

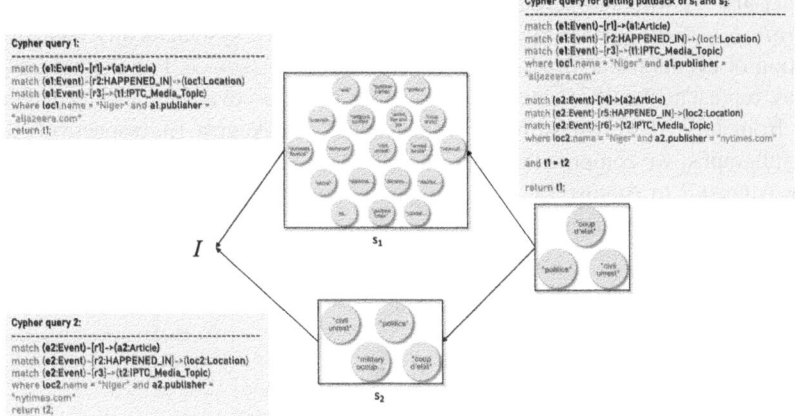

Fig. 5. Computing pullback with Cypher query [15].

the news stories covered by the two publishers. Specifically, Fig. 5 presents a Cypher query that combines two separate queries to compute the pullback object of the two subgraphs extracted from the graph database. To ensure that the diagram commutes, the condition $t1 = t2$ is specified in the query. Since the two subgraphs S_1 and S_2 include only nodes of type $IPTC\_MediaTopic$, we include $IPTC\_MediaTopic$ nodes in the result pullback object. Figure 5 shows a cypher query expression to compute the pullback object of $S_1 \to I$ and $S_2 \to I$. The perspectives of the publishers are computed from the difference of the subgraphs S_1 and S_2 with the pullback object. Here we have demonstrated the perspective analysis with respect to *IPTC* media topics but the other dimensions can also be used for perspective analysis.

3.3 Analyzing the Progression of Events

Analyzing the progression of events is a crucial task in computational journalism, essential for understanding how news stories develop and change over time. As global media coverage grows more abundant, journalists and researchers face the challenge of dis-

tilling complex and evolving narratives from vast amounts of data. The need to analyze event progression stems from the desire to uncover how events unfold, identify
emerging trends, and understand the dynamics and causal relationships among different phases of an event. However, this task is complicated by the dynamic nature of
news coverage and the vast amount of information from diverse sources. A major challenge in this process is managing and interpreting data from numerous publishers, each
offering unique and sometimes conflicting narratives. There is a lack of tool support in
computational journalism to systematically record events and analyze their progression
to extract meaningful insights. We propose (1) to use features such as names, locations
and *IPTC* topics to group news articles covering stories about closely related topics
and, then, (2) to use category theory to analyze the progression of events by means of
analyzing contents in news articles. We reuse the concept presented in Fig. 4 where we
adapt S_1 and S_2 with a selection of events capturing situations from $time_{x1} - time_{y1}$
and $time_{x2} - time_{y2}$ respectively. From S_1 and S_2 we systematically compare the
evolution of events from $time_{x1} - time_{y1}$ to $time_{x2} - time_{y2}$. For example, S_1 and
S_2 may represent the *IPTC* media topics being used to cover the news events about
Niger from July 31 to August 6 and from August 7 to August 13, respectively. From
these subgraphs, we compute the emerging *IPTC* media topics in the reports published
during August 7 to August 13. This comparative analysis allows journalists to get an
overview of the progression of events.

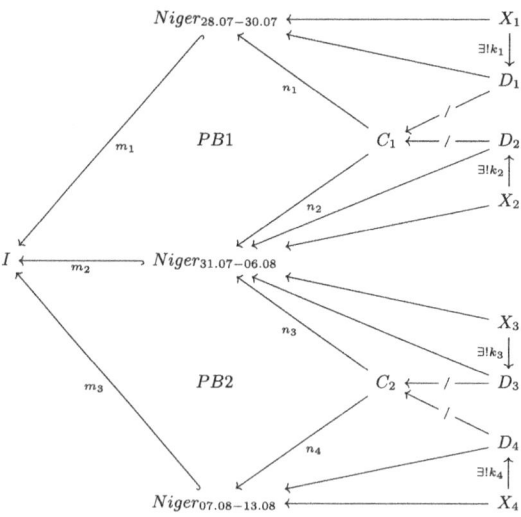

Fig. 6. Capturing the progression of events with pullback operation [15].

The progression of events can be represented as a transformation of *IPTC* media
topics being covered by the publishers. Let us consider that in Fig. 6, $Niger_{28.07-30.07}$
, $Niger_{31.07-06.08}$ and $Niger_{07.08-13.08}$ are representing the *IPTC* media topics being
used to cover the news events in $Niger$ for periods July 28 to July 30, July 31 to August

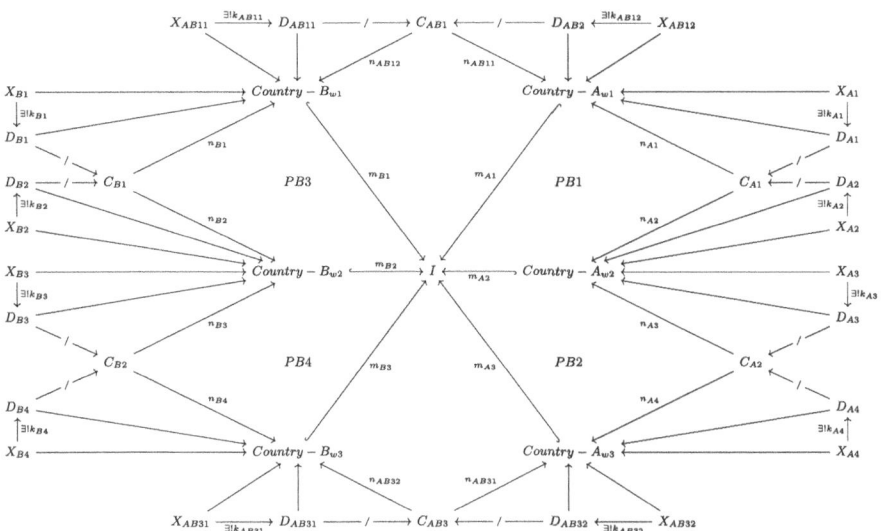

Fig. 7. Comparison of progression of events [15].

6 and August 7 to August 13 respectively. The pullback object C_1 and C_2 represents the commonality of the events (with respect to *IPTC* media topics) in $Niger_{28.07-30.07}$, $Niger_{31.07-06.08}$ and $Niger_{31.07-06.08}$, $Niger_{07.08-13.08}$ respectively. The object D_1 would capture the media topics being removed from the reporting during July 31 to August 6; D_2 would capture the media topics being newly added during July 31 to August 6. Similarly, D_3 would capture the media topics being removed from the reporting during August 7 to August 13 and D_4 would capture the media topics being added during August 7 to August 13.

Similar categorical operations can be employed to analyze the progression of events across two different countries. For instance, consider the task of analyzing the weekly progression of events in *Niger* and *Gabon* since the start of coups in these two countries. Figure 7 illustrates a computational model for such analysis. The pullback object C_{AB1} captures the commonality in the progression of events between the two countries $Country - A$ and $Country - B$, where $Country - A_{w1}$ and $Country - B_{w1}$ represent contextual information of events (such as *IPTC* media topics or involved countries or individuals) reported in the first week. For brevity we did not show C_{AB2} (pullback object between $Country - A_{w2}$ and $Country - B_{w2}$) in the diagram. By examining the pullback objects C_{AB1}, C_{AB2}, C_{AB3}, and so forth, common patterns in the event progression between the two countries can be identified.

Figure 8 illustrates a computation model for the comparison of progression of events at a higher level of abstraction. $\alpha_1, \alpha_2, \beta_1, \beta_2$ represents contextual information of events specified at a certain abstraction level j; In our running example we only have a hierarchical data model for *IPTC* Media topics, therefore, all the *IPTC* Media topics in $\alpha_1, \alpha_2, \beta_1, \beta_2$ are at level j in the *IPTC* Media topic ontology. $\alpha_1', \alpha_2', \beta1', \beta2'$ represents contextual information of events specified at a higher level of abstraction. The

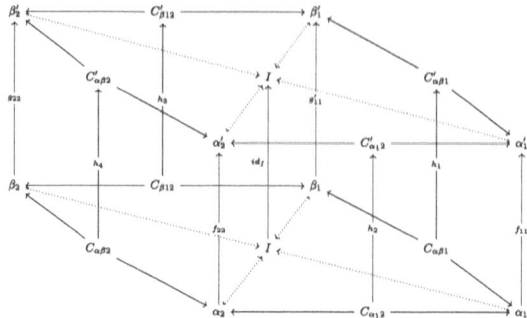

Fig. 8. Comparison of progression of events at a higher level of abstraction [15].

pullback objects $C_{\alpha\beta i}$ (where $i = 1, 2$) in the bottom layer represent the commonality of the progression of events. The arrows between layers represent graph homomorphisms between corresponding elements from lower to higher levels of abstraction in the knowledge graph I.

Theorem: For any non-empty pullback object $C_{\alpha\beta i}$ (where $i = 1, 2$) at level j, the corresponding pullback objects $C'_{\alpha\beta i}$ at level $k < j$ is non-empty.

Proof Sketch: Consider a non-empty pullback object $C_{\alpha\beta i}$ (where $i = 1, 2$) at level j; this would require at least one element $n_a \in \alpha_i$ and one element $n_b \in \beta_i$ where n_a and n_b are mapped to the same element in the knowledge graph. If n'_a (with level k) is a parent of n_a, and n'_b (with level k) is a parent of n_b, then n'_a and n'_b must also map to the same element in the knowledge graph. The pullback objects $C'_{\alpha\beta i}$ should at least contain an element that maps to n'_a and n'_b and therefore cannot be empty.

3.4   Temporal Analysis

The temporal aspect of events in journalism is crucial as events are continuously evolving. Journalistic events are often interconnected, with causal relationships influencing their progression. For instance, a *political crisis* can increase the likelihood of subsequent *armed conflict*. Additionally, events can evolve over time, involving new entities such as international organizations or humanitarian groups in ongoing conflicts or crises. Therefore, capturing the temporal dynamics of events provides valuable insights for journalists.

Linear Temporal Logic (LTL) offers a framework to capture these temporal aspects. We propose enhancing LTL in two ways. First, we incorporate the concept of duration, building on our previous work [7]. Second, we integrate the Diagram Predicate Framework (DPF) and category theory into our LTL definition, thereby enabling a richer representation of the temporal and structural properties of events.

Linear temporal logic (LTL) [10] is a modal temporal logic with modalities referring to (temporal) order of events. We propose LTL_{DGP} (Dynamic Graph Patterns) that models the temporal aspects of the events in our news framework incorporating category theoretical concepts. A well-formed LTL_{DGP} formula with time, ϕ, is therefore recursively defined by the BNF formula below:

$$\phi := \top \mid \bot \mid U \mid \neg\phi \mid \phi \wedge \phi \mid \phi \vee \phi \mid$$
$$\bigcirc_{(TimeInterval)} \phi \mid \Diamond_{(TimeInterval)} \phi \mid$$
$$\Box_{(TimeInterval)} \phi \mid \phi \cup_{(TimeInterval)} \phi$$
$$U := P.n = Atom$$

where P denotes an arbitrary predicate listed in Table 1. Table 2 illustrates how these predicates are mapped to the underlying model. We borrow the notation $P.n$ from the object oriented programming in order to refer to a node n from the extracted portion of a graph based on the predicate P.

$$TimeInterval := \; < Time \mid \; \leq \; Time \mid$$
$$> Time \mid \; \geq \; Time \mid \; = Time$$
$$Time := INT \; second \mid INT \; minute \mid INT \; hour \mid INT \; days \mid$$
$$INT \; week \mid INT \; month \mid INT \; year \mid Time \; and \; Time$$

We also define the time difference between event instances:

$$diff_{Time}((S_i, m_i), (S_{i+1}, m_{i+1})) =$$
$$InstanceTime(S_{i+1}, m_{i+1}) - InstanceTime((S_i, m_i)) \tag{3}$$

where $InstanceTime(x)$ is a function that returns the time associated with event instance x.

Definition 1. *Given a formula ϕ, and an arbitrary path $\pi_E = ((S_1, m_1), (S_2, m_2), (S_3, m_3) \dots)$ π encompasses a sequence of all reports on an arbitrary event E. Each S_i along with its corresponding graph morphism m_i, represents an instance of the schema shown in Fig. 1 at time i. The satisfaction relation $\models$ is defined as follows:*

- $\pi \models \top$
- $\pi \not\models \bot$
- $\pi \models U$ *iff for $P \in \Pi^{\Sigma_1}$, $m_1^* \in [\![P]\!]$ the following diagram commutes, and $O_1^*.n = Atom$:*

$$
\begin{array}{ccc}
P & \xrightarrow{\;\delta\;} & I \\
{\scriptstyle m_1^*}\big\uparrow & & \big\uparrow{\scriptstyle m} \\
O_1^* & \xrightarrow[\;\delta^*\;]{} & S_1
\end{array}
$$

- $\pi \models \neg\phi$ *iff $\pi \not\models \phi$*
- $\pi \models \phi_1 \wedge \phi_2$ *iff $\pi \models \phi_1$ and $\pi \models \phi_2$*
- $\pi \models \phi_1 \vee \phi_2$ *iff $\pi \models \phi_1$ or $\pi \models \phi_2$*
- $\pi \models \phi_1 \rightarrow \phi_2$ *iff $\pi \models \phi_2$ whenever $\pi \models \phi_1$*

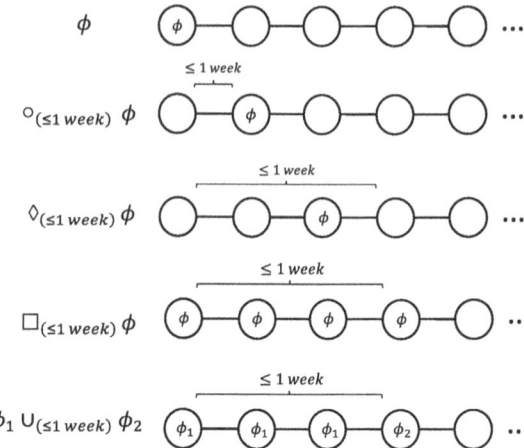

Fig. 9. Example of paths with events and time intervals [7].

- $\pi \models \bigcirc_{(TimeInterval)} \phi$ iff $\pi^2 \models \phi$ and $diff_{Time}(S_1, S_2)$ complies with $TimeInterval$
- $\pi \models \square_{(TimeInterval)} \phi$ iff, for all $i \geq 1, \pi^i \models \phi$ and $diff_{Time}(S_1, S_i)$ complies with $TimeInterval$
- $\pi \models \Diamond_{(TimeInterval)} \phi$ iff, there is some $i \geq 1$ such that for $j \leq i, \pi^j \models \phi$, and $diff_{Time}(S_1, S_i)$ complies with $TimeInterval$
- $\pi \models \phi_1 \cup_{(TimeInterval)} \phi_2$ iff, there is some $i \geq 1$ such that $\pi^i \models \phi_2$ and for all $j = 1, 2, ...i - 1$ we have $\pi^j \models \phi_1$ and $diff_{Time}(S_1, S_i)$ complies with $TimeInterval$.

Figure 9 visualizes the semantics of some operations of our proposed temporal logic. The enhanced expressiveness of LTL_{DGP} empowers us to formulate a diverse range of formulas, allowing for the identification of patterns of interest within the event paths. In the following few example are presented.

- "Eventually, in less than 4 d, there will be an event where an *armed conflict* *(IPTC=20000056)* occurs involving *protesters*." In simpler terms, this formula asserts that within the time interval of 4 days or more, there should be an occurrence of an event classified under the *IPTC* media topic "armed conflict" and involving "protesters". Figure 10a shows an event-set that is satisfied by this formula. The gray area represents the 4 day time interval.

$$\Diamond_{(\geq 4\,days)}(([\texttt{IPTC}].IPTC\_Topic = "20000056")$$
$$\wedge ([\texttt{Person}].Person = "Protesters")) \tag{4}$$

- "Always, in the next 8-day interval, if *political dissent (IPTC=20000648)* occurs at a specific point of time, then *political process (IPTC=20000649)* must occur." In other words, this formula asserts that within an interval of 8 days, if there is an event classified under the *IPTC* media topic 20000648, it must be followed (or accompanied) by an event classified under the *IPTC* media topic (*IPTC*=20000649). Figure 10b shows an event-set that is satisfied by this formula.

$$
\Box_{(\geq\ 8\ \text{days})}(([\texttt{IPTC}].IPTC\_Topic = "20000648")
$$
$$
\rightarrow ([\texttt{IPTC}].IPTC\_Topic = "20000649")) \tag{5}
$$

- "If at any time we encounter a *political crisis* (*IPTC*=20000647), then it should even-tually be followed by an *armed conflict* within a duration of six days." The formula is a conjunction of 2 terms, The first term in the conjunction ensures that at some point in the future, a *political crisis* must be reported. This term uses the diamond oper-ator to assert the eventual occurrence of the event, making it a necessary condition for the subsequent implications to be meaningful. This prevents the formula from holding vacuously by ensuring that the condition of a *political crisis* being reported is an unavoidable event. The second term in the conjunction specifies the temporal relationship that must hold once a *political crisis* occurs. The box operator indicates that the enclosed condition must always hold true for every instance of time follow-ing the initial event. Specifically, it states that whenever a *political crisis* is reported, it must always be followed by an *armed conflict* within the next six days. The gray area represents the 4 day time interval.

$$
(\Diamond_{(\geq\ 0\ \text{seconds})}([\texttt{IPTC}].IPTC\_Topic = "20000647")) \wedge
$$
$$
(\Box_{(\geq\ 0\ \text{seconds})}([\texttt{IPTC}].IPTC\_Topic = "20000647" \rightarrow \tag{6}
$$
$$
\Diamond_{(\leq\ 6\ \text{days})}([\texttt{IPTC}].IPTC\_Topic = "20000056")))
$$

- "If at any point in the future a *political crisis* is reported in *Myanmar*, then within the following 6 days, there must be a report involving *Government*." This formula asserts that if there is an event located in Myanmar and it is classified under the *IPTC* media topic 20000647, then within the next 6 days, there must be an event involving the government.

$$
\Box(\geq\ 0\ \text{seconds})(([\texttt{Location}].Location = "Myanmar" \wedge
$$
$$
[\texttt{IPTC}].IPTC\_MediaTopics = "20000647") \rightarrow \tag{7}
$$
$$
\Diamond_{(\leq\ 6\ days)}([\texttt{Person}].Person = "Government"))
$$

3.5 Variant Analysis

In this section, we introduce a technique for variant analysis based on the computation results from Sect. 3. We apply statistical methods to detect variations in news articles. Section 3.3 detailed techniques for retrieving data from a knowledge graph across var-ious dimensions and abstraction levels. We use this data selection process to identify variants by applying statistical methods. Here, we present *Exploratory Data Analysis* (EDA) for identifying trends in time and space, which serves as the foundation for our variant analysis.

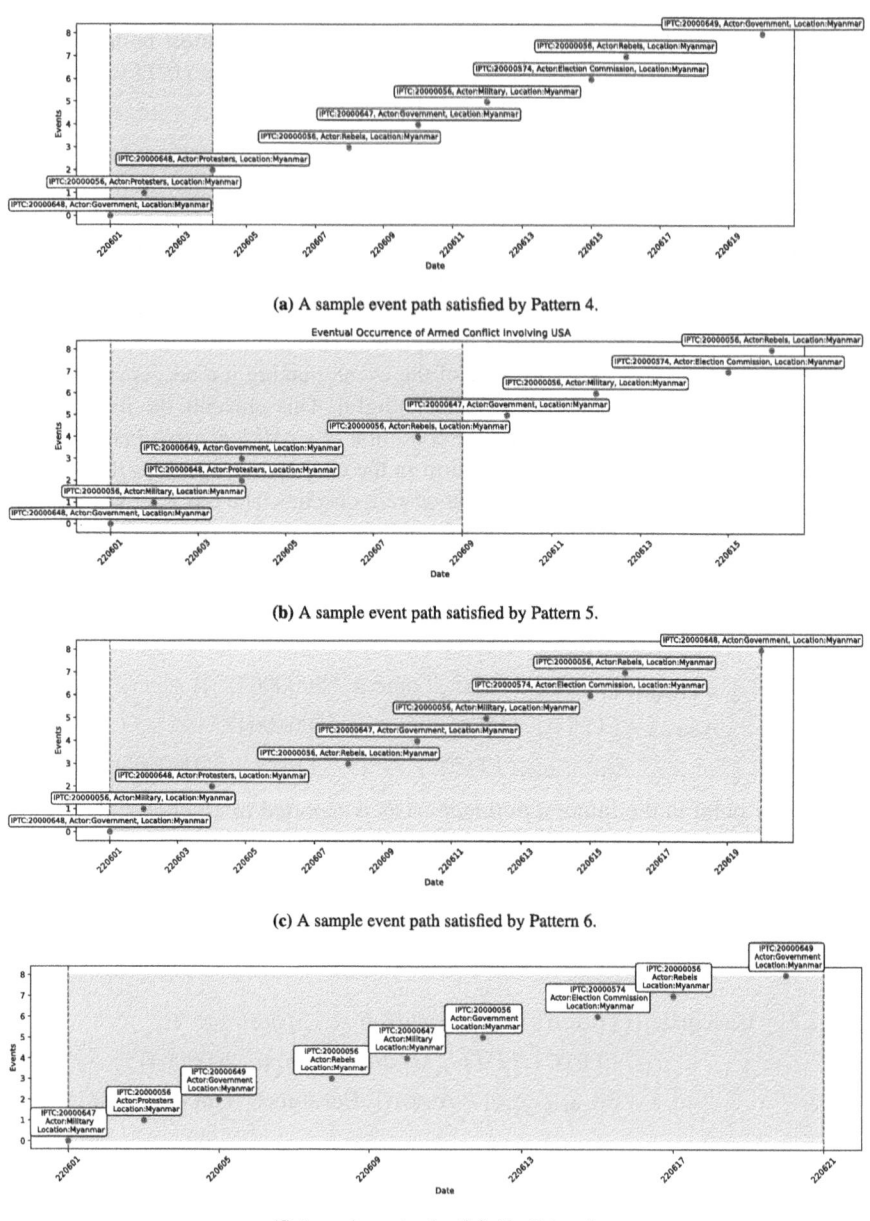

(a) A sample event path satisfied by Pattern 4.

(b) A sample event path satisfied by Pattern 5.

(c) A sample event path satisfied by Pattern 6.

(d) A sample event path satisfied by Pattern 6.

Fig. 10. Timeline Visualization of Event Sequences Satisfying LTL_{DGP} Formulas.

To identify trends in reporting across different topics, a dimension and an abstraction level are first selected, and relevant data is then extracted from the knowledge graph. For instance, to analyze trends in the reporting of *civil unrest* in *Niger* from

August 1 to August 20, 2023, events corresponding to the *civil unrest* topic in the *IPTC* Media topic ontology are retrieved from the knowledge graph. The extracted data is subsequently used for statistical analysis, such as frequency distribution, and for visualizing trends over time using a timeline. Through the visualization of these events on a timeline, patterns of reporting by different publishers are illustrated, and the reporting activity throughout the specified period is tracked.

Figure 11 highlights the duration of engagement of individual publishers (*aljazeera.com*, *theguardian.com*, *reuters.com*, *independent.co.uk*, *nytimes.com*, *washingtontimes.com*, and *cnn.com*) in reporting about *civil unrest* in *Niger*. In the figure, the background represents the co-limit, which is a categorical representation of the union of all events reported by these publishers on the topic of *civil unrest* in *Niger*. From this figure, various aspects of the news coverage can be analyzed, such as the identification of similarities between publishers. For example, it may be observed that *Independent.co.uk* and *WashingtonTimes.com* display similar reporting patterns during the period of *civil unrest* in *Niger*. Such similarities may reveal insights into the approaches of different publishers to the same topic. Beyond the comparison of reporting patterns for a specific topic, the proposed method can be adapted to explore other dimensions of the news dataset. For instance, trends related to the involvement of specific countries in conflicts can be identified by retrieving and analyzing data on different types of conflicts involving various countries. We leverage ontological hierarchies to ensure that we extract events at the appropriate level of abstraction. For example, using the *IPTC* Media topic ontology, we can gather data on coups in African nations and identify common trends in how foreign countries are involved in these events.

4   Discussion and Future Work

In this paper, we have introduced a model-based framework for content analysis in computational journalism. By leveraging knowledge graphs and category theory, our approach enables detailed comparative and temporal analysis of news content across various dimensions and abstraction levels.

In the landscape of news content analysis, various systems such as GDELT [12] have been developed for identifying and organizing news events from vast data streams in structured formats. While GDELT efficiently aggregates and quantitatively analyzes vast volumes of news data, a new approach is needed to enable researchers to dive deeper into individual news events, one which also holds the potential to promote transparency and accountability in news analysis in order to foster more responsible journalism practices.

Our framework for content analysis introduces a novel approach that goes beyond traditional text mining and semantic technologies [11], [18]. In this paper, our primary focus has been on the analysis of various reports pertaining to a specific event, particularly in terms of perspectives. One can furthermore include the intricacies of opinions, reporting angles, tones, and the framing of articles, enriching our understanding of news narratives. We also presented a logical framework that leverages Linear Temporal Logic (LTL) in the context of knowledge graphs to capture and analyze temporal patterns within news storylines. By formulating formulas, we can represent and query

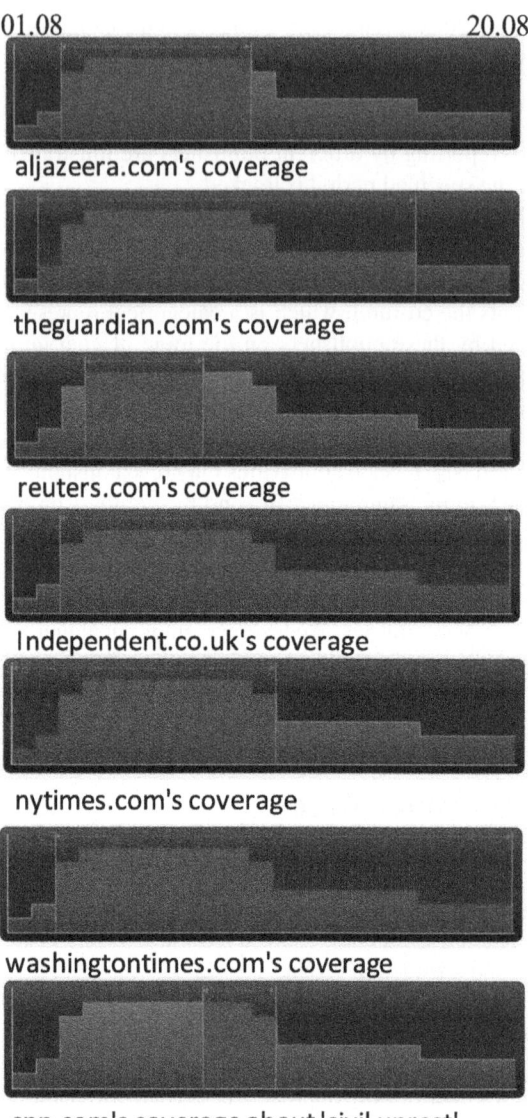

Fig. 11. Timeframe showing the engagement of news publishers in reporting about *civil unrest* in *Niger* [15].

various temporal aspects of event progression. Additionally, we have employed a systematic approach to track the evolution and progression of these events over time which provides insights into how events unfold and transform over time.

While we have presented an analysis technique using category theory, there is much more to explore and develop in this field. We believe that the integration of generative

AI and category theory can contribute to the evolution of journalism in the digital age, fostering transparency, accountability, and enriched news content for both journalists and readers. Particularly, our approach has the capacity to assist in tasks that involve the comparison of news items. For instance, it can be particularly useful in multilingual news comparison, where it can facilitate cross-cultural analysis of news events by overcoming language barriers. It can also be utilized in fact checking and verification, aiding in the assessment of news source credibility. Additionally, it is well-suited for bias and framing analysis, enabling the exploration of different perspectives presented in the media. By addressing these future directions, we hope to enhance the capabilities of the news analysis frameworks and contribute to the advancement of media studies.

Acknowledgement. This research is funded by SFI MediaFutures partners and the Research Council of Norway (grant number 309339).

References

1. Cypher query language (2023). https://neo4j.com/developer/cypher/. Accessed 25 Sept 2023
2. Ethical journalism network (2023). https://ethicaljournalismnetwork.org/who-we-are. Accessed 26 Sept 2023
3. GDELT (2023). https://www.gdeltproject.org/data.html. Accessed 12 Sept 2023
4. Barr, M., Wells, C.: Category Theory for Computing Science. Prentice-Hall Inc., Upper Saddle River (1990)
5. Berven, A., Christensen, O.A., Moldeklev, S., Opdahl, A.L., Villanger, K.J.: A knowledge-graph platform for newsrooms. Comput. Ind. **123**, 103321 (2020). https://doi.org/10.1016/j.compind.2020.103321. https://www.sciencedirect.com/science/article/pii/S0166361520305558
6. Ehrig, H., Ehrig, K., Prange, U., Taentzer, G.: Fundamentals of Algebraic Graph Transformation. Monographs in Theoretical Computer Science. An EATCS Series, Springer (2006)
7. Fatemi, B., Rabbi, F., MacCaull, W.: A validated learning approach to healthcare process analysis through contextual and temporal filtering, pp. 108–137. Springer, Heidelberg (2024). https://doi.org/10.1007/978-3-662-68191-6_5
8. Fatemi, B., Rabbi, F., Opdahl, A.L.: Evaluating the effectiveness of gpt large language model for news classification in the iptc news ontology. IEEE Access **11**, 145386–145394 (2023). https://doi.org/10.1109/ACCESS.2023.3345414
9. Fatemi, B., Rabbi, F., Tessem, B.: Fairness in automated data journalism systems. NIKT: Norsk IKT-konferanse for forskning og utdanning (2023). https://doi.org/10.13140/RG.2.2.30374.19522. https://www.researchgate.net/publication/365127564_Fairness_in_automated_data_journalism_systems
10. Gabbay, D.M., Hodkinson, I., Reynolds, M.A.: Temporal logic: mathematical foundations and computational aspects (1994)
11. Leban, G., Fortuna, B., Brank, J., Grobelnik, M.: Event registry: learning about world events from news. In: Proceedings of the 23rd International Conference on World Wide Web, pp. 107–110. ACM (2014). https://doi.org/10.1145/2567948.2577024
12. Leetaru, K., Schrodt, P.A.: Gdelt: global data on events, location, and tone, 1979–2012. In: ISA Annual Convention, vol. 2, pp. 1–49. Citeseer (2013)
13. Liu, D., Bai, T., Lian, J., Zhao, X., Sun, G., Wen, J.R., Xie, X.: News graph: an enhanced knowledge graph for news recommendation. In: KaRS@ CIKM, pp. 1–7 (2019)

14. Opdahl, A.L., Al-Moslmi, T., Dang-Nguyen, D.T., Gallofré Ocaña, M., Tessem, B., Veres, C.: Semantic knowledge graphs for the news: a review. ACM Comput. Surv. **55**(7), 1–38 (2022)
15. Rabbi, F., Fatemi, B., Lamo, Y., Opdahl, A.L.: A model-based framework for news content analysis. In: MODELSWARD, pp. 99–107 (2024)
16. Rospocher, M., et al.: Building event-centric knowledge graphs from news. J. Web Semant. **37**, 132–151 (2016)
17. Rossini, A.: Diagram predicate framework meets model versioning and deep metamodelling (2011)
18. Rudnik, C., Ehrhart, T., Ferret, O., Teyssou, D., Troncy, R., Tannier, X.: Searching news articles using an event knowledge graph leveraged by wikidata. In: Companion Proceedings of the 2019 world Wide Web Conference, pp. 1232–1239 (2019)
19. Rutle, A.: Diagram predicate framework: a formal approach to mde (2010)
20. Savelka, J., Ashley, K.D.: The unreasonable effectiveness of large language models in zero-shot semantic annotation of legal texts. Front. Artif. Intell. **6** (2023)
21. Schudson, M.: Journalism: Why it Matters. Polity Press, London (2020)

Analyzing Side-Tracking of Developers Using Object-Centric Process Mining

Saimir Bala[1]([⊠])(iD), Thanh Nguyen[1], and Jan Mendling[1,2](iD)

[1] Humboldt Universität zu Berlin, Berlin, Germany
{saimir.bala,thanh.nguyen,jan.mendling}@hu-berlin.de
[2] Weizenbaum Institute, Berlin, Germany

Abstract. Managers need to analyze the software development process to proactively make decisions that meet quality, budget and time objectives. To aid this analysis, a number of data-driven approaches exist, which can be used for specific purposes, such as computing target key performance indicators (KPIs). In particular, process analysis techniques, like process mining, can analyze data from event logs of information systems and deliver actionable insights on how the *process* is conducted. However, traditional process mining techniques make strong assumptions on the structure of event logs, requiring the existence of a *case* identifier, used to group the traces. As a result, the output of such techniques only provides a narrow view of the reality, leading the manager towards wrong interpretations in cases of *side-tracking*, when a developer is involved in different processes that interleave one another. To account for these cases, we investigate the use of object-centric process mining (OCPM) to analyze software repositories. Our results help to explain performance issues by revealing the contributing factors that hinder the progress of development tasks.

Keywords: Process analysis · Software repositories · Object-centric process mining

1 Introduction

Monitoring the software development process is a complex task as it involves many actors who must coordinate their work effectively. Fortunately, there are vast amounts of data collected in the system logs of software repositories that keep track of the work done by developers. To analyze these data from a *process* perspective, process mining techniques have been used [8]. Recently, object-centric process mining (OCPM) [2] has emerged as a new paradigm that allows for multi-dimensional process analysis [22]. OCPM approaches are particularly affine to data from software. Contrary to traditional process mining approaches, they do no require a notion of *case* (which is not present in software development processes [9]), but rather focus on capturing all relevant entities and their relations.

While approaches from literature have tackled the problem of monitoring tasks in software development in a myriad of ways [4,31,39,42], there is still a lack of process analysis techniques. One reason for this, is given by the multi-dimensionality of the

© The Author(s), under exclusive license to Springer Nature Switzerland AG 2026
F. José Domínguez Mayo et al. (Eds.): MODELSWARD 2024, CCIS 2547, pp. 23–42, 2026.
https://doi.org/10.1007/978-3-031-96841-9_2

software process that includes various perspectives such as time, resource, control-flow (hand-over of work), and so on. In this context, literature has analyzed these perspective separately [8]. However, this is not sufficient to understand inter-perspective behavior and may lead to wrong interpretation of the results by the manager [2].

In this paper, we extend previous work [36] to adapt multi-dimensional process analysis techniques from OCPM to analyze software data. We show how to process the input gathered from real-world GitHub repositories to construct event knowledge graphs. We use these graphs to both compute key performance indicators (KPIs) and to perform process analysis. Our approach is able to provide deeper insights in the software development process than traditional process mining. In particular, it is able to uncover inter-perspective behavior such as developer *side-tracking*. With this work, we increase the manager's ability to make informed decisions and show the applicability of OCPM to software data.

The remainder of the paper is structured as follows. Section 2 illustrates the problem at hand, reviews the related literature and derives the research questions. Section 3 describes the research methodology, the goals and details all the steps towards the creation of an artifact to achieve the defined goals. Section 4 provides the results of our artifact applied to a real-world repository from GitHub. Section 5 discusses the results against the research questions and Sect. 6 concludes the paper.

2   Background

This section provides the background of our research. It is divided in three subsections. Section 2.1 states the problem addressed. Section 2.2 presents existing contributions from literature that tackle the problem. On this basis, Sect. 2.3 derives our research questions.

2.1   Problem Statement

Software development is complex and includes many processes aimed at targetting specific aspects that contribute to the engineering of a working artifact. In reality, building a software product is rarely a sequential process. In fact, this is rather a creative endeavour that depends, among other things, on what is the current status of the development and what issues arise along the way.

This nature of software creates a problem for *managers*, who want to help the team and make the best decisions, but do not have precise information about the progress. Therefore, questions like *will we meet the deadline* or *is there more workforce required in a specific task* become hard to answer. Wrong evaluation of the current development status may, among others issues, lead to loss of revenue, trust in the customer, low quality of the delivered product, increased maintenance cost, higher technical debt and other issues [11, 17, 50].

To aid the analysis of software projects, trace data generated from software development is used [8, 18]. Specifically, the software development methodology is analyzed in the details of its constituting elements [30, 47]. Especially, data analysis techniques, such as process mining [1, 2, 49] are used to provide results that are best understood

by managers. In particular, process analysis helps to address key difficulties [49] by
i) providing means to handle the complexity of information via filering techniques; *ii)*
measuring key performance indicators (KPIs); and *iii)* providing a model that is easier
to understand by the manager.

Figure 1 illustrates a common scenario in software development. To implement a
specific feature, an actor (e.g., senior software developer) from the development team
starts to *Implement functionality A*. While working on this task, the developer is called
by a second team because complex issue has occured which needs their expertise. The
actor, after finishing their current task in the *Feature development* process, starts to
work on the activity *Enter Issue to Backlog*, belonging to the *Issue resolution* process.
Working on the issue also requires reporting. The actor does this via completing activity
Report issue which belongs to the *Issue reporting* process. Then, the senior developer
helps the team by contributing to *Resolve current issue* and *Resolve related issues*.
Finally, the senior developer can go back to work in *Feature development* by moving to
activity *Implement functionality B*.

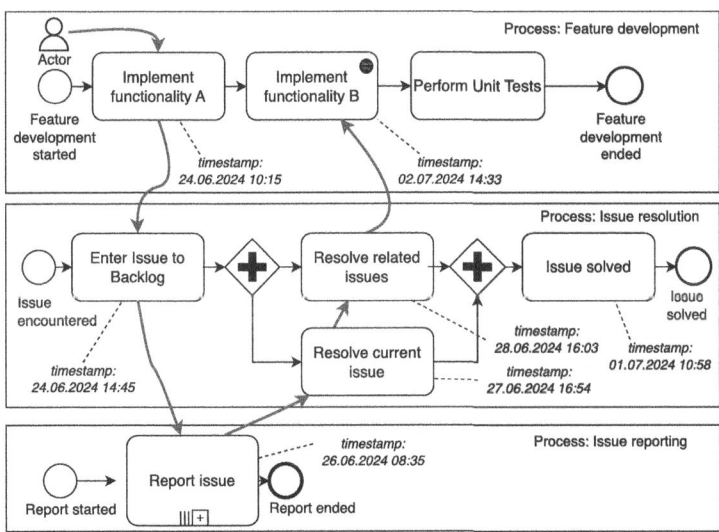

Fig. 1. Illustration of the problem of understanding the progress of a specific software development process. Only the process view is not sufficient to explain why Implement functionality B
takes longer.

In this context, a manager needs to analyze the *Feature development* process to
understand how long it normally takes to perform the activities that require implementation. Thus, the data about this process would be collected and analyzed. Specifically, the manager can see that *Implement functionality A* was finished at the time
marked by timestamp=24.06.2025 10:15 and *Implement functionality B* was finished at timestamp=02.07.2024 14:33. As traditional process mining tools force
the choice of the process to analyze via the requirement of a *case*, the manager has

only the information about these two timestamps and no information about any event that happened outside the *Feature development* process. Therefore, while in reality the actor performed a number of activites, the manager can only see that it took roughly one week to reach the status in which *Implement functionality B* is done. In this scenario the actor peformed useful activities (connected by blue sequence flows) to help the team, but this is not always the case. Performing different actities by developers is also referred to as *side–tracking*. Side–tracking by developers is not always a desired behavior. Furthermore, it makes it hard for managers to assess the current status and the effort that is put in the development, thus hindering their effectiveness.

2.2   Literature Review

Related to the problem illustrated above, there are three research stream upon which we can draw: *i)* Mining Software Repositories; *ii)* Information Systems Research on Open Source Development; and *iii)* Process Analysis and Object-Centric Process Mining.

Mining Software Repositories. In this research stream fall those works which use data mining techniques to compute quantitative analysis (e.g., KPIs) about the software. In this context, the focus is to learn how users relate to the artifacts in the repositories [37], or at analyzing the evolution of changes over time [55]. To achieve that, these techniques are based on identifying process events [54] from the software repository data and abstracting them onto higher-level activities [37]. The goal is to measure aspects of software such as the type of work (i.e., what kind of files are being worked on) [48], the type of resources [5] or measure KPIs [42]. All these works provide valuable insights into the software development efforts done in the project, but focus on low-level indicators or relations.

Furthermore, there are works that target more the managers, by applying process analysis. Pasuksmit et al. [39] evaluate the state of the art on log parsing to prepare input for process mining techniques. Milewicz et al. [34] look into who is driving the evolution of scientific software in collaborative reserach projects. Schipper et al. [43] propose the use process mining for bottlenecks in sprint planning. All these works only take into account traditional process mining, and are therefore not able to directly detect side-tracking.

Information Systems Research on Open Source Development. There is a substantial body of literature in information systems that uses software data, particularly from open source development, to theorize about the process.

Key theoretical works and empirical studies include the following. Carlo et al. [16] studied the impact of adoption timing on innovation outcomes during disruptive innovation cycles, demonstrating how early and late adoption of new technologies influence innovation performance and strategic decision-making. Crowston [19] applied coordination theory to analyze software change processes, identifying mechanisms for task assignment, resource sharing, and managing dependencies in large-scale software development. Adolph et al. [4] examined how individuals' perspectives about a software project converge towards a common understanding, highlighting the importance of reconciling diverse viewpoints for effective collaboration in open source projects. Yu and Petter [53] used shared mental models theory to explain how teams work together to complete common tasks, emphasizing the need for effective communication and shared understanding, especially in virtual and distributed open source teams. Lindberg et al. [31] investigated coordination mechanisms for resolving pull requests in open source projects, providing practical guidelines for integrating contributions from multiple developers.

Furthermore, Sedano et al. [44] studied waste in software development, developing a taxonomy that identifies nine types of waste, including overproduction, waiting, and defects. This research is valuable for enhancing efficiency in open source projects. Werner and Berry [51] highlighted the use of trace data in analyzing large development projects, showing how detailed trace data can provide insights, identify bottlenecks, and improve project management practices. These studies provide a foundation for designing and developing effective approaches to analyzing the software development process.

Process Analysis and Object-Centric Process Mining. Works in this area aim at understanding how events in software development unfold over time. For that they take into account various elements [49] of the software development. There are approaches to transform software development data in process-mining compatible event-logs [29, 41]. There are also approaches that enable process analytics of fine-grained events from evolving artifacts [13]. More complex approaches use repository data to analyse well-known processes. The work from [32] uses process mining [1] to analyze bug resolution processes, while [7, 10, 26] use version data to analyse commits, and gather insights respectively about the project timeline, hidden dependencies and *de-facto* teams.

Most of the techniques in the process mining stream require the input data to have well-defined attributes (i.e., an event log with defined case, activity, and timestamp). These works cannot be readily applied to data from software development [46]. As well, they only focus on discovering and analyzing predefined relations, by fixing the notion of case and following its traces in the data. However, the notions of case and activity of a process, especially in software data, are in practice loosely defined [9].

In recent years, process mining approaches are moving toward multi-dimensional analysis. Indeed, concepts like object-centric process mining (OCPM) [2] and standards like OCEL [23] are increasingly gaining interest. Thus, the tendency is to use as much information as possible. One way to holistically capture the information contained in the event logs is through the use of so-called *event knowledge graphs* [28] and store them in graph databases [20].

2.3   Research Questions

Given the opportunities arising by the multi-dimensional process analysis offered by OCPM, we derive the following research question *How can we exploit process analysis to analyze software development traces in a repository?*. As OCPM is a rather new technique, it makes sense to first test its applicability on software data. Furthermore, OCPM should specifically address the scenario illustrated in the problem statement (Sect. 2.1). Therefore, we divide our main research question into the following two.

RQ1. *How can we exploit Object-Centric Process Mining (OCPM) to analyze software development traces in a repository?*

RQ2. *How can we exploit OCPM to discover developer side-tracking?*

In other words, **RQ1** wants to investigate the applicabilty of OCPM to software development data and its effectiveness to deliver useful input for the manager and **RQ2** wants to test whether OCPM can help identify developer side-tracking, which is not possible to detect with traditional process mining techniques.

3 Approach

In the following, we describe our methlogical approach. Section 3.1 describes design science research method (DSRM) [25]. Section 3.2 details the Design and Development of the artifact created through DSRM. Section 3.3 describes how the input is preprocessed to be consumed by the artifact. Section 3.4 describes how the information is linked together and event-knowledge graphs are built. Section 3.5 shows what types of analyses are delivered to the manager.

3.1 Research Method

Design Science Reserach Methodology (DSRM) [25] is a research paradigm that focuses on the creation and evaluation of *artifacts* designed to solve identified organizational problems. Originating from the fields of engineering and computer science, DSRM emphasizes the development of innovative solutions through iterative processes of design, implementation, and refinement [40,52].

Key elements of DSRM include the following. *Problem Identification and Motivation*: Clearly defining the problem to be addressed, including its importance and relevance to stakeholders. This step ensures the research is grounded in real-world needs. *Objectives of a Solution*: Establishing criteria for what constitutes a successful solution. These objectives guide the development and assessment of the artifact. *Design and Development*: Creating the artifact, which can be a model, method, construct, or instantiation. This phase involves leveraging existing theories and technologies to craft a novel solution. *Demonstration*: Showing how the artifact can solve the problem through experiments, case studies, or simulations. This step provides initial evidence of the artifact's utility. *Evaluation*: Systematically assessing the artifact's effectiveness and efficiency against the predefined objectives. Various methods, including analytical, experimental, and observational techniques, are employed to validate the artifact. *Communication*: Disseminating the results to both technical and managerial audiences. Effective communication ensures that the findings and artifacts can be utilized by others and contribute to the broader knowledge base.

Figure 2 summarizes the design science research process. DSRM is iterative, often cycling through these steps multiple times to refine and enhance the artifact. Its rigorous approach ensures that the solutions developed are both innovative and practical, addressing the specific needs of organizations while contributing to academic knowledge [25,40]. This research uses design science to develop a software artifact. The

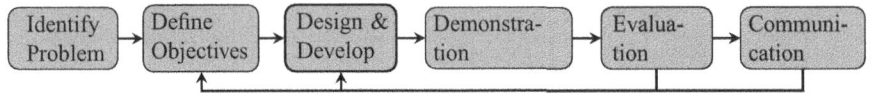

Fig. 2. Design Science Research Process (Peffers et al., 2007 [40]).

contribution serves the purpose of applying a process mining solution to a new domain, also referred to as exaptation [24]. Next, we describe the details of the design and development phase.

3.2   Design and Development of the Artifact

To implement the Design and Development step of DSRM, we followed a four-steps approach. These steps consist in pre-processing the repository data to extract event, building a knowledge-graph from these events, analysing them via multiple queries, and presenting the results to the end user. Next, we present the goals of our approach following the Goal-Question-Metric (GQM) paradigm from [12]. Then, we describe each step of our approach.

We define the following three main goals and related questions.

GQ1. *Goal 1*: analyze the development of individual modules, especially those showing signs of delay, to identify potentially problematic areas. For instance, if `developerA` discontinues work on `moduleA`, understanding the reasons behind such disruptions is crucial to address underlying workflow or project management issues and provide timely solutions. *Question 1*: What are the reasons behind discontinued work?

GQ2. *Goal 2*: comprehend the impacts of shifting developer attention or side-tracking, thus addressing and mitigating impacts on overall productivity. *Question 2:* How to trace task transitions and discern whether such shifts arise from urgent issues or mismanaged priorities?

GQ3. *Goal 3*: inform long-term planning and resource allocation, especially for specialized knowledge areas. *Question 3*: How to investigate code complexity and recurrent issues in files that necessitate frequent developer attention?

The following five *metrics* are identified to gauge progress towards our goals-questions. As metrics can be used to address more than one question, we provide a their description separately and map them to the relative goal-question (GQ). *Module/Task Progress* [38] measures the completion rate of tasks or modules, focusing on indicators like "task completion time" (GQ1). *Developer Activity* [45] assesses a developer's activity on a project by evaluating the number and frequency of commits (GQ1). *Code Churn* [45] examines the amount of code rewritten or revised, indicating issues with code complexity or quality (GQ1, GQ3). *Issue Tracking* [33] metrics (e.g.,"Number of Open Issues") signal potential problems within the software (GQ1, GQ3). *Task Switching* [14] records instances of developers switching tasks, aiding in identifying its frequency and impact (GQ1, GQ2, GQ3).

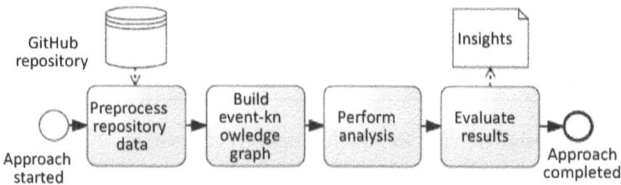

Fig. 3. Artifact for Analyzing Side-Tracking in Software Development Projects.

An overview of the steps involved in the artifacts' design are illustrated in Fig. 3. The approach takes as input a reference to a software repository and performs four steps. First, it pre-processes the data stored in the repository in order to extract various events. Second, these event data are employed to populate an event-knowledge graph. Third, various analyses are performed on the event-knowledge graph by means of queries. Fourth, the results are collected and presented to a user. In the following sections, we will detail the first three steps, while the evaluation follows in the next section.

3.3   Preprocessing Repository Data

We focused on feature selection from the GitHub API to shape our event knowledge graph, choosing parameters that reflect various dimensions of the development process. Thus, we fetch the datasets from the software repository (e.g., GitHub) and select the most relevant dimensions for our purpose. We include *commit data, issue event data, pull requests* and *branch data*.

When extracting commit data we include fields like SHA, committer, author's name, commit message, verification status, commit parents, merge status, URL, stats, files involved, author-login, repos, URL, organizations URL, and branch name. These parameters are chosen to visualize the essence, trajectory, and workflow of the software development process based on file modifications over time after each commit.

When extracting issue event data, we include data about both open and closed issues from the chosen repository, and their correlated events. We fetch information about the issue, event type, commit-id, event-creator, state, and a timestamp indicating whether the issue was closed and when.

When extracting the data of pull requests we include the pull-request number, title, state (closed, open or all), user who made the PR, creation time of the PR, merge time (if merged), and the merge commit's SHA code. With these parameters, we can get a better understanding of what transpires when a developer decides to merge a pull request from one branch into another and how commits are being handled for both the merging branches. We can also compare the data of two states: what data are being generated when users open a pull request versus what data are being recorded after it gets closed.

Finally, when extracting the branch data, we include the branch name for the purpose of better navigation the data from commits and subsequently from pull requests. To fetch the data in a systematic manner, we wrote a Python script and used it together with the requests library. These data served as the foundation for our event knowledge graph and were critical in reflecting the intertwined relationships among different software development events and activities.

3.4 Building an Event Knowledge Graph

In the following, we describe the steps to convert the acquired data from the repository into the event knowledge graph. In order to do so, we rely on Neo4j[1] graph database and its Cypher query language.

Creating Nodes. The first phase consists of loading event data extracted from the repository during the pre-processing step and stored into CSV files. That is, for each of the four datasets *commit data, issue event data, pull requests* and *branch data*, we have a corresponding .csv file. With these we create the primary nodes of the knowledge graph. Each type of node represents a unique entity in the software development process.

We used a Cypher query[2] to create entities from the *commits* dataset (i.e., `commit.csv` file). From this dataset we can create the following nodes: `Commit`, `Author`, and `File`. Each `Commit` node is associated with an `Author` node representing the individual who made the commit and several `File` nodes representing the files that were altered in the commit. The `Commit` nodes include properties such as `commit_id`, `message`, `URL`, `stats`, `date`, and `merge`, which provide detailed information about each commit while `Author` nodes contain information or each individual. Nodes for `File` help to show the state of each file after a modification has been done by a commit.

Queries for creating entities from the issue, events and pull requests nodes are similar. For commits we create `Author` nodes and for issue events we create `Users` nodes to distinguish the different type of GitHub's users. `Author` are the GitHub users or developers that are actively involve in the process of the development process. `Users` are the people from the open community that contributed to the issue through activities such as comment or reference.

Creating Relationships. Next we describe how we create the relationships.

Branches, Authors, Files and Commits. In this step, relationships `:COMMITTED` (between an `Author` and a `Commit`) and `:BELONGS_TO` (between a `Commit` and a `Branch`) are formed and each commit is linked to the files (`File`) it modifies through the `:MODIFIES` relationship. These are established by connecting the `Author` node who `:COMMITTED` to the `Commit` node and linking each `Commit` to the `Branch` node it belongs to. This will relatively show which commit belongs to which branch and eventually who worked on a specific branch or file.

---

[1] https://neo4j.com.

[2] All the queries can be found in our GitHub repository https://anonymous.4open.science/r/Multi-Dimensional-Process-Analysis-on-Software-Data-F33F.

Directly Follows Relation for Commits. This relationship, represented as :DF, connects two commit nodes that directly follow one another in time, regardless of the branch they belong to. This is similar to the commit history displayed on GitHub but not limited to a specific branch. The :DF relationship makes it possible to trace the chronological sequence of commits across all branches.

Directly Follows Relation of Commits-Modification. This relationship, symbolized as :DF_M, connects two commit nodes that directly follow each other only if they have modified the same file. Like :DF, this relationship also tracks the sequence of commits, but it narrows down the scope to those modifying the same file. This allows a detailed view of how individual files evolve over time. It also helps at detecting patterns to highlight developers who stop working on the file.

The relationships :DF and :DF_M enrich the structure of the event knowledge graph by adding a time dimension. Queries for creating Issue, Event and PullRequest relationships can be found in our GitHub repository.

3.5 Performing the Analysis

We leverage graph databases to extract the following Key Performance Indicators (KPIs) and process models.

Basic KPIs. We start with describing the general (i.e., not process oriented) software development KPIs our approach offers.

Code Churn Analysis. Code churn [35] is the measure of lines of code added and removed from a file over time. The code churn can be calculated using the formula Code Churn = Lines Added + Lines Deleted. We compute this for all the developers. This also allows to rank the developers by contribution (e.g., by sorting the respective churn value in decreasing order).

Ratio of Closed and Open Issues. This metric provides insight into the project's issue management efficiency and effectiveness [33]. Assesses the project's issue management efficiency and effectiveness and indicates well-managed projects and areas for improvement in the development process.

We compute this metric as Ratio (State) $= \frac{\text{Issues (State)}}{\text{Total Issues}}$, where the input parameter *State* can take the values *Open* or *Close* to indicate respectively opened or closed issues.

Cycle Time. This is a performance-related software development metric, representing the time taken to implement, test, and correct a piece of work from the moment work begins until it is ready for delivery [6]. It measures the time taken from beginning work to delivery, providing a more granular view of the development process.

The *cycle time* in software development can be calculated using the formula Cycle Time = Completion Date − Start Date. We do this for all the issues. We are also able to compute the cycle time of each user that has worked on a given issue. With this, we allow for identifying patterns or anomalies in cycle times associated with specific users, providing a more granular view of the development process.

KPIs for Process Analysis. Next, we provide some metrics for process analysis. We focus on, i) issue resolution time, ii) collaboration, iii) file/commit dependency, and iv) issue escalation.

Issue Resolution Time Analysis. With this metric we analyze how long it takes to resolve different types of issues. Specifically, we look into two aspects: the individual issues that take the longest to resolve, and the users who, on average, take longer to complete issues. Utilizing a Cypher query we can perform the analysis by extracting information of issues or users with the longest cycle time with simple queries. More specifically, this is computed as the cycle time of each user that is associated to an issue. That is, it computes the amount of time elapsed between the first and last events of that user on the issue.

Collaboration Analysis. Analyzing collaboration [15] between team members reveals patterns in how team members interact on issues and files. For example, we can identify which team members often work on the same issues or files.

We compute this as two KPIs regarding respectively the issues and the files that were collaboratively worked on. We consider all the *collaborative* events from two users u1, u2 that were recorded within the same issue. We apply the same logic for what concerns the commonly modified files. We return the number of shared issues as the collaboration value. Same holds for the shared files.

File/Commit Dependency Analysis. This metric helps to identify relationships between different parts of the codebase [10]. For instance, it makes it possible to identify files that are frequently modified together, revealing areas of the codebase that are tightly coupled and may benefit from refactoring to improve modularity. We compute this KPI by considering the set of shared commits among the various files. Files that appear together in more commits have a higher dependency with one another.

Issue Escalation Analysis. Analyzing issue escalation [27] helps to identify patterns in issue evolution over time. We identify issues that undergo a larger number of events and consider them potentially problematic as they may require more management attention. To do so, we navigate the event knowledge graph and collect all the issues along with their related events, sorted in decreasing order.

Extracting a Process Model. To extract a process model we construct : DF (directly-follows) relationships between event nodes correlated to the same entity node. These relationships link together events of the same type that follows one another according to their timestamps. We repeat this for all the processes or dimension we want to investigate. Then, we classify the event nodes to event classes and retrieve a multi-entity directly-follows graphs (DFGs) through aggregation. Ultimately, through this approach we can obtain a process model that represents multi-entity DFGs.

We applied the techniques from [20, 22]. Hence, we could aggregate the graph nodes to class nodes. Then we constructed filtered directly-follows relationships and retrieved a *proclet* model [3] that provides one distinct behavioral model per entity. We aggregate the event class nodes for branch and commits nodes, after analyzing the resulting graph.

Next, we raise the level of abstraction. We adapt the query for DFG discovery to aggregate : DF relationships between classes. To obtain the *proclet* model, we proceed by adding synchronized edges between event classes of the same activity in different entity types.

Finally, we simplify the resulting proclet model by raising again the level of abstraction. We create a higher-level class node for branch (that could be considered as an *activity* in a process) corresponding to how the event nodes and class nodes were constructed.

This concludes the steps required to perform the analysis of the software development process. The evaluation of the results can then be carried out by a domain expert (e.g., a manager or a senior software developer) who can then use the extracted KPIs and models to gather insights into the status of the project.

4   Evaluation

To demonstrate the insights gathered by our approach, we tested it on the GitHub repository of Microsoft Visual Studio Code[3] (vscode).

4.1   KPIs and Process Analysis

We start with showing the applicability of our approach to generate custom KPIs. Given the underlying graph-structure, it is possible to define both custom and well-known software engineering KPIs. One commonly used KPI for process analysis is *cycle time*. Cycle time for an issue, means the time it take from its opening to its closing (resolved). Listing 1.1 shows Cypher query to retrive the issues that took the longest times to be closed. The result of this query can also be combined with another query that retrieves the people associated to the issue. Table 1 reports the values of the issue resolution time analysis KPI in the vscode repository. We can observe the user who spent more time on average on resolving issues. All the Cypher queries and analyses to achieve these results can be found in our GitHub repository.

4.2   Process Model

We derived a process model after filtering the entire database to focus on the progression of a specific file over time. For the purpose of demonstration we picked the file quickInput.ts. Using a Cypher query, we connect, label by category and display the events that happened on the file on the different dimensions. The resulting model can be seen in Fig. 4.

In this model, we used branches to represent 6 process activities, focusing mainly on the progression of File nodes, the associated Commits and their Authors. Additionally, Issue nodes are also involved in the process where they got raised to signify that a file needed to be worked on and areas that need attention. Here we could also see the cycle time of each resolved issue as well as the users that were involved in helping to solve the issue.

---

[3] https://github.com/microsoft/vscode.

Listing 1.1. Issue nodes with `opened_at` and `closed_at` timestamps.

```
MATCH (i:Issue)
WHERE i.state = 'closed'
RETURN
  i.issue_id,
  i.closed_at - i.opened_at
    as resolution_time
ORDER BY resolution_time DESC
LIMIT 10
```

Table 1. Top 10 Users with the Longest Average Cycle Times [36].

User	Hours	Minutes
aeschli	23	44
bhavyaus	23	11
Danielmelody	23	11
weinand	23	11
dtroberts	18	56
christian-bromann	18	44
JacksonKearl	18	34
jzyrobert	18	34
joelday	18	34
AmitPr	18	34

In Fig. 4 we can also observe that in Activity T3 and T4, there are some commits that belong to different branches, a deeper investigation revealed these as revert commits from T4, occurring post-merge of the T3 working branch into the main branch, signaling an issue necessitating further work on the file. The author that was responsible for this action is highlighted in the Figure, and we can observe that he continued to work on the process in the next Activity T5 as well before pausing for a significant time period until there was an issue that require the process to be merged into the main branch. In Activity t6 we can also see that there were another few direct changes by 2 other authors before finishing the workflow for this file.

Further insights were sought on why the author from T4 and T5 paused before merging their work into the main branch. By filtering the workflow for this specific author during that timeframe, we can delve into the cause of this side-tracking and visualize their work progression during this period.

Figure 5 reveals the author worked on another branch during the hiatus. The graph depicts the states of the file in question (yellow nodes) and the other files the author worked on during that period (brown nodes). The multi-dimensional process analysis enabled us to identify the side-tracking issue and explain it by the help of another dimension with one simple query.

After utilizing the metric *code churn*, and filtering the time and the name of the author in question, we obtained a comprehensive list of what the author was working on or side-tracking during that time period in a relational form of data. This is shown is Table 2.

The relational database results can be exported in formats like `csv` or `json`. This allows for subsequent data loading into tools such as Python Library or NumPy, facilitating further analyses and visualizations by creating charts or statistics.

4.3   Proclet Model

Next, we provide details on user behavior. When developers encounter an issue in their projects, their typical response is to create a separate branch to work on the file or

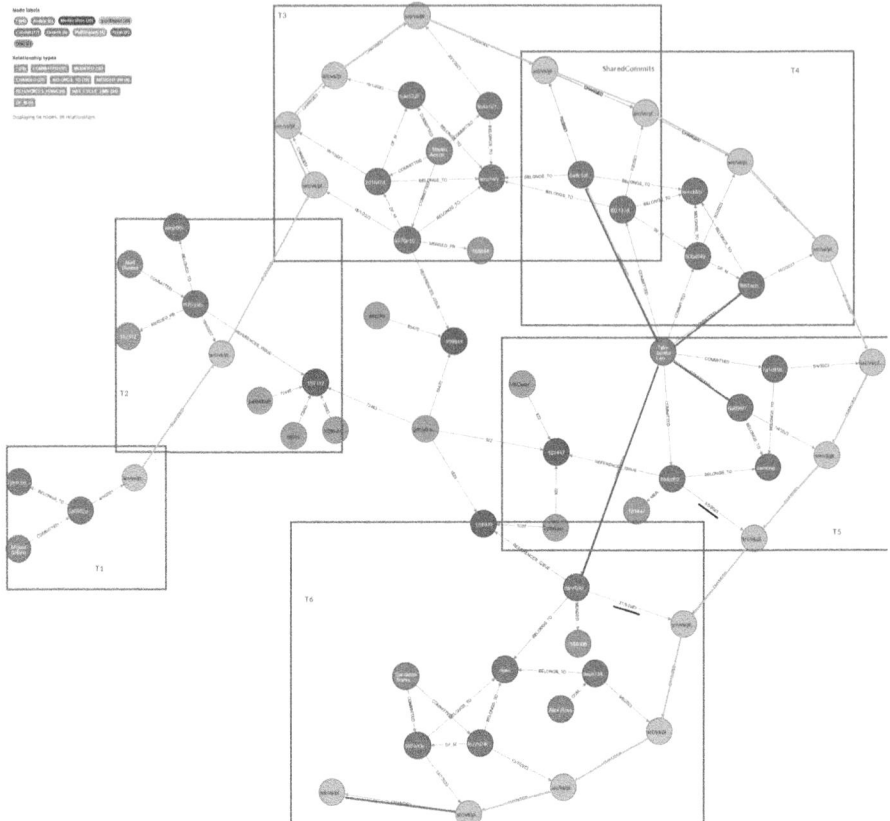

Fig. 4. The process of developing file `quickInput.ts` [36].

Table 2. Total churn of developer TJL. File path prefixes are left out [36].

File	Total Churn (lines)	Most Churning Dev
.../mainThreadAuthentication.ts	105	TJL
.../authenticationService.ts	105	TJL
.../vscode.d.ts	105	TJL
.../extHostAuthentication.ts	105	TJL
.../authentication.ts	105	TJL
.../vscode.proposed.getSessions.d.ts	105	TJL
.../extHost.protocol.ts	105	TJL
.../githubServer.ts	44	TJL
.../github.ts	44	TJL
.../quickInput.ts	10	TJL

module in question. From this perspective, a branch could be considered an *activity* of the process. To allow for better investigation of these extra activities, we resort to the notion of *proclets* [3].

Figure 6 shows the extraction of two proclet models (following the idea presented in [21]) related to the file quickInput.ts analyzed previously. We focused on two perspectives: i) the commits that were made to the file by actors (Fig. 6a) and ii) the branches created before including changes to the main branch (Fig. 6b). By observing Fig. 6a we can notice that file quickInput.ts that after its creation, it is handed over to a next actor. Aftewards, it undergoes to a number of changes by the same actor as seen in the big connected component of the graph. This actor is also the one who then pushes the changes to the main branch. Subsequently, another actor works on subsequent changes and also pushes them to the main branch. Similarly, Fig. 6b shows the change activites made to the, which do not appear in the main branch, but rather in a separate branch.

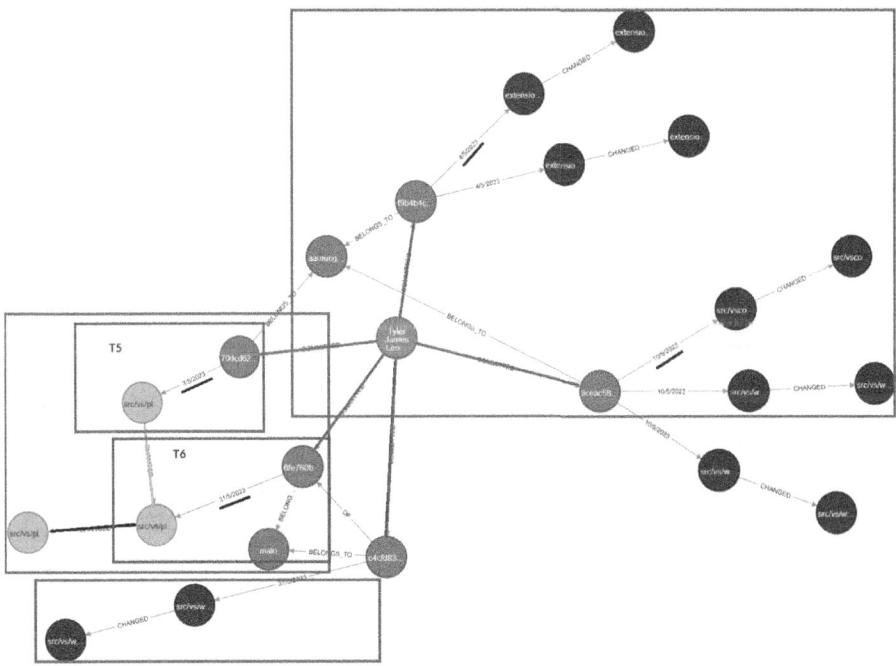

Fig. 5. Author side-tracking problem [36].(Color figure online)

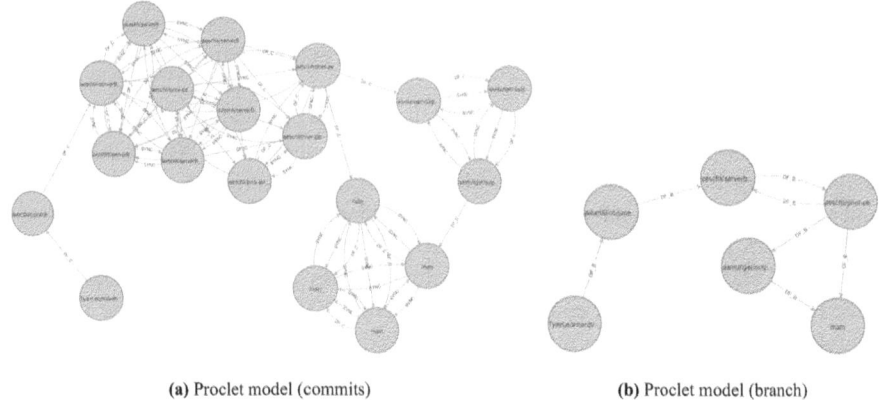

(a) Proclet model (commits)   (b) Proclet model (branch)

Fig. 6. Proclet models of `quickInput.ts` based on different dimensions.

5 Discussion

The work presented in this paper is driven by the overall research question: *How can we exploit multi-dimensional process analysis to analyze software development traces in a repository?*. To answer this question we used multi-dimensional process mining.

With regard to **RQ1:** *How can we exploit Object-Centric Process Mining (OCPM) to analyze software development traces in a repository?*, we found that OCPM is applicable and useful to analyze software repositories. This is inline with previous work from [41] who applied traditional process mining. This work overcomes issues of applying traditional process mining such the project-orientation of development processes [7] and the non existence of clear case and activities [9]. With regard to **RQ2:** *How can we exploit OCPM to discover developer side-tracking?*, we found that OPCM can uncover these situations. This is due to the fact that all entities and interaction are linked together in the event-knowledge graph.

Key findings of this paper are that i) multi-dimensional process mining is suitable for analysing software repository data; and ii) it is possible to obtain a comprehensive view of the overall process that happens behind software development. The first point (i) is shown by the queries presented in the first part Sect. 3. Another evidence of the suitability of this approach for software development analysis is the fact that various KPIs can be reproduced by means of Cypher queries. The second point is evident by the analysis of Fig. 4. In this picture, it is possible to observe not only the sequence of commit activities performed by one user to a file, but also other activities that influenced the user behavior. This, for instance, enables the explanation of why certain files took longer to be developed. In this case, we see that the reasons are that more developers were involved (purple nodes) and that some developers also worked on other files before continuing to contribute on the file `quickInput.ts`.

Compared to previous studies that focus on extracting a process workflow from their repositories, we argue that this study is a first attempt on gathering a multi-perspective view. Well-known approaches such as [29,41] only tackle one dimension (i.e., they force the notion of a process case). Existing process mining approaches that output DFGs tend to make this assumption. Instead, our approach can show information beyond the discussed KPIs. For example, we can to observe in Fig. 4 that certain users (like Tyler) contribute to more commits than others – suggesting that these maybe senior users – or that certain issues are more complex to solve because they are related to busy users or they simply require more work.

6 Conclusion

To overcome the problems of existing data-driven analysis techniques, we explore the use of Object-Centric Process Mining for software development data. More specifically, we designed and developed an open-source artifact that we applied to real-world data from GitHub. We show OCPM is applicable to such data and can deliver valuable results for the managers. In particular, it can be used as a basis to compute commonly used KPIs and also to show process models that capture complex information. As an added value of OCPM over traditional process mining technique, we showed that it can well-capture inter-process behavior such as side-tracking. This helps to explain why determinate activites take longer.

Future work aims to delve deeper into possibilities for analyses that open up thanks to object-centricity. Therefore, we plan to assess the potentials of OCPM for software development data-analysis. Furthermore, we plan to exploitn the entities and relationships stored into the event-knowledge graph to support the development and testing of information systems theories (e.g., on coordination).

Acknowledgments. This research was supported by the Einstein Foundation Berlin under grant EPP-2019-524 and the Weizenbaum Institute under grant 16DII133

References

1. van der Aalst, W.M.P.: Process Mining - Data Science in Action, 2nd edn. Springer, Heidelberg (2016)
2. Aalst, W.M.P.: Object-centric process mining: dealing with divergence and convergence in event data. In: Ölveczky, P.C., Salaün, G. (eds.) SEFM 2019. LNCS, vol. 11724, pp. 3–25. Springer, Cham (2019). https://doi.org/10.1007/978-3-030-30446-1_1
3. van der Aalst, W.M.P., Barthelmess, P., Ellis, C.A., Wainer, J.: Proclets: a framework for lightweight interacting workflow processes. Int. J. Cooperative Inf. Syst. **10**(4), 443–481 (2001)
4. Adolph, S., Kruchten, P., Hall, W.: Reconciling perspectives: a grounded theory of how people manage the process of software development. J. Syst. Softw. **85**(6), 1269–1286 (2012)
5. Agrawal, K., Aschauer, M., Thonhofer, T., Bala, S., Rogge-Solti, A., Tomsich, N.: Resource classification from version control system logs. In: EDOC Workshops, pp. 1–10. IEEE Computer Society (2016)
6. Agrawal, M., Chari, K.: Software effort, quality, and cycle time: a study of CMM level 5 projects. IEEE Trans. Softw. Eng. **33**(3), 145–156 (2007)

7. Bala, S., Cabanillas, C., Mendling, J., Rogge-Solti, A., Polleres, A.: Mining project-oriented business processes. In: Motahari-Nezhad, H.R., Recker, J., Weidlich, M. (eds.) BPM 2015. LNCS, vol. 9253, pp. 425–440. Springer, Cham (2015). https://doi.org/10.1007/978-3-319-23063-4_28
8. Bala, S., Mendling, J.: Monitoring the software development process with process mining. In: Shishkov, B. (ed.) BMSD 2018. LNBIP, vol. 319, pp. 432–442. Springer, Cham (2018). https://doi.org/10.1007/978-3-319-94214-8_34
9. Bala, S., Mendling, J., Schimak, M., Queteschiner, P.: Case and activity identification for mining process models from middleware. In: Buchmann, R.A., Karagiannis, D., Kirikova, M. (eds.) PoEM 2018. LNBIP, vol. 335, pp. 86–102. Springer, Cham (2018). https://doi.org/10.1007/978-3-030-02302-7_6
10. Bala, S., Revoredo, K., de A.R. Gonçalves, J.C., Baião, F., Mendling, J., Santoro, F.: Uncovering the hidden co-evolution in the work history of software projects. In: Carmona, J., Engels, G., Kumar, A. (eds.) BPM 2017. LNCS, vol. 10445, pp. 164–180. Springer, Cham (2017). https://doi.org/10.1007/978-3-319-65000-5_10
11. Balasubramanian, L., Mnkandla, E.: An evaluation to determine the extent and level of agile software development methodology adoption and implementation in the botswana software development industry. In: 2016 International Conference on Advances in Computing and Communication Engineering (ICACCE), pp. 320–325. IEEE (2016)
12. Basili, V.R., Caldiera, G., Rombach, H.D.: The goal question metric approach. In: Encyclopedia of Software Engineering, pp. 528–532 (1994)
13. Beheshti, S.-M.-R., Benatallah, B., Motahari-Nezhad, H.R.: Enabling the analysis of cross-cutting aspects in ad-hoc processes. In: Salinesi, C., Norrie, M.C., Pastor, Ó. (eds.) CAiSE 2013. LNCS, vol. 7908, pp. 51–67. Springer, Heidelberg (2013). https://doi.org/10.1007/978-3-642-38709-8_4
14. Benbunan-Fich, R., Adler, R.F., Mavlanova, T.: Measuring multitasking behavior with activity-based metrics. ACM Trans. Comput. Hum. Interact. 18(2), 7:1–7:22 (2011)
15. Biazzini, M., Baudry, B.: "may the fork be with you": novel metrics to analyze collaboration on github. In: WETSoM, pp. 37–43. ACM (2014)
16. Carlo, J.L., Gaskin, J.E., Lyytinen, K., Rose, G.M.: Early vs. late adoption of radical information technology innovations across software development organizations: an extension of the disruptive information technology innovation model. Inf. Syst. J. 24(6), 537–569 (2014)
17. Chan, F.K.Y., Thong, J.Y.L.: Acceptance of agile methodologies: a critical review and conceptual framework. Decis. Support Syst. 46(4), 803–814 (2009)
18. Choetkiertikul, M., Dam, H.K., Tran, T., Ghose, A., Grundy, J.: Predicting delivery capability in iterative software development. IEEE Trans. Softw. Eng. 44(6), 551–573 (2018)
19. Crowston, K.: A coordination theory approach to organizational process design. Organ. Sci. 8(2), 157–175 (1997)
20. Esser, S., Fahland, D.: Multi-dimensional event data in graph databases. J. Data Semant. 10(1–2), 109–141 (2021)
21. Fahland, D.: Describing behavior of processes with many-to-many interactions. In: Donatelli, S., Haar, S. (eds.) PETRI NETS 2019. LNCS, vol. 11522, pp. 3–24. Springer, Cham (2019). https://doi.org/10.1007/978-3-030-21571-2_1
22. Fahland, D.: Multi-dimensional process analysis. In: BPM. Lecture Notes in Computer Science, vol. 13420, pp. 27–33. Springer, Heidelberg (2022). https://doi.org/10.1007/978-3-031-16103-2_3
23. Ghahfarokhi, A.F., Park, G., Berti, A., van der Aalst, W.M.P.: OCEL: a standard for object-centric event logs. In: Bellatreche, L., et al. (eds.) ADBIS 2021. CCIS, vol. 1450, pp. 169–175. Springer, Cham (2021). https://doi.org/10.1007/978-3-030-85082-1_16
24. Gregor, S., Hevner, A.R.: Positioning and presenting design science research for maximum impact. MIS Q. 37(2), 337–355 (2013)

25. Hevner, A.R., March, S.T., Park, J., Ram, S.: Design science in information systems research. MIS Q. 75–105 (2004)
26. Jooken, L., Creemers, M., Jans, M.: Extracting a collaboration model from VCS logs based on process mining techniques. In: Di Francescomarino, C., Dijkman, R., Zdun, U. (eds.) BPM 2019. LNBIP, vol. 362, pp. 212–223. Springer, Cham (2019). https://doi.org/10.1007/978-3-030-37453-2_18
27. Keil, M.: Pulling the plug: software project management and the problem of project escalation. MIS Q. **19**(4), 421–447 (1995)
28. Khayatbashi, S., Hartig, O., Jalali, A.: Transforming event knowledge graph to object-centric event logs: a comparative study for multi-dimensional process analysis. In: ER (2023)
29. Kindler, E., Rubin, V.A., Schäfer, W.: Activity mining for discovering software process models. In: Software Engineering. LNI, vol. P-79, pp. 175–180. GI (2006)
30. Kneuper, R.: CMMI: Improving Software and Systems Development Processes Using Capability Maturity Model Integration. Rocky Nook (2008)
31. Lindberg, A., Berente, N., Gaskin, J., Lyytinen, K.: Coordinating interdependencies in online communities: a study of an open source software project. Inf. Syst. Res. **27**(4), 751–772 (2016)
32. Marques, R., da Silva, M.M., Ferreira, D.R.: Assessing agile software development processes with process mining: a case study. In: CBI (1), pp. 109–118. IEEE Computer Society (2018)
33. Meneely, A., Corcoran, M., Williams, L.A.: Improving developer activity metrics with issue tracking annotations. In: WETSoM, pp. 75–80. ACM (2010)
34. Milewicz, R., Pinto, G., Rodeghero, P.: Characterizing the roles of contributors in open-source scientific software projects. In: MSR, pp. 421–432. IEEE / ACM (2019)
35. Munson, J.C., Elbaum, S.G.: Code churn: A measure for estimating the impact of code change. In: ICSM, p. 24. IEEE Computer Society (1998)
36. Nguyen, T., Bala, S., Mendling, J.: Multi-dimensional process analysis of software development projects. In: MODELSWARD, pp. 179–186. SCITEPRESS (2024)
37. Oliva, G.A., Santana, F.W., Gerosa, M.A., de Souza, C.R.B.: Towards a classification of logical dependencies origins: a case study. In: EVOL/IWPSE, pp. 31–40. ACM (2011)
38. Paasivaara, M., Lassenius, C.: Collaboration practices in global inter-organizational software development projects. Softw. Process. Improv. Pract. **8**(4), 183–199 (2003)
39. Pasuksmit, J., et al.: Improving agile planning for reliable software delivery. In: MSR, pp. 25–26. IEEE (2023)
40. Peffers, K., Tuunanen, T., Rothenberger, M.A., Chatterjee, S.: A design science research methodology for information systems research. J. Manag. Inf. Syst. **24**(3), 45–77 (2007)
41. Poncin, W., Serebrenik, A., van den Brand, M.: Process mining software repositories. In: CSMR, pp. 5–14. IEEE Computer Society (2011)
42. Rastogi, A., Gupta, A., Sureka, A.: Samiksha: mining issue tracking system for contribution and performance assessment. In: ISEC, pp. 13–22. ACM (2013)
43. Schipper, D., Aniche, M.F., van Deursen, A.: Tracing back log data to its log statement: from research to practice. In: MSR, pp. 545–549. IEEE/ACM (2019)
44. Sedano, T., Ralph, P., Péraire, C.: Software development waste. In: ICSE, pp. 130–140. IEEE/ACM (2017)
45. Shin, Y., Meneely, A., Williams, L.A., Osborne, J.A.: Evaluating complexity, code churn, and developer activity metrics as indicators of software vulnerabilities. IEEE Trans. Softw. Eng. **37**(6), 772–787 (2011)
46. Tsoury, A., Soffer, P., Reinhartz-Berger, I.: A conceptual framework for supporting deep exploration of business process behavior. In: Trujillo, J.C., et al. (eds.) ER 2018. LNCS, vol. 11157, pp. 58–71. Springer, Cham (2018). https://doi.org/10.1007/978-3-030-00847-5_6
47. Van Loon, H.: Process Assessment and ISO/IEC 15504: A Reference Book, vol. 775. Springer, Heidleberg (2004)

48. Vasilescu, B., Serebrenik, A., Goeminne, M., Mens, T.: On the variation and specialisation of workload - a case study of the gnome ecosystem community. Empir. Softw. Eng. **19**(4), 955–1008 (2014)
49. Vavpotic, D., Bala, S., Mendling, J., Hovelja, T.: Software process evaluation from user perceptions and log data. J. Softw. Evol. Process. **34**(4) (2022)
50. Vavpotic, D., Hovelja, T.: Improving the evaluation of software development methodology adoption and its impact on enterprise performance. Comput. Sci. Inf. Syst. **9**(1), 165–187 (2012)
51. Werner, C.M., Berry, D.M.: An empirical study of the software development process, including its requirements engineering, at very large organization: how to use data mining in such a study. In: Kamalrudin, M., Ahmad, S., Ikram, N. (eds.) APRES 2017. CCIS, vol. 809, pp. 15–25. Springer, Singapore (2018). https://doi.org/10.1007/978-981-10-7796-8_2
52. Wieringa, R.J.: Design Science Methodology for Information Systems and Software Engineering. Springer, Heidelberg (2014)
53. Yu, X., Petter, S.: Understanding agile software development practices using shared mental models theory. Inf. Softw. Technol. **56**(8), 911–921 (2014)
54. Zimmermann, T., Weißgerber, P.: Preprocessing CVS data for fine-grained analysis. In: MSR, pp. 2–6 (2004)
55. Zimmermann, T., Weißgerber, P., Diehl, S., Zeller, A.: Mining version histories to guide software changes. IEEE Trans. Softw. Eng. **31**(6), 429–445 (2005)

Enhancing Scenario-Based Modeling Using Large Language Models

David Harel[1], Guy Katz[2(✉)], Assaf Marron[1], and Smadar Szekely[1]

[1] The Weizmann Institute of Science, Rehovot, Israel
[2] The Hebrew University of Jerusalem, Jerusalem, Israel
guykatz@cs.huji.ac.il

Abstract. Manually modeling complex systems is a daunting task. Although numerous methods have been proposed for mitigating this issue, this difficult problem persists. Recent breakthroughs in generative AI and large language models have led to the creation of general-purpose chatbots, which can assist software engineers and modelers in various tasks. Still, these chatbots are often inaccurate or incorrect, and so using them in an unstructured manner might result in erroneous system models. Here, we outline a method designed for integrating chatbots into the modeling process, in a safer and more structured way. To facilitate this integration, we advocate the use of the scenario-based modeling paradigm, which has been shown to facilitate the automated analysis of models. We suggest that through the iterative invocation of a chatbot, combined with manual and automatic inspection of the models it produces, one can obtain a more robust and accurate system model. We report on favorable preliminary results, which showcase the potential of this approach.

Keywords: Large language models · Generative AI · Chatbots · Scenario-based modeling · Rule-based specifications

1 Introduction

The manual modeling of complex systems is an error-prone and daunting endeavor. Moreover, even after the initial modelling of the system is done, ongoing tasks such as repair and modification continuously tax human engineers. Creating methodologies and tools for facilitating and streamlining this process has been the topic of extensive research. Still, many aspects of this problem remain unsolved [5,44].

In recent years, the deep learning revolution has brought about dramatic changes in many domains, including computer science. This trend has recently intensified with the release of ChatGPT, the learning-based chatbot [43], which appears to be a significant step towards general-purpose AI. ChatGPT, and other tools like it [13,42], can be applied in countless kinds of tasks—and particularly, as part of the modeling and coding of complex software systems [45]. Using

F. José Domínguez Mayo et al. (Eds.): MODELSWARD 2024, CCIS 2547, pp. 43–68, 2026.
https://doi.org/10.1007/978-3-031-96841-9_3

ChatGPT, engineers might provide a natural-language description of the system being developed, and then receive from the chatbot a model of this system, or even the source code that implements it. Using iterative invocations of ChatGPT, the system can later be modified or enhanced, as the need arises. This kind of technique has already been successfully used on systems from various application domains [6,39,45].

Even though the ability to leverage ChatGPT[1] as part of the software development cycle can significantly empower software engineers, it also presents potential pitfalls that should be considered. One potential drawback of using chatbots in this way is that the answers they produce are often incomplete or inaccurate, and sometimes overlook various aspects of the input query [39]. Further, the input query presented to the chatbot might itself be imperfect, and the engineering team might overlook this fact until the system is deployed. Consequently, if we assume that human engineers will become increasingly dependent on chatbots for performing various tasks, the associated risk that such errors might find their way into the final, deployed models and code of the system at hand increases. Consequently, we face the following challenge: how can we harness modern chatbots in a way that lifts significant loads of work off the engineer's shoulders, but which results in system models that are accurate and sound?

In this paper, we advocate for the design of an encompassing modeling scheme, which would allow engineers to combine chatbots such as ChatGPT with more manual, "traditional" techniques for systems modeling [5,44], in such a way that will achieve the aforementioned goal. The core idea is to make use of ChatGPT in a more controlled way; i.e., by repeatedly invoking it for various tasks, but to also repeatedly analyze and inspect its results, in order to ensure their accuracy and soundness. We believe that such schemes, if properly designed, could allow software engineers to benefit from the capabilities of Chat-GPT without jeopardizing the quality of the resulting systems. In the longer run, we argue that such a scheme could constitute a step towards the vision of *Wise Computing* [25], which includes the turning of the computer into a proactive member of the engineering team—which can propose possible courses of action, detect under-specified sections of the model, and support the various routine actions that arise as part of the development cycle of modern software.

To construct such a modeling scheme, we propose here to leverage some of the extensive work that has been carried out within the modeling community over the years. Specifically, we focus here on such modeling frameworks that afford two benefits which, in our view, complement the capabilities of ChatGPT: (i) models produced by the modeling framework are highly aligned with the way humans perceive the systems under development. This, we argue, could facilitate the manual inspection of ChatGPT's output by the engineers; and (ii) models produced by the framework are amenable to automated analysis techniques, e.g.,

---

[1] We will often use the term *ChatGPT* somewhat generically, to represent an arbitrary, modern chatbot.

model checking. This is needed to support the automated detection of inconsistencies and errors in models that are automatically generated by ChatGPT.

Multiple existing modeling framework fit these requirements and could probably be used in our context. Still, for the initial evaluation results discussed here, we chose to focus on *scenario-based modeling (SBM)*. SBM is modeling technique that produces models comprised of simple *scenarios*. Each such scenario corresponds to a single aspect of the system being modeled [9,33]. As we later discuss, this fact facilitates a smoother collaboration between human engineers and chatbot.

In order to demonstrate the potential of this combined framework, we study here some few tasks that naturally arise within a system's life cycle. More concretely, we focus on the model's initial design phase; its testing; the verification of its various properties; its later repair or enhancement, possibly due to the discovery of inconsistencies; and also the search for under-specified portions within the model. Our results are preliminary, but are highly promising. We hope that this paper could form the basis for further research in this important direction.

In the rest of the paper, we discuss the key concepts of our proposed approach, and lay out a high-level plan for future steps. We start with an introduction to the concepts of SBM and language model-based chatbots, in Sect. 2. We then present the proposed integration of ChatGPT and SBM in Sect. 3, and continue with a discussion of the more advanced aspects of such an integration in Sect. 4. In Sect. 5 we present technical and methodological challenges that emerged in our experiments as well as directions for addressing these challenges in further refinement of the methodology. Next, we discuss related work in Sect. 6, followed by a conclusion in Sect. 7.

2   Background

2.1   Large Language Model-Based Chatbots

Chat Generative Pre-trained Transformer (ChatGPT), by OpenAI [7,43], is a large language model (LLM) based chatbot. ChatGPT is sufficiently powerful to conduct an iterative conversation of variable format, style, length, level of detail, and language. At each stage of the conversation, the user presents ChatGPT with a fresh prompt, and the chatbot then replies—based on all previous prompts that appeared in that conversation (also referred to as the *context*). Since its debut in 2022, ChatGPT has quickly become profoundly successful, and has inspired several other companies to create their own chatbots [3,13,42].

Internally, ChatGPT is comprised of a proprietary series of generative pre-trained transformer (GPT) models. These models are, in turn, based on Google's transformer architecture [46]. ChatGPT has been fine-tuned for conversational applications, through a combination of reinforcement and supervised learning techniques, followed by manual adjustments by human engineers. The chatbot's training, and also its inference, are considered very costly in terms of processing resources and power consumption.

As far as functionality is concerned, ChatGPT is extremely versatile. Some of its numerous uses include writing and debugging computer programs [45], generating student essays [2], and also composing music [40]. However, it may sometimes produce plausible-sounding but completely incorrect answers—which is a known limitation for large language models [16].

2.2   Scenario-Based Modeling

Scenario-based modeling [33] (SBM) is an approach for modeling complex, reactive systems. The main building block in a scenario-based (SB) model is called a *scenario object*, and it describes a single behavior of the system being modeled—whether desirable or undesirable—which can be specified as allowed, necessarily, or forbidden. Each of the model's scenario object does not interact with its counterparts directly, and is created in isolation. Cross-scenario interaction is supported, but only through a global execution mechanism, which may execute a set of scenarios in a way that produces global, cohesive behavior.

Multiple flavors of SBM have been proposed, each with its own mechanism for cross-scenario interactions. Here, we focus on a particular set of idioms, which are common in many of the SBM frameworks: the *requesting, waiting-for* and *blocking* of discrete event sets [33]. As the mode is executed, each of the scenario objects repeatedly visits designated *synchronization points*; and in each of these points, the global execution mechanism triggers a single event. Each scenario object may declare sets of events that it wishes to see triggered (*requested* events), events that it would like to avoid (*blocked* events), and events that it does not request itself, but which it would like to monitor (*waited-for events*). The global execution mechanism then collects these declarations from each of the scenario objects in the system (or, possibly, a subset thereof [19]), selects a single event that is requested and not blocked, and then broadcasts this selection to all relevant scenario objects.

In each synchronization point there may be multiple events that are requested and not blocked; and multiple strategies have been put forth for selecting one of these events. Possible strategies include arbitrary or random event selection, a round-robin mechanism, and also look-ahead schemes that simulate the possible progression of the execution, and then select events in order to optimize an objective specified a-priori (e.g., the avoidance of deadlocks). Executing a scenario-based model in this way is termed play-out [31]).

Figure 1 illustrates a simple SB model. It represents a system that controls the water level of a water tank, which is equipped with cold and hot water taps. Each of the scenario objects is depicted as a transition system, wherein nodes correspond to the predetermined points of synchronization. The ADDHOTWA-TER scenario object repeatedly waits for events of type WATERLOW, and whenever such an event is triggered, the scenario object requests three times the event ADDHOT. Symmetrically, the ADDCOLDWATER scenario object requests the addition of cold water. When the SB model includes only the objects ADD-COLDWATER and ADDHOTWATER, three ADDCOLD events and three ADDHOT events may be triggered, in any order, during the model's execution. If maintaining a more stable water temperature within the tank is important, this could be achieved by adding the scenario object STABILITY, which enforces the interleaving of ADDHOT and ADDCOLD events—through the use of the event blocking idiom. An execution trace of the SB model that contains all three objects appears in the event log.

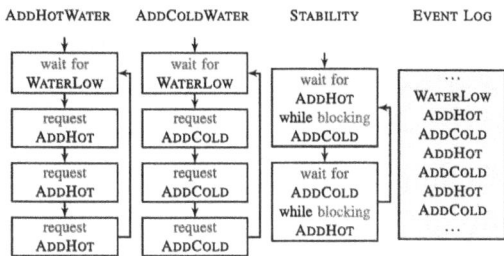

Fig. 1. (Borrowed from [26, 28].) An SB model that controls the water level in a tank with hot and cold water taps.

Scenario-based modeling has been implemented on top of several high-level languages, such as C++ [21], Java [32], JavsScript [4], Python [47], and ScenarioTools [14]. Moreover, scenario-based modeling has been applied to various complex systems, including cache coherence protocols [23], a web-server [21], and robotic controllers [17]. To keep the presentation simple in the coming sections, we will usually describe SB models as transitions systems.

We follow here the formal definitions of SBM as they appear in [36]. A scenario object O over event set E is given as a tuple $O = \langle Q, \delta, q_0, R, B \rangle$, where the components are defined as follows:

- Q is a set of states. Each state in Q represents a single, predetermined synchronization point;
- $q_0 \in Q$ is the initial state;
- $R : Q \to 2^E$ and $B : Q \to 2^E$ are mappings from states to the respective sets of events requested and blocked at these states; and
- $\delta : Q \times E \to 2^Q$ is a transition function, which serves to indicate how the scenario object transitions between states in response to the triggering of events from E.

A set of individual scenario objects can be composed, in a pairwise fashion, according to the rules that appear below. Let $O^1 = \langle Q^1, \delta^1, q_0^1, R^1, B^1 \rangle$ and $O^2 = \langle Q^2, \delta^2, q_0^2, R^2, B^2 \rangle$ be two scenario objects, specified over a common event set E. These two objects are composed into a single scenario object $O^1 \parallel O^2 = \langle Q^1 \times Q^2, \delta, \langle q_0^1, q_0^2 \rangle, R^1 \cup R^2, B^1 \cup B^2 \rangle$, where:

- $\langle \tilde{q}^1, \tilde{q}^2 \rangle \in \delta(\langle q^1, q^2 \rangle, e)$ if and only if $\tilde{q}^1 \in \delta^1(q^1, e)$ and $\tilde{q}^2 \in \delta^2(q^2, e)$; and

– the composite labeling function is defined as the union of its constituents; i.e., $e \in (R^1 \cup R^2)(\langle q^1, q^2 \rangle)$ if and only if $e \in R^1(q^1) \cup R^2(q^2)$, and $e \in (B^1 \cup B^2)(\langle q^1, q^2 \rangle)$ if and only if $e \in B^1(q^1) \cup B^2(q^2)$.

Through the $\|$ composition operator, we define a *behavioral model* M as a set of scenario objects, $M = \{O^1, O^2, \ldots, O^n\}$. The executions of model M are defined to be precisely the executions of the composite object $O = O^1 \| O^2 \| \ldots \| O^n$. Consequently, each execution of M starts from O's initial state, which, in turn, is the n-tuple of initial states of the individual objects of which O is comprised; and throughout M's run, in each state q one enabled event $e \in R(q) - B(q)$ is selected for triggering, if such an event exists. The execution then transitions to a state $\tilde{q} \in \delta(q, e)$, and the process is repeated.

3 Integrating ChatGPT and SBM

3.1 Basic Integration

As the first step towards integrating SBM and ChatGPT, we present a straightforward methodology for generating scenario objects from free-text, using ChatGPT. To get ChatGPT to present its output in scenario object form, we propose to include, in the prompts presented to the chatbot, a *preamble* that describes SBM's semantics, as presented in Sect. 2. This preamble is used to instruct ChatGPT to produce its output as transition systems, wherein each state is labeled with requested/blocked events; and has also a set of transition rules that indicate its successor state, for each event that could be triggered. Note that such a preamble only needs to be designed once, and that it can then be used with any subsequent query. Whenever a specific SBM implementation is in use (e.g., C++, Java), the chatbot's output can be adjusted to match the required syntax of that implementation.

The simple preamble, which we used in our some of our initial experimentation, is as follows:[2]

> I would like you to help me create a scenario-based model. A scenario-based model is comprised of a finite set of events, and scenarios. Each scenario is a sequence of states. In each state the scenario can request events, wait-for events, and block events. Afterwards, one event that is requested by at least one scenario, but is blocked by no scenario, is selected for triggering. Scenarios that requested or waited-for this event may then change states, and the process repeats itself. Scenarios cannot have internal loops or variables; these must be expressed using additional states.
>
> To display scenarios, please use the following format. For each state, mention the state's name, and the sets of requested and blocked events. Also, mention the transitions to other states. For example:
> – s1: request X, block Y. If X is triggered, go to state s2.

---

[2] This preamble and several other prompts are borrowed from [26]. In some of the experiments, we used other descriptions of SBM; but as it turned out, ChatGPT was able to handle very well the great variability in such descriptions.

> – s2: request Y, block X. If Y is triggered, go to state s2.
> Now, here are the details of the specific scenario-based model I'd like you to create...

Through this preamble, we could get ChatGPT to generate the model we described in Sect. 2. For the ADDHOTWATER scenario, we used the following prompt:

> Consider the event set WaterLow, AddHot, AddCold.
> Please suggest a scenario that waits for event WaterLow (without requesting it). When WaterLow is triggered, the scenario performs the following, 3 times in a row: request the event AddHot, and wait for it to be triggered (both in a single state). When the 3rd AddHot event occurs, the scenario transitions back to its initial state.

The chatbot then replied to this prompt as follows:

> – s1: wait for WaterLow. If WaterLow is triggered, go to state s2.
> – s2: request AddHot, wait for AddHot. If AddHot is triggered, go to state s3.
> – s3: request AddHot, wait for AddHot. If AddHot is triggered, go to state s4.
> – s4: request AddHot, wait for AddHot. If AddHot is triggered, go to state s1.

Which is indeed equivalent to the transition system that appeared in Fig. 1. The ADDCOLDWATER scenario could also, be generated using the symmetrical prompt. Next, if we wished to incrementally modify the system through the introduction of the STABILITY scenario, we could issue the final prompt:

> Please suggests a scenario that uses blocking to ensure that no two consecutive AddHot events can be triggered, and that no two consecutive AddCold events can be triggered; that is, once AddHot is triggered, AddCold must be triggered before AddHot can be triggered again, and vice versa. This scenario should not request any events, and should work regardless of any WaterLow events.

And in response, ChatGPT would produce the STABILITY scenario, precisely as described in Fig. 1.

We point out that there is a subtle difference between the prompts we used to obtain the first two scenarios, ADDHOTWATER and ADDCOLDWATER, compared to the prompt used to obtain STABILITY. For the first two cases, our prompt included information that approximately described the transition system that we desired; whereas in the last case, our prompt was more high-level, and did not contain the word "state". Still, in all cases, the chatbot successfully produced the desired outcome. This further demonstrates the wide specification range that ChatGPT can successfully handle; and it suggests that a chatbot can be used even in cases where the engineers themselves are not entirely certain of what the scenario that they desire looks like. While it is reasonable to assume that the more accurate description, the more accurate result, it seems that even high-level descriptions can prove useful, especially when enhanced by techniques for automated analysis, as we discuss next.

3.2   The Proposed Methodology

Further extending the basic integration between SBM and ChatGPT, we now propose an outline for a structured, language-agnostic and LLM-agnostic methodology for creating complex models of reactive systems that interact with their environment repeatedly, and may receive external inputs [35]. Many critical, modern systems can be regarded as reactive [1], and as a result there has been extensive work on devising methods and tools for modeling such systems. In spite of this tremendous effort, there still remain significant gaps; and these could result in models that are either inaccurate or difficult to maintain, or both. In this paper, which can be regarded as an element within the Wise Computing vision [25], we seek to mitigate these gaps, by creating advanced and intelligent tools, which will begin to undertake system development tasks that are traditionally reserved for humans. The approach is based on having system components generated, incrementally and iteratively, through the use of an LLM; and to have the LLM's outputs checked systematically, and semi-automatically, using various methods and tools (see Fig. 2).

1. Describe, textually and in natural language, the problem and its environment.
2. Choose a scenario-based, compositional modeling language, which affords well-defined execution semantics, and which is suitable for incrementally developing the system at hand.
3. Obtain a chatbot that is familiar with the general application domain, or which can readily become familiar with the domain through external knowledge, and which can be made to produce code in the selected scenario-based language.
4. Create a preamble that iteratively describes the semantics of the scenario-based language to the LLM. In order to confirm that the LLM has successfully internalized the details of the language semantics, have it execute (i.e., play out [31]) systems described as rules or scenarios in the selected language. Specifically, have the LLM output logs of scenario states, triggered events, composite system states, the values of environment variables, etc.
5. In an iterative manner, add scenarios and refine existing ones, as follows:
   (a) Use prompts to describe certain not-yet-specified requirements or aspects of the system as scenarios.
   (b) Have the chatbot generate the actual scenarios for the prompt, in the selected language.
   (c) Have the chatbot generate natural language descriptions of executable test cases and properties to be verified (perhaps as assertions for formal verification tools), per the original requirements. This entails stating the requirements at hand, from different perspectives.

(d) Carry out initial validation and testing within the chatbot, by challenging it to independently find gaps and incorrect execution paths. If needed, correct the natural language specification and prompts.

(e) Systematically check the output produced by the LLM, externally, by using the following (or part thereof): unit testing of individual scenarios, code reviews by human engineers, model checking of the new scenarios, as well as those of the composite system, subsystem testing with some or all of the already-developed scenarios, etc. Such testing is intended to be carried out in the execution environment of the language, whereas model checking is intended to be carried out using an adequate formal verification tool. Most importantly, both should be independent of the LLM's environment. As a possible enhancement, automate the subjecting of generated scenarios to model checking and testing.

(f) When errors are discovered, do not alter the generated code; instead, alter the LLM prompts, until the correct system scenarios and testing and verification properties are successfully generated. This step is crucial for ensuring that the stakeholder's (i.e., customer's) view of the requirements is well aligned with the developer's understanding, as well as with the actual code.

(g) Once the set of generated scenarios appears ready, repeat step (d), by having the LLM find potential failures or gaps in this set of scenarios. Specifically, attempt to find, through the LLM's suggestions, new environment considerations that might prevent the system from functioning correctly. This step is intended to mimic common system engineering task of having potential customers or external experts review some of the advanced system prototypes. Then, repeat earlier steps as needed.

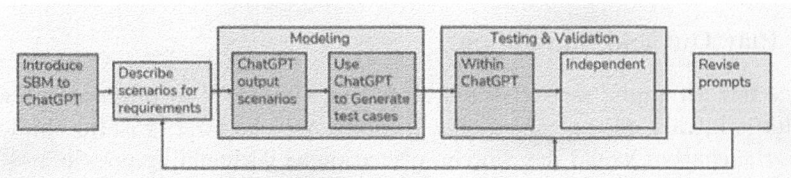

Fig. 2. Methodology overview: Development is iterative; testing and validation are carried out both within and outside of the LLM; when issues are identified with LLM-generate code, problematic code blocks are replaced using new or revised prompts.

Next, we elaborate on some of these steps, and provide illustrative, simple examples.

4   Using the Method in the Development Cycle

4.1   Code Generation

Code generation is one of the most straightforward capabilities of chatbots that we propose to integrate into a system's development cycle. In Sect. 3 we demonstrated that ChatGPT can generate an executable, scenario-based model—and similar capabilities have been demonstrated with other languages [6,39,45]. One advantage in the context of scenario-based systems is that it is possible to generate stand-alone scenarios, which can then be tested and reviewed separately, and later be added, incrementally, to the system at hand. In our preliminary experimentation for this paper, we tested code generation for requirements in the realms of algorithms on data structures, autonomous vehicles, control systems, and simulating natural phenomena. For each of these realms, the chatbot/SBM integration proved useful.

4.2   Modeling

Once ChatGPT successfully digested the underlying principles of SB models, it was indeed successful in combining logic with its knowledge of the problem domain and of the world at large, in order to enhance or develop an SB model. For example, it was successful in introducing new environment events, in describing the sensor scenarios required for triggering such events, and also in adding the corresponding application scenarios that react to these events. In one case, we considered a robot moving numbered tiles on a sequence of cells, and asked the chatbot to generate SB code for a bubble-sort algorithm to be used by this system. ChatGPT was able to introduce events corresponding to the arrival of a tile at the tail-end of the array, and it was also able to generate scenarios for reacting to such events.

4.3   Play Out and Simulation

After a few attempts, we succeeded in getting ChatGPT to produce execution logs for arbitrary SB specifications. Initially, we observed "wishful thinking", where the chatbot would describe an execution as it should be per the problem description. By iteratively refining our prompts, as illustrated in Fig. 3, we eventually got ChatGPT to follow the execution steps correctly and to display the event and transition leading to each synchronization point; as well as a table of all scenarios, indicating for each scenario its event declarations and whether or not it had requested or waited-for the event that was eventually triggered.

4.4   SMT-Like Model Analysis

A key advantage of SB modeling is its amenability to automated formal verification, and the availability of tools that perform this—either through exhaustive model checking that traverses all paths, or by using a domain-specific

Scenario descriptions in user prompts to ChatGPT:

```
GL:   Repeat three times: request the event "Flash Green Light"
RL:   Repeat three times: request the event "Flash Red Light"
ALTG: Repeat forever : Wait for "Flash Green Light" and after it happens,
      block "Flash Green Light" while waiting for "Flash Red Light"
ALTR: Repeat forever : Wait for "Flash Red Light" and after it happens,
      block "Flash Red Light" while waiting for "Flash Red Light"
```

Excerpts from ChatGPT playout output:

Upon initialization, all scenarios are allowed to reach their first stable state.

Scenario Short name	Wake-up	Requested	Blocked	Waited for
GL	Y	Flash Green Light		
RL	Y	Flash Red Light		
ALTG	Y			Flash Green Light
ALTR	Y			Flash Red Light

Let's proceed with the next step following the event "Flash Green Light":

Scenario Short name	Wake-up	Requested	Blocked	Waited for
GL	Y	Flash Green Light		
RL	N	Flash Red Light		
ALTG	Y		Flash Green Light	Flash Red Light
ALTR	N			Flash Red Light

Fig. 3. (Borrowed from [26].) *Simulating the execution of an SB model with ChatGPT.* Top: user prompts describing the scenarios at hand. Middle and bottom: The first couple of entries in the chatbot's output, when requested to play out the system's execution. These show the triggered events, the scenarios that reacted to these events, and the event-set declarations of each of the scenarios at the following synchronization point.

verification approach through the use of Satisfiability Modulo Theory (SMT) engines [20,30,37]. This is achieved through the abstraction and encapsulation of domain-specific processes, conditions and actions as states and events. The result is a set of relatively small intuitive scenarios that reflect individual requirements, and whose composition produces the complex system—as opposed to complexities that rise from the intricate conditional flow of sensitive and delicate processes, each with numerous steps.

In our experiments, we observed that ChatGPT is able to leverage these kinds of encapsulation and abstraction in identifying cases where a specification has either been omitted, or is handled incorrectly. In one case involving an autonomous vehicle system, we presented the chatbot with the following three requirements: (i) always stop when the light is red; (ii) always obey instructions from a police person; and (iii) never injure a person. ChatGPT readily reported that these requirements may be conflicting. With regards to the safety requirement of not entering an intersection when the traffic light is red, the chatbot pointed out that the autonomous vehicle may fail to stop if the road is icy; that it may involuntarily enter the intersection if, after stopping, it is hit from behind by another vehicle that did not stop; and, furthermore, that it may cause injury to a person even without moving, e.g., if a person who is walking behind the AV gets hit by another vehicle and is thrust against the AV.

In another case, using a mathematical, SMT-like analysis, ChatGPT successfully identified a particularly interesting execution path. Here, we presented the chatbot with a system comprised of the following four scenarios: the first scenario waits for an external time tick event, then requests flashing a red light briefly, and then waits for any event; the second scenario does the same, but requests to flash a green light; the third scenario counts time ticks modulo 3, and blocks the red light from flashing every third tick; and the fourth scenario another blocks flashing the green light, every five ticks. Next, we added the requirement that between any two consecutive time ticks, at least one light must be flashed. When prompted, ChatGPT responded that the requirement is not satisfied—and that every 15 time ticks ($3 \cdot 5$) both red and green flash events will be blocked. The chatbot apparently reached this conclusion through an arithmetic calculation, as opposed to a step-by-step simulation, which allowed it to quickly reach similar conclusions for arbitrarily large numbers.

Below is an excerpt from this conversation (borrowed from [26]), after the scenarios had already been described. When prompted with

now a new requirement came in: always, after every tick, *at least one light* must be flashed. Does the combined system of red flashing and green flashing with the 3 and 5 restrictions satisfy the requirement?

To this, ChatGPT replies:

To analyze whether the combined system satisfies the new requirement that at least one light must flash after every tick, we must consider the synchronization points of both the red and green systems with their respective restrictions:

The red system flashes on every tick, except every third one. The green system flashes on every tick, except every fifth one. If we consider the sequence of ticks and apply both restrictions, the combined system would not flash a light on a tick that is both a multiple of three and five — specifically, on ticks that are multiples of fifteen, since 15 is the least common multiple of 3 and 5. At such ticks, both systems would be blocking their respective lights from flashing due to their individual restrictions.

Therefore, on ticks that are multiples of fifteen (like the 15th, 30th, 45th tick, and so on), neither light would flash, violating the new requirement that at least one light must flash after every tick.

In conclusion, the combined system of red flashing and green flashing with the restrictions of not flashing on ticks divisible by three and five, respectively, does not satisfy the requirement that at least one light must be flashed after every tick.

Further, the chatbot was successful in discussing possible generalizations of this computation, including the calculation of the number of states of the composite system that an exhaustive model checker would have to traverse.

However, this capability is limited and should be used with care. For example, when we presented a similar case, where event E1 occurs every 3 s, in seconds 0,3,6,9, etc., and event E2 occurs at second 77 and then every 75 s, it toook several interactions and correction by humans for ChatGPT to realize that E1 and E2 can never occur at the same second since the time stamp of E2 events is always 2 modulo 3. This deficiency does not completely erase the value of ChatGPT in such SMT-like analyses. When checking global assertions, counter examples yielded by ChatGPT can be readily checked, and may identify potential bugs. Incorrect counterexamples may highlight gaps in the specification which may have led to the incorrect computations. Plain errors by ChatGPT in this context are not too expensive. Partial or incorrect attempts by ChatGPT at proofs that certain properties always hold, can help guide humans in carrying out rigorous analysis, whether mentally or with the help of tools, independent of an LLM.

Interestingly enough, while the chatbot successfully applied its logic to discover system execution paths with special properties, it failed to perform as well when required to list *all* possible execution paths that possess a certain property. In one case, we presented ChatGPT with a 4-by-4 cell grid, and prompted it for the steps that a robot may take from the bottom-left cell (0,0) to the top-right cell (3,3), using the usual events for up, down, left and right motions. We also instructed the chatbot to only look for paths that remained within the grid. ChatGPT produced paths such as *right, right, right, up, up, up* or *right, up, right, up, right, up*, but when instructed to list all possible paths that go through cell (1,3) it failed, and instead listed several paths that did not reach the desired target at all, such as *up, up, up, right, down, down, right, up, right*. We thus conclude that ChatGPT is not yet able to carry out exhaustive model checking on SB systems. However, this is not a severe limitation, because our proposed methodology for verifying the LLM's outputs entails carrying out such analysis independently of the LLM environment.

4.5 Identifying Under-Specification

Even in cases where an existing model addresses all stated requirements perfectly, it is possible that there are additional areas of the broader problem domain that are currently not handled properly—possible due to synthetic or reduced problem descriptions. When presented with appropriate prompts, ChatGPT was able to significantly improve an already developed model, or, conversely, to help in explicitly stating the expected scope and boundaries of the intended system.

In one example [18], we presented the chatbot with an SB model that had been developed for science teaching purposes. The model contained information on how bees depend on the ambient temperature in order to switch between being active and hibernating; how flower plants rely on hours of daylight in order to start blooming; and how active bees depend on blooming flowers for their survival. In the original model, the number of daylight hours and the average temperatures were mutable parameters, which students could adjust in order to check how certain combinations of settings could sustain the bees, whereas other settings could cause the bees to die out due to hunger.

When we prompted ChatGPT for possible enhancements to the education model, it returned with a suggestion that we consider also weather-related variations, as these might modify the pre-specified fixed number of daylight hours and average temperature for a given time of year.

4.6 Explainability

Once the chatbot is provided with a certain expected or observed behavior of the system, it is often able to explain the cause of that behavior, in natural language. Further, it is often able to reasonably balance between providing the overly detailed, complete execution trace, and the overly simplistic explanation that "this is what the system is supposed to do".

In one case we provided the chatbot with details on the semantics of SB modeling, and then prompted it as follows (borrowed from [26]):

In a system with two scenarios, one waits for time tick events and after each time tick requests a short beep (100 ms). The other scenario waits for time ticks, and after each such event requests a long beep (500 ms). Each of these scenarios waits for both the short and long beep events, so that after each time tick, exactly one beep occurs. Actuator scenarios actually cause the respective beeping action. Time tick events are injected by the environment every one second. A user reported that it watched the system for 20 s, and never heard a long beep. Can you explain why this may have happened?

ChatGPT's response was:

The user's report of not hearing a long beep in a system with two scenarios—one requesting a short beep after each time tick, and the other requesting a long beep after each time tick—can be explained through the principles of Scenario-based Modeling (SBM).

In SBM, when multiple scenarios request different events after a shared trigger event, the execution environment selects one of these requested events to occur. The selection can be arbitrary or follow a specific strategy, such as alphabetic or lexical order, priority, random, round-robin, etc. In this case, if the event selection strategy prioritizes the short beep over the long beep (for example, due to alphabetic order, where "short beep" comes before "long beep"), then the short beep will always be selected to occur after each time tick, and the long beep will never be executed. Since time tick events are injected by the environment every second, and both scenarios are waiting for this event, each time tick leads to both scenarios being activated. However, if the system consistently selects the short beep event over the long beep event after each time tick, the scenario requesting the long beep will never progress to the state where it actually triggers the long beep. As a result, only short beeps will be heard.

In summary, the user's observation of not hearing any long beeps can be attributed to the event selection mechanism within the SBM framework, which in this case consistently favors the short beep event over the long beep event. This could be due to the selection strategy used by the system (like alphabetic order) or other operational logic specifics.

We then challenged the chatbot again:

Thank you. Assume that the developers changed the selection algorithm and they now select events randomly. The user tested the system many times, for hours, and never heard a long beep. Can you try to explain?

And in response to this, ChatGPT returned with a highly comprehensive answer, which covered many possible issues with the execution infrastructure, human-machine interactions, and the application scenarios. Here are a few excerpts, borrowed from [26]:

If the event selection algorithm was changed to randomly select between the short beep and long beep events, but the user still never hears a long beep, there are several potential explanations:

Implementation Error in Random Selection: The most straightforward explanation could be a bug or implementation error in the random selection algorithm. It might not be truly random, or it could be incorrectly favoring the short beep event due to a coding mistake.

Issue with the Long Beep Scenario: There might be a problem with the scenario that requests the long beep. This could be a coding error or a logical flaw in the scenario itself, preventing it from properly requesting the long beep event.

User Perception or Reporting Error: Finally, there could be an issue with how the user is perceiving or reporting the beeps. They might be missing the long beep due to distraction, ambient noise, or misunderstanding what constitutes a long beep in the context of this system.

To diagnose the issue accurately, developers would need to conduct thorough testing and debugging, looking into each of these potential areas to find where the problem lies.

Although these explanations were quite impressive, they were also imperfect. In some cases, we presented the chatbot with well-specified scenarios accompanied by a detailed description of an observed event sequence, but ChatGPT was unable to describe a step-by-step execution (play-out) of the scenarios that would result the given event sequence; instead, it provided incorrect explanations for how the event sequence might occur. Such issues could sometimes be resolved by repeatedly providing ChatGPT with reminders and pin-pointing its mistakes. This is a significant caveat that serves as a reminder that outputs produced by the LLM must be formally inspected and verified.

4.7   Accommodating Semantic Flexibility

Many software engineering teams are tied to specific programming and modeling languages, and their associated semantics. In our experimentation, ChatGPT was in many cases able to discuss and accommodate alternative semantics, demonstrating flexibility that human engineers sometimes lack.

For example, consider again the water tap example, first described in Sect. 2. Observe the ADDHOTWATER scenario: when it is in any of the states where it requests ADDHOT, it is not waiting for event WATERLOW, and consequently cannot react to its triggering. However, if we consider the semantics of the Live Sequence Charts [9], which is another SB formalism, every scenario constantly waits for all events that were waited-for in its starting state. When such a waited-for event occurs, the LSC infrastructure instantiates a fresh copy of the scenario. As it turns out, from our initial textual description of SBM, ChatGPT concluded that this semantics were the default.

In another example, we tried to get ChatGPT to generate a scenario-based implementation of Quicksort. Before starting, the chatbot remarked that this will be hard, because classical solutions are recursive. To assist the chatbot, we then pointed out that there was actually an alternative, published implementation for Quicksort, which was iterative instead of recursive [34]. Further, this implementation was structured as a set of instructions to human workers that needed to arrange cars in an automobile dealership parking lot, according to window-sticker prices. Each employee in this implementation was assigned one, narrow role, which coincides nicely with how SB modeling works. ChatGPT readily accepted this new "mindset", and was able to produce the sought-after SB specification.

4.8   Interactive Mutual Learning

Through our experimentation with the proposed approach, we observed that ChatGPT could often achieve better results when it was provided with multiple prompts, explorations and discussions, compared to when it was provided with a single, concise, detailed description. We believe that this might be a general rule worth following when a chatbot is used as part of the software and system development cycle. Thus, this style of work might be a good fit for an agile development process, which inherently involves a great deal of trial and error as it spirally converges towards the specified (or, sometimes, under-specified) goal. From the chatbot's point of view, this is a highly constructive process, in which developers and stakeholders iteratively describe their wishes and plans, as they slowly refine their own understanding of the system and its environment, as well as their own needs and intended future interactions with the system.

An integral part of this refinement is the production of increasingly explicit definitions of elements that are within the scope of the system's environment.

Such definitions, which may be highly useful to both chatbots and humans, are often quite absent from classical system specifications.

4.9 Generating New Formal Assertions and Testable Properties

Given an LLM-generated component, generating test cases based on the original specification is a straightforward activity. Furthermore, it is only natural to ask the LLM to generate the code for such a test case. However, the generated programs, or scenarios, must be tested also from additional perspectives. Specification and execution of these tests may be carried out both with and without the help of the LLM.

To illustrate these additional perspectives, consider the following examples.

We have asked ChatGPT to produce a stand-alone Python program that flashes a green light for half a second every 3 s, i.e., in seconds 0, 3, 6, 9, etc., when counting time from zero. ChatGPT returned an acceptable program. When asked to generate a test case, it created a reasonable program that examined an execution log and confirmed that indeed one would observe repetition of periods of half a second of the green light being on, followed by 2.5 s of that light being off. However, as may often happen, if the on and off periods are not exactly 0.500 and 2.500 respectively, but say, 0.501 and 2.501, the program may still pass the test, but over time, the timestamps of when the light is flashed will be quite far from a multiple of 3. This is another property that must be checked as it was in the specification. Generating the code for this test may be done by a human or by ChatGPT (of course, the test case must be checked in either case).

One technique for generating new perspectives is to generate alternative designs and implementations, and examining the differences. We have asked ChatGPT to generate code for a robot to navigate a two dimensional grid of cells from an origin cell to a destination cell with steps of right, left, up and down, and where some cells are marked as obstacles, and can be sensed only from an adjacent cell. We then asked ChatGPT to generate a materially different program. ChatGPT generated a breadth-first search, replacing its choice of depth-first search in the first program. When asked about the externally visible effects it listed resource usage and performance aspects, opportunity for parallelization, and more. We then clarified to ChatGPT that the grid data structure is not to be used as a map in advance route planning, and that the scenarios should simulate actual movement, including back-tracking. While such simulation seems very similar to a depth first search, the path that the program outputs would be different: in the simulated traversal, the backtracking steps are part of the path, where in the search they are only part of the planning until a path with no backtracking is found. A developer can examine these issues and determine whether any of them should be included in the specification or in the testing or formal verification of the component.

Another approach for generating new perspectives does not involve code generation, but explores possible behaviors. Going back to the light flashing program from the first example in this subsection, we asked ChatGPT whether a program could comply literally with every aspect of the specification, and still produce undesired results. In its first response, ChatGPT suggested that a program that flashes a red light between consecutive flashing of the green light may comply literally with the specification, but may not behave as expected. Similarly ChatGPT suggested that if the device producing the green light also creates a sound, the behavior may be undesired. The developers can then consider whether to enhance the specification accordingly to avoid these cases, and/or whether to create test cases, using cameras, microphones, and appropriate software, to check that indeed the behavior of the system in the world is as intended.

The properties to be checked can be formulated by the LLM in natural language, as executable test cases, or as we show below, as formal assertions for verification tools. For example, we prompted ChatGPT to analyze the following scenario: An autonomous vehicle (the ego car) is at a red traffic light. It senses that car B, that was approaching fast behind it, noticed the red light late, and hit its brakes. B is screeching to a halt. It is not clear whether B will be able to stop before it hits the ego car. Further, parts of the intersection are "clear". With some interaction, ChatGPT produced reactive code for the ego car to move forward when both needed and possible. Clearly, it is not enough that the ego car should eventually reach a point beyond the stopping point of car B, and we asked ChatGPT to refine and formalize this requirement. Referring to variables in the program, it offered two variants, one for SPIN/Promela:

$$ltl \ \ no\_collision\{[\ ]((d\_E - d\_B) >= \text{safe\_distance})\}$$

and one for NuSMV:

$$\text{SPEC AG}((d\_E - d\_B) >= \text{safe\_distance})$$

5 Methodology and Technology Notes

In this section we document several issues and challenges that came up in our experiments in using an LLM according to the methodology outline described above. For each issue we list possible approaches for addressing it in further formalization or refinement of the methodology, in developing tools around it, and/or in the way engineers apply the methodology. The discussion refers to experiments with development of a scenario-based program for grid traversal.

5.1 The Methodology Focuses on One Aspect of the Development Cycle

The use of an LLM in building software applications is already wide-spread, and will likely grow, in analysis, requirement specification, design, coding, testing, etc. The methodology discussed here focuses particularly on the *development* task (which is largely code development), as contrasted, say, with requirement specification or integration testing; it can be employed within an agile-development sprint, and within other approaches to the system development cycle.

5.2   Prompt Engineering for Scenario Generation

What should a prompt that requests an LLM to generate one scenario look like?

Ideally, one would like to specify the desired function in a natural manner, as in "Do not allow the robot to move into a grid cell that is marked as an obstacle", and let the LLM take care of the details of SBM. Alternatively, one could specify "Please create a scenario that, before the robot moves out of a grid cell, checks the cells to the right, left, above and below the current cell, and if any of those adjacent cells is an obstacle, block the respective, Right, Left, Up, and Down move events, until the robot exits the current cell.". However, if the LLM is able to add fine details to the actual code, it means that the code is more distant from the requirement specification, and may contain decisions and choices that a domain specialist may not be aware of. For example, following multiple prompts, the LLM may make application-related assumptions (as in the case of carrying out a map-based search instead simulated traversal as described in Sect. 4.9). Of course, such LLM decisions would turn out in code review, and then either be accepted or rejected by the developer. Clearly, in a methodology that aims for intuitive executable specifications, the natural language prompts should be as close as possible to the actual code. Hence, when the LLM indeed enhances the generated module beyond the original prompt specification, the developer should update the prompt to either request or exclude these enhancements specifically.

One could also start with a functional description of a scenario, and once this is complete, after several iterations, have the LLM generate, in addition to the SBM code, a natural language description of the scenario. In addition to serving as documentation, the description may serve as an LLM prompt in another scenario-generation iteration (which of course must be tested).

5.3   Watching Out for Scenario Regression

The output of an LLM is never predictable. Small and focused changes in a prompt, or new prompts requesting a small change in an existing code block may cause larger, or unpredictable, changes in one or more scenarios. Our conclusion is that with each iteration of producing one or more artifacts one should (a) compare the result with prior artifacts; and (b) run tests and a comprehensive manual (i.e., human-driven) review over a larger set of artifacts and components. Tools that readily compare and display all differences between multiple LLM-generated code blocks would be very useful for this purpose. It is not enough to observe the desired change in the expected location in the code, or the changed behavior in the problematic section in an execution log. While this is an intuitive methodological requirement and common practice, recall that the entire methodology is about the coding stages in application development and not about application testing stages.

5.4   Dealing with Context Dependencies

As stated earlier, scenarios implicitly start with the word "always", as in: "Always when event E1 occurs, request event E2". However, this universal rule may have exceptions that depend on the context, i.e. a variety of system and environment conditions. For example, when hurrying to a hospital, transporting a patient in a critical condition, on a deserted street, when no other vehicle is in sight, a human driver may (cautiously) run a red light, and an autonomous, SBM-based vehicle might need to do the same. Or, in our grid traversal example, the robot creates its own context, and the path should not loop into itself. Should the necessary information be tracked in each scenario separately? Should there be a data structure that is shared between the scenarios? Or, should the environment inject external sensor events to indicate relevant information?

There has been research about context oriented programming in general [8], and implementing context awareness in behavioral programs in particular [11]. In the present example, we chose to have several shared data structures for this purpose, but the more general question of what are the best ways to weave context dependencies SB designs, and therefore into LLM prompts, is still open.

5.5   Dealing with LLM-Generated Bugs

The LLM may generate incorrect code even for the most precise prompt. Here are a few examples from our experiments: (i) when checking certain properties of adjacent cells, the scenario used the previous location of the robot (which was accessed for another function in the same scenario) instead of the current location; (ii) when needing to block multiple events, the scenario incorrectly issued several different YIELD commands instead of accumulating multiple blocked events in a set, and passing the set to the single yield; (iii) an IF statement that should have controlled only a few code lines, instead dominated and conditioned the rest of the scenario; (iv) a scenario that should have had a single YIELD command, waiting each time for the next move of the robot, incorrectly waited for the move both at the beginning and the end of each of its iteration. These (and other) errors were caught in testing, and the code was corrected using revised or new, corrective prompts. However, since these errors were not a result of prompt vagueness or ambiguity, one may ask how the principle of not manually modifying the code, and only changing the prompt, should be applied in this case. One approach could be to add these originally corrective actions as emphases and notes in the prompt; such notes may be reminiscent of when an experienced programmer explains a code module to a novice, sharing stories about past bugs and omissions, to emphasize the need for close attention to details.

5.6   Issues Around Direct Code Changes

It is often very tempting to change the code directly and not via an LLM prompt. Two examples from our experiments are changing a printed string, from "CURRENT LOCATION" to "CURRENT LOCATION:", or inserting a PRINT() in a particular point for debug purposes. Unfortunately, such manual code changes are lost the next time the scenario is generated using the LLM, or, conversely, they cause the abandonment of the methodology.

5.7   Mapping Prompts to Scenarios

While in SBM scenario specifications can align with requirement specifications, our experiments show that in incremental scenario development this is not always the case. For example, initially, we separated the three functions of physically moving the robot, updating the robot's location, and printing the robot's actual path, into separate scenarios. To enforce a particular event order, we combined these three functions into one scenario (an alternative solution was to keep the scenarios separate and rely on event blocking). To generate the scenario, we prompted the LLM to create one scenario that consolidates the functions of these three scenarios in a certain order, without repeating the details of each operation. In another case, ChatGPT, on its own, added the logic that prevents the robot from stepping outside the grid boundaries, to the scenario that checks for obstacles; this created a redundancy with the scenario that was responsible for checking for grid boundaries; hence, we prompted ChatGPT to delete the unneeded scenario.

We also occasionally prompted for application-wide changes affecting all scenarios, such as changing the parameters to the YIELD command from the format that appears in the SBM preamble that we used (borrowed verbatim from [48]), to the format required by the BP Python execution environment of [47]. The entire chat dialog can than serve in having the LLM generate a concise description of each of the scenarios in the final application.

5.8   Emerging Requirements

One of the characteristics of agile approaches to software development is the emergence of new requirements as part of iterative sprints. In the first block of code for the robot-on-grid application, the coordinate system for grid cells that ChatGPT chose was different from how the user tacitly visualized them: (row,column) as is common in matrix description versus (horizontal,vertical), as in an (x,y) Cartesian system; in the former, a move up increases the second coordinate, and in the latter, it decreases the first coordinate. This choice, or decision, by the LLM, for an application detail that was not specified, triggered the documenting of a new requirement.

5.9   Low-Level Programming Choices

Some of the dialogs with ChatGPT were on specific programming style issues, like whether to rely on particular semantics of the Python language (e.g., when the compiler or interpreter exits the computation of an OR condition when one of the sub-conditions is computed to be true), or when and how to use temporary variables for streamlining the program's appearance and flow. This question is outside of the scope of the current methodology; the LLM may be taught to comply with the developer's preferences as a rule, as opposed to dealing with specific changes to already-generated code blocks.

6   Related Work

In recent years, LLM-based chatbots have progressed significantly, and have had a considerable impact on a diverse range of domains. Engineers and researchers are just now beginning to tap the potential applications of this technology in music [40], education [2], healthcare [38], academia and libraries [41], and many other areas.

Within the software engineering domain, which is our focus here, there have already been attempts made to harness chatbots for tasks such as evaluating the quality of code [6], correcting bugs [45], and generating code semi-automatically or completely automatically [10,12]. The general sentiment is that chatbots will play a significant role in the future of code generation; although the specifics are not yet clear. Our work here is an attempt to outline one possible path forward, which, we believe, will help bring about this integration in a safe and controlled manner.

The methodology that we advocate here for the integration of LLMs into the software development cycle relies on the large body of existing work on the topic of scenario-based modeling [9,33]. Concretely, we propose to leverage the SBM's amenability to formal analysis techniques [22,29], such as automatic repair [27], synthesis [15], and verification [20,30]. Additional, recent work has also identified the benefits that SBM affords in this context [48]. Although we focus here on SBM, additional modeling approaches, with similar traits, could likely be used in a similar manner.

Finally, this paper can be regarded as yet another step towards the overarching vision of *Wise Computing* [23–25]. Wise computing is an attempt to transform the computer into a proactive member of the software engineering team—making suggestions and observations, raising questions, and even carrying out verification-like processes without an explicit request from a human engineer.

7   Conclusion

The appearance of LLMs, and the subsequent release of advanced, general-purpose chatbots, is a huge step forward, and is very likely to revolutionize the domain of software engineering in the decades to come. Still, because of errors and inaccuracies that are abundant in the outputs of such chatbots, this kind of integration must be carried out with care. Here, we outline one possible method for such an integration, which leverages the diverse capabilities of chatbots; but which at the same time also emphasizes that a careful analysis and inspection of their outputs is crucial to perform such an integration safely. It is our hope that this work will form a basis for additional research on this important topic.

As our next steps, we intend to continue this work along several directions. First and foremost, we plan to create an implementation of the environments and tools needed to fully integrate SBM and ChatGPT; and then, through this tools and environments, carry out a large, real-world evaluation of case studies of interest. These case studies will hopefully demonstrate the usefulness of the approach as a whole.

In addition to the above, we find it highly likely that this kind of work will mandate enhancements and modifications to existing tools—chatbots and SBM frameworks alike. For example, with the current ChatGPT version, every conversation starts from a blank slate; whereas for a system that is undergoing iterative development, e.g. as part of the Wise Computing vision, it would likely be of better use to have the chatbot memorize, and utilize, previous conversations. Such an integration could be achieved, e.g., by summarizing concluded conversation and then providing these summaries back to the chatbot, as part of the preamble, whenever a new conversation is about to begin. A more elegant solution would be to customize ChatGPT specifically for the task of developing SB models and programs, and to have it remember key points of previous chats automatically. Ideally, LLMs will be able to perform such learning selectively, and over time, using their knowledge of the system being developed to determine which information from past conversation should be retained, and for how long.

Going beyond system development, the developments described above could also prove useful in a broader perspective: the same prompt engineering methods that would be useful for incremental and interactive system development could be used, e.g., to teach computers about other domains, and also in improving the training and day-to-day communications of human engineers.

Acknowledgements. We thank Dan Aleksandrowicz for valuable discussions and insights.

The work of Harel, Marron and Szekely was funded in part by an NSFC-ISF grant to DH, issued jointly by the National Natural Science Foundation of China (NSFC) and the Israel Science Foundation (ISF grant 3698/21). Additional support was provided by a research grant to DH from the Estate of Harry Levine, the Estate of Avraham Rothstein, Brenda Gruss, and Daniel Hirsch, the One8 Foundation, Rina Mayer, Maurice Levy, and the Estate of Bernice Bernath.

The work of Katz was partially funded by the European Union (ERC, VeriDeL, 101112713). Views and opinions expressed are however those of the author(s) only and do not necessarily reflect those of the European Union or the European Research Council Executive Agency. Neither the European Union nor the granting authority can be held responsible for them.

References

1. Aceto, L., Ingólfsdóttir, A., Larsen, K., Srba, J.: Reactive Systems: Modelling, Specification and Verification. Cambridge University Press, Cambridge (2007)
2. AlAfnan, M., Dishari, S., Jovic, M., Lomidze, K.: ChatGPT as an educational tool: opportunities, challenges, and recommendations for communication, business writing, and composition courses. J. Artif. Intell. Technol. **3**(2), 60–68 (2023)
3. Anthropic: Claude (2024). https://www.anthropic.com/claude

4. Bar-Sinai, M., Weiss, G., Shmuel, R.: BPjs: an extensible, open infrastructure for behavioral programming research. In: Proceedings 21st ACM/IEEE International Conference on Model Driven Engineering Languages and Systems (MODELS), pp. 59–60 (2018)

5. Biolchini, J., Mian, P., Natali, A., Travassos, G.: Systematic Review in Software Engineering. technical Report. System Engineering and Computer Science Department COPPE/UFRJ, Report ES 679 (2005)

6. Burak, Y., Ozsoy, I., Ayerdem, M., Tüzün, E.: Evaluating the code quality of AI-assisted code generation tools: an empirical study on GitHub copilot, Amazon CodeWhisperer, and ChatGPT (2023). https://arxiv.org/abs/2304.10778/

7. Chang, Y., et al.: A Survey on Evaluation of Large Language Models, technical Report (2023). https://arxiv.org/abs/2307.03109/

8. Costanza, P., Hirschfeld, R.: Language constructs for context-oriented programming: an overview of ContextL. In: Proceedings of Symposium on Dynamic Languages (DLS), pp. 1–10 (2005)

9. Damm, W., Harel, D.: LSCs: breathing life into message sequence charts. J. Formal Methods Syst. Des. (FMSD) 19(1), 45–80 (2001)

10. Dong, Y., Jiang, X., Jin, Z., Li, G.: Self-collaboration code generation via Chat-GPT, technical Report (2023). https://arxiv.org/abs/2304.07590/

11. Elyasaf, A.: Context-oriented behavioral programming. Inf. Softw. Technol. 133, 106504 (2021)

12. Feng, Y., Vanam, S., Cherukupally, M., Zheng, W., Qiu, M., Chen, H.: Investigating code generation performance of Chat-GPT with crowdsourcing social data. In: Proceedings of 47th IEEE Computer Software and Applications Conf. (COMPSAC), pp. 1–10 (2023)

13. Google: Bard (2023). https://bard.google.com/

14. Greenyer, J., Gritzner, D., Gutjahr, T., König, F., Glade, N., Marron, A., Katz, G.: ScenarioTools—a tool suite for the scenario-based modeling and analysis of reactive systems. J. Sci. Comput. Program. (J. SCP) 149, 15–27 (2017)

15. Greenyer, J., Gritzner, D., Katz, G., Marron, A.: Scenario-based modeling and synthesis for reactive systems with dynamic system structure in ScenarioTools. In: Proceedings of 19th ACM/IEEE International Conference on Model Driven Engineering Languages and Systems (MODELS), pp. 16–23 (2016)

16. Gregorcic, B., Pendrill, A.M.: ChatGPT and the Frustrated Socrates. Phys. Educ. 58(2) (2023)

17. Gritzner, D., Greenyer, J.: Synthesizing executable PLC code for robots from scenario-based GR(1) specifications. In: Seidl, M., Zschaler, S. (eds.) STAF 2017. LNCS, vol. 10748, pp. 247–262. Springer, Cham (2018). https://doi.org/10.1007/978-3-319-74730-9_23

18. Harel, D., Assmann, U., Fournier, F., Limonad, L., Marron, A., Szekely, S.: Toward methodical discovery and handling of hidden assumptions in complex systems and models. In: Engineering Safe and Trustworthy Cyber Physical Systems—Essays Dedicated to Werner Damm on the Occasion of His 71st Birthday (2023)

19. Harel, D., Kantor, A., Katz, G.: Relaxing synchronization constraints in behavioral programs. In: McMillan, K., Middeldorp, A., Voronkov, A. (eds.) LPAR 2013. LNCS, vol. 8312, pp. 355–372. Springer, Heidelberg (2013). https://doi.org/10.1007/978-3-642-45221-5_25

20. Harel, D., Kantor, A., Katz, G., Marron, A., Mizrahi, L., Weiss, G.: On composing and proving the correctness of reactive behavior. In: Proceedings of 13th International Conference on Embedded Software (EMSOFT), pp. 1–10 (2013)

21. Harel, D., Katz, G.: Scaling-up behavioral programming: steps from basic prin-
    ciples to application architectures. In: Proceedings of 4th SPLASH Workshop on
    Programming Based on Actors, Agents and Decentralized Control (AGERE!), pp.
    95–108 (2014)
22. Harel, D., Katz, G., Lampert, R., Marron, A., Weiss, G.: On the succinctness of
    idioms for concurrent programming. In: Proceedings of 26th International Confer-
    ence on Concurrency Theory (CONCUR), pp. 85–99 (2015)
23. Harel, D., Katz, G., Marelly, R., Marron, A.: An initial wise development envi-
    ronment for behavioral models. In: Proceedings of 4th International Conference
    on Model-Driven Engineering and Software Development (MODELSWARD), pp.
    600–612 (2016)
24. Harel, D., Katz, G., Marelly, R., Marron, A.: First steps towards a wise develop-
    ment environment for behavioral models. Int. J. Inf. Syst. Model. Des. (IJISMD)
    7(3), 1–22 (2016)
25. Harel, D., Katz, G., Marelly, R., Marron, A.: Wise computing: toward endowing
    system development with proactive wisdom. IEEE Comput. **51**(2), 14–26 (2018)
26. Harel, D., Katz, G., Marron, A., Szekely, S.: On augmenting scenario-based model-
    ing with generative AI. In: Proceedings of 12th International Conference on Model-
    Driven Engineering and Software Development (MODELSWARD), pp. 235–246
    (2024)
27. Harel, D., Katz, G., Marron, A., Weiss, G.: Non-intrusive repair of reactive pro-
    grams. In: Proceedings of 17th IEEE International Conference on Engineering of
    Complex Computer Systems (ICECCS), pp. 3–12 (2012)
28. Harel, D., Katz, G., Marron, A., Weiss, G.: Non-intrusive repair of safety and
    liveness violations in reactive programs. Trans. Comput. Collect. Intell. (TCCI)
    16, 1–33 (2014)
29. Harel, D., Katz, G., Marron, A., Weiss, G.: The effect of concurrent programming
    idioms on verification. In: Proceedings of 3rd International Conference on Model-
    Driven Engineering and Software Development (MODELSWARD), pp. 363–369
    (2015)
30. Harel, D., Lampert, R., Marron, A., Weiss, G.: Model-checking behavioral pro-
    grams. In: Proceedings of 9th ACM International Conference on Embedded Soft-
    ware (EMSOFT), pp. 279–288 (2011)
31. Harel, D., Marelly, R.: Specifying and executing behavioral requirements: the play
    in/play-out approach. Softw. Syst. Model. (SoSyM) **2**, 82–107 (2003)
32. Harel, D., Marron, A., Weiss, G.: Programming coordinated scenarios in java.
    In: Proceedings of 24th European Conference on Object-Oriented Programming
    (ECOOP), pp. 250–274 (2010)
33. Harel, D., Marron, A., Weiss, G.: Behavioral programming. Commun. ACM
    (CACM) **55**(7), 90–100 (2012)
34. Harel, D., Marron, A., Yerushalmi, R.: Scenario-based algorithmics: coding algo-
    rithms by automatic composition of separate concerns. Computer **54**(10), 95–101
    (2021)
35. Harel, D., Pnueli, A.: On the development of reactive systems. Logics Models
    Concurr. Syst. **F-13**, 474–498 (1985)
36. Katz, G.: On module-based abstraction and repair of behavioral programs. In:
    McMillan, K., Middeldorp, A., Voronkov, A. (eds.) LPAR 2013. LNCS, vol.
    8312, pp. 518–535. Springer, Heidelberg (2013). https://doi.org/10.1007/978-3-
    642-45221-5_35

37. Katz, G., Barrett, C., Harel, D.: Theory-aided model checking of concurrent transition systems. In: Proceedings of 15th International Conference on Formal Methods in Computer-Aided Design (FMCAD), pp. 81–88 (2015)

38. Li, J., Dada, A., Kleesiek, J., Egger, J.: ChatGPT in healthcare: a taxonomy and systematic review, technical Report (2023). https://www.medrxiv.org/content/10.1101/2023.03.30.23287899v1

39. Liu, J., Xia, C., Wang, Y., Zhang, L.: Is your code generated by ChatGPT really Correct? Rigorous evaluation of large language models for code generation, technical Report (2023). https://arxiv.org/abs/2305.01210/

40. Lu, P., et al.: MuseCoco: generating symbolic music from text, technical Report (2023). https://arxiv.org/abs/2306.00110/

41. Lund, B., Wang, T.: Chatting about ChatGPT: how may AI and GPT impact academia and libraries? Libr. Hi Tech News **40**(3), 26–29 (2023)

42. MetaAI: LLaMa (2023). https://ai.meta.com/llama/

43. OpenAI: ChatGPT (2022). https://chat.openai.com/

44. Pettersson, O., Andersson, J.: A survey of modeling approaches for software ecosystems. In: Maglyas, A., Lamprecht, A.-L. (eds.) Software Business. LNBIP, vol. 240, pp. 79–93. Springer, Cham (2016). https://doi.org/10.1007/978-3-319-40515-5_6

45. Surameery, N., Shakor, M.: Use chat GPT to solve programming bugs. Int. J. Inf. Technol. Comput. Eng. (IJITC) **3**(1), 17–22 (2023)

46. Vaswani, A., et al.: Attention is all you Need. In: Proceedings of 31st Conference on Advances in Neural Information Processing Systems (NeurIPS) (2017)

47. Yaacov, T.: BPPy: behavioral programming in python. SoftwareX **24** (2023)

48. Yaacov, T., Elyasaf, A., Weiss, G.: Boosting LLM-based software generation by aligning code with requirements. In: Proceedings of 14th International Model-Driven Requirements Engineering Workshop (MoDRE) (2024)

Model-Driven Development of Chatbot Microservices

Adel Vahdati⬤ and Raman Ramsin$^{(\boxtimes)}$ ⬤

Department of Computer Engineering, Sharif University of Technology, Azadi Avenue, Tehran,
Iran
{adel.vahdati97,ramsin}@sharif.edu

Abstract. Conversational agents and chatbots are gaining prominence in software systems by providing functionalities beyond traditional GUIs. These intelligent assistants facilitate software development tasks such as deployment, error handling, and scheduling. However, chatbot development remains challenging due to productivity, reusability, scalability, and maintainability issues.

We propose a model-driven methodology for chatbot development in four phases: computation-independent model construction, platform-independent model construction, platform-specific model construction, and code generation. The methodology enhances productivity by automating code generation and improves reusability through computation-independent and platform-independent definitions. Additionally, it introduces a novel approach to categorizing, enumerating, parameterizing, and representing user intents. We obtain data for training natural language understanding services and leverage microservice architecture and architectural design patterns to enhance scalability, maintainability, and interoperability. The methodology has been evaluated based on three groups of criteria: criteria relevant to the generic software development lifecycle, criteria specific to model-driven development, and criteria relevant to chatbots.

Keyword: Model-driven methodology · Chatbot microservice · Natural Language processing

1 Introduction

Software systems are now adopting a new type of interface beyond the traditional GUI. Conversational agents, intelligent assistants, and conversational user interfaces (CUI) are becoming increasingly popular [1]. Additionally, conversational agents are already aiding software development activities such as automating deployment tasks, assigning errors and issues to team members, and scheduling tasks [2]. Their integration into social networks as communication channels has enhanced stakeholder participation in task automation and collaborative modeling [2, 3].

In conversational agents, user interaction occurs through text, voice messages, or interactive images (as in Gesture Bots). The agent always has a dialogue mechanism, with the only difference being the interface or medium through which this dialogue happens [1].

F. José Domínguez Mayo et al. (Eds.): MODELSWARD 2024, CCIS 2547, pp. 69–87, 2026.
https://doi.org/10.1007/978-3-031-96841-9_4

A chatbot mimics human conversation through two-way communication using natural language. To provide a useful conversation, a chatbot platform must offer the following features [4]:

- Natural language processing (NLP) and natural language understanding (NLU): understanding user input and extracting relevant information.
- Conversation flow management
- Performing necessary actions: such as searching a database or calling other services.

Leading companies like Google (Dialogflow), Microsoft (Microsoft Bot Framework), Amazon (Amazon Lex), and IBM (Watson) have provided various tools and frameworks to create conversational agents [5]. These tools offer a framework, cloud environment, and GUI to define the conversation flow. Existing frameworks utilize machine learning (ML) algorithms to identify the user's intention based on the message sent by the user; for instance, Amazon provides services such as Lex, Comprehend, and Polly to help create intelligent assistants [6].

In model-driven development (MDD), a system is modeled at different levels of abstraction. Model transformations are used to refine high-level abstract models into lower-level models or code [7, 8]. In chatbot development, MDD can help reduce accidental complexity [8], leading to higher productivity, performance, and reusability [9].

We propose a model-driven methodology that guides the process of creating a chatbot. This methodology encompasses four phases: construction at the computation-independent modeling (CIM) level, construction at the platform-independent modeling (PIM) level, construction at the platform-specific modeling (PSM) level, and construction at code level; sets of activities and products have been specified for each phase, and metamodels have been defined at different levels of abstraction to describe the problem/solution domains.

The CIM-level construction phase of our proposed methodology focuses on understanding the problem domain and user goals through natural language conversations. This phase involves creating CIM models to analyze the problem domain and requirements, resulting in a requirements model. User goals are then extracted to form an intent model. Our approach is generic and adaptable to various contexts, categorizing and enumerating user intents, identifying necessary parameters, and using a metamodel for intent representation. We also introduce the CRAC method (Concept, Responsibilities, Asynchronous Collaboration) for analyzing the problem domain and extracting the requirements, modeling domain concepts and system functions, and capturing asynchronous system interactions through events.

The PIM-level construction phase focuses on designing the chatbot microservice and its interactions with essential services, using PIM models that are platform-agnostic. This phase involves identifying user intents, extracting necessary information, and employing AI and ML algorithms for training. We leverage MDD techniques, including a domain-specific language (DSL) for describing questions and model-to-text transformations for seamless integration with the NLU microservice. The architecture of the chatbot microservice is defined using patterns like CQRS and API Controller, with metamodels abstractly describing the design aspects. Additionally, we define a bidirectional conversation flow between the chatbot and users, ensuring effective communication through a proposed dialogue flow metamodel.

The PSM-level construction phase involves implementing solutions and generating code in C# within the.NET framework. This phase introduces two metamodels for describing the solution domain using class and interface concepts, and the metamodel for configuring software projects, including external services like NLU and Messaging microservices.

The code-level construction phase introduces a metamodel to model project structures, folders, files, and their contents. PSM-level models are transformed into the solution model using model-to-model (M2M) transformations, and solution code is subsequently generated from this model by model-to-text (M2T) transformations.

This paper is structured as follows: Sect. 2 provides a review of the research background; the challenges of chatbot development are discussed in Sect. 3; in Sect. 4, the proposed methodology and architecture are introduced; the proposed methodology is evaluated in Sect. 5; and in Sect. 6, conclusions and directions for future work are presented.

2 Related Works

Several frameworks have emerged to simplify the creation and deployment of chatbots. Notably, Xatkit [10] is a chatbot development framework that leverages MDD and DSLs. Designers define user intentions and behaviors, binding them to actions and responses. The runtime engine deploys the chatbot, registers intents, establishes connections, and launches external services.

Another web-based environment, CONGA [5], employs a DSL for modeling conversational agents. Specifications are analyzed and compiled into tools like Rasa or Dialogflow. A recommendation component assists in selecting the most suitable tool for chatbot creation.

Mahmood et al. [6] focus on dynamic user interfaces by utilizing microservice architecture and the flexibility of natural languages. User intentions are identified based on requirements, and utterances are mapped to these intents. Open API specifications orchestrate microservices according to their capabilities and availability.

Matic et al. [4] propose an architecture that allows using various natural language understanding (NLU) services without vendor lock-in. They provide a general NLU metamodel and specific metamodels for Dialogflow and Rasa NLU services, along with mapping rules for automatic object creation.

Perez-Soler et al. [3] introduce an automated solution for modeling conversational agents using natural language. Users can express incomplete or inaccurate ideas, and the framework refines the model accordingly.

Ed-douibi et al. [11] suggest a chatbot interface for querying Open Data resources. Users ask questions in natural language, and the chatbot converts them into API requests. The annotated API model configures the chatbot for querying Web APIs, with Xatkit as the generation tool.

Lastly, Perez-Soler et al. [2] demonstrate using a chatbot as an interface for querying domain-specific models, catering to non-technical users. The chatbot model is automatically generated based on the domain metamodel, implemented using Xatkit.

3   Challenges of Chatbot Development

Developing chatbots presents several significant challenges. First, reliance on proprietary components and services during design and runtime creates dependency on service providers [5]. Ensuring compatibility across platforms and different tool providers is also a critical concern [9].

Model-driven development (MDD) can simplify the process of describing various types of user interfaces (UIs) and creating rich UI experiences [1]. However, metamodeling and language engineering remain complex tasks. Additionally, techniques are needed to analyze model quality and tools that can reflect changes in requirements [9].

Current MDD methodologies often lack sufficient focus on requirements engineering [9]. To create chatbots using the MDD approach, employing design patterns and quality metrics becomes essential [9]. Furthermore, chatbots must be maintained and synchronized with evolving requirements, necessitating methods to enhance maintainability, adaptability, and scalability [9]. Table 1 outlines some of the critical questions that arise during chatbot development [12].

Table 1. Critical questions that arise during chatbot development [12].

1	How to find the most suitable tool for creating a chatbot based on its requirements?
2	How to design a chatbot independent of the development tool and platform?
3	How to analyze and evaluate a chatbot before implementation?
4	How to keep up with the rapid growth of the ecosystem and tools for developing chatbots?
5	How to support the migration process of chatbots to a new tool or platform?
6	How to integrate a chatbot with new NLU services provided by different vendors?
7	How to integrate chatbots with new communication channels provided by different vendors?
8	How to solve the coupling between a chatbot and a specific intent recognition service?
9	How to obtain training phrases for ML algorithms to recognize user intents?

4   Proposed Chatbot Development Methodology

Our proposed methodology for chatbot development emphasizes modeling at various abstraction levels, model transformations, and code generation. The abstraction levels provide a structured way to represent chatbot-related concepts and behaviors. We start with high-level conceptual models (CIM-level) that capture user intents, system responses, and domain-specific knowledge. As we refine the models, we move to platform-independent models (PIM-level) that consider architectural patterns and interaction flows. Then, we reach platform-specific models (PSM-level) that address implementation details and technology choices. Finally, code artifacts are generated at the lowest level of abstraction.

Model-to-model transformations play a crucial role in our methodology. They create lower-level models from higher-level ones. For instance, transforming a CIM-level intent model into a PIM-level interaction model bridges the gap between user requirements and system behavior. These transformations ensure consistency and traceability across abstraction levels.

Beyond models, we generate solution code using model-to-text transformations. These transformations map models to actual implementation artifacts. Based on the desired architecture and design patterns, we produce code snippets, service interfaces, and communication protocols. Our overall solution architecture follows the microservice paradigm. Figure 1 shows the overall solution based on the microservice architecture. It includes three essential microservices:

1. Chatbot Microservice: Handles user interactions, natural language understanding (NLU), and context management, and delegates request fulfillment to the relevant Business services.
2. NLU Microservice: Focuses on intent recognition, entity extraction, and language processing.
3. Messaging Microservice: Manages communication channels and message routing.

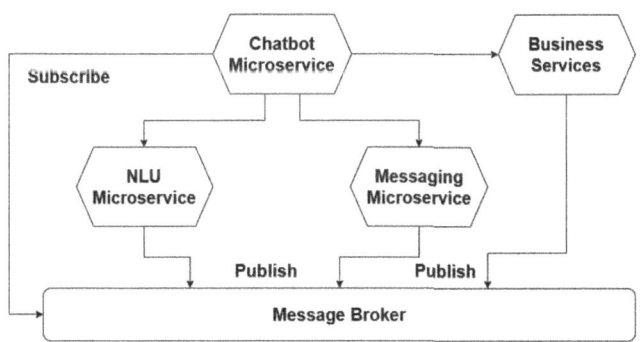

Fig. 1. Overall solution architecture.

Building upon our previous methodology [12], we have tailored the process specifically for developing chatbot microservices. Figure 2 provides an overview of the methodology and the modeling process across different abstraction levels. As seen in this figure, the methodology spans four phases: CIM-level construction, PIM-level construction, PSM-level construction, and Code-level construction. While this paper primarily focuses on the chatbot microservice, the same principles apply to developing the NLU and Messaging microservices: at the CIM level, we create CRAC models specific to NLU and Messaging; the PIM level involves designing CQRS and Controller models tailored for each microservice; based on the desired platform and technology stack, we transform these models to the PSM level; and finally, using model-to-text transformation, solution code is generated for both NLU and Messaging microservices. In summary, our model-driven methodology provides a comprehensive framework for building intelligent conversational agents, extending seamlessly to the auxiliary microservices critical for chatbot functionality.

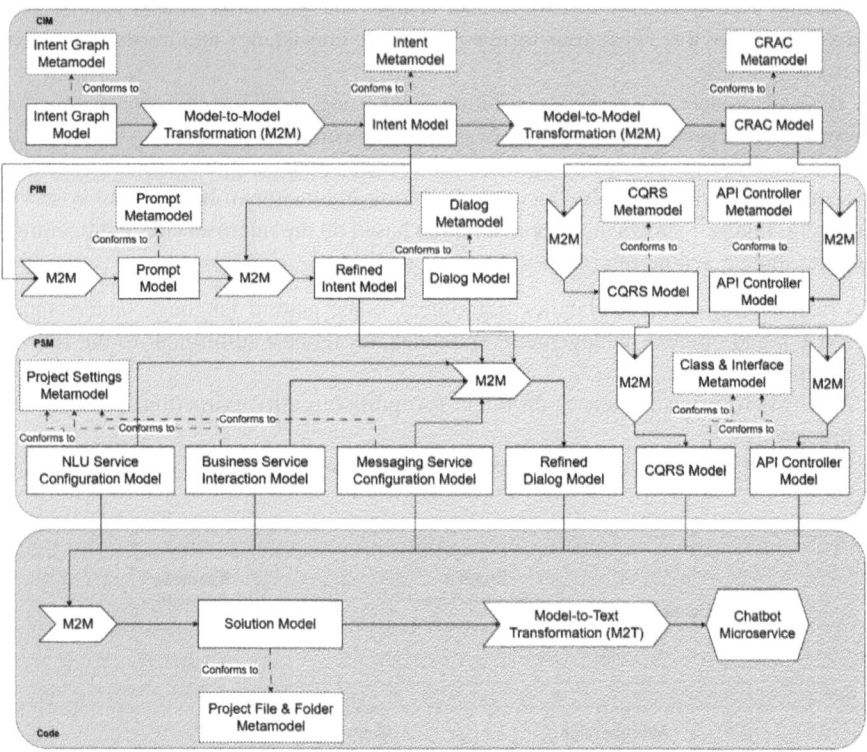

Fig. 2. MDD methodology for developing chatbot microservices.

4.1 CIM-Level Construction

This phase aims to explore the problem domain and understand user goals through natural language conversations. Models are described at the highest level of abstraction, known as the computation-independent model (CIM). Initially, the problem domain and requirements undergo analysis, resulting in a requirements model. Subsequently, user goals are extracted from this model using model transformations, leading to the creation of the intent model.

We propose a generic approach to automatically model user intents expressed through natural language conversations with chatbots. Unlike domain-specific methods, our approach is not tied to any particular problem domain. Instead, it can adapt to various contexts where users interact with chatbots to achieve specific tasks. The key steps in our approach are as follows:

1. Intent Categorization
2. Intent Enumeration
3. Parameter Identification
4. Intent Representation

We begin by categorizing user intents based on the context of the conversation. These intents represent high-level actions or requests that users express. For instance, in the context of infrastructure provisioning, we identify categories such as "Provisioning Resources," "Configuration Management," "Deployment Automation," and "Orchestration." Each category represents a distinct aspect of resource management. Table 2 shows a prompt template for user intent categorization, instructing ChatGPT's response format based on the intent graph metamodel shown in Fig. 3.

Within each category, we enumerate the specific intents that users express. These intents correspond to high-level tasks or actions that users want to perform. For example in the "Provisioning Resources" category, we identify the list of intents as "Create Virtual Machine (VM) (CreateVM)", "Create Container Cluster (CreateCluster)", "Create Load Balancer (CreateLB)", and "Create Database Instance (CreateDB)". Table 3 shows a prompt template for user intent enumeration.

For each intent, we identify the necessary parameters. These parameters capture the essential information required to fulfill the user's request. For example, common parameters of "Create Virtual Machine (VM) (CreateVM)" intent include "vmName", "vmSize", "image", "network", and "storage".

Table 4 shows a prompt template for intent parameters identification.

To capture the essence of user intents, we introduce an intent metamodel (Fig. 4). This metamodel serves as a structured representation that encapsulates the intent, its associated parameters, and their relationships. By leveraging this metamodel, we can automatically generate intent models from conversational data.

We propose a method for analyzing problem domains and extracting the requirements that we call the CRAC method (Concept, Responsibilities, Asynchronous Collaboration); this method provides a structured approach to understanding domain-specific concepts and their associated responsibilities [12].

Table 2. Categorizing user intents (intent categorization).

Template
Categorize user intents within a specific problem domain: {problem_domain}. Provide your answer in json format, including the problemDomain and list of catgories (the name and description of each category).
Prompt
Categorize user intents within a specific problem domain: "Infrastructure as Code". Provide your answer in json format, including the problemDomain and list of catgories (the name and description of each category).
Answer

{
  "problemDomain": "Infrastructure as Code",
  "categories": [
    {
      "name": "Provisioning Resources",
      "description": "Creating, managing, and scaling infrastructure resources using code"
    },
    {
      "name": "Configuration Management",
      "description": "Defining and maintaining consistent configurations for infrastructure components"
    },
    {
      "name": "Deployment Automation",
      "description": "Automating the deployment process for applications and services"
    },
    {
      "name": "Orchestration",
      "description": "Coordinating and managing complex workflows involving multiple resources"
    }
  ]
}

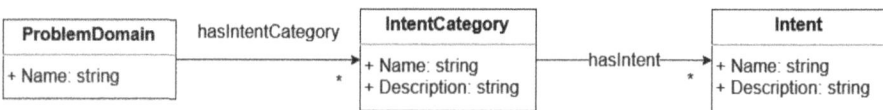

Fig. 3. Intent graph metamodel.

According to CRAC, domain concepts are modeled as instances of the Domain-Concept class, representing fundamental elements. These concepts serve as building

Table 3. Finding the intents related to a specific category (intent enumeration).

Template
Find the list of user intents in the {problem domain} problem domain related to {category} category. Provide your answer in json format, including the problemDomain, category, and list of intents (the name and description of each intent).
Prompt
Find the list of user intents in the "Infrastructure as Code" problem domain related to "Provisioning Resources" category. Provide your answer in json format, including the problemDomain, category, and list of intents (the name and description of each intent).
Answer

{
  "problemDomain": "Infrastructure as Code",
  "category": "Provisioning Resources",
  "intents": [
    {
      "name": "Create Virtual Machine (VM) (CreateVM)",
      "description": "Provision a virtual machine with specified configuration"
    },
    {
      "name": "Create Container Cluster (CreateCluster)",
      "description": "Provision a container cluster for deploying containerized applications"
    },
    {
      "name": "Create Load Balancer (CreateLB)",
      "description": "Provision a load balancer to distribute incoming traffic"
    },
    {
      "name": "Create Database Instance (CreateDB)",
      "description": "Provision a database instance with specified settings"
    }
  ]
}

blocks for the problem domain. Additionally, high-level system functions are captured as Commands. These commands are responsible for transitioning the system between valid states. For example, a "Create Virtual Machine" command triggers the provisioning process, resulting in an event that alters the system state.

Table 4. Identifying parameters required to fulfill the user's request (parameter identification).

Template
Can you provide me with the required parameters for performing the {intent} intent in the {problem domain} problem domain related to {category} category? Provide your answer in json format, including the problemDomain, category, intent, and list of parameters (the name and description of each parameter).
Prompt
Can you provide me with the required parameters for performing the "Create Virtual Machine (VM) (CreateVM)" intent in the "Infrastructure as Code" problem domain related to "Provisioning Resources" category? Provide your answer in json format, including the problemDomain, category, intent, and list of parameters (the name and description of each parameter).
Answer

```
{
  "problemDomain": "Infrastructure as Code",
  "category": "Provisioning Resources",
  "intent": "Create Virtual Machine (VM) (CreateVM)",
  "parameters": [
    {
      "name": "vmName",
      "description": "The name of the virtual machine"
    },
    {
      "name": "vmSize",
      "description": "The desired size or configuration for the VM"
    },
    {
      "name": "image",
      "description": "The base operating system image for the VM"
    },
    {
      "name": "network",
      "description": "The network configuration for the VM"
    },
    {
      "name": "storage",
      "description": "The storage options for the VM"
    }
  ]
}
```

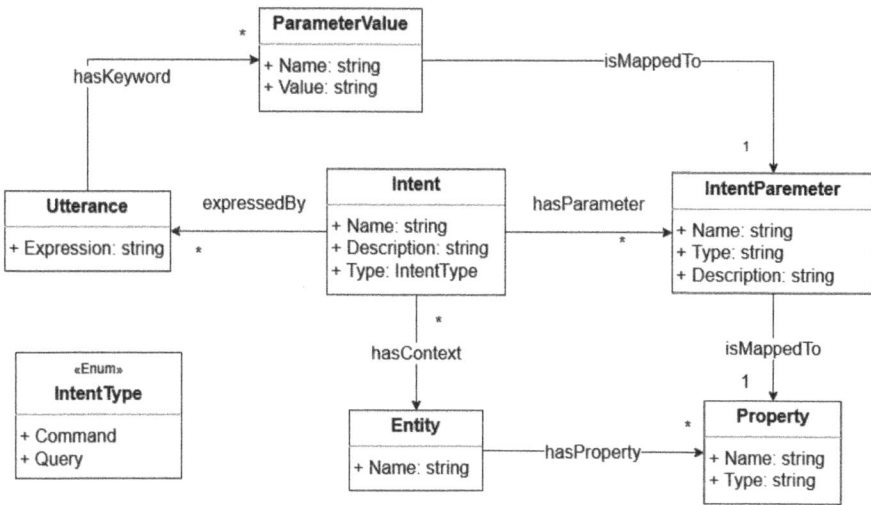

Fig. 4. Intent metamodel.

The CRAC method acknowledges that system interactions are often asynchronous. Events play a crucial role in capturing these collaborations. When a command is executed, it generates an Event that reflects the outcome of the action. These events provide a way to track system changes, notify relevant components, and maintain consistency across distributed systems.

Figure 5 shows the CRAC metamodel. To bridge the gap between user intents and the CRAC model, model-to-model transformations (M2M) is executed. These transformations map intent-related information to corresponding CRAC elements (Table 5). By aligning the intent model with the CRAC representation, we ensure context-aware responses and facilitate efficient system design.

4.2 PIM-Level Construction

In this phase, our objective is to design the chatbot microservice and establish its interactions with essential services. The platform-independent models (PIM) created during this stage remain agnostic to specific platforms and service providers.

We begin by identifying user intents and extracting the necessary information to fulfill their requests. An AI model and machine learning (ML) algorithm are typically employed for training. Tasks involve finding training phrases for each intent, identifying key parameters, and mapping them to generic or custom entities. In our previous work [12], we illustrated the approach, demonstrated prompt generation, and leveraged model-driven development techniques. By describing questions using a DSL and converting them via model-to-text transformations, we facilitate seamless integration with NLU microservices. We've introduced a metamodel to describe these questions, as depicted in Fig. 6.

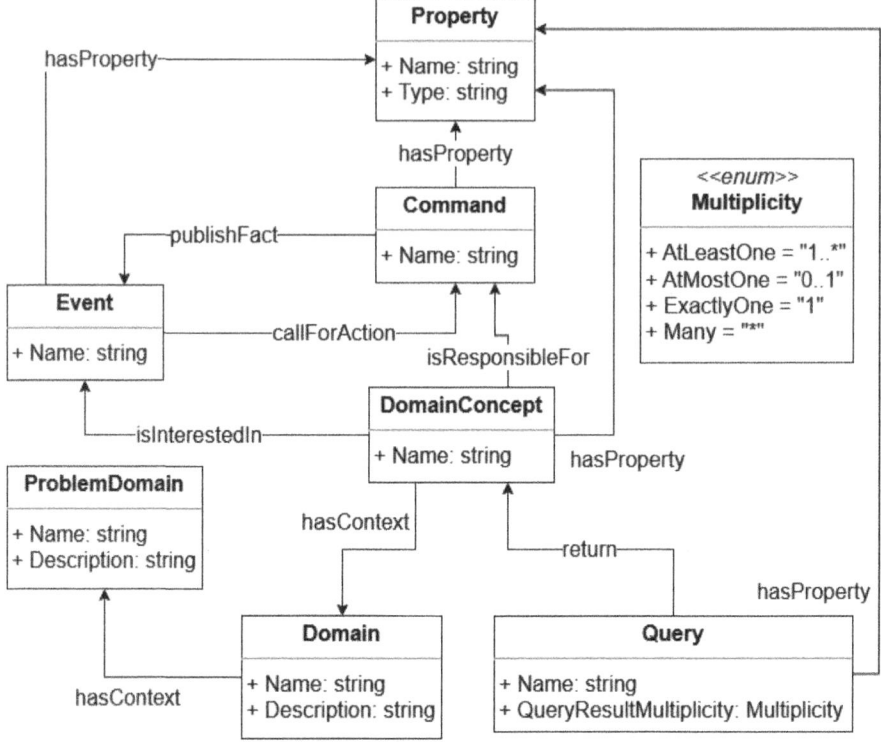

Fig. 5. CRAC metamodel.

The second activity focuses on defining the chatbot microservice architecture. We employ various architectural patterns, including the CQRS (Command Query Responsibility Segregation) and API Controller patterns. The CQRS metamodel abstractly describes design aspects related to CQRS, such as command handlers, query handlers, events, and queries. Similarly, the API Controller metamodel provides an abstract syntax for describing web request entry points and their distribution via controller patterns. Table 6 and Table 7 show transformation rules for converting the CRAC model to CQRS and API Controller models.

The third activity involves defining the bidirectional conversation flow between the chatbot microservice and the user. For each intent in the model, we outline how the chatbot interacts with users and specify actions to fulfill their requests. To achieve this, we propose a metamodel for describing the dialogue flow, ensuring effective bidirectional communication between the chatbot microservice and users, as shown in Fig. 7.

Table 5. Intent-to-CRAC model transformation rules.

Intent Metamodel	CRAC Metamodel
Entity	DomainConcept
Intent {Intent.Type = Command}	Command
Intent {Intent.Type = Query}	Query
Property	Property
IntentParameter	Property
Entity ➜ Property: hasProperty	DomainConcept➜Property: hasProperty
Intent {Intent.Type = Command}➜IntentParameter: hasParameter	Command➜Property: hasProperty
Intent {Intent.Type = Query}➜ntentParameter: hasParameter	Query➜Property: hasProperty
Intent {Intent.Type = Command}➜Entity: hasContext	DomainConcept➜Command: isResponsibleFor
Intent ➜ Entity: hasContext	Query➜DomainConcept: return

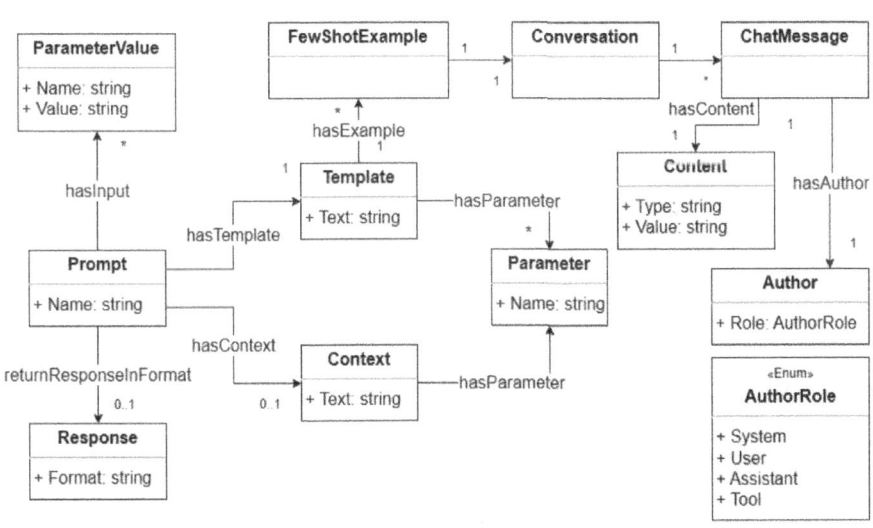

Fig. 6. Prompt metamodel.

4.3 PSM-Level Construction

At the PSM level, two metamodels have been provided for implementing solutions and generating code in the C# language within the .NET framework. The goal of the "Class & Interface" metamodel (a partial view of which is provided in Fig. 8) is to provide an

Table 6. CRAC-to-CQRS model transformation rules.

CRAC Metamodel	CQRS Metamodel
Command	CommandHandler➜Command: canHandle
Query	QueryHandler➜Query: canHandle
DomainConcept➜Event: isInterestedIn	EventHandler➜Event: canHandle

Table 7. CRAC-to-APIController model transformation rules.

CRAC Metamodel	API Controller Metamodel
DomainConcept➜Command: isResponsibleFor	APIController➜Command: dispatchCommand
Query➜DomainConcept: return	APIController➜Query: dispatchQuery

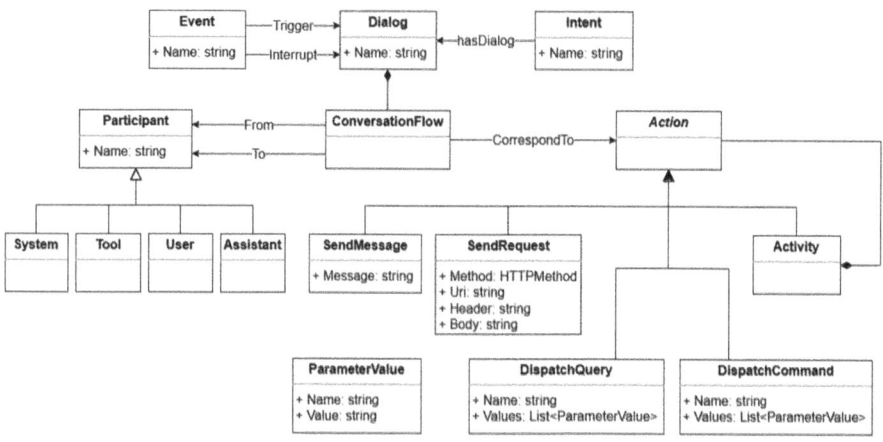

Fig. 7. Dialog metamodel.

abstract syntax that allows describing the solution domain using class and interface concepts in the C# programming language. The purpose of the "Project Settings" metamodel (Fig. 9) is to provide an abstract syntax for describing the settings and configuration of a software project in the .NET framework, including external services such as NLU and Messaging microservices.

By combining information from the Business Service Interaction Model, NLU Service, and Messaging Service Configuration Models at the PSM level with the Refined Intent Model and Dialog Model at the PIM level, we generate the Refined Dialog Model. Additionally, the CQRS and API Controller models at the PIM level are transformed into corresponding models at the PSM level using model-to-model transformation.

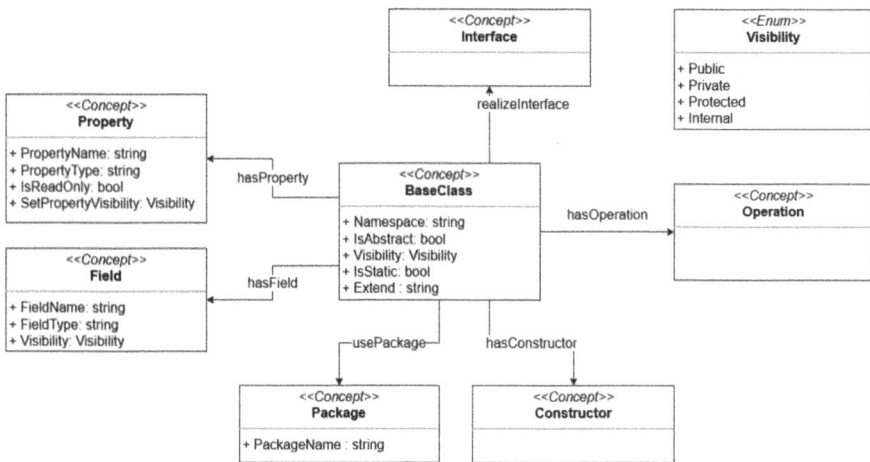

Fig. 8. Partial Class & Interface metamodel (from the 'BaseClass' perspective).

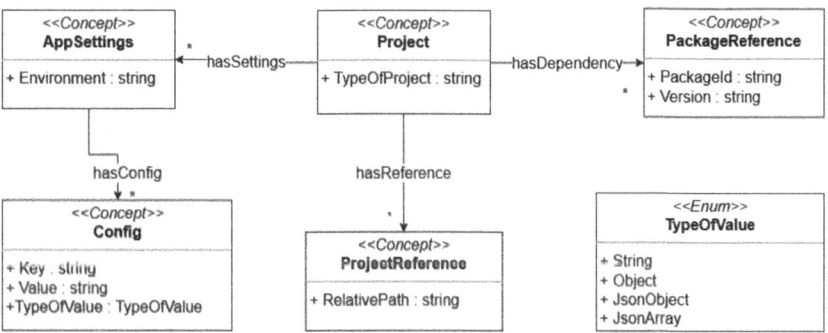

Fig. 9. Project Settings metamodel.

4.4 Code-Level Construction

At the code level, a simple metamodel called the "Project File & Folder" metamodel has been established to model project structure, folders, files, and their content, as shown in Fig. 10. Through model-to-model transformation, PSM-level models are converted into the "Solution Model," which adheres to the "Project File & Folder" metamodel. Subsequently, solution code is generated from the "Solution Model" using model-to-text transformation.

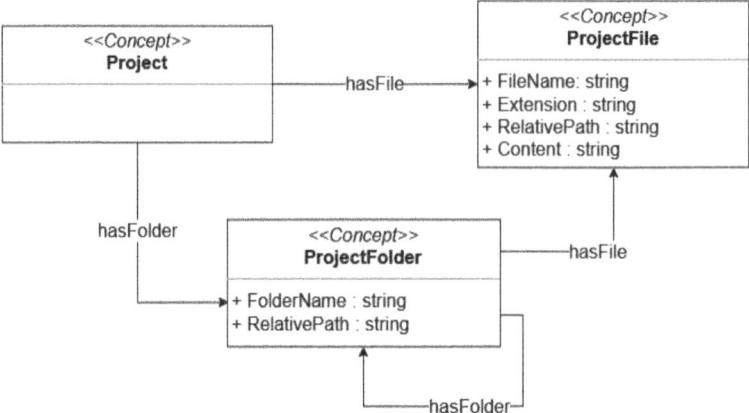

Fig. 10. Project File & Folder metamodel.

5   Evaluation

We have used a criteria-based approach to evaluate the effectiveness of our proposed methodology. The evaluation criteria fall into three distinct categories: criteria related to the generic software development lifecycle (SDLC), criteria specific to model-driven development (MDD), and criteria directly applicable to chatbots. The results of evaluating the proposed methodology based on these three categories of criteria are presented in Table 8.

For problem domain analysis, our approach fully supports understanding the domain-specific requirements, facilitating effective solution design. Regarding the generic SDLC, our methodology fully supports Requirements Engineering, Analysis, Design, and Implementation phases. However, it does not provide complete coverage of the entire lifecycle, as Test, Deployment, and Maintenance phases are not explicitly addressed. In terms of umbrella activities, our methodology partially supports cross-cutting concerns, which play a crucial role in software development.

Reusability is a key aspect, and our methodology leverages the model-driven development (MDD) approach, promoting the creation of reusable artifacts. Specifically related to MDD, our methodology supports modeling at different levels of abstraction (CIM, PIM, PSM, and Code). It also enables seamless Model-to-Model transformation across these levels and model-to-text transformation at the Code level.

In the context of chatbots, our methodology addresses domain knowledge modeling, user intent modeling, and conversation flow modeling. Additionally, it covers essential tasks for setting up Natural Language Understanding (NLU) services and architectural design, and satisfies essential quality attributes such as scalability, flexibility, and interoperability. Furthermore, it excels in handling conversation aspects, including understanding user queries and providing relevant responses.

Table 8. Criteria-based evaluation results.

Category	Criteria		Level
Generic SDLC Criteria	Coverage of Generic Lifecycle	Requirements Engineering	●
		Analysis	●
		Design	●
		Implementation	●
		Test	◐
		Deployment	○
		Maintenance	○
	Coverage of Umbrella Activities	Project Management	○
		Quality Assurance	◐
		Risk Management	◐
	Reusability		●
	Adaptability		◐
MDD-related Criteria	CIM / PIM / PSM Creation		●
	Model Transformation		●
	Metadata Management		○
	Verification & Validation		◐
	Automatic Testing		○
	Traceability between Models		◐
	Tool Support		○
Chatbot-related Criteria	Chatbot Input / Output		Text
	Domain		Closed-Domain
	Approaches		AI-based
	Knowledge Data Structures		(Semi)Structured
	Domain Knowledge Modeling		●
	User Intent Modeling		●
	Conversation Flow Modeling		●
	Training Phrase Elicitation / Annotation		●
	NLU Service Providers		Vendor-Independent
	Communication Channels		Vendor-Independent
	Architectural Design		●
	Quality Attributes	Scalability	●
		Flexibility	●
		Maintainability	●
		Interoperability	●
		Usability	◐
		Availability	◐
		Performance	◐
		Security	◐
	Conversational Aspects	Understanding	◐
		Answering	◐
		Navigation	◐
		Error handling	◐
		Relevance	◐
		Consistency	◐

Legend: Full support ● ; Partial support ◐ ; No Support ○

6 Conclusions

We have introduced a model-driven methodology for chatbot development, addressing challenges related to productivity, reusability, scalability, and maintainability. By leveraging computation-independent models (CIMs), platform-independent models (PIMs), and platform-specific models (PSMs), our approach guides developers through the chatbot creation process. We emphasize seamless transitions between these levels of abstraction, enabling efficient model-to-model and model-to-text transformations.

Our methodology not only automates code generation but also introduces a novel approach to user intent representation. By categorizing, enumerating, parameterizing, and representing user intents, we enhance the effectiveness of natural language understanding (NLU) services. Additionally, we adopt microservice architecture and architectural design patterns to improve scalability, maintainability, and interoperability. As chatbots continue to evolve, our model-driven approach offers a valuable framework for building intelligent conversational agents.

Future research will focus on providing tool support for our methodology and defining metamodels for common communication platforms and NLU services.

References

1. Planas, E., Daniel, G., Brambilla, M., Cabot, J.: Towards a model-driven approach for multiexperience AI-based user interfaces. Softw. Syst. Model. **20**(4), 997–1009 (2021). https://doi.org/10.1007/s10270-021-00904-y
2. Perez-Soler, S., Daniel, G., Cabot, J., Guerra, E., de Lara, J.: Towards automating the synthesis of chatbots for conversational model query. In: Enterprise, Business-Process and Information Systems Modeling, (pp. 257–265) (2020). https://doi.org/10.1007/978-3-030-49418-6_17
3. Perez-Soler, S., Guerra, E., de Lara, J.: Flexible modelling using conversational agents. In: 2019 ACM/IEEE 22nd International Conference on Model Driven Engineering Languages and Systems Companion (MODELS-C), 478–482 (2019). https://doi.org/10.1109/MODELS-C.2019.00076
4. Matic, R., Kabiljo, M., Zivkovic, M., Cabarkapa, M.: Extensible chatbot architecture using metamodels of natural language understanding. Electronics **10**(18), 2300 (2021). https://doi.org/10.3390/electronics10182300
5. Perez-Soler, S., Guerra, E., de Lara, J.: Creating and Migrating Chatbots with Conga. 2021 IEEE/ACM 43rd International Conference on Software Engineering: Companion Proceedings (ICSE-Companion), 37–40 (2021). https://doi.org/10.1109/ICSE-Companion 52605.2021.00030
6. Mahmood, R., Joshi, A., Lele, A., Pennington, J.: Dynamic Natural Language User Interfaces Using Microservices. HAI-GEN+ User2agent@ IUI (2020). https://ceur-ws.org/Vol-2848/user2agent-paper-1.pdf
7. Rodrigues da Silva, A.: Model-driven engineering: a survey supported by the unified conceptual model. Comput. Lang., Syst. Struct. **43**, 139–155 (2015). https://doi.org/10.1016/j.cl.2015.06.001
8. Alam, O., Corley, J., Masson, C., Syriani, E.: Challenges for reuse in collaborative modeling environments. MODELS Workshops, pp. 277–283 (2018)
9. Martínez-Gárate, Á.A., Aguilar-Calderón, J.A., Tripp-Barba, C., Zaldívar-Colado, A.: Model-driven approaches for conversational agents development: a systematic mapping study. IEEE Access **11**, 73088–73103 (2023). https://doi.org/10.1109/ACCESS.2023.3293849

10. Daniel, G., Cabot, J., Deruelle, L., Derras, M.: Xatkit: a multimodal low-code chatbot development framework. IEEE Access **8**, 15332–15346 (2020). https://doi.org/10.1109/ACCESS.2020.2966919
11. Ed-douibi, H., Cánovas Izquierdo, J.L., Daniel, G., Cabot, J.:. A model-based chatbot generation approach to converse with open data sources. In: Web Engineering (Vol. 12706, pp. 440–455) (2021). https://doi.org/10.1007/978-3-030-74296-6_33
12. Vahdati, A., Ramsin, R.: "Model-driven methodology for developing chatbots based on microservice architecture". In: Proceedings of the 12th International Conference on Model-Based Software and Systems Engineering (MODELSWARD'24), 2024, pp. 247–254 (2024)

DynaTool: A Tool for Optimizing Hybrid Software Process

María Cecilia Bastarrica[1] , Luis Silvestre[2]([⊠]) , Andrés Wallberg[2],
and Daniel González[1]

[1] Department of Computer Science, University of Chile, Santiago, Chile
cecilia@dcc.uchile.cl, daniel.gonzalez.2@ug.uchile.cl
[2] Department of Computer Science, Faculty of Engineering, Universidad de Talca, Curicó, Chile
lsilvestre@utalca.cl

Abstract. Hybrid software processes that integrate agile and traditional practices are currently the most commonly used in the industry. Typically, development activities employ agile practices, while management tasks rely on more traditional methods. However, the optimal combination of practices depends not only on project attributes, such as team size, but also on the specific characteristics that need to be emphasized, such as time to market or early value addition. DynaTail was introduced as a method for integrating hybrid process tailoring with practice selection to optimize specific characteristics. While it received positive feedback in industry evaluations, users noted the need for a supporting tool to simplify the process for software developers, allowing them to focus on process elements rather than the technical details of the method. In response, we developed DynaTool, a model-driven engineering (MDE)-based support tool designed to meet this need. DynaTool offers interactive interfaces for specifying processes, context, and practices. In this paper, we refine DynaTail's optimization strategy to clearly identify the practices that should be applied to each process activity to maximize the desired characteristic. We also update DynaTool to incorporate these enhancements.

Keywords: Hybrid software process · MDE-based tool · Software process evaluation

1 Introduction

A software process is defined as a combination of roles, activities and work products [2, 14]. Processes have been valued by software companies as a means for managing development in an organized manner so that it is possible to plan, schedule and provision software projects [23]. However, a single process does not fit all kinds of projects, even within the same organization. For example, the required developer experience depends largely on the complexity of the product, or the type of technologies that need to be used for its development [5, 6]. Similarly, a small project could skip building several work products. The activity of adjusting the company's process to the particular characteristics of the project being addressed is called tailoring.

F. José Domínguez Mayo et al. (Eds.): MODELSWARD 2024, CCIS 2547, pp. 88–104, 2026.
https://doi.org/10.1007/978-3-031-96841-9_5

Agile methods propose a series of practices that software development teams adopt and adapt to address project development. These methods are specially appropriate to promote productivity in projects with high uncertainty but they do not provide strong support for project management [29]. Therefore, most companies follow hybrid processes, i.e., a combination of agile and traditional practices. Large companies used to define traditional software processes with strictly specified activities, responsibilities, workflow, work products, etc., but lately most of them start adopting some agile practices. Conversely, small companies that tried to follow a completely agile methodology, soon realized that some structure is required for managing projects under control [19]. However, it is not easy to assess which combination of agile and traditional practices adopted is the most appropriate one provided that this depends on the intended project characteristic as well as the project context [11, 17].

The DynaTail method is designed for companies that must frequently adapt their hybrid processes to meet the diverse needs of their clients [31]. Tailoring, in this context, goes beyond simply adjusting the general process to fit a specific context; it also involves selecting different practices based on the characteristics that need optimization. DynaTail accomplishes this through two stages. First, the general process is tailored to align with the project's specific context. Second, it identifies the optimal combination of agile and traditional practices for executing the tailored process activities according to the desired characteristics.

DynaTail has been validated in a real software development company [21]. Although the company's process engineer highly appreciated the method, he highlighted the complexity of applying DynaTail without a supporting tool. We built DynaTool to support DynaTail based on the formal models defined in [31]. A first version of this tool was reported in [37]. Nevertheless, we argue that the complexity of the method, and not only the tool, could have also prevented the process engineer to fully grasp the potential and some of the features that could actually provide real hybrid optimized processes. In particular the first version did not explicitly defined the process along with the particular practices that should be applied for carrying out each activity.

We here present a refined version of DynaTail that automatically selects the set of practices for implementing the tailored process that optimizing the desired characteristic. We also present an updated implementation of DynaTool taking into account this improvement.

The rest of the paper is structured as follows. Section 2 presents background on software process improvement and tailoring, hybrid processes, and a general description of the DynaTail method. Section 3 describes DynaTool, its supporting models and transformations as well as the process for applying it [21] now using DynaTool. Finally, we describe our ongoing work and draw some conclusions in Sect. 4.

2   Background

2.1   Process Tailoring and Improvement

Software process improvement (SPI) is the area in software engineering that deals with the evaluation of software development processes, to assess and potentially improve them [13]. SPI used to follow strategies based on models such as CMMI and standards such as ISO that define a series of process areas that should be considered in order to reach a certain maturity level. This approach added repeatability but they have shown to be rigid for some kinds of applications, e.g. innovation projects.

Software process tailoring is the act of adjusting the activities of a process in order to create a new process suited to a different (and likely narrower) context [12]. But the context is not all that matters. Peng Xu and Balasubramaniam [39] and Vijayasarathy and Butler [36] found that tailoring is not only influenced by the project context, but also a set of environmental factors, challenges, project goals and process tailoring strategies.

Pedreira et al., in a systematic review [25], found that while most software process tailoring approaches involve some level of formality, the majority are only suitable for large organizations. Kalus and Kuhrmann [16] also conducted a systematic review on the criteria used for tailoring software processes. Their findings highlight the significance of specific organizational factors, which can serve as guidelines for selecting appropriate agile methods.

Software & Systems Process Engineering Metamodel (SPEM)[1] and Business Process Model & Notation (BPMN)[2] are the OMG standards for specifying software processes and business processes, respectively. Although SPEM is expressive for capturing subtleties of software processes, it lacks supporting tools. On the other hand, BPMN counts on a plethora of tools but it is not expressive for certain particularities of software development [9] such as modeling activities where several roles are involved or identifying variation points. However, in most cases BPMN supporting tools are enough.

SPEM and BPMN are the OMG standards for specifying software and business processes, respectively. While SPEM is well-suited for capturing the particularities of software processes, it lacks sufficient tool support. In contrast, BPMN benefits from a wide range of tools but falls short in expressing certain specific aspects of software development [9], such as modeling activities involving multiple roles [28] or identifying variation points. Nevertheless, in most cases, the tools available for BPMN are adequate. Pillat et al. [26] introduced BPMNt, an extension of BPMN designed to define variability in software processes modeled with BPMN. While this approach leverages BPMN's more user-friendly notation, deviating from the standard creates incompatibility with existing tools, hindering automatic transformations.

Hurtado et al. [15] propose a MDE-based strategy for software process tailoring. They consider a process specified in SPEM and a tailoring transformation that takes the process and the context models as input and yields a project specific process also specified in SPEM. This approach makes use of SPEM's variation primitives for identifying the process variation points.

Improving Agile processes involves optimizing how teams plan, execute, deliver, and gather feedback on development projects to streamline workflows and enhance efficiency [30]. Agile methodologies offer a framework for continuous improvement, empowering teams to respond to evolving business needs through the use of metrics, practices, and technology [4].

Campanelli et al. [3] conducted a systematic literature review on the tailoring of agile methods, including the various approaches used. Their analysis and classification

---

[1] http://www.omg.org/spec/SPEM/.

[2] https://www.omg.org/bpmn/.

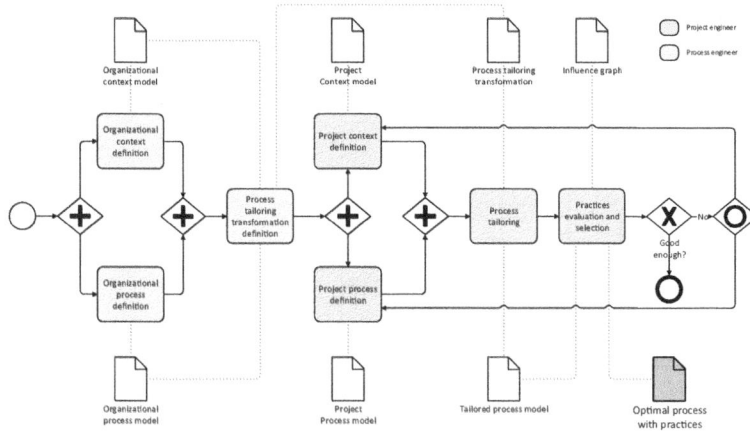

Fig. 1. DynaTail's process (extended from [37]).

revealed that most agile method tailoring techniques were independent of the specific agile method employed by the organization. They also found that the tailored methods were primarily based on Scrum or XP, the tailoring approaches were grounded in method engineering (a meta-method process), and the tailoring criteria were largely driven by internal factors such as project type and communication.

Thiemich and Puhlmann [34] propose an integrated BPM project methodology framework that merges BPM with Scrum, focusing on the technical implementation of business processes. Martins and Zacarias [22] introduce an agile BPM methodology consisting of three key steps: process discovery, supervision, and assessment. They also compare various BPM methodologies, such as AGILIPO and Agile BPM Project. Zacarias et al. [40] compare four meta-models and propose an agile BPM meta-model. Von Bernardo et al. [1] link agility with BPM by presenting an agile BPM management method that spans four areas—analysis, planning, design, and building—where business, application, and technology goals are integrated into the analysis and planning phases.

Ozdenizci et al. [24] investigate the use of business process management methodologies to enhance agile software processes and agility maturity. Giachetti et al. [10] propose a model-driven approach for selecting agile practices, ensuring development processes align with quality standards.

2.2 Hybrid Software Process Improvement

Traditional software processes intend to bring structure into software development so that projects are easily managed. They define steps in order to avoid uncertainty and improvisation. However, in projects for innovative domains or not well defined requirements, these processes do not result effective. Agile software development methods have been proposed to deal with these difficulties.

Several companies have adopted agility, but completely agile projects are difficult to provision and schedule. Hybrid software processes that combine some agile and some

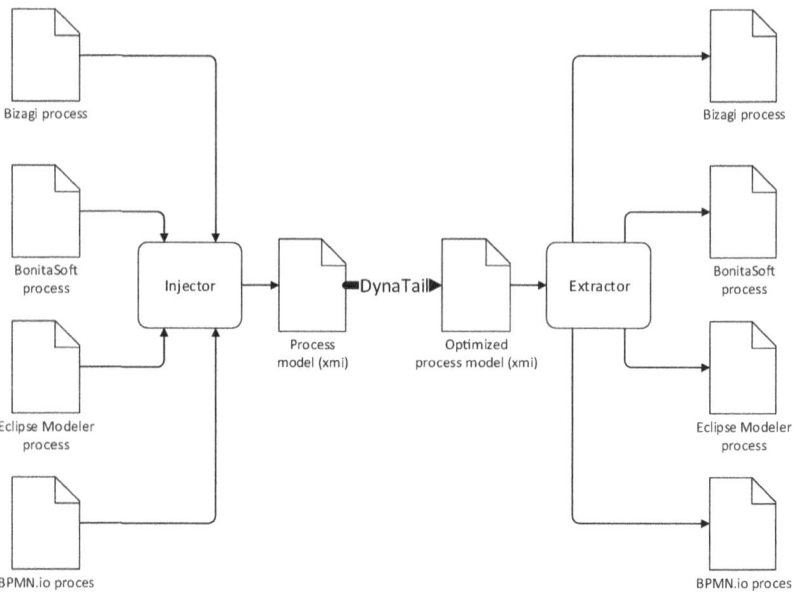

Fig. 2. DynaTool's architecture.

traditional practices are a trade-off approach. Kuhrmann et al. [19] defined a hybrid software process as "any combination of agile and traditional approaches that an organizational unit adopts and customizes to its own context needs". One of the first proposal for hybrid software processes is "Water-Scrum-Fall" [38] where management activities are addressed with traditional practices while software development follows Scrum. But not any combination of practices is appropriate [27] for the organization and the project goals.

Evaluating each combination of practices presents a significant challenge [35]. Determining the appropriate level of agility is equally complex [7]: which activities should be handled by each approach, and which practices should be applied to each activity? While some empirical guidelines exist [33], both the desired characteristics of processes and the available practices evolve over time. Therefore, selecting the optimal combination of practices requires ongoing adjustment [17].

2.3   DynaTail

DynaTail acknowledges that context-based tailoring is not enough for process improvement, since two or more tailored processes may be consistent with the context but they improve different attributes. Moreover, the practices - either traditional or agile - that are applied for executing each activity, will also have an influence. Therefore, DynaTail explicitly considers these three dimensions: context, practices and desired attribute to be improved for generating the appropriate process to be applied in a particular project with the purpose of optimizing certain particular characteristic.

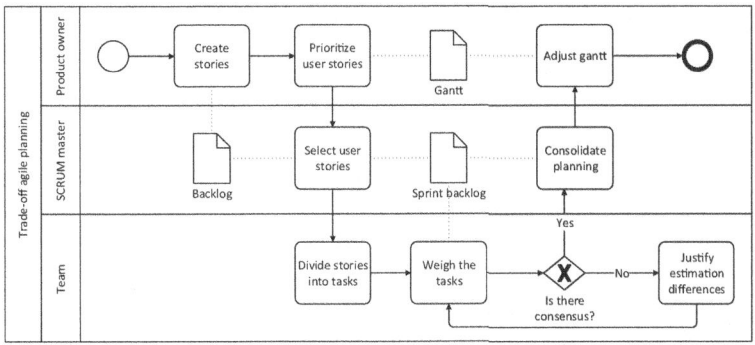

Fig. 3. Trade-off Agile Planning Process (from [37]).

The method involves two main activities: tailoring the process to the context, and choosing the appropriate practices that optimize the desired characteristic for implementing the activities of the tailored process. DynaTail defines tailoring as a model transformation that takes the process and context models and yields an adapted process model. The selection and evaluation of the most appropriate practices is carried out by computing the combination of practices in an influence graph that optimize the intended characteristic.

Here, the attributes that influence the intended characteristic to be improved are specified along with the weight of their influence. Similarly, the set of activities in the tailored process model may influence each of these attributes with different weights. Finally, each activity may be implemented with different practices, each one with its own influence weight. There is a different influence graph for each characteristic, and they are also specific to the organization since the included activities are those in the process model and the practices are the ones regularly applied in the organization.

The weights used in the evaluation are organization-specific, ranging from -2 to 2, as suggested by Diebold et al. [8]. A weight of -2 signifies a highly negative influence, while 2 indicates a highly positive influence. These weights are initially assigned by experienced developers within the organization and may be adjusted over time based on empirical results from previous projects. After evaluating the tailored process and its selected practices, the process engineers may determine whether the outcome is satisfactory. If not, they might choose to manually adjust the process or its context. Such modifications would also affect the selection of practices for implementing each activity. Activities and artifacts involved in DynaTail's process are identified in Fig. 1.

3 DynaTool

In order to build a user-friendly supporting tool for DynaTail, the method has been fully formalized. An initial version of these DynaTail's models has already been presented in [31] where all activities and artifacts identified in Fig. 1 are formalized.

DynaTool is based on these models and a first version was presented in [37]. In this paper we present a refinement of this tool that improves the evaluation activity in order to compute the optimal set of practices for implementing the process. This is represented in Fig. 1 as "Practice evaluation and selection" updating what was originally activity called "Process evaluation". In this section, we replicate the process and context from the running example in the previous paper, providing a more detailed explanation of each element. Additionally, we introduce several new components: (1) an enhanced version of the tailoring rules definition interface, (2) an updated completely formalized influence graph model, and (3) the newly added "Practice Evaluation and Selection" activity, accompanied by two application scenarios.

3.1   Process Definition and Modeling

Organizations often establish specific processes to guide different types of projects. For instance, there might be distinct processes for system quality assurance, requirements specification, or project planning. These general processes should be tailored and adapted to fit the unique needs of each individual project. DynaTool uses BPMN for process formalization, provided that this notation is widely used in industry for process specification. Figure 3 illustrates the *Trade-off Agile Planning Process* process included in [21].

There are several modeling tools for specifying processes in BPMN such as BonitaSoft, Eclipse Modeler, BPMN.io and Bizagi. This has both benefits and drawbacks. Companies may choose any tool for modeling their processes but each of them implements its own *flavor* of BPMN adding some extra characteristics that are not necessarily compatible with BPMN 2.0 that is the strict standard.

To address this issue, we have built a set of projectors. First, an injector that transforms the BPMN process (BPMN file), that may be defined in any commercial BPMN modeling tool, into a BPMN 2.0 standard process model (XMI file). Second, an extractor that transforms the BPMN process model of the configured process (XMI file) back into a BPMN process description (BPMN file). This is necessary for visualizing in any BPMN modeling tool the result of applying DynaTool for obtaining the process to be applied in the particular project. Figure 2 describes DynaTool's architecture with respect to these projectors.

The projectors consider matching elements between the BPMN process and the BPMN process model. In this sense, there are process elements in BPMN processes that are not used for the injector such as those related to their layout, but that need to be preserved because they will be later needed for the extractor.

The injector applies the following steps: (1) Identify elements of the BPMN process that are relevant for building the process model, (2) Semantic analysis of the labels in the BPMN file, (3) Establish a dictionary that implements the matching elements, (4) Create a hierarchical structure from the BPMN 2.0 metamodel, (5) Build the process model (XMI file).

Figure 3 shows the same Trade-off Agile Planning process presented in [37] defined using BonitaSoft while Fig. 4 shows the BPMN process model generated after applying the injector. This BPMN process model conforms to the BPMN 2.0 metamodel and can be manipulated using EMF tools. However, this BPMN process model does not consider the graphical elements (only standard process elements).

The goal of DynaTail is to provide the process engineer or project manager the actual process that should be applied in a particular project including the details about

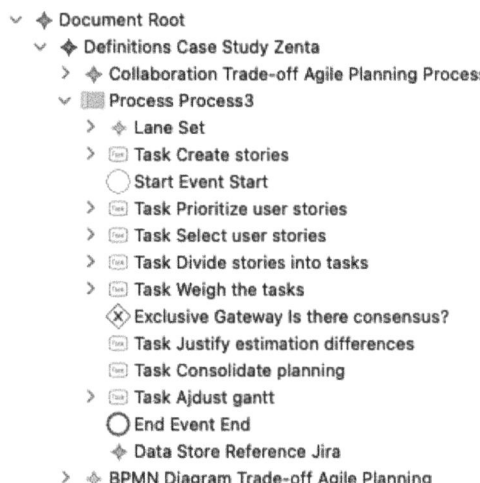

Fig. 4. Trade-off Agile Planning Process Model (from [37]).

the practices to be used for executing each activity. Therefore, this process should be displayed in a human understandable notation. To this end, the extractor that takes the process model resulting from applying DynaTail back to a process model that can be displayed in a BPMN modeling tool. The extractor applies the following steps: (1) Identify elements of the BPMN process model for building the BPMN process, (2) Semantic analysis of the labels in the XMI file, (3) Establish a dictionary that implements the matching elements, (4) Create a hierarchical structure from the BPMN description, (5) Build the BPMN process model (BPMN file). Provided that the XMI file does not contain information about process elements sequencing, the original BPMN file is also used as input in order in order to make use of the elements' graphical layout to build the BPMN file for displaying the process.

3.2   Influence Graph Definition

Each organization counts on an *Influence graph* for each potential characteristic that may need to be optimized. Here, the set of practices - either agile or traditional - that may implement each activity in the process are specified. Also, this graph specifies how much each of these practices influences the corresponding activity. Provided that BPMN does not count on variability primitives, we specify the process variability in this influence graph (Fig. 5).

Figure 10 shows the *Influence graph model* for the process in Fig. 3. The graph is structured in four levels. First, the characteristic to be optimized that in our example is "Customer value". A second level of attributes that, according to the literature, have an influence on that characteristic. In our case, these are "Valuable delivery" and "Delivery on time". Third, we have the set of activities on the process model that influence each attribute. And finally, the set of agile practices that may be used for implementing each of these activities. Each of these influences is quantified with a value between -2 and

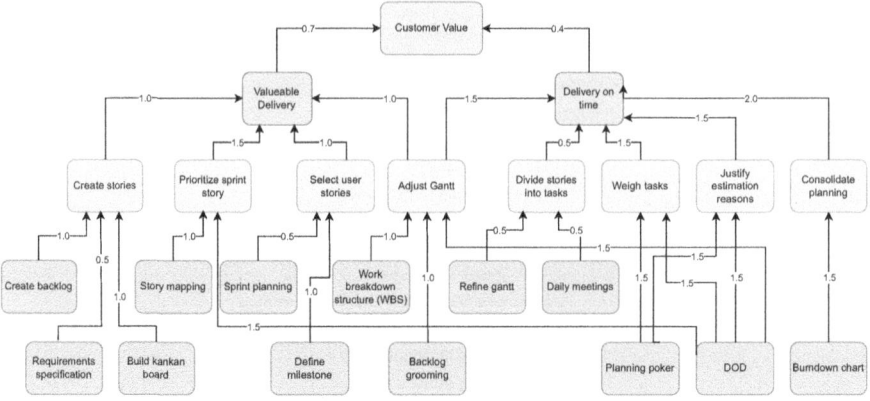

Fig. 5. Influence Graph.

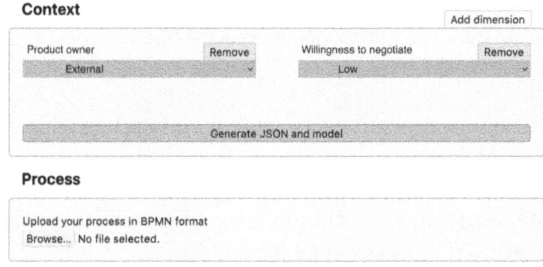

Fig. 6. Context definition tool user interface (from [37]).

2 that is initially defined by experts that usually apply the process and then they are adjusted according to empirical results. This graph conforms to an Influence graph metamodel that refines that presented in [37] for including practices explicitly relating them to the activities they may implement.

In order to better illustrate the way this *Influence graph* is used to obtain the optimized process, we have significatively extended the graph by adding several alternative practices that may be used for implementing each activity. Each of these practices has a different influence weight on the activity. For example, "Valuable delivery" has an influence of 0.7 on "Customer value", while "Delivery on time" has an 0.4 influence. Relating activities, the "Adjust Gantt" activity may implemented with three different practices, each one with its own weight: "DOD" 1.5, "Backlog grooming" 1.0, and "Work breakdown structure" 1.0.

3.3   Context Definition and Modeling

A project's context is defined by the characteristics of its environment. Common characteristics in software development projects include system size, software complexity, development team size, and domain knowledge, among others. While a company may

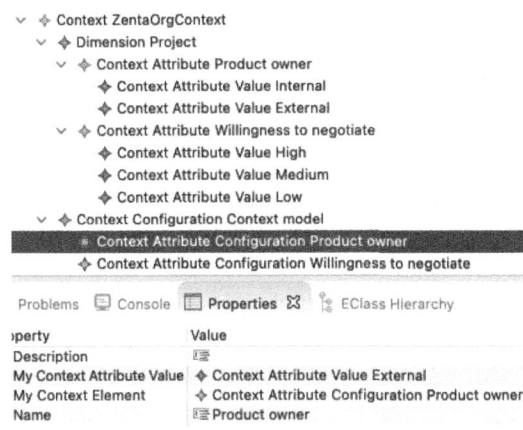

Fig. 7. Context model (from [37]).

establish a standardized development process and apply it consistently, it can also take contextual characteristics into account to select or tailor the process, making it more suitable for each specific project. Although any characteristic could theoretically be used to define the context for process tailoring, research has shown that project/product size and application domain are the most commonly considered dimensions [18]. In this paper, we adopt a broad perspective and consider any type of dimension.

To develop DynaTool, we formally represent the project context as a model that integrates seamlessly into the tool. We have created a custom context definition interface that enables the process engineer to specify the context attributes to be considered, while the project engineer can assign values to these attributes for a specific project. Additionally, we have developed an injector that takes the context, defined as a JSON file generated by this tool, and converts it into a context model.

In order to replicate the running example presented in [37], we show in Fig. 1 the same context. Figure 6 shows the interface through which the project manager defines the context, while Fig. 7 illustrates the resulting context model after applying the injector. The context model comprises two sections: the *Organizational Context Model*, which defines all context attributes and their potential values, and the *Project Context Model*, which configures these attributes with specific values for a given project context. Only attributes defined in the Organizational Context Model can be configured. As indicated in the interface, the *Project Owner* attribute in the context model is set to "External", as specified at the bottom part of the model. Similarly, the *Willingness to Negotiate* attribute is set to "Low".

In the lower part of the context definition interface there is the possibility of uploading the BPMN process file and lounge first the injector and then the tailoring transformation described in the following section.

3.4   Process Tailoring Definition and Modeling

We developed a new interactive tool for defining transformation rules for process model tailoring. The generated transformations follow the same syntax as before. Using a separate model injector, these rules are then transformed into an ATL transformation model, which takes both the process and context models as input and produces a tailored process model as output. In what follows we describe each of these activities, their user interfaces and their supporting models.

Writing tailoring rules in a formal language is highly complex and could pose a significant barrier to making DynaTool applicable across various processes and contexts in industry. To address this, we designed a even more user-friendly interface that allows process engineers to define these tailoring rules interactively.

To this end, the *Process model* and *Context model* must be defined in advance. First, DynaTool retrieves all activities from the Process model (see Fig. 8a). The process engineer can then select an activity that may be implemented differently based on specific context values. A rule will define for example that in certain contexts, the activity should not be necessary to be performed as part of the optimized process.

For instance, in this example, "Prioritize user stories" has been selected. A specific rule for this activity can then be defined using the user interface shown in Fig. 8b. Figure 9 presents three rules defined by the process engineer for this activity. For example, rule 3 is the one generated according to the specification in Fig. 8: *Product owner*

(a) Selecting variable activity   **(b)** Defining transformation rules

Fig. 8. Transformation rules user interface.

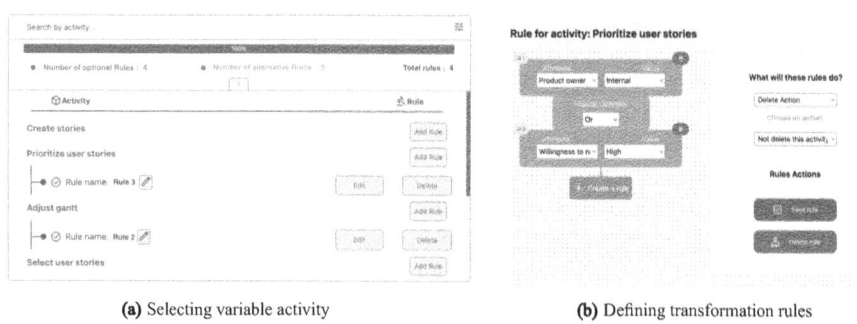

```
helper def:ruleOpt1():Boolean=
    if(thisModule.getValue('Project owner type') = 'external'
        and thisModule.getValue('Willingness to negotiate') = 'low' )
    then true else false endif;


helper def:ruleOpt2():Boolean=
    if((thisModule.getValue('Project owner type') = 'external'
        and thisModule.getValue('Willingness to negotiate') = 'medium')
        or (thisModule.getValue('Project leader type') = 'internal'
            or thisModule.getValue('Willingness to negotiate') = 'high') )
    then true else false endif;

helper def:ruleOpt3():Boolean=
    if(thisModule.getValue('Project owner type') = 'internal'
        and thisModule.getValue('Willingness to negotiate') = 'high' )
    then true else false endif;
```

Fig. 9. Tailoring rules automatically generated (adapted from [37]).

is classified as "internal" or their *Willingness to negotiate* is "high," as outlined in the context specification of the previous section, then the *Prioritize stories* activity must be included in the tailored process. In this case, if no other rule applies, the process will remain as shown in Fig. 3, with no activities removed. Similarly, the first rule is the one that would be applied in the context defined in Fig. 6.

Once all the desired rules have been defined, the transformation shown in Fig. 9 can be automatically generated. It is important to note that this operation is a higher-order transformation, which is highly complex and challenging to perform manually.

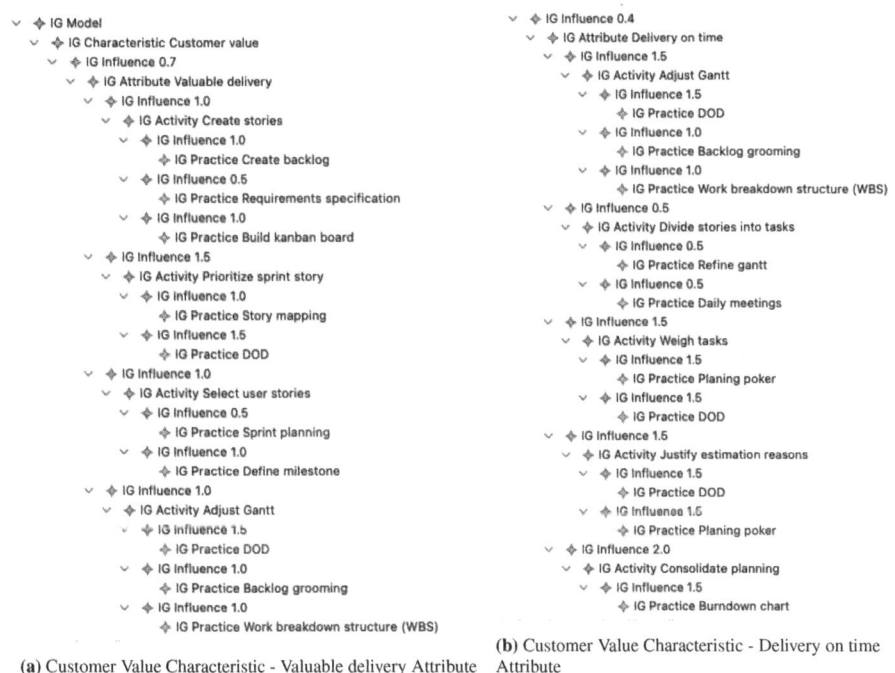

(a) Customer Value Characteristic - Valuable delivery Attribute   (b) Customer Value Characteristic - Delivery on time Attribute

Fig. 10. Influence Model.

3.5 Practice Evaluation and Selection

The *Practice evaluation and selection* activity extends the *Process evaluation* activity introduced in the first version of DynaTool [37]. This step is implemented as a model transformation that takes the *Influence graph* and the *Tailored process model* as inputs, producing a process optimized with a specific set of practices aimed at enhancing the desired characteristic. In this step, the practices that most effectively contribute to optimizing the targeted characteristic are selected. It is important to note that only the activities included in the tailored process will be evaluated and considered for the final output.

Table 1. I(Prac,Act): Matrix of influences of practices on activities.

Practice	Activity			
	Create stories	Prioritize sprint story	Select user stories	Adjust gantt
Create backlog	1.0	0	0	0
Requirements specification	0.5	0	0	0
Build kanban board	1,0	0	0	0
Story mapping	0	1.0	0	0
DOD	0	1.5	0	1.5
Sprint planning	0	0	0.5	0
Define milestone	0	0	1.0	0
Backlog grooming	0	0	0	1.0
Work breakdown structure (WBS)	0	0	0	1.0
Refine gantt	0	0	0	0
Daily meetings	0	0	0	0
Planing poker	0	0	0	0
Burndown chart	0	0	0	0

Table 2. I(Prac,Act): Matrix of influences of practices on activities.

Practice	Activity			
	Divide stories into tasks	Weigh the tasks	Justify estimation reasons	Consolidate planning
Create backlog	0	0	0	0
Requirements specification	0	0	0	0
Build kanban board	0	0	0	0
Story mapping	0	0	0	0
DOD	0	1.5	1.5	0
Sprint planning	0	0	0	0
Define milestone	0	0	0	0
Backlog grooming	0	0	0	0
Work breakdown structure (WBS)	0	0	0	0
Refine gantt	0.5	0	0	0
Daily meetings	0.5	0	0	0
Planing poker	0	1.5	1.5	0
Burndown chart	0	0	0	1.5

The characteristic can either be maximized or minimized. If the goal is to maximize it, as in the case of adding value to the client, the practices selected should have the greatest positive influence on the relevant activities. Conversely, if the characteristic needs to be minimized, such as reducing time to market, the chosen practices should be those with the least influence on their corresponding activities.

Tables 1 and 2 show the influence of all the practices on the process activities. This information is the same included in the *Influence graph* depicted in Fig. 10.

In order to maximize the desired characteristic (value added in the example), the value of the attributes that influence it directly must be also maximized. Provided that

Table 3. Influence of activities and practices on attributes - First evaluation -Agile practices.

Activity	Practice	Valuable delivery	Delivery on time
Create stories	Build kanban board	1.0 * 1.0	0
Prioritize sprint story	DOD	1.5 * 1.5	0
Select user stories	Define milestone	1.0 * 1.0	0
Adjust gantt	DOD	1.5 * 1.0	1.5 * 1.5
Divide stories into tasks	Daily meetings	0	0.5 * 0.5
Weigh the tasks	Planning poker	0	1.5 * 1.5
Justify estimation reasons	Planning poker	0	1.5 * 1.5
Consolidate planning	Burndown chart	0	1.5 * 2.0
		0.84	1.25

the activities are those that are part of the process, the practice chosen for implementing each activity will be that also maximizes the influence of the activity over the attribute.

The value of the attributes is computed as the average influence of all the influence of the activities along with their chosen practices as shown in Table 3 and Table 4 (we consider two possible evaluations).

Finally, the characteristic value is obtained as the average of the value of these attributes. In this case is 1.35. If the value obtained is considered good enough, the method ends and the best process for optimizing the intended characteristic is the "Hybrid process model" that defines not only the activities to be followed but also the practices that should be applied in each step.

On the contrary, if the process engineer considers that the resulting value is not good enough, he/she may proceed to *Change process* or *Change context* and restart whole method. Modifying the process could be for example, adding new steps or roles not present in the previous process, while modifying the context could be for example, adding more developers to the team in charge of the project. Moreover, another potential change could be adding new practices to the influence graph that can potentially be applied for performing certain activities.

Finally, we apply the extractor that takes as input the XMI tailored process and generates the BPMN process. The BPMN process is automatically generated and can be visualized from a BPMN tool as Bizagi, BonitaSoft, BPMN.io or Eclipse Process Modeler.

Since the primary goal of DynaTail is to define the optimal setup for a given project encompassing the process, context, and practices that best achieve the desired characteristic—the notion of "good enough" is largely subjective and depends on the process engineer's judgment. However, a more objective approach can be taken using a *what-if* strategy, which allows for comparing different configurations. Ultimately, it is still up to the process engineer to decide, for example, whether the organization has the resources to configure a specific context or implement certain practices.

Table 4. Influence of activities and practices on attributes - Second evaluation - Hybrid practices.

Activity	Practice	Valuable delivery	Delivery on time
Create stories	Requirements specification	0.5 * 1.0	0
Prioritize sprint story	DOD	1.5 * 1.5	0
Select user stories	Define milestone	1.0 * 1.0	0
Adjust gantt	WBS	1.0 * 1.0	1.0 * 1.5
Divide stories into tasks	Refine gantt	0	0.5 * 0.5
Weigh the tasks	DOD	0	1.5 * 1.5
Justify estimation reasons	DOD	0	1.5 * 1.5
Consolidate planning	Burndown chart	0	1.5 * 2.0
		0.59	1.17

4   Conclusions

A software process is considered effective not only if it aligns with its context but also if it helps achieve a desired goal, such as minimizing development time or maximizing value added. While agile software development encourages the adoption and adaptation of various practices, it is not immediately clear which combination of practices will be most suitable for reaching the project's specific objectives.

We have developed DynaTail, a strategy for determining the optimal configuration of agile and traditional practices to achieve a desired value for a specific characteristic. To facilitate the application of DynaTail, we created DynaTool, a model-driven engineering (MDE)-based support tool. This tool was initially introduced in [37].

In this work, we have enhanced the metamodels and refined the tool's calculation methods to make it more powerful and user-friendly. Additionally, and most importantly, the updated version provides project managers with precise guidance on which practices should be applied to each activity—a feature that was less clear in the previous version.

Although the new version of the tool has not yet been fully applied in industry, we have successfully replicated all the processes from our previous work [20,21,32,37].

References

1. Bernardo, J.R., de Padua, S.I.D.: Toward agile business process management: description of concepts and a proposed definition. Knowl. Process Manag. **30**(1), 14–32 (2023)
2. Braude, E.J., Bernstein, M.E.: Software Engineering: Modern Approaches. Waveland Press (2016)
3. Campanelli, A.S., Parreiras, F.S.: Agile methods tailoring a systematic literature review. J. Syst. Softw. **110**(C), 85–100 (2015). https://doi.org/10.1016/j.jss.2015.08.035
4. Choraś, M., et al.: Measuring and improving agile processes in a small-size software development company. IEEE Access **8**, 78452–78466 (2020)
5. Clarke, P., O'Connor, R.V.: The situational factors that affect the software development process: towards a comprehensive reference framework. Inf. Softw. Technol. **54**(5), 433–447 (2012)

6. Dayyala, N., Walstrom, K.A., Bagchi, K.K., Udo, G.: Factors impacting defect density in software development projects. Int. J. Inf. Technol. Syst. Approach (IJITSA) **15**(1), 1–23 (2022)
7. Diebold, P., Zeher, T.: The Right Degree of Agility in Rich Processes. In: Managing Software Process Evolution, pp. 15–37. Springer, Heidelberg (2016)
8. Diebold, P., Zehler, T.: The agile practices impact model: idea, concept, and application scenario. In: Proceedings of the 2015 International Conference on Software and System Process, pp. 92–96. ACM (2015)
9. Werner, C.M., Berry, D.M.: An empirical study of the software development process, including its requirements engineering, at very large organization: how to use data mining in such a study. In: Kamalrudin, M., Ahmad, S., Ikram, N. (eds.) APRES 2017. CCIS, vol. 809, pp. 15–25. Springer, Singapore (2018). https://doi.org/10.1007/978-981-10-7796-8_2
10. Giachetti, G., de la Vara, J.L., Marín, B.: A model-driven approach to adopt good practices for agile process configuration and certification. Computer Standards & Interfaces **86**, 103737 (2023)
11. Gill, A.Q., Henderson-Sellers, B., Niazi, M.: Scaling for agility: a reference model for hybrid traditional-agile software development methodologies. Inf. Syst. Front. **20**, 315–341 (2018)
12. Ginsberg, M.P., Quinn, L.H.: Process tailoring and the software capability maturity model. Citeseer (1995)
13. Humphrey, W.: A Discipline for Software Engineering. SEI Series in Software Engineering, Addison Wesley, Boston (1995)
14. Humphrey, W.S.: The software engineering process: definition and scope. In: Proceedings of the 4th International Software Process Workshop on Representing and Enacting the Software Process, pp. 82–83 (1988)
15. Hurtado Alegría, J.A., Bastarrica, M.C., Ochoa, S.F., Simmonds, J.: MDE software process lines in small companies. J. Syst. Softw. **86**(5), 1153–1171 (2013)
16. Kalus, G., Kuhrmann, M.: Criteria for software process tailoring: a systematic review. In: International Conference on Software and System Process, pp. 171–180. ACM (2013)
17. Klünder, J., et al.: Catching up with method and process practice: an industry-informed baseline for researchers. In: 2019 IEEE/ACM 41st International Conference on Software Engineering: Software Engineering in Practice (ICSE-SEIP), pp. 255–264. IEEE, IEEE/ACM (2019)
18. Klünder, J., et al.: Determining context factors for hybrid development methods with trained models. In: International Conference on Software and System Processes, ICSSP'2020, pp. 61–70. ACM (2020)
19. Kuhrmann, M., et al.: Hybrid software and system development in practice: waterfall, scrum, and beyond. In: Proceedings of the 2017 International Conference on Software and System Process, ICSSP 2017, pp. 30–39. Association for Computing Machinery, New York (2017)
20. Marín, J., Bastarrica, M.C., Hurtado, J.A., Silvestre, L.: Dynatail: a method for hybrid software process tailoring. Technical Report. TR/DCC-2021-1, Computer Science Department, University of Chile (2021). https://www.dcc.uchile.cl/reportes
21. Marín, J., Hurtado, J.A., Bastarrica, M.C., Silvestre, L.: Tailoring hybrid software processes in a medium-size software company. In: Proceedings of the 38th ACM/SIGAPP Symposium on Applied Computing, SAC, pp. 1042–1050. ACM (2023)
22. Martins, P.V., Zacarias, M.: An agile business process improvement methodology. Procedia Comput. Sci. **121**, 129–136 (2017)
23. Münch, J., Armbrust, O., Kowalcyzk, M., Soto, M.: Software Process Definition and Management. Springer-Verlag, Heidelberg (2012)
24. Ozdenizci Kose, B.: Business process management approach for improving agile software process and agile maturity. J. Softw. Evol. Process **33**(4), e2331 (2021)

25. Pedreira, O., Piattini, M., Luaces, M.R., Brisaboa, N.R.: A systematic review of software process tailoring. SIGSOFT Softw. Eng. Notes **32**(3), 1–6 (2007)
26. Pillat, R.M., Oliveira, T.C., Alencar, P.S.C., Cowan, D.D.: BPMNt: a BPMN extension for specifying software process tailoring. Inf. Softw. Technol. **57**, 95–115 (2015). https://doi.org/10.1016/j.infsof.2014.09.004
27. Prenner, N., Unger-Windeler, C., Schneider, K.: Goals and challenges in hybrid software development approaches. J. Softw. Evol. Process **33**(11), e2382 (2021)
28. Pulgar, J., Bastarrica, M.C.: Transforming multi-role activities in software processes into business processes. In: Dumas, M., Fantinato, M. (eds.) BPM 2016. LNBIP, vol. 281, pp. 372–383. Springer, Cham (2017). https://doi.org/10.1007/978-3-319-58457-7_27
29. Raharjo, T., Purwandari, B.: Agile project management challenges and mapping solutions: a systematic literature review. In: Proceedings of the 3rd International Conference on Software Engineering and Information Management, pp. 123–129. ACM (2020)
30. Santana, C., Queiroz, F., Vasconcelos, A., Gusmão, C.: Software process improvement in agile software development a systematic literature review. In: 2015 41st Euromicro Conference on Software Engineering and Advanced Applications, pp. 325–332. IEEE (2015)
31. Silvestre, L., Bastarrica, M.C., Hurtado, J.A., Marín, J.: Formalizing the goal-directed and context-based software process tailoring method. In: XLVII Latin American Computing Conference, CLEI, pp. 1–9 (2021)
32. Silvestre, L., Bastarrica, M.C., Ochoa, S.F.: A model-based tool for generating software process model tailoring transformations. In: 2014 2nd International Conference on Model-Driven Engineering and Software Development (MODELSWARD), pp. 533–540. IEEE (2014)
33. Tell, P., et al.: What are hybrid development methods made of?: an evidence-based characterization. In: Proceedings of the International Conference on Software and System Processes, ICSSP 2019, Montreal, QC, Canada, 25–26 May 2019, pp. 105–114. IEEE/ACM (2019)
34. Thiemich, C., Puhlmann, F.: An agile BPM project methodology. In: Daniel, F., Wang, J., Weber, B. (eds.) BPM 2013. LNCS, vol. 8094, pp. 291–306. Springer, Heidelberg (2013). https://doi.org/10.1007/978-3-642-40176-3_25
35. Unterkalmsteiner, M., Gorschek, T., Islam, A.M., Cheng, C.K., Permadi, R.B., Feldt, R.: Evaluation and measurement of software process improvement–a systematic literature review. IEEE Trans. Softw. Eng. **38**(2), 398–424 (2012). https://doi.org/10.1109/TSE.2011.26
36. Vijayasarathy, L.R., Butler, C.W.: Choice of software development methodologies: do organizational, project, and team characteristics matter? IEEE Softw. **33**(5), 86–94 (2016)
37. Wallberg, A., González, D., Silvestre, L., Bastarrica, M.C.: A tool for modeling and tailoring hybrid software processes. In: Proceedings of the 12th International Conference on Model-Based Software and Systems Engineering, MODELSWARD 2024, Rome, Italy, 21–23 February 2024, pp. 264–271. SCITEPRESS (2024)
38. West, D., Gilpin, M., Grant, T., Anderson, A.: Water-scrum-fall is the reality of agile for most organizations today. Forrester Res. **26**(2011), 1–17 (2011)
39. Xu, P., Ramesh, B.: Software process tailoring: an empirical investigation. J. Manag. Inf. Syst. **24**(2), 293–328 (2007). http://www.jstor.org/stable/40398686
40. Zacarias, M., Martins, P.V., Gonçalves, A.: An agile business process and practice metamodel. Procedia Comput. Sci. **121**, 170–177 (2017)

Modeling Languages, Tools and Architectures

Specifying, Analysing and Implementing Decision-Support System Architectures

Mert Ozkaya[1]([✉])[iD], Mehmet Alp Kose[2][iD], and Egehan Asal[3][iD]

[1] Department of Computer Engineering, Yeditepe University, Istanbul, Turkey
mozkaya@cse.yeditepe.edu.tr
[2] Istanbul, Turkey
[3] DFDS, Istanbul, Turkey
egehasa@dfds.com

Abstract. Nowadays, decision-support systems (DSSs) are considered as one of the most crucial parts of many systems whose goal is to use a set of data and make the optimum decisions. To develop high-quality DSSs that can easily be maintained, an architecture-centric software development process can be followed. However, we observed that the literature lacks an architecture modeling language for the high-level specifications of DSS architectures that can be automatically analysed and transformed into an executable code. So, in this paper, we propose a novel architecture modeling language called *DSSGen* which offers a set of component types (i.e., problem, diagnosis and action) for the high-level specifications of DSS architectures. We developed a toolset for DSSGen, which enables for *(i)* the modeling of DSSGen architectures via a modeling editor, *(ii)* simulating the architectural models using Modelica, *(iii)* generating quality Java code from the architectural models, and *(iv)* visualising the code structure using UML class diagram. We evaluated DSSGen in two parts. First, we measured DSSGen's impact on the development time performance via four different case-studies that have been performed by a group of practitioners. Then, we conducted a survey with the same group of practitioners to understand their perspectives on DSSGen.

Keywords: Decision support systems · Model-driven engineering · Modeling language · Model simulation · Code-generation

1 Introduction

Decision support systems (DSSs) have been used since the early nineties for the purpose of automating the decision making processes in diverse industries [18,22,23]. With DSSs, optimum decisions can be made quickly using the data set available, compared with the manual approaches that lead to subjective decisions based on opinions. As indicated in [23], the term *decision* here indicates the role of DSSs as decision makers rather than collecting, analysing and reporting data and information. The term *support* indicates that the DSSs not always make decisions on behalf of humans but rather support their decision making process. The term *system* indicates that the DSSs

---

M. A. Kose—Independent Researcher.

F. José Domínguez Mayo et al. (Eds.): MODELSWARD 2024, CCIS 2547, pp. 107–131, 2026.
https://doi.org/10.1007/978-3-031-96841-9_6

consists of different components that interact with each other such as data generators, diagnosis makers, decision makers, and action takers.

The literature includes several different studies on DSSs that reveal the applications of DSSs in different domains, such as [38] for healthcare, [8] for logistics, [35] for disaster management, [39] for agriculture and [17] for traffic management. The high popularity of DSSs among various industries makes it crucial to develop quality DSSs with the least development effort. To this end, a software architecture-centric development approach can be adopted [12,33], which promotes making high-level architectural decisions about the system under development, reasoning about those decisions and then using those decisions to perform low-level design and implementation. By doing so, DSSs that better meet the quality needs can be developed in a way that can easily be maintained. Architecture-centric development can be supported with the model-driven engineering (MDE) technique [2,20,32,36], which promotes the development of modeling languages and tools for facilitating the high-level specifications of software architectures in a way that can automatically be analysed, simulated and further generated into some useful artefacts (e.g., executable code).

As we discussed our literature search discussed in Sect. 2, the literature includes some reference architectures that can be used as a guide on specifying the architecture of DSSs for different domains. However, the literature lacks in any approach that reveals the use of modeling languages and their toolset for the specifications of DSS architectures that can easily be simulated and generated into executable code automatically.

In this paper, we propose a novel architecture modeling language called *DSSGen*, which offers a set of component types (i.e., Problem, Diagnosis, and Action) and connector types. DSSGen can be used for specifying the high-level architecture of any DSSs in an understandable, precise, and highly-analysable way. Practitioners can specify different concerns using different component types and connect the components using connectors. The problem components encapsulate the domain data collected from the environment and are needed by the diagnosis component(s) to make any diagnosis. So, whenever the problem data change, an event occurs for the diagnosis component which process their patterns to make any diagnosis. Whenever any diagnosis is made, an event is generated for the action components which can then get the expected tasks to be performed. The events herein are generated and transmitted by the connectors. We developed a toolset for DSSGen using the Metaedit+ meta-modeling technology [19], which enables for *(i)* the modeling of DSSGen architectures, *(ii)* simulating the architectural models using Modelica [10], *(iii)* generating quality Java code from the architectural models, and *(iv)* visualising the code structure using UML class diagram.

In the rest of the paper, we initially give our literature analysis. Then, we introduce the *DSSGen* language. Next, we introduce the *DSSGen* toolset and that is followed by our comprehensive evaluation of the language and its toolset. Lastly, we give the conclusion.

2 Related Work

The literature includes several approaches that can be considered as a reference for designing the DSS architectures on specific domains including healthcare [7,30], manufacturing [14,29,31], and traffic management [6]. Those reference architectures can aid in understanding the types of components and connectors and any constraints and rules on their behaviours and interactions for the effective specifications of the DSS architectures so that the DSSs realised accordingly can easily be communicated, reused and maintained. While those reference architectures can be considered very useful, most of them are essentially applicable for a particular domain only. Also, the reference architecture specifications are not supported with any modeling languages with *(i)* a concrete notation set for specifying DSS architectures accordingly and *(ii)* a tool support for editing and processing the architecture models. Therefore, it is not so easy to evaluate the use of the reference architectures.

Besides the reference architectures, the literature includes several modeling languages that can be considered for the specifications of DSS architectures [25]. The de-facto software modeling languages such as UML [4] and SysML [3] can aid in specifying high-level models that are independent from each other focus on different aspects of decision-support systems (e.g., structural, behaviour, and interaction). However, since those languages are general-purpose and do not provide DSS-specific notation sets, the models specified may not be so useful for communicating the DSS decisions. Also, the UML/SysML modeling tools do not aid in performing DSS-specific analyses (e.g., simulating the DSS behaviours) and code-generation (e.g., pattern-centric code). Besides UML and SysML, general-purpose architecture description languages (ADLs), such as ArchiMate [21], C4 [34], and XCD [26], which support the architectural modeling from different perspectives can also be used. With those ADLs, one can specify the structural models of DSSs at different levels of details and associate the structural models with some behaviour and interaction models. However, none of those ADLs aid in specifying the DSS architectures with specialised notation sets and provide any useful tool support for simulating the DSS behaviours and generating executable code.

The literature also includes tens of different domain-specific languages (DSLs) through which different domain problems can be addressed at an architectural level. Some popular DSLs are *(i)* AADL for the specification and analysis of embedded system architectures, *(ii)* the DSLs for the internet-of-things domain [1], *(iii)* WebDSL for the web applications [13], and *(iv)* DeepDSL for deep learning network applications [40]. DSLs each essentially focus on a particular problem that may be solved with a DSS development, and therefore some DSLs may indeed include notations for specifying the DSS components and connectors. Note however that one may not use DSLs for the high-level specifications of DSS architectures in a way that can be analysed and transformed into an executable DSS code.

3   DSSGen Language Definition

DSSGen has been proposed as an extension of our early initial attempt called *DecSup* [27]. The feedback that we received from industry and academia about *DecSup* lead us to propose a new, improved language for the facilitated specifications and communications of high-level DSS architectures. While *DSSGen* and *DecSup* both use the same set of component and connector types, the structure and attributes of the component and connector types have been highly improved with *DSSGen* that are discussed in the rest of this section. Moreover, unlike *DecSup*, *DSSGen* is supported with a Java code generator and code visualiser in UML that are discussed in Sect. 4.

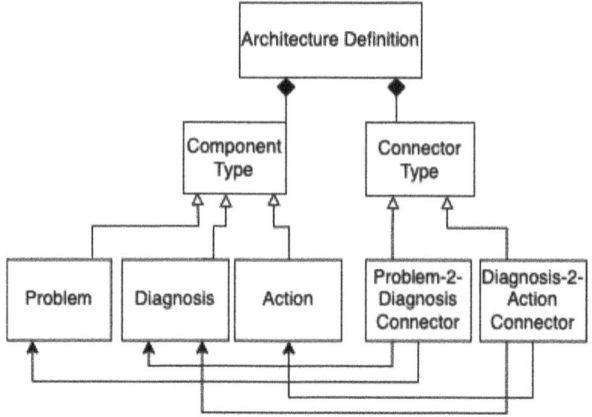

Fig. 1. The component and connector types supported by DSSGen.

3.1 DSSGen Concepts

DSSGen offers a set of component and connector types for the high-level specifications of any DSS architectures, which are depicted in Fig. 1. So, any DSS architectures are specified with the components of three types (i.e., problem, diagnosis, and action) and those components interact via the connectors of two types (i.e., one for connecting a problem component with a diagnosis component and the other for connecting a diagnosis component with an action component).

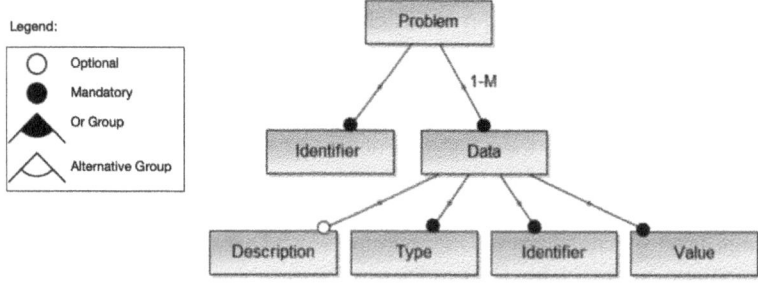

Fig. 2. The feature diagram for the problem component type.

Problem Component Type. The very first stage of the decision making process is to define any problem in terms of a data set that represent the occurrence of some phenomena in the environment. Upon the occurrence of a phenomenon in the problem environment, a set of data specified for the problem component are expected to be assigned with some proper values which can then be used for making diagnoses and the corresponding decisions.

The problem component type is therefore considered as an abstraction for the domain data set that represent any problem. Figure 2 shows the problem component type definition. The problem component type consists of an identifier and a set of domain data. An identifier gives a name for the problem component type. A problem component may have 1 or more data. Each data is specified with a description, type, identifier, and a value. The data type can be either primitive (e.g., int, char, bool) or complex (e.g., string or some user-defined structure).

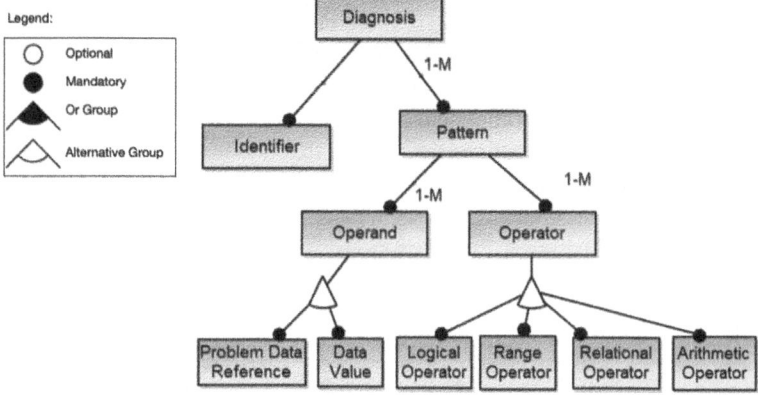

Fig. 3. The feature diagram for the diagnosis component type.

Diagnosis Component Type. Given the data indicating the existence of a problem, a diagnosis is expected to be made that directly impacts on decision(s) for the actions to be taken.

The diagnosis component type is considered as an abstraction that represents a unit for making a diagnosis using some patterns. As Fig. 3 shows, a diagnosis component type consists of an identifier and 1 or more pattern specifications. A pattern here essentially represents a single expression or the logical combinations of a set of expressions where each expression can be either relational or arithmetic. To specify a pattern, one or more operands and operators are therefore considered. An operand can either be a variable that refers to a problem domain data or just a literal value. The operator can

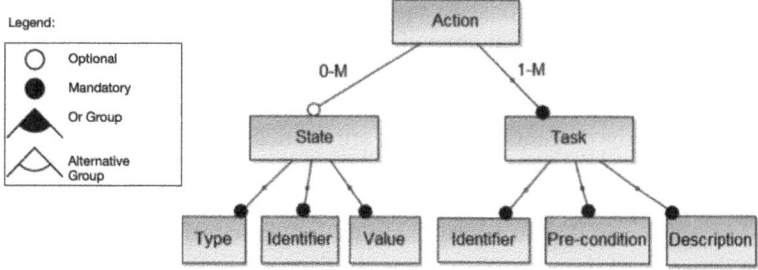

Fig. 4. The feature diagram for the action component type.

be either a logical operator (AND, OR, NOT), range operator (e.g., 1–5), relational operator ($<$, $>$, $<=$, $>=$, and $==$), or arithmetic operator ($+$, $-$, $*$, $/$).

Action Component Type. Once any diagnosis is made via the diagnosis component (i.e., one of its patterns is satisfied), an action needs to be operated and the task(s) of that action needs to be performed.

The action component type is an abstraction that represents an action which takes place upon any diagnosis detected. As shown in Fig. 4, the action component type consists of zero or more state data and one or more tasks. A state data represents an action state, which is specified with a type (i.e., integer, double, boolean, string and char), identifier, and a value. Each task represents any activity to be performed and is specified with an identifier, pre-condition and description. Here, the pre-condition statement indicates the condition on an action state(s) data that needs to be satisfied for the task to be performed. The task description gives the informal explanation of the task.

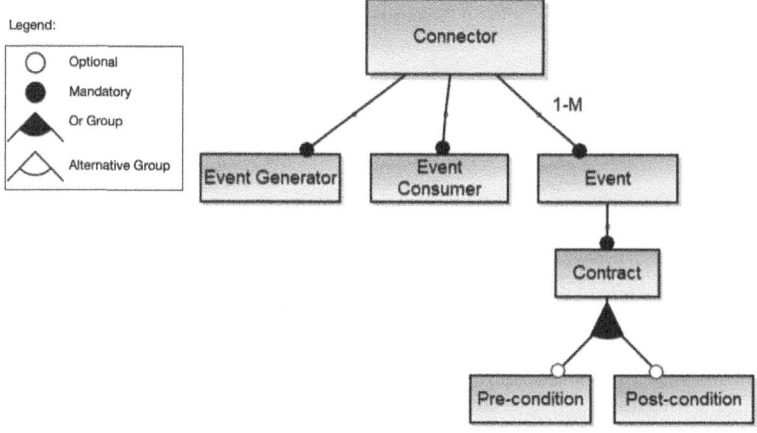

Fig. 5. The feature diagram for the connector type.

Connector Type. The components of the problem, diagnosis, and action component types interact with each other so as to compose any DSS architectures. Whenever the data of a problem component changes, an event occurs and the diagnosis component(s) that are interested in the problem are notified. The diagnosis component processes all the data received from the problem component with its patterns. If any diagnosis is made (i.e., a pattern is satisfied), another event occurs and the action component(s) that are associated with the diagnosis component are notified. The event-driven interactions between the problem and diagnosis components and the interactions between the diagnosis and action components are all coordinated via the connectors.

As depicted in Fig. 1, two types of connectors are considered in DSSGen both of which derive from the same abstraction. As depicted in Fig. 5, the connector type abstraction consists of a generator, a consumer and 1 or more events. The generator herein represents the role played by the component that is connected with the connector and causes an event to be occurring. The consumer herein represents the role played by the component that is connected with the connector and are notified due to the event occurring. So, each connector derived from the connector type abstraction here connects one component playing the generator role with another component playing the consumer role. Whenever a data in the problem component changes, a connector event is generated and the generated event is consumed by the diagnosis component via the connector. Whenever a diagnosis pattern is evaluated, another connector event is generated and the generated event is to be consumed by the action component via the connector. Any connector event consumed by the action components consists of a contract specification which is a pair of pre- and post-conditions. With the event contracts, one can specify when the generated event should be accepted (i.e., the pre-condition) and how the state of the consuming component should change (i.e., the post-condition). Note that *(i)* not each event has to have a contract specification, and *(ii)* an event contract may just have a pre-condition or post-condition exclusively.

3.2 DSSGen's Concrete Notation Set

Figure 6 shows the concrete symbols for the problem, diagnosis, and action component types and connector types. So, the component types are basically specified with colored circles and the connector types with a black directed arrow. Component and connector symbols are supported with graphical user interfaces.

Whenever any component is clicked, a new dialog box opens for specifying the component attributes. Clicking any problem component symbol enables for specifying the domain data set that represent the problem. Clicking a diagnosis component symbol enables for specifying the diagnosis pattern(s). Clicking an action component enables for specifying the action state data and tasks.

Each type of connector is specified with a directed arrow, which connects the components playing the event generator and event consumer roles. For a connector that connects a problem with diagnosis, the problem component plays the role of an event generator while the diagnosis component plays the role of an event consumer. For a connector that connects a diagnosis with an action, the diagnosis component is the event generator while the action component is the consumer. In this case, users are expected to click on the arrow symbol and use the dialog box opening to specify the event contracts in terms of the pre-condition and post-condition. The former states the condition under which an event can be generated and the post-condition indicates the state change for the action component after receiving the event.

Figure 7 shows the notation set for specifying the diagnosis patterns. So, different types of notations consisting of the logical, relational, arithmetic, range, and sequence operators can be used. Moreover, the *data* notation can be used for specifying a reference to a problem data that needs to be processed (e.g., compared with some value or used as part of an arithmetic expression).

4 DSSGen's Modeling Toolset

Figure 8 shows the architecture of the DSSGen modeling toolset, which consists of an editor and a set of model transformation tools. The modeling editor depicted in Fig. 9

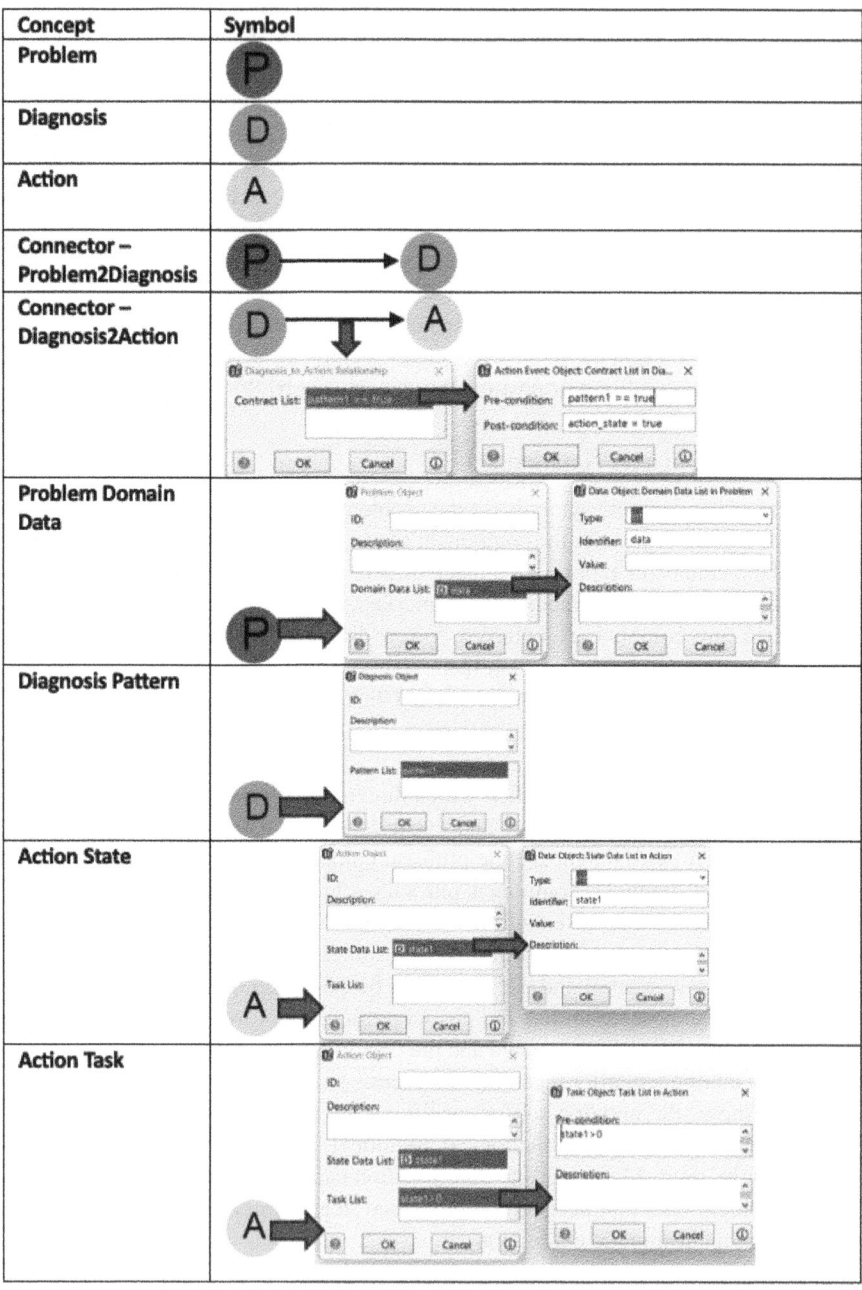

Fig. 6. The concrete symbols for the DSSGen language concepts.

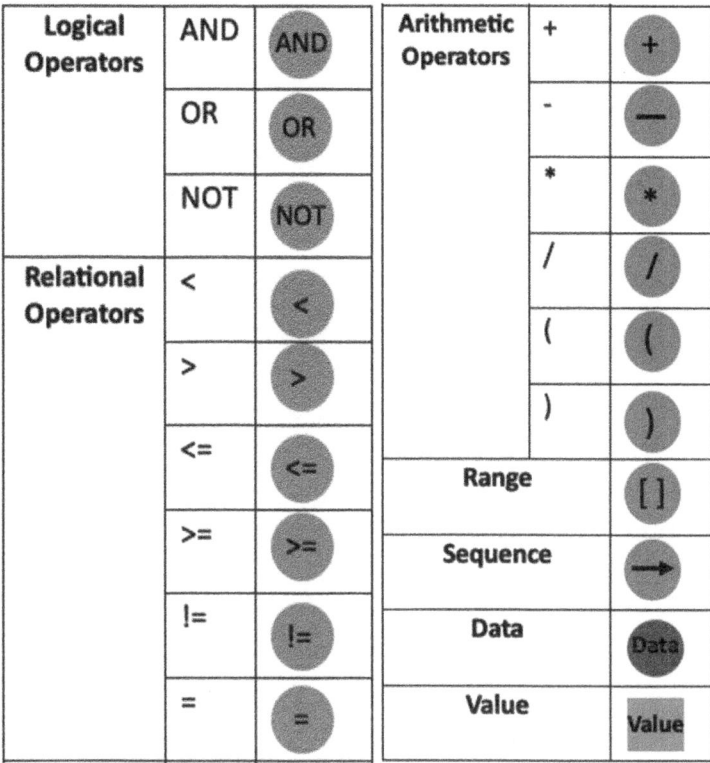

Fig. 7. The concrete symbols for the DSSGen language concepts - pattern specification.

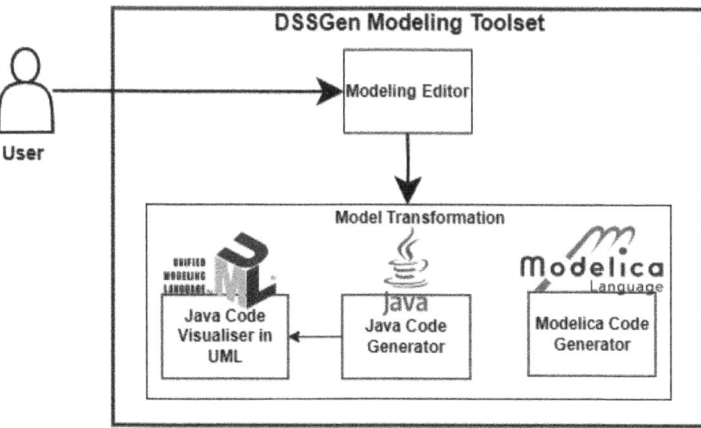

Fig. 8. The tool architecture for DSSGen.

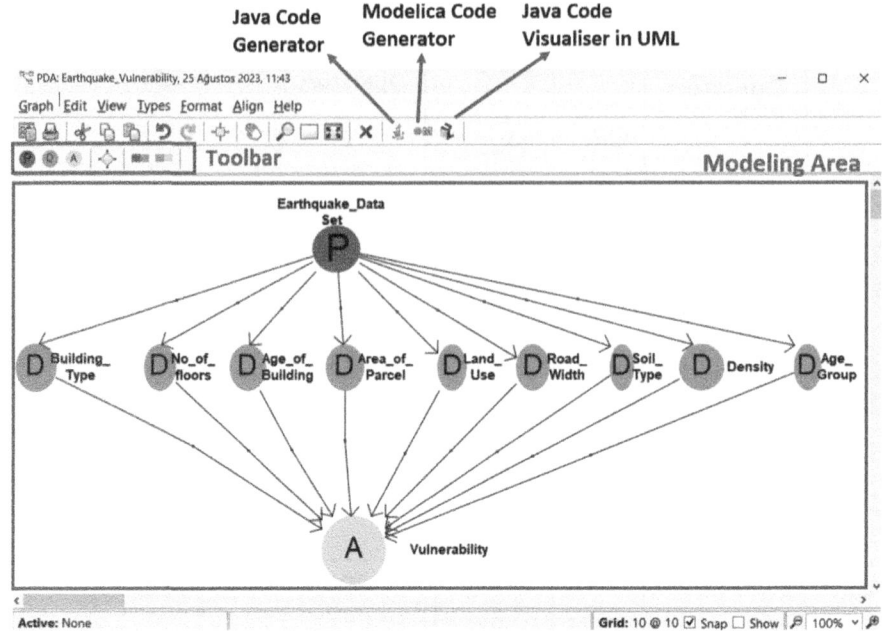

Fig. 9. DSSGen's modeling editor.

can be used to specify the DSSGen architecture models that can then be transformed by clicking on the editor icons. The editor consists of three essential areas, which are toolbar, modeling area, generator icons. After specifying the *DSSGen* models with the editor, users can use the editor generator icons to generate executable Java code or simulator code in Modelica. Users can also visualise the generated Java code in UML class diagram so as to understand the generated code structure.

In the rest of the section, we initially introduce the Java code generator and code visualiser. Then, we introduce the Modelica code generator. We use some case-studies to facilitate the discussion of each generator.

4.1   Java Code Generator

The Java code generator works as integrated with the modeling editor and transforms any DSSGen architecture model into a fully executable GUI application in Java. In Fig. 10, we consider the DSSGen model for the respiratory illness detection and treatment. The generated GUI application from the DSSGen model here prompts the user to input the problem domain data and then returns the decision automatically.

The generated GUI application consists essentially of a user interface module and a logic module. The user interface module includes a Java class that represents the graphical user interfaces through which the users type their inputs and view the results. The logic module consists of a set of Java classes that reflect the architectural model specified. In the rest of this section, we focus on the logic module of the generated GUI

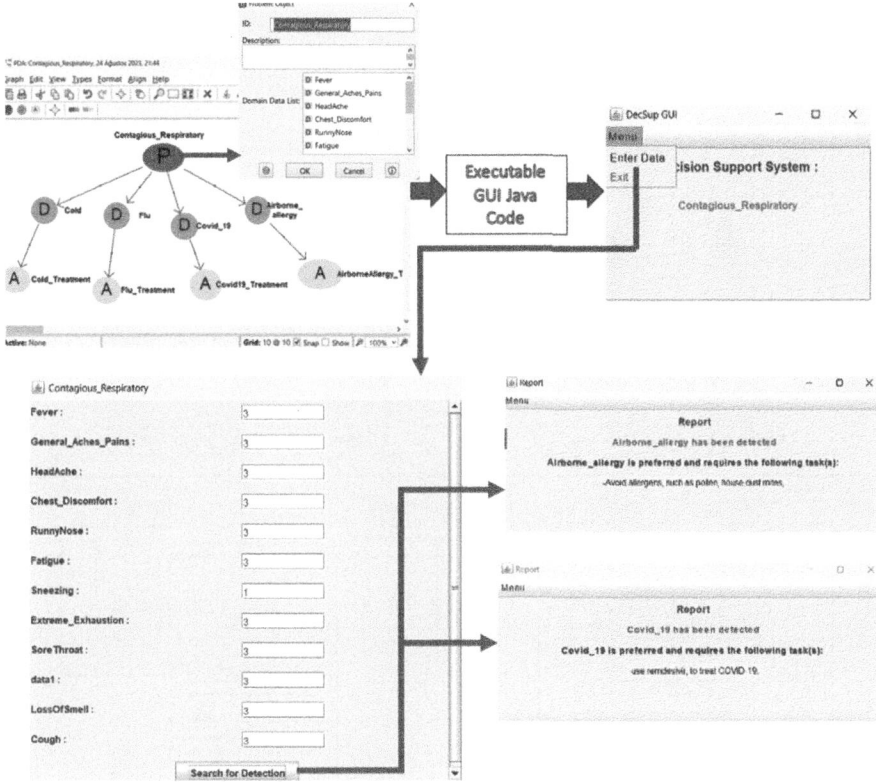

Fig. 10. Running DSSGen's Java code generator on the DSSGen specification for detecting respiratory illnessses.

applications that serves for processing the data, making any diagnosis and choosing the right action.

Figure 11 shows the code structure for the Java code that is generated from the DSSGen specification for the respiratory illness detection system given in Fig. 10. In the respiratory illness detection, a set of data are processed to make the right detection (i.e., Flu, Covid, Airborne Allergy, or Cold) and then suggest the appropriate treatment. The editor visualises the code structure in UML whenever the user clicks on the "Java Code Visualiser in UML" icon on the editor.

As also depicted in Fig. 11, we used Gang of Four's observer design pattern [11] to implement the DSSGen specifications in Java and designed the code generator algorithms accordingly. This is essentially because the *DSSGen* architecture models are event-driven and prompt the components of different types (i.e., problem, diagnosis and action) to interact whenever some events occur, which can best be implemented using the observer design pattern. The generated code from any DSSGen specification includes a Java class for keeping the problem domain data specified via the problem components (i.e., *OBSERVABLE_PROBLEM*), which plays the observable role in the

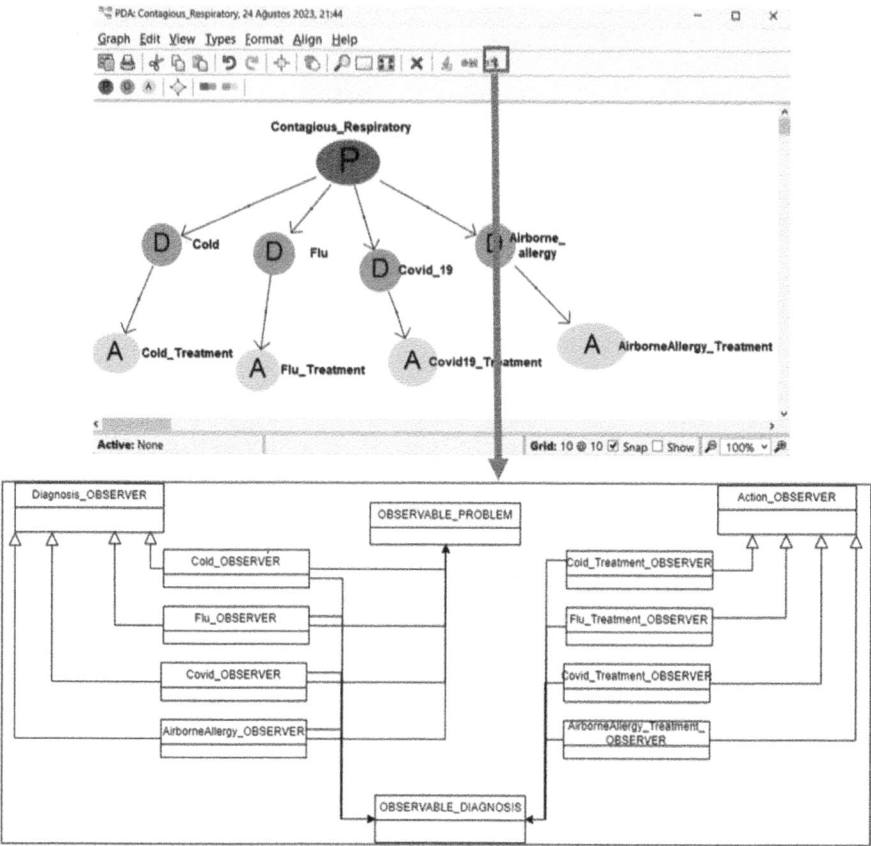

Fig. 11. Visualising the code structure for the generated code in Fig. 10 based on the observer design pattern.

code architecture. Indeed, the problem domain data for any DSS are to be observed by the diagnosis components. The diagnosis components are each transformed into a separate Java class, whose instance plays the observer role (the classes that inherit *Diagnosis_Observer*). Each diagnosis observer class is associated with the observable class that represents the problem components specified. That way, the diagnosis class instances can be notified by the associated problem class instance acting as an observable upon any problem data changed. Note also that any diagnosis components are observed by some action components with which they are connected in the architectural model. Therefore, while any diagnosis component is an observer for the problem components, the same diagnosis component acts as an observable for the action components. So, the observer classes for the diagnosis components are all associated with an observable class (i.e., *OBSERVABLE_DIAGNOSIS*) through which the observers for the action components can obtain the diagnosis data (e.g., the pattern results). Whenever any diagnosis pattern is satisfied, the associated diagnosis class instance updates the diagnosis class instance acting as the observable and that triggers a notification for the class instance(s) for the action components. Note that for each action component, a Java class is transformed and that is associated with the observable diagnosis class.

```
1      ∀ d  ∈ diagnosisComponentSet
2         model d.name
3            ∀ connection ∈ d. problemConnectionSet
4               ∀ data ∈ connection. problem. DataSet
5                  input data.type data.name;
6                  data.type data.name "_STATE";
7            ∀ connection ∈ d. actionConnectionSet
8               ∀ contract ∈ connection. contractSet
9                  output "senderEvent" "senderEvent_" contract.id;
10           equation
11              ∀ connection ∈ d. problemConnectionSet
12                 ∀ data ∈ connection. problem. DataSet
13                    data.name "_STATE" = data.name;
14           algorithm
15              ∀ connection ∈ d. actionConnectionSet
16                 ∀ contract ∈ connection. contractSet
17                    if ( contract.pre-condition )  then
18                       "senderEvent_" contract.id = true;
19                    end if;
20        end d.name;
21     ∀ a  ∈ actionComponentSet
22        model a.name
23           ∀ connection ∈ a. diagnosisConnectionSet
24              ∀ contract ∈ connection. contractSet
25                 input "receiverEvent" "receiverEvent_" contract.id;
26           ∀ data ∈ a. stateDataList
27              data.type data.name = data.initial;
28           algorithm
29              ∀ connection ∈  a. diagnosisConnectionSet
30                 ∀ contract ∈ connection. contractSet
31                    if ( "receiverEvent_" contract.id == true)  then
32                       contract.post-condition;
33                    end if;
34              ∀ task ∈ a. taskList
35                    if ( task.pre-condition == true)  then
36                       display (task.description);
37                    end if;
38        end a.name;
39     model "architecture"
40        ∀ problem ∈ problemComponentSet
41           ∀ data ∈ problem. DataSet
42              input data.type data.name;
43        ∀ diagnosis ∈ diagnosisComponentSet
44           diagnosis.name diagnosis.name "_instance";
45        ∀ action ∈ actionComponentSet
46           action.name action.name "_instance";
47        equation
48           ∀ d  ∈ diagnosisComponentSet
49              ∀ connection ∈ d. problemConnectionSet
50                 ∀ data ∈ connection. problem. DataSet
51                    connection.diagnosis.name  "_instance" . data.name =
52                                    connection.problem.data.name;
53              ∀ connection  ∈ d. actionConnectionSet
54                 ∀ contract ∈ connection. contractSet
55                    connect ( connection.action.name "_instance" . "receiverEvent_" contract.id,
56                              connection.diagnosis.name "_instance" . "senderEvent_" contract.id );
57     end "architecture"
```

Fig. 12. DSSGen's translation algorithm for Modelica.

4.2 Modelica Simulator

The modeling editor depicted in Fig. 9 is supported with another generator that transforms the DSSGen architecture models in the Modelica simulation modeling language [10] for model simulation.

Figure 12 gives the algorithm description for the Modelica translations from DSS-Gen. We use the *model* element (i.e., the main building block in Modelica) to transform the components specified in the DSSGen architectures. The *model* definition for a diagnosis component (lines 1–20 in Fig. 12) includes *(i)* an *input* statement for receiving each problem domain data, *(ii)* a variable for each problem domain data received as input for keeping a copy of its value, *(iii)* an *output* statement for each contract specification of the connector(s) that connect the diagnosis with the action component(s), *(iv)* an *equation* block for assigning the inputs to the variables, and lastly *(v)* an *algorithm* block for checking the contract pre-conditions of the connectors and activating the output statements accordingly (i.e., setting *true*). The *model* definition for an action component (lines 21–38 in Fig. 12) includes *(i)* an *input* statement for each diagnosis associated with the action component, *(ii)* a variable for each state data of the action component, and lastly *(iii)* an *algorithm* block. The *algorithm* block here includes a separate *if* statement for each contract specification of the associated connectors where the input that is received from the diagnosis and represents the contract pre-condition is checked, and if that is satisfied, the action state is updated using the contract post-condition. Also, the *algorithm* block includes a separate if statement for each action task. That is, the tasks whose pre-condition on the action state is satisfied are displayed on the simulator. The last *model* definition (lines 39–57 in Fig. 12) represents the system architecture and therefore creates the instances of the model definitions corresponding

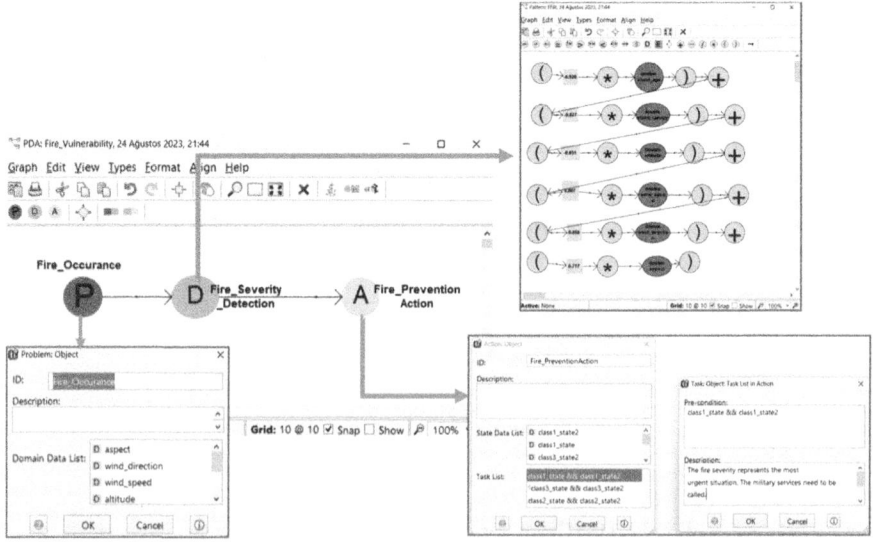

Fig. 13. The DSSGen specification for the fire severity.

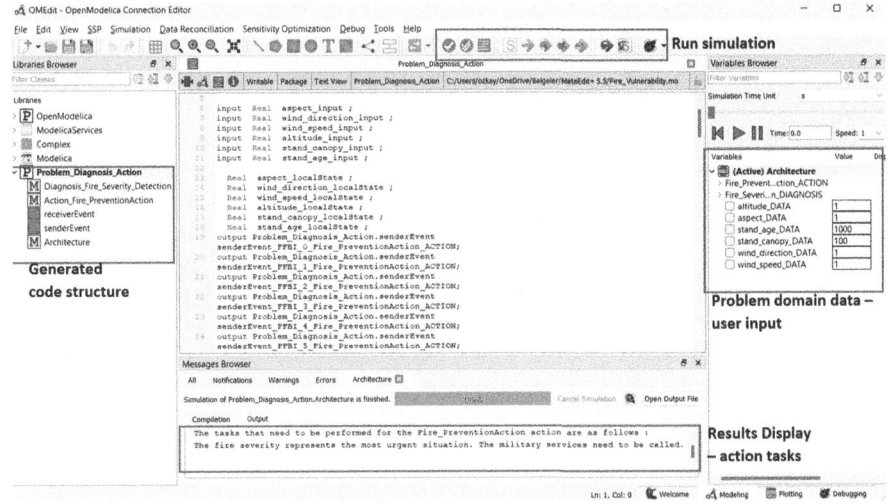

Fig. 14. Using OpenModelica to execute the automatically generated Modelica code from the fire severity model given in Fig. 13.

to the diagnosis and action components that together compose the system architecture. The *model* definition here includes an *input* statement for each problem domain data and those input statements are assigned with the diagnosis inputs. Lastly, a separate *connect* statement is defined for connecting the output statement of each diagnosis with an input statement of an action so as to enable the data flow from the diagnosis to the action components.

To show how the simulation works, we consider the DSSGen specification given in Fig. 13 for the fire severity detection [5]. Here, given a set of problem domain data, the fire severity level is intended to be detected using a pattern (i.e., the equation shown in Fig. 13) and the necessary action(s) is taken by the action component. In Fig. 14, we show the OpenModelica simulator [9] that we used for running the Modelica code which has been automatically generated from the fire severity model specified in Fig. 13 via the DSSGen editor. The left window on the simulator displays the Modelica code structure, where the model definitions generated from the architectural components (i.e., the problem, diagnosis, and action components) are shown. The right window gives the list of the data variables that correspond to the problem domain data which need to be assigned values by the users. The bottom window displays the results upon running the simulation in terms of the action(s) enabled and their tasks to be performed.

5 Evaluation

To evaluate *DSSGen* and its toolset, we considered measuring the development time that can be reduced with *DSSGen* and the user perspectives on the language and its toolset. Therefore, we focused on investigating two research questions given as follows:

RQ1. To what extent does *DSSGen* reduce the development time for DSSs?

RQ2. What are the thoughts of the practitioners about the *DSSGen* language and its toolset?

We performed *DSSGen*'s evaluation in the DFDS development center in Turkey[1]. DFDS is based in Denmark, which is one of the biggest logistics and transportation companies in Europe. DFDS owns several transportation and cruise ships and terminals in important harbours (e.g., Istanbul Pendik in Turkey and Trieste in Italy) and enables the quick and efficient transportation of any types of goods between Middle East and Europe. The DFDS development center in Turkey offers software solutions to various problems about the supply chain management, B2B cargo delivery and pickup, ground transportation, sea logistics and warehouse management, and sea terminal transfer operations.

5.1 Development Performance

To answer RQ1, we aimed to understand to what extent the development time can be reduced with *DSSGen*. To this end, 4 different software engineers working for the R&D center of the DFDS development center in Turkey have been involved in the evaluation processes. Firstly, we asked each engineer to develop a DSS without using *DSSGen*. Given that *DSSGen* produces pattern-centric code, we also asked the engineers to develop quality code that is based on the observer design pattern. In the second stage, the engineers have been asked to use *DSSGen* and perform model-driven engineering to develop the same system. The engineers each have B.S.c degree on computer engineering and considerable experience in developing DSSs. The engineers have abstract knowledge on modeling and none of them performed any model-driven activities before.

We started the evaluation process with a series of tutorials on model-driven engineering that took 8 h in total. By doing so, we intended to ensure that the engineers have the necessary knowledge on such related topics as modeling, meta-modeling, modeling languages, model analysis and model transformation. We also organised another tutorial for introducing the *DSSGen* language and demonstrating its toolset We further introduced here the Metaedit+ technology, with which the toolset has been developed. The second tutorial took 3 h to complete. Lastly, we conducted a 3-h session for introducing the four case-studies that the engineers are intended to use for the evaluation process. For each case study considered, first we explained the domain of the case-study and the aim(s) of the decision making process in that domain. Then, we explained the *(i)* concepts and their relationships required to develop a DSS for that specific case-study, *(ii)* any needed formulas, equations, and statements for making the necessary diagnoses, and *(iii)* any action(s) that can take place upon any diagnosis made. The case-studies are summarised as follows.

Respiratory Illnesses: In this case-study, the article published by the National Institutes of Health (NIH) - i.e., part of the U.S. Department of Health and Human Services - about the respiratory illness detection and treatment has been considered[2]. The goal is to *(i)* detect various types of respiratory illnesses (e.g., COVID19, flu, cold, and airborne

---

[1] DFDS Development Center in Turkey: https://www.dfds.com.tr/.
[2] NIH Web-site: https://newsinhealth.nih.gov/2022/01/it-flu-covid-19-allergies-or-cold.

allergy) using a common set of data including fever, headache, runny nose, sneezing, exhaustion, sore throat, cough, and loss of smell and *(ii)* recommend the most suitable treatment(s).

Fire Behaviour: In this case-study, Dasdemir et al.'s work [5] on managing the fire behaviours is considered. Fire behaviours can be measured using several different data including wind direction, wind speed, and stand canopy. Dasdemir et al. propose a fire behaviour index which is essentially an equation of the data variables and enables for determining the fire behaviour category (e.g., very high, high, and medium). Determining the fire behaviour category further enables for determining the most suitable actions to be taken.

Delivery Vulnerability: In this case-study, Wu et al.'s work [37] on managing the logistics risks by measuring the delivery vulnerability is considered. Delivery vulnerability can be measured by using such data as the accident type, accident region, vehicle type, product type, severity level and accident time. Wu et al. propose a set of patterns which enable for determining the severity level of the delivery vulnerabilities (i.e., accidents) that can then be acted upon differently.

Earthquake Vulnerability: In this case-study, Ishita et al.'s work [15] on determining the buildings' earthquake vulnerability is considered. Earthquake vulnerability can be measured by considering different factors such as building type, number of floors, age of building, area of parcel, land use, road width, soil type, density and age group. Ishita et al. further prioritise the factors considered using the analytical hierarchy process method and propose a formula for calculating the earthquake vulnerability of the buildings given the data corresponding to the factors.

Results. Figure 15 shows the time spent for the development of the four case-studies (i.e., earthquake vulnerability, fire behaviour, delivery vulnerability, and respiratory illnesses). We measured the time spent in terms of four development phases which are analysis, modeling & design, implementation and testing. The top bar-chart gives the time spent when *DSSGen* was not used by the engineers, while the bottom bar-chart gives the time spent when *DSSGen* was used.

Analysis: The analysis phase of the 4 case-studies took essentially similar amount of times when *DSSGen* was not used - i.e., 20–30 min. We think that this is because the case-studies have already been introduced at the beginning and thus, the problem domain and the regarding concepts and relationships have been discussed in detail with the engineers. So, this made the engineers already have a clear idea about the software requirements and spend less effort for the analysis phase. When the *DSSGen* language and its toolset was used, it took 5 min to perform the analysis phase. The time spent here is just to do with going through the concepts and relationships of the case-studies that have been discussed at the beginning.

Modeling & Design: Modeling & design was not the main focus of the engineers while developing the DSSs without using *DSSGen*. The engineers basically sketched some diagrams (i.e., simple boxes and lines) supplemented with some texts to figure out the structure of the source-code to be developed. Therefore, the time spent changes between 30–40 min. On the other hand, the modeling & design phase represents the

Development time without using DecSup (mins)

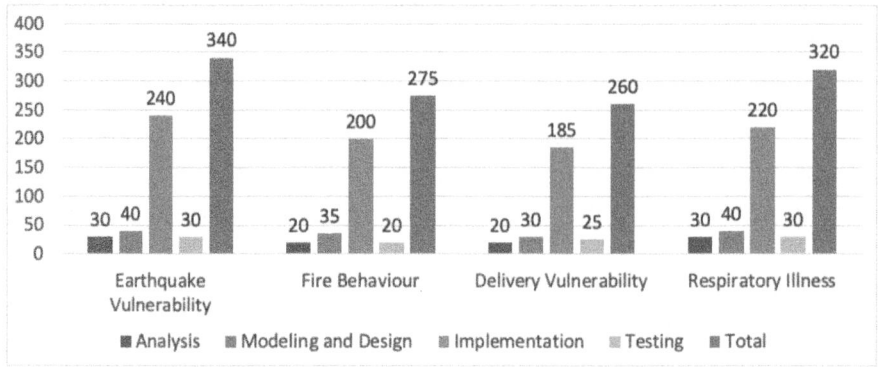

Development time using DecSup (mins)

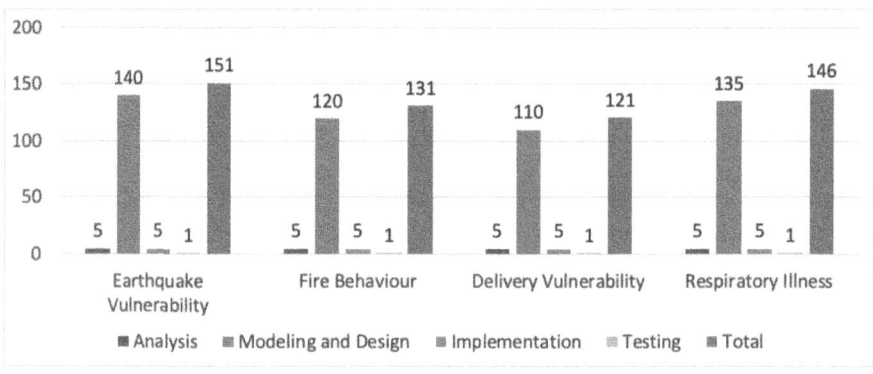

Fig. 15. Evaluating the development time performance.

main part for the development when *DSSGen* is used. Here, the engineers specified the DSS architectures and validated their specifications using the *DSSGen* modeling language and its modeling toolset. Therefore, the modeling & design phase here took between 110–140 min (i.e., 126 min in average).

Implementation: The implementation phase is the main part of the development process when *DSSGen* was not used. Here, the engineers performed their main effort in the manual coding of the desired systems in accordance with the software requirements and design sketches. The average amount of time spent for the manual coding is 211 min. Note that the implementation phase took negligible time when *DSSGen* was used. This is because the engineers used the code generators integrated with the modeling editor and transformed the architecture specifications into a fully executable code immediately. The very small amount of time spent here is essentially to do with running the code generators.

Testing: In the testing phase, the engineers had to separate some time on testing their code to make it working when *DSSGen* was not used. This essentially required 20–30 min. When *DSSGen* was used, the engineers did not need to test their software code as the fully executable pattern-centric code was produced by the tool automatically.

Total: When *DSSGen* was not used by the engineers, the total average time for developing the decision support systems is 298 min. When *DSSGen* was used, the total average development time has been reduced to 137 min. So, the *DSSGen* language and its toolset improved the development time performance and we observed approximately a 2.2 times faster development.

5.2   User Survey

In this part of the evaluation, we considered the second research question (RQ2) and intended to conduct a user survey to understand the practitioners' thoughts about the *DSSGen* language and its toolset. To design the survey questions, we used the framework for the qualitative assessment of the languages proposed by Kahraman et al. [16]. So, we ended up with 26 different questions about 10 different aspects of software quality. These are functional suitability, usability, reliability, maintainability, productivity, extensibility, compatibility, expressiveness, reusability, and integrability. Besides, we also included in the survey 4 different open-ended questions for learning the users' thoughts about the language and tool usabilities.

The survey has been executed with the 4 engineers who have been involved in the development time performance evaluation.

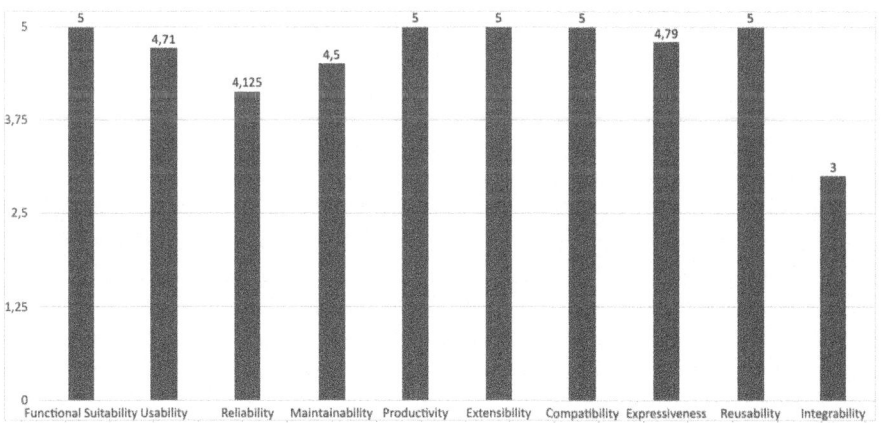

Fig. 16. Evaluating the *DSSGen* language and its toolset via the user survey from different perspectives.

Results. Figure 16 shows the survey results for 10 different perspectives and the general total average of scores is 4.7 out of 5, which shows the high satisfaction of the users with regard to the *DSSGen* language and its toolset.

Concerning the functional suitability, the engineers fully agree that *DSSGen* offers the suitable concepts for specifying the DSS architectures that can be processed for suitable services such as simulation and code generation. Concerning usability, the engineers mostly agree that *DSSGen* aids in designing and implementing DSSs in an effective way. Concerning reliability, the engineers in general agree that *DSSGen* aids in producing reliable (i.e., correct) models. Note that the total reliability score is relatively lower (i.e., 4.125), which might be because *DSSGen*'s toolset focuses more on the user-guided model simulation rather than the automated validation of models against some pre-defined properties. With maintainability, the engineers agree that the *DSSGen* language and its toolset can be maintained easily with the help of the Metaedit+ meta-modeling technology. With productivity, the engineers fully agree that *DSSGen*'s code generator improves the development time considerably. With extensibility, the engineers fully agree that the *DSSGen* language can easily be extended using the Metaedit+ technology. With compatibility, the engineers fully agree that the *DSSGen* language and its toolset are compatible with the DSS domain and its development processes. With expressiveness, the engineers mostly agree that the *DSSGen* language is expressive enough for the specifications of the high-level architectures of any DSSs. With reusability, the engineers fully agree that the *DSSGen* language concepts and symbols can easily be reused via the Metaedit+ technology. Lastly, integrability has been given the least score, which is to do with integrating the language with any other languages. This is essentially because the *DSSGen* language and its toolset has been developed using Metaedit+ and therefore only the languages developed with Metaedit+ can be integrated.

We also asked the following 4 questions to the engineers:

1- Does *DSSGen* make the development of DSSs easier?

2- Do you find *DSSGen* useful for the development of DSSs?

3- Do you think that the *DSSGen* toolset is easy to use?

4- Are there any difficulties you encountered while using *DSSGen*? If so, do you have any suggestions to solve it?

Concerning the first question, the engineers all stated that *DSSGen* facilitates the development of DSSs with its support for the model-driven development. Indeed, *DSSGen*, gives a high-level modeling language through which highly abstract DSS architecture models can be specified, analysed, and automatically transformed into a fully executable quality (i.e., pattern-centric) code. As the engineers indicated, one just needs to make the high-level decisions for any DSS to be developed including the components of different types (i.e., problem, diagnosis and action) and their attributes without having to realise those decisions in Java and any low-level tasks (i.e., using design patterns at code-level, the algorithms and data structures). Concerning the second question, the engineers found *DSSGen* highly useful. The engineers stated that they have not used (and even heard about) before such a model-driven development platform which liberates practitioners from having to be a programming expert (i.e., those performing pattern-centric development for quality coding). The engineers have especially been impressed with the reduced development time that they had experienced. Also, the engineers stated that *DSSGen* enables for experimenting with different configurations of system architectures and adding/removing components without dealing with any implementation details. Concerning the third question, the engineers find the *DSSGen* toolset easy to use. As the engineers indicated, using the *DSSGen* editor did not require any learning curve as they quickly figured out how to create/delete Metaedit+ projects, edit and save models, run the generators that are integrated with the editor and thus easily accessible, and even other interesting facilities such as collaborative modeling and importing/exporting models.

In the last question, the engineers indicated some issues that they face with. Firstly, integrating the *DSSGen* toolset with external tools is not possible as the *DSSGen* toolset can only be accessible over the Metaedit+ technology and not be used as standalone. Another problem is the lack of support for customising the editor user interfaces (e.g., changing the location of the toolbar or the appearances of the editor icons for the generators). It should however be noted that it is highly difficult to develop such a modeling tool as *DSSGen* using any programming technologies rather than using the meta-modeling technologies [28].

5.3 Threats to Validity

The evaluation of *DSSGen* that we have discussed in Sect. 5 may raise some threats to the validity of the evaluation results obtained.

We involved 4 engineers for evaluating the *DSSGen* language and its toolset who have participated in both the development performance evaluation and user survey. The reason why we have involved just 4 practitioners is that our expectations from the evaluators require considerable amount of time and effort to be separated and thus not many engineers were willing to participate. Indeed, the evaluators had to *(i)* study the case-studies, *(ii)* implement their solutions using programming technologies, *(iii)* use *DSS-Gen* to perform model-driven engineering, and *(iv)* be involved in the interview sessions and answer several survey questions. However, it should also be noted that the number of the evaluators here is quite satisfying according to Nielsen's framework for usability [24].

Another threat can be to do with our choice of involving a single evaluator group for the development performance evaluation. The engineers who have been involved in the first stage (i.e., manual implementation of the case-studies) are those who have also been involved in the second stage (i.e., the model-driven development of the case-studies using *DSSGen*). This can cause a threat as the engineers have used their knowledge and experience from first stage during the second stage. It should however be noted that we needed the engineers to be involved in both the manual implementation and using *DSSGen* for the automated code generation. This is because in the user survey, the engineers have been asked questions to learn about their opinions on the language and tool usabilities which can be answered precisely if the engineers were involved in both the first and second stages of the development performance evaluation.

Lastly, to minimise any potential threats, we used different case-studies in our evaluation that vary in their level of complexities.

6 Conclusion

In this paper, we discussed a novel architecture modeling language called *DSSGen* for the high-level specifications of the DSS architectures in a precise and analysable way. *DSSGen* offers three types of components, which are problem, diagnosis and action. The problem components encapsulate the domain data collected from the environment and are needed by the diagnosis component(s) to make any diagnosis. Whenever the problem data change, an event occurs for the diagnosis component which process their patterns to make diagnosis. Whenever any diagnosis is made, an event is generated for the action components which can then get the expected tasks to be performed. We developed a toolset which enables for *(i)* the modeling of architectures, *(ii)* simulating the architectural models using Modelica, *(iii)* generating quality Java code from the architectural models, and *(iv)* visualising the code structure using UML class diagram.

To evaluate *DSSGen*, we performed both quantitative and qualitative analyses. Concerning quantitative analysis, we measured the development time performance gained with the use of the *DSSGen* toolset. We asked 4 software engineers who work for DFDS to work on one of the distinct case studies suggested, which are earthquake vulnerability, fire behaviour, delivery vulnerability, and respiratory illness. Each engineer first used the toolset to specify the architecture model for the chosen case-study and generate the executable code automatically. Then, the engineers developed the software implementation manually for the chosen case-study. We compared the time differences and observed that using the toolset improves the development time more than twice. Concerning the qualitative analysis, we conducted a survey among the DFDS engineers to understand their perspectives on *DSSGen*. To this end, we asked 26 rating questions and 4 open-ended questions. So we observed that the engineers found *DSSGen* as of high-quality in terms of different aspects including functional suitability, usability, reliability, maintainability, productivity, extensibility, compatibility, expressiveness, reusability, and integrability.

We are now working on extending *DSSGen* for the model-driven engineering of digital twin applications. To this end, we aim to extend the languages with the necessary concepts for specifying the components of any digital twin applications. Also, we aim to develop a code-generator that can produce pattern-centric quality code from the digital twin architecture models.

References

1. Arslan, S., Ozkaya, M., Kardas, G.: Modeling languages for internet of things (IoT) applications: a comparative analysis study. Mathematics **11**(5) (2023). https://doi.org/10.3390/math11051263. https://www.mdpi.com/2227-7390/11/5/1263
2. Atkinson, C., Kuhne, T.: Model-driven development: a metamodeling foundation. IEEE Softw. **20**(5), 36–41 (2003). https://doi.org/10.1109/MS.2003.1231149
3. Balmelli, L.: An overview of the systems modeling language for products and systems development. J. Obj. Tech. **6**(6), 149–177 (2007). www.sysml.org
4. Booch, G., Rumbaugh, J.E., Jacobson, I.: The Unified Modeling Language User Guide - Covers UML 2.0, 2nd edn. Addison Wesley Object Technology Series, Addison-Wesley (2005)
5. Daşdemir, İ, Aydın, F., Ertuğrul, M.: Factors affecting the behavior of large forest fires in Turkey. Environ. Manage. **67**, 162–175 (2021)

6. Dunkel, J., Fernandez, A., Ortiz, R., Ossowski, S.: Event-driven architecture for decision support in traffic management systems. Expert Syst. Appl. **38**(6), 6530–6539 (2011). https://doi.org/10.1016/J.ESWA.2010.11.087

7. El-Sappagh, S.H.A., El-Masri, S.: A distributed clinical decision support system architecture. J. King Saud Univ. Comput. Inf. Sci. **26**(1), 69–78 (2014). https://doi.org/10.1016/J.JKSUCI.2013.03.005

8. Fanti, M.P., Iacobellis, G., Ukovich, W., Boschian, V., Georgoulas, G.K., Stylios, C.D.: A simulation based decision support system for logistics management. J. Comput. Sci. **10**, 86–96 (2015)

9. Fritzson, P., et al.: OpenModelica - a free open-source environment for system modeling, simulation, and teaching. In: 2006 IEEE Conference on Computer Aided Control System Design, 2006 IEEE International Conference on Control Applications, 2006 IEEE International Symposium on Intelligent Control, pp. 1588–1595 (2006). https://doi.org/10.1109/CACSD-CCA-ISIC.2006.4776878

10. Fritzson, P.A.: Principles of Object-Oriented Modeling and Simulation with Modelica 2.1. Wiley (2004)

11. Gamma, E., Helm, R., Johnson, R., Vlissides, J.: Design Patterns: Elements of Reusable Object-Oriented Software. Addison Wesley (1994). ISBN-13 978-0201633610

12. Georgas, J.C., Dashofy, E.M., Taylor, R.N.: Architecture-centric development: a different approach to software engineering. XRDS **12**(4), 6 (2006). https://doi.org/10.1145/1144359.1144365

13. Groenewegen, D.M., Hemel, Z., Kats, L.C.L., Visser, E.: WebDSL: a domain-specific language for dynamic web applications. In: Harris, G.E. (ed.) Companion to the 23rd Annual ACM SIGPLAN Conference on Object-Oriented Programming, Systems, Languages, and Applications, OOPSLA 2008, Nashville, TN, USA, 19–13 October 2007, pp. 779–780. ACM (2008). https://doi.org/10.1145/1449814.1449858

14. Guo, Z., Ngai, E., Yang, C., Liang, X.: An RFID-based intelligent decision support system architecture for production monitoring and scheduling in a distributed manufacturing environment. Int. J. Prod. Econ. **159**, 16–28 (2015). https://doi.org/10.1016/j.ijpe.2014.09.004. https://www.sciencedirect.com/science/article/pii/S0925527314002825

15. Ishita, R.P., Khandaker, S.: Application of analytical hierarchical process and GIS in earthquake vulnerability assessment: case study of ward 37 and 69 in Dhaka city. J. Bangladesh Inst. Plan. (2010). ISSN 2075-9363

16. Kahraman, G., Bilgen, S.: A framework for qualitative assessment of domainspecific languages. Softw. Syst. Model. **14**(4), 1505–1526 (2015). https://doi.org/10.1007/s10270-013-0387-8

17. Kazak, J., Chalfen, M., Kamińska, J., Szewrański, S., Świąder, M.: Geo-dynamic decision support system for urban traffic management. In: Ivan, I., Horák, J., Inspektor, T. (eds.) Dynamics in GIscience, pp. 195–207. Springer, Cham (2018)

18. Keen, P.G.: Decision support systems: a research perspective. In: Decision support Systems: Issues and Challenges: Proceedings of An International Task Force Meeting, pp. 23–44 (1980)

19. Kelly, S., Lyytinen, K., Rossi, M.: MetaEdit+ a fully configurable multi-user and multi-tool CASE and CAME environment. In: Jr., J.A.B., Krogstie, J., Pastor, O., Pernici, B., Rolland, C., Sølvberg, A. (eds.) Seminal Contributions to Information Systems Engineering, 25 Years of CAiSE, pp. 109–129. Springer (2013). https://doi.org/10.1007/978-3-642-36926-1_9. http://dx.doi.org/10.1007/978-3-642-36926-1_9

20. Kent, S.: Model driven engineering. In: Butler, M.J., Petre, L., Sere, K. (eds.) Integrated Formal Methods, Third International Conference, IFM 2002, Turku, Finland, 15–18 May 2002, Proceedings. LNCS, vol. 2335, pp. 286–298. Springer (2002). https://doi.org/10.1007/3-540-47884-1_16

21. Lankhorst, M.M., Proper, H.A., Jonkers, H.: The anatomy of the archimate language. Int. J. Inf. Syst. Model. Des. 1(1), 1–32 (2010)
22. Marakas, G.M.: Decision Support Systems in the Twenty-First Century. Prentice-Hall Inc, USA (1998)
23. Moore, J.H., Chang, M.G.: Design of decision support systems. ACM SIGOA Newsl. 1(4–5), 8–14 (1980). https://doi.org/10.1145/1017672.1017658
24. Nielsen, J.: How many test users in a usability study? (2012). https://www.nngroup.com/articles/how-many-test-users/
25. Ozkaya, M.: The analysis of architectural languages for the needs of practitioners. Softw. Pract. Exper. 48(5), 985–1018 (2018). https://doi.org/10.1002/spe.2561
26. Ozkaya, M., Kloukinas, C.: Design-by-contract for reusable components and realizable architectures. In: Seinturier, L., de Almeida, E.S., Carlson, J. (eds.) CBSE 2014, Proceedings of the 17th International ACM SIGSOFT Symposium on Component-Based Software Engineering (part of CompArch 2014), Marcq-en-Baroeul, Lille, France, June 30–July 4 2014, pp. 129–138. ACM (2014). https://doi.org/10.1145/2602458.2602463. http://doi.acm.org/10.1145/2602458.2602463
27. Ozkaya., M., Kose., M., Asal., E.: DecSup: an architecture description language for specifying and simulating the decision support system architectures. In: Proceedings of the 12th International Conference on Model-Based Software and Systems Engineering - MODELSWARD, pp. 89–98. INSTICC, SciTePress (2024). https://doi.org/10.5220/0012231200003645
28. Ozkaya, M., Musayev, K., Kose, M.A.: Practitioners' experiences on developing graphical modeling editors: a survey. In: Fill, H., Mayo, F.J.D., van Sinderen, M., Maciaszek, L.A. (eds.) Proceedings of the 18th International Conference on Software Technologies, ICSOFT 2023, Rome, Italy, 10–12 July 2023, pp. 276–286. SCITEPRESS (2023). https://doi.org/10.5220/0012062400003538
29. POurbabai, B.: Components of a decision support system for computer integrated manufacturing. Int. J. Comput. Integr. Manuf. 1(4), 253–261 (1988). https://doi.org/10.1080/09511928808944370
30. Robbins, D.E., Gurupur, V.P., Tanik, J.: Information architecture of a clinical decision support system. In: 2011 Proceedings of IEEE Southeastcon, pp. 374–378 (2011). https://doi.org/10.1109/SECON.2011.5752969
31. Salama, S., Eltawil, A.B.: A decision support system architecture based on simulation optimization for cyber-physical systems. Procedia Manuf. 26, 1147–1158 (2018). https://doi.org/10.1016/j.promfg.2018.07.151. https://www.sciencedirect.com/science/article/pii/S2351978918308278, 46th SME North American Manufacturing Research Conference, NAMRC 46, Texas, USA
32. Selic, B.: The pragmatics of model-driven development. IEEE Softw. 20(5), 19–25 (2003). https://doi.org/10.1109/MS.2003.1231146
33. Taylor, R.N., Medvidovic, N., Dashofy, E.M.: Software Architecture - Foundations, Theory, and Practice. Wiley (2010)
34. Vázquez-Ingelmo, A., García-Holgado, A., García-Peñalvo, F.J.: C4 model in a software engineering subject to ease the comprehension of UML and the software. In: 2020 IEEE Global Engineering Education Conference, EDUCON 2020, Porto, Portugal, 27–30 April 2020, pp. 919–924. IEEE (2020). https://doi.org/10.1109/EDUCON45650.2020.9125335
35. Wallace, W.A., Balogh, F.D.: Decision support systems for disaster management. Publ. Admin. Rev. 45, 134–146 (1985). http://www.jstor.org/stable/3135008
36. Whittle, J., Hutchinson, J.E., Rouncefield, M.: The state of practice in model-driven engineering. IEEE Softw. 31(3), 79–85 (2014). https://doi.org/10.1109/MS.2013.65
37. Wu, P.J., Chaipiyaphan, P.: Diagnosis of delivery vulnerability in a logistics system for logistics risk management. Int. J. Logist. Manage. 31(1), 43–58 (2020)

38. Yin, H., Jha, N.K.: A health decision support system for disease diagnosis based on wearable medical sensors and machine learning ensembles. IEEE Trans. Multi-Scale Comput. Syst. **3**(4), 228–241 (2017). https://doi.org/10.1109/TMSCS.2017.2710194
39. Zhai, Z., Martínez, J., Beltran, V., Martínez, N.L.: Decision support systems for agriculture 4.0: survey and challenges. Comput. Electron. Agric. **170**, 105256 (2020). https://doi.org/10.1016/J.COMPAG.2020.105256
40. Zhao, T., Huang, X.: Design and implementation of deepDSL: a DSL for deep learning. Comput. Lang. Syst. Struct. **54**, 39–70 (2018). https://doi.org/10.1016/J.CL.2018.04.004

An Approach for the Comparative Evaluation of Requirements Formalisation Approaches

Shekoufeh Kolahdouz Rahimi[1]([⊠])[ID], Kevin Lano[2][ID], Sobhan Yassipour Tehrani[3][ID], Chenghua Lin[4][ID], Yiqi Liu[4][ID], and Muhammad Aminu Umar[2][ID]

[1] School of Arts, University of Roehampton, London, U.K.
`shekoufeh.rahimi@roehampton.ac.uk`
[2] Department of Informatics, King's College London, London, U.K.
`{kevin.lano,aminu.umar}@kcl.ac.uk`
[3] Department of Computer Science, University College London, London, U.K.
`sobhan.tehrani@ucl.ac.uk`
[4] Department of Computer Science, The University of Manchester, Manchester, U.K.
`{chenghua.lin,yiqi.liu}@manchester.ac.uk`

Abstract. Various approaches have been proposed to automate the formalisation of software requirements from semi-formal or informal documents. However, this area of research lacks well-established case studies to serve as benchmarks for comparing different methods. Additionally, there is a need for clear, objective criteria to effectively assess the outcomes of these formalisation approaches. These gaps make it challenging to identify which techniques are most suitable for specific formalisation tasks. This paper addresses these issues by introducing a set of standardized case studies and a structured framework for evaluating the performance of requirements formalisation techniques using measurable criteria. We apply this evaluation framework to assess five different formalisation methods, which include both rule-based and machine learning-driven approaches.

Keywords: Requirements formalisation · Model-driven engineering · NLP · Machine learning

1 Introduction

Requirements formalisation (RF) is a process in requirements engineering which defines a precise requirements specification based on informal or semi-formal requirements documentation. Typically, RF involves producing a software model such as a UML class diagram or other UML model, or a specification in a domain-specific language (DSL), from natural language requirements documents in text format. The RF process or result can also provide useful analysis information about the requirements statement, i.e., to detect duplicated or invalid requirements.

Requirements formalisation can be a high resource process if performed manually, so there has been much research interest in the automation of requirements formalisation. RF automation has significant potential as a means of reducing software development costs, accelerating development processes, and increasing the rigour of requirements engineering processes. Many approaches have been proposed for automated or

© The Author(s), under exclusive license to Springer Nature Switzerland AG 2026
F. José Domínguez Mayo et al. (Eds.): MODELSWARD 2024, CCIS 2547, pp. 132–150, 2026.
https://doi.org/10.1007/978-3-031-96841-9_7

semi-automated formalisation of software requirements, typically involving some form of natural language processing (NLP) or machine learning (ML) [28,37]. However, the research field lacks widely-recognised benchmark case studies to support comparative evaluation of different approaches on the same requirements cases, and the most widely-used evaluation technique, based on estimating precision/recall and F-measure accuracy of a formalised model with respect to a manually-produced reference model, is subjective.

F-measure gives the degree to which a proposed formalised model correctly expresses the model elements implied by the source text, and has the definition

$$F \ = \ 2 * \frac{precision * recall}{precision + recall}$$

$$recall \ = \ \frac{correctly\ identified\ elements}{total\ identified}$$

$$precision \ = \ \frac{correctly\ identified\ elements}{total\ correct\ elements}$$

The judgement as to the correctness of the model elements has a subjective aspect, for example, it may be based on agreement with a 'gold standard' model produced by a human expert. However different modelers may produce significantly different gold standard models. Our view is that evaluation of RF approaches should use objective measures where possible, and also take into account the software engineering context of use of formalised models. In general, software developers should be able to effectively use the formalised models for further development stages, and should be able to relate the models to the original requirements statement. Thus the quality and internal consistency of the formalised model is important (e.g., there should not be duplicated class or use case names in formalised models, and names of model elements should adhere to name style conventions for the respective model kinds). There should also be a high degree of traceability between the formalised requirements and the source text.

To effectively compare different RF approaches, objective measures of accuracy are needed, which are aligned to the SE context of use of the formalised model. Thus we propose the evaluation model of Fig. 1, which involves three aspects: (i) an objective measure of similarity between the formalised model and a rigorously produced 'gold standard' reference model; (ii) measures of completeness and consistency of the formalised model wrt the source requirements document; (iii) a measure of internal quality of the model.

The reference model could be produced by agreement between two or more human experts, with an independent review by a further expert, to improve its validity and appropriateness as a correctness standard.

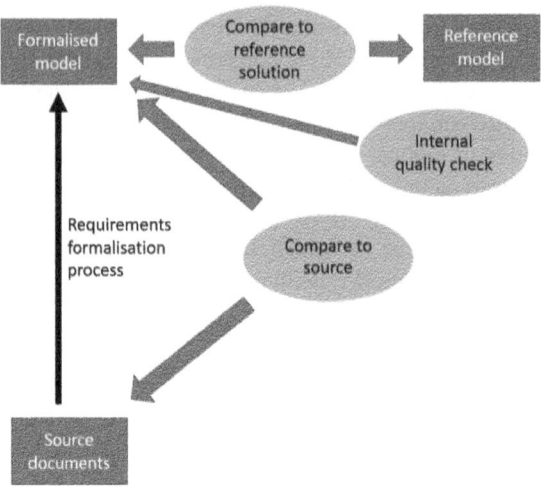

Fig. 1. Evaluation strategies for requirements formalisation [31].

1.1   Natural Language Processing (NLP)

NLP is a collection of techniques for the processing of natural language text, including part-of-speech (POS) tagging/classification, tokenisation and segmentation, lemmatisation, parsing, chunking, dependency analysis and reference correlation. NLP tools include Stanford NLP [36], Apache OpenNLP [4], iOS NLP Framework, Python's NLTK, and WordNet [30].

The standard parts of speech include [32]:

- Determiners – usually tagged as DT, e.g., "a", "the";
- Nouns – NN for singular nouns and NNS for plural;
- Proper nouns – NNP and $NNPS$;
- Adjectives – JJ for general adjectives, JJR for relative adjectives, JJS for superlatives;
- Possessives – $\_PRP\$$;
- Modal verbs – MD such as "should", "must";
- Verbs – VB for the base form of a verb, VBP for present tense except 3rd person singular, VBZ for present tense 3rd person singular, VBG for gerunds, VBD for past tense;
- Adverbs – RB;
- Prepositions/subordinating conjunctions – IN.

For specialised purposes or domains, additional parts of speech may also be defined, as in [39]. NLP has been a key element of automated RE approaches [28]. However, the trained models available for POS-tagging and parsing with the existing NLP tools are usually oriented towards general English text, which can differ significantly from the English typically used in software requirements statements. The existing POS-tagger models may therefore sometimes mis-classify words in requirements statements (e.g., "stores" may be mis-classified as a noun, even when used as a verb, and "existing" used as an adjective may be mis-classified as a gerund).

An important technique for RF is chunking: the recognition of groups of adjacent words which form a semantic unit. These can be expressed as regular expressions in terms of tags. For example the chunk pattern

$$(DT)?(JJ) * (NN|NNS) +$$

characterises simple noun phrases on non-proper nouns, such as "The principal surgeon" or "A large data repository". Chunking depends upon the accuracy of the applied POS-tagging.

1.2 Machine Learning (ML)

Machine learning covers a wide range of techniques by which knowledge about patterns and relationships between data is learned and encoded as implicit or explicit rules in a software system. ML can be used for classification, translation or prediction, and also for image or text generation. In particular, ML is used to create the part-of-speech and other classification models used in NLP tools. ML techniques include K-nearest neighbours (KNN), decision trees, random forests, inductive logic programming (ILP) and various forms of neural nets. A key distinction can be made between techniques such as decision trees and ILP where explicit rules are learnt from data, and techniques such as neural nets where the learned knowledge is in an implicit form (consisting of the weights of connections in the trained network). In recent years there have been substantial advances in neural networks (such as recurrent neural networks or RNNs) which possess a 'memory' of a sequence of inputs, enabling them to perform prediction tasks and process data (such as natural language texts or programs) that consist of a connected sequence of elements (sentences) [19]. A major advance was the introduction of the Transformer neural net architecture [38], utilising the concept of *attention* to prioritise the key relationships between input data elements that are relevant for a particular task. Transformer is used as the basis for most large-scale neural net systems in the natural language processing domain, such as text summarisers or machine translators.

Large scale neural net systems are also termed *deep learning* systems. These include pre-trained language models (PLMs) and large language models (LLMs). For such systems a large-scale unsupervised (pre-)training process is typically applied, using training datasets consisting of a wide range of input texts such as books, web pages, program code, etc. The models can then be specialised for particular language tasks using supervised learning (fine-tuning) on selected examples. The increasing power of PLMs and LLMs such as BERT [14], Codex [8] and the GPT series [40] has already led to innovative software assistants such as Copilot [13] and program translators such as CodeT5. The appropriate pre-training and fine-tuning of LLMs to support software engineering tasks is an area of active research [16]. There have been a few recent works on using LLMs for requirements formalisation, these have concluded that existing LLM-based tools are limited in their capabilities in this area, but that there is potential for further improvements [1,2,7]. It could be expected that LLMs would be effective for RF because of their vast general knowledge of a wide range of domains, however they can lack knowledge of modelling languages, and also suffer from unreliability – their outputs will vary from one time to another even when given the same inputs [29]. They may also present incorrect results in a plausible manner [5]. Thus they are best utilised as assistants for semi-automated RF, rather than enabling full automation.

Toolsets for ML include Google MLKit, Tensorflow, Keras, ScikitLearn and Theano.

2   Comparing Requirements Formalisation Approaches

In this study we illustrate our proposed evaluation framework by comparing five alternative approaches for formalising behavioural system requirements expressed in unstructured English text or as semi-structured user stories.

The approaches are:

Hamza and Hammad [15]: based on segmentation, POS-tagging, chunking, grammar patterns.
Elallaoui, Nafil and Touahni [9]: based on POS-tagging
AgileUML [22]: based on POS-tagging, chunking, semantic analysis and word-similarity matching
Simple Heuristic. As a baseline for comparison, a simple heuristic approach based on POS-tagging and chunking is defined and evaluated
ChatGPT. We utilise GPT 4.0[1] to create UML class and use case models from textual requirements, using the prompting approach of [6].

User stories are widely-used in agile methods to express functional requirements. They have the semi-structured format

As a/an [actor], I [wish/want/...] to [action], [purpose]

where the stakeholder requiring the functionality is identified in the first part, then the functionality action in the second part, and an optional purpose is described in the third part.

An example user story could be:

As a doctor, I wish to view the patient's EHR

User stories are appropriate to express units of application functionality, and can usually be formalised as UML use cases. They are not suited to express domain constraints or non-functional properties such as "The system should respond to requests within 10 s". Thus, it is preferable for a RF approach to be able to process a wide range of input sentences, not only those in the format of user stories.

2.1   Hamza and Hammad Approach [15]

The approach starts from a textual specification of requirements in English text, this is spell-checked to eliminate erroneous text, then segmented into sentences. POS-tagging is applied, and this information is used to chunk the text into sequences of closely-associated words. For example the sequence of adjectives associated with a noun are

---

[1] chat.openai.com.

grouped with it: this is the chunk pattern JJ^*NN and related chunk patterns. Stemming is used to identify the root form of words in the text. Grammar knowledge patterns (GKP) are used to recognise expected sentence structures, and provide a corrective to semantic errors arising from incorrect POS-tagging.

To identify actors and actions of a use case, different rules are applied to handle variation in the way that these can be expressed in unstructured text.

The approach is evaluated on four case studies of requirements statements, of small size (each case has between 11 to 23 functional requirements). It is not clear if these are real systems or artificial examples. Precision and recall are evaluated, however it is unclear how the correctness of the formalisation is determined, i.e., how the correct reference model was constructed. They find an average recall of 69% and precision of 72%, which indicates that the approach tends to produce both incorrect formalisations, and fails to produce correct formalisations. The reasons for these errors are mainly due to linguistic variability and ambiguity/incompleteness in the requirements statements. Another factor is that the requirements statements also express constraints, such as "all fields of an edited asset can be modified except Ids", which do not correspond to use cases. The approach could be extended by adding recognition of these different forms of requirement, e.g., by classifying requirements statements.

On the example sentence, the approach produces the result:

```
class doctor { }

usecase viewpatient'ehr
{ actor = doctor; }
```

The use case is correct, but the name of the use case contains an invalid character.

2.2 Elallaoui, Nafil and Touahni Approach [9]

In contrast to the preceding approach, this approach takes as input semi-structured user stories, and applies POS-tagging as its main NLP technique. The input text sentences are POS-tagged and the words of each sentence are filtered to remove adjectives and auxiliary words, retaining only nouns and verbs. The first noun/compound noun in each sentence is assumed to be the actor of the use case. The following verbs and nouns then make up the action of the use case.

The evaluation uses a single case, but of large size (168 user stories). Recall and precision compared to a manually-constructed use case model are calculated, with high precision and recall values for actors (p = 98%, r = 98%), use cases (p = 87%, r = 85%) and their relationships (p = 87%, r = 85%).

On the example sentence, the approach produces the result:

```
class doctor { }

usecase wishviewpatientEHR
{ actor = doctor; }
```

This is a valid formalisation.

2.3   AgileUML [22]

This approach operates on either unstructured or semi-structured behaviour specifications. It performs segmentation into sentences and POS-tagging, and uses a decision tree classifier to distinguish sentences that express user stories from those that express data requirements or general constraints. Both class definitions and use cases are derived from the classified sentences, using heuristics to recognise the class names, attribute names, actors and actions in the text. A thesaurus/glossary is used to classify words/phrases. Approximate matching using text edit distance [23] is used in order to allow for variation in word form.

The evaluation is performed on 27 cases, including 24 real-world cases. There are 10 large cases (over 75 user stories), 2 small and 15 of medium size (25 to 74 use cases). The average F-measure is 94%, based on comparison of the automatically formalised models with manually-derived models.

On the example sentence, the approach produces the result:

```
class Doctor {
  stereotype originator="1";
}

class Patient {
  stereotype originator="1";
}

usecase viewThePatient : void {
    parameter doctorx : Doctor;
    parameter patientx : Patient;
    stereotype originator="1";
    stereotype actor="Doctor";
    stereotype read;

    ::
      true => patientx->display();
}
```

Here, tracing information is embedded into the model using the *originator* tag. Executable behaviour is produced for use cases where possible, so that they can be immediately used for prototyping. However the key noun 'EHR' is missing from the use case name.

The authors find that a major cause of poor formalisation results is incorrect tagging and incorrect parsing by the NLP tools used (Stanford NLP and Apache OpenNLP). Thus the formalisation algorithms fail because the input they are given is semantically incorrect (e.g., 'existing' mis-classified as a verb in a phrase 'the existing files').

2.4   Simple Heuristic Approach

This approach operates on semi-structured user stories as input. It tokenises the input sentences and applies POS-tagging. For each sentence it attempts to recognise the entities (classes) referenced in the sentence as those noun phrases $DT?JJ^*NN+$ which have a noun in a predefined glossary of 'entity' nouns. Use cases are recognised from those sentences which contain both a verb and a modal verb. Chunking of the sentence according to the pattern

$$[\sim VB]^*VB^*MD[\sim VB]^*(VB[\sim VB]^*)$$

is performed,where the first block of non-verbs is used to form the actor name, and the second block starting with the first verb following the modal verb is taken as the use case action. Finally, the category of this verb in a verb glossary is used to classify the kind of use case as 'create', 'edit', 'read', 'delete' or 'other'.

For example, "As a doctor, I wish to view the patient's EHR" would be chunked as [As, a, doctor, I], [wish], [to], [view, the, patient's, EHR]. This would produce the use case

```
usecase view_the_patient_EHR {
  stereotype actor="doctor";
  stereotype "read";
}
```

Doctor and *Patient* would become classes. Attributes of class C are recognised from the other nouns occurring in the same sentences as the class name C.

2.5   ChatGPT (GPT 4.0)

ChatGPT is an LLM designed to operate via conversational interaction with users. Users submit queries, termed *prompts*, to elicit results from the LLM. In the work of [6], GPT 3.5 was used, with the prompt:

Please generate a UML class diagram model for the following requirements:

We made use of the latest published version of ChatGPT, based on GPT 4.0, and extended the prompt to also ask for the creation of a use case model:

Please generate a UML class diagram model and a use case model for the following software requirements:

ChatGPT will usually produce both a textual and graphical model result, with the graphical output rendered using ASCII characters. We have used the textual model output in the analysis of the results.

Figure 2 shows the graphical models output by ChatGPT on the doctor-patient example. The class diagram illustrates a distinctive feature of ChatGPT as a RF approach, in that it may add extra elements to the formalised model which were not present in the requirements statement (e.g., *medicalHistory* and *labResults* attributes for an EHR), based on its pre-existing domain knowledge. This may be an undesirable feature if close consistency between the requirements and model is required.

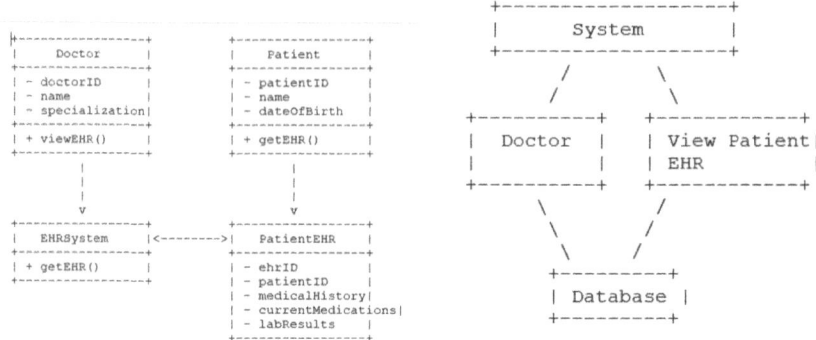

Fig. 2. ChatGPT output: (a) class diagram, (b) use case model.

2.6   Summary

The first four approaches all use POS-tagging and segmentation of the text into sentences as key NLP processes. They differ in their strategies for extracting use case elements from the resulting text, although some form of chunking based on the expected form of behavioural requirements is an essential part of each strategy. The evaluations of each approach all use the concepts of accuracy based on recall/precision and F-measure, but the number, scale and provenance of evaluation examples differ, as does the basis for computing accuracy. This approach to compute accuracy also depends upon the subjective judgement of the evaluator as to whether a formalised element is correct or not.

3   Evaluation Framework

In order to provide a platform for consistently comparing different requirements formalisation approaches, we define an evaluation framework which consists of:

- A domain-specific language (DSL) for expressing NLP pipelines [21]
- An instantiation of the DSL in Python, using the Python NLTK NLP library, together with a specific library of utility functions for requirements formalisation
- A set of evaluation examples taken from real-world requirements documents, together with manually-derived 'gold standard' formalised models produced by a rigorous process
- Evaluation tools, to perform a threefold evaluation of the models created by each RF approach (Fig. 1).

This framework has the benefit of a high degree of automation: the evaluations can be performed without human subjectivity entering into the assessment, as could occur if precision/recall figures are estimated based on manual comparison of two models.

The DSL includes statement constructs for loading datasets, filtering and transforming datasets, and performing analysis operations on them, and for saving datasets. The syntax is based on SQL. A novel facility is the ability to specify chunking transformations by regular expressions. Thus a regular expression formed from POS names or generalised POS names can be written in order to specify that a POS-tagged text is to be split into chunks that match the expression.

The evaluation examples for the requirements formalisation of user-story format requirements include 1 large (FABSucs) and 1 medium sized example (k3ucs) of real-world requirements specifications, taken from different sources [17,25], and written using different styles. We also provide two evaluation examples which are not formatted in user stories. These are the real-world R49_Tcs and R59_Telescope cases from [6]. Table 1 summarises the information about these cases.

Table 1. Evaluation cases.

Case	Domain	Structure	Size (LOC)
k3ucs	Education	User stories	61
FABSucs	Finance	User stories	189
R49_Tcs	Military	Unstructured	65
R59_Telescope	Science	Unstructured	40

The evaluation tools are as follows:

- $checkModelNames.py$ – this checks the names of model elements, i.e., whether attributes, use cases and classes have valid names, including checks for duplicate names, overlong names, and a check that class names should be a singular noun. This check helps to ensure that the models are suitable for use as the specification for an application.
- $compareModel2Source.py$ – checks the percentages of source document nouns and verbs which also appear in the generated models. This helps to ensure that all information from the source document has been represented in the formalised model. Specifically, *noun completeness* is defined as

$$\frac{\#(source\ document\ nouns\ that\ occur\ in\ model)}{\#(source\ document\ nouns)}$$

and likewise for *verb completeness*.

In addition, a consistency check is made that all names used in the formalised model also occur in the requirements – this addresses the issue which occurs with LLM-based approaches where the LLM may invent additional content not present in the requirements. *Noun consistency* is defined as

$$\frac{\#(model\ class/attribute\ names\ that\ occur\ as\ nouns\ in\ source)}{\#(model\ class/attribute\ names)}$$

Verb consistency is:

$$\frac{\#(model\ usecase\ names\ that\ occur\ as\ verbs\ in\ source)}{\#(model\ usecase\ names)}$$

– *compareModels.bat* – compares the reference 'gold standard' model for a case to the model produced by a formalisation approach. This generalises the usual precision/recall estimates by (i) comparing classes and attributes in the two models, in addition to use cases; (ii) allowing partial matches between names of elements, based on string edit distance.

The tools may be accessed at [20].

We also include the F-measure accuracy estimation, based on the standard definition but with a 0.5 correctness score for an element which is identified but with significant differences to the correct version (e.g., its name includes several superfluous words or omits necessary words).

We do not evaluate the efficiency/time performance of approaches because these are implemented on different platforms and hence comparing execution times would not give information about the intrinsic efficiency of the approaches.

4   Evaluation of Selected Approaches

We apply the three comparisons of Fig. 1 to each of the approaches of Sect. 2, for the k3ucs and FABSucs requirements cases, which are expressed in terms of user stories. We also estimate our modified F-measure accuracy for recognising use cases. In addition, we apply the simple heuristic, AgileUML and ChatGPT approaches to the R49 and R59 general requirements documents from [6]. All artefacts and results of these evaluations may be accessed at [20].

Tables 2 and 3 show the model quality scores for each RF approach applied to the two user-story evaluation cases. The FABSucs case was too large for processing by ChatGPT.

Table 2. Formalised model quality: k3ucs.

Approach	Class validity	Attribute validity	Use case validity	Flaws
Hamza/Hammad	0	0	1	0
Elalloui et al.	0.33	0	0.42	17
AgileUML	0.88	1	1	3
Simple heuristic	0.95	0	1	1
ChatGPT	1	0	0	26

Tables 4, 5 show the model quality analysis for the RF approaches applied to the R49_Tcs and R59_Telescope cases.

Tables 6 and 7 show the model completeness and consistency scores for each RF approach applied to the two user-story evaluation cases.

Tables 8, 9 give the model completeness and consistency results for the R49_Tcs and R59_Telescope cases.

Table 3. Formalised model quality: FABSucs.

Approach	Class validity	Attribute validity	Use case validity	Flaws
Hamza/Hammad	0	0	1	0
Elalloui et al.	0.57	0	1	6
AgileUML	0.96	1	1	3
Simple heuristic	0.96	0	1	2
ChatGPT	–	–	–	–

Table 4. Formalised model quality: R49_Tcs.

Approach	Class validity	Attribute validity	Use case validity	Flaws
AgileUML	0.98	0.76	1	25
Simple heuristic	0.86	1	1	3
ChatGPT	1.0	0.93	0	24

Table 5. Formalised model quality: R59_Telescope.

Approach	Class validity	Attribute validity	Use case validity	Flaws
AgileUML	0.98	0.73	1	18
Simple heuristic	1	1	0.625	3
ChatGPT	1	1	0	7

Table 6. Formalised model completeness and consistency: k3ucs.

Approach	Noun completeness	Verb completeness	Noun consistency	Verb consistency
Hamza/Hammad	0	0.4	0	0
Elalloui et al.	0.08	1.0	1.0	0.64
AgileUML	0.51	1.0	0.98	1.0
Simple heuristic	0.45	0.93	1.0	1.0
ChatGPT	0.11	0.73	1.0	0.95

Tables 10 and 11 show the model accuracy scores for each RF approach applied to the two user-story evaluation cases.

Table 12 shows the modified F-measure for use case recognition for each approach and both user-story cases.

Table 7. Formalised model completeness and consistency: FABSucs.

Approach	Noun completeness	Verb completeness	Noun consistency	Verb consistency
Hamza/Hammad	0	0.32	0	0.02
Elalloui et al.	0.09	1.0	1.0	0.37
AgileUML	0.41	0.86	1.0	0.99
Simple heuristic	0.36	1.0	1.0	1.0
ChatGPT	–	–	–	–

Table 8. Formalised model completeness and consistency: R49_Tcs.

Approach	Noun completeness	Verb completeness	Noun consistency	Verb consistency
AgileUML	0.73	0.93	1.0	1.0
Simple heuristic	0.8	0.97	1.0	1.0
ChatGPT	0.29	0.65	0.78	0.79

Table 9. Formalised model completeness and consistency: R59_Telescope.

Approach	Noun completeness	Verb completeness	Noun completeness	Verb completeness
AgileUML	0.77	1.0	0.96	0.97
Simple heuristic	0.24	1.0	1.0	1.0
ChatGPT	0.18	0.44	0.92	1.0

Table 10. Formalised model accuracy: k3ucs.

Approach	Class similarity	Attribute similarity	Usecase similarity
Hamza/Hammad	0	0	0.47
Elalloui et al.	0	0	0
AgileUML	0.04	0.002	0.68
Simple heuristic	0.007	0	0.57
ChatGPT	0.034	0	0.56

Table 11. Formalised model accuracy: FABSucs.

Approach	Class similarity	Attribute similarity	Usecase similarity
Hamza/Hammad	0	0	0.6
Elalloui et al.	0.01	0	0.56
AgileUML	0.02	0	0.75
Simple heuristic	0	0	0.57
ChatGPT	–	–	–

Table 12. F-measures for user-story cases.

Approach	k3ucs	FABSucs
Hamza/Hammad	0.23	0.15
Elalloui et al.	0.35	0.23
AgileUML	0.69	0.81
Simple heuristic	0.71	0.55
ChatGPT	0.65	–

4.1 Discussion

The accuracy of all the RF approaches on the user-story cases, as estimated by model similarity (Tables 10, 11) is below 70%, which indicates that they need to be used in conjunction with human expertise to refine or correct their results, and that they do not provide a fully automated solution. The formalisation completeness results for nouns is quite low (Tables 6 and 7), indicating that information on data elements is being ignored or lost by the formalisation processes. The completeness for verbs is generally high except for the Hamza/Hammad approach. On inspection the low results for this approach are due to verb stemming, so that the original version of the verb is lost and only the stem retained in the resulting model. On the other hand, the AgileUML approach adds the purpose of the user story into the use case name, resulting in excessively long and complex names. The simple heuristic approach sometimes adds the actor part of the user story into the use case name: in cases such as "The system should allow a staff member to ...", the actor is wrongly assigned as 'The system'. The Ellaloui et al. approach also has the same flaw. It should be a user-configurable choice whether certain terms such as 'System' or 'Application' can be accepted as actors.

Although the Hamza/Hammad and AgileUML approaches aim to recognise a range of different textual formats for user stories, there are still some cases which they fail to process correctly. Only the ChatGPT approach is able to recognise use cases that involve two or more actors. The AgileUML approach instead creates use cases with a single actor, linked to other actors via data usage relationships.

The first four approaches primarily use heuristic rules to recognise use case and class model elements. The only explicit use of machine learning (ML) is the decision tree classifier used by AgileUML to distinguish different categories of requirements. It may be difficult to use ML to learn the derivation from user stories to use cases because of the relatively small amounts of data available for training.

The use of tools such as WordNet or Word2Vec [26] to compute word similarity scores could also be of potential use to improve the heuristic approaches.

Regarding the general requirements documents R49_Tcs and R59_Telescope, for the R49 case, both the simple heuristic and AgileUML approaches are able to abstract suitable classes and use cases, however the simple heuristic approach does not recognise inheritance relationships between classes, and the classes tend to have too many attributes. The AgileUML approach creates some classes which are too general and not application-specific (such as $Type$ and $Communication$). The ChatGPT approach produces meaningful models, which however lack detail and sometimes also omit significant elements of the input texts. There are also spurious elements in the produced models, which were not in the requirements statements, such as $latitude$ and $longitude$ attributes for R49.

R59 is a more challenging case than R49, because the description is in a more discursive format, and it also refers to a diagram, which is not included in the (text only) input to the requirements formalisation approaches.

The simple heuristic approach is able to abstract appropriate classes and use cases for R59, however there are many missing attributes, hence a low noun completeness score. The AgileUML approach creates more complete classes, however it does not recognise separate use cases, but combines the complete system functionality into a single use case. The ChatGPT approach performs well on this case, extracting both meaningful classes and use cases, however with significant omissions, hence the low completeness scores for the approach in Table 9.

5   Related Work

Prior to 2020 the main approaches for requirements formalisation involved simple NLP techniques together with heuristic rules. Examples of such approaches are [9, 15, 35]. Since 2020 there has been a noticeable increase in the number of papers that apply NLP together with DL techniques for the automatic generation of UML diagrams from requirements.

The automation of natural language analysis for extraction of UML diagrams is emphasised in [24]. The main focus of this work is to apply NLP techniques and heuristic rules to generate usecase and activity diagrams. The Stanford CoreNLP tool is used to perform NLP tasks. Following these, heuristic rules are applied individually for generation of activity and usecase diagrams. The applicability of the approach is evaluated using the Qualification Verification System (QVS) case study. The result indicates the productivity of the approach in generating diagrams, in comparison to the existing approaches. In [39] a utilities permitting system based on an NLP algorithm is designed to formalise the requirements of road agencies in UML and OCL formats. The input requirements are in textual format. The NLP process includes a pre-processing step, which tokenises and splits sentences. In this step words are classified into parts of speech and labeled according to POS tags. Then occurrences of the terms in the sentences are recognised and in the third step by applying a chunking technique the sentence structure is analysed and represented as tree structures. Finally, five rules are applied to generate target information from tree structures. The system is validated in terms of performance and applicability by using random cases. The Requirement Transformation (RETRANS) approach is presented in [18], this generates usecase and activity diagrams from requirements in text format by applying model transformation and NLP techniques. An NLP algorithm is designed in [3] to generate sequence and class diagrams from scenario-based requirements. A software tool called automatic generation of UML (AGUML) is presented to perform all the tasks automatically. Experimental results are reported to show the applicability and performance of the approach. In [33] an automatic approach for generation of class diagrams from semi-structured text inputs is presented. Some keywords are used to structure the input. NLP techniques and heuristic rules are used to generate the result by applying the procedure in four steps. In the first step classes are extracted followed by generation of attributes in the next step. Following that methods and relations are extracted. The last three steps depend on the first step in this procedure.

A ML approach for extraction of classes and attributes from unstructured plain text is introduced in [10]. Two classifiers are used to classify each word into class and attributes. To relate appropriate attributes to classes dependency parsing is used. A public requirements dataset is used throughout this research [11]. NLP techniques are used in the pre-processing and post-tagged phases to transfer data to the ML tasks. Then the machine learning algorithms of Support Vector Machine (SVM) and Naive Bayes (NB) are applied for extracting classes and attributes. A text-to-model transformation framework for mapping textual requirements to UML models is presented in [34]. The authors emphasise on integrating machine learning methods, word embedding, heuristic rules, statistical and linguistic knowledge to increase the quality of the outcome. A web application for generation of use case and class diagrams from English text is presented in [27]. In this research NLP and ML techniques are used. Tokenization, POS tagging, chunking and splitting are NLP techniques that are applied in this process. Finally, the visual representation of diagrams are provided using Visual studio.

RF using LLMs to create UML models from natural language is investigated (using ChatGPT) by [7]. The results show that some basic requirements formalisation ability is present in ChatGPT, however specific fine-tuning of a suitable LLM (pre-trained with datasets including software models) by instruction training for the formalisation task would be necessary to improve this capability. The approach of [1,2] uses prompt engineering with GPT-4 to formalise natural language assertions as OCL constraints. However, in this work an existing UML class model is assumed, and used as context information to enable constraint formalisation. Thus this only addresses a part of a complete RF process. Few-shot learning using GraphGPT is used by [12] to create graphical models from natural language system descriptions. They found generally good results for the creation of class diagrams in PlantUML format (which is known by the LLM) from natural language descriptions, however only small-scale examples were investigated. The paper of [6] compares ChatGPT with a heuristic RF approach on 30 evaluation cases, and finds that these approaches have similar average accuracy in terms of F-measure, but that the LLM approach has greater variability in its results.

5.1 Summary of Related Work

Although many different research works have investigated RF by applying NLP, heuristic or DL techniques, the field remains at an experimental stage. Most of the works in the field applied heuristic approaches, however these were not evaluated on a broad range of input cases. Therefore, it is not possible to determine the applicability of such approaches in alternative domains. Only a few approaches have applied DL in the RF domain, this limited use is likely to be due to the limited quantity of available appropriate training data (i.e., relating requirements text to formalised models). In general most of the ML approaches do not apply the whole potential of DL in the domain. Furthermore, there is no standard benchmark and evaluation criteria for comparing different RF cases. Therefore, in our research we provide a set of standard evaluation tools and selected requirement statements representative of real-world cases, to compare the effectiveness of RF approaches according to objective criteria. In order to address the reliability issues of DL approaches, particularly of LLMs, we introduced consistency checking between the formalised model and the original source text, to identify cases where the DL technique has created extraneous model elements not derived from the requirements.

6   Future Work

We intend to enlarge the set of evaluation cases to include a wider range of requirements documents, and to expand the evaluation to more approaches, including formalisation of dynamic behaviour (creating state machines or activities).

Further evaluation criteria could be added, for example, some measure of how configurable and adaptable an approach is: to what extent it permits users to modify any parameters, strategies or knowledge bases used in its formalisation process. Another form of comparison could be a 'blindfolded taste test' where a group of independent software engineers evaluate and rank alternative formalisations of a requirements statement, without knowing the identity of the approach which produced the formalisation.

7   Conclusions

In this paper, we introduced a robust framework aimed at systematically and objectively evaluating various requirements formalisation methodologies. By applying the framework to five distinct approaches to software requirements formalisation, including both traditional and machine-learning-based methods, we have uncovered critical factors influencing formalisation accuracy, scalability, and applicability across diverse software development contexts. The study also highlights the challenges posed by LLM-based techniques, particularly in terms of maintaining model consistency with original requirements. These findings underscore the need for continued refinement in AI-based formalisation tools, offering a foundation for future research to enhance the reliability and usability of automated formalisation in practice.

References

1. Abukhalaf, S., Hamdaqa, M., Khomh, F.: On Codex prompt engineering for OCL generation: an empirical study. arXiv:2303.16244v1 (2023)
2. Abukhalaf, S., Hamdaqa, M., Khomh, F.: PathOCL: path-based prompt augmentation for OCL generation with GPT-4. arXiv:2405.12450v1 (2024)
3. Alashqar, A.M.: Automatic generation of UML diagrams from scenario-based user requirements. Jordanian J. Comput. Inf. Technol. **7** (2021)
4. Apache: Apache openNLP toolkit (2021). https://opennlp.apache.org
5. Borg, M.: Requirements engineering and large language models: insights from a panel. IEEE Softw. (2024)
6. Bozyigit, F., et al.: Generating domain models from natural language using NLP: a benchmark dataset and experimental comparison of tools. SoSym (2024)
7. Camara, J., Troya, J., Burgueno, L., Vallecillo, A.: On the assessment of generative AI in modeling tasks. SoSyM **22** (2023)
8. Chen, M., et al.: Evaluating large language models trained on code. arXiv preprint **2107:03374v2** (2021)
9. Elallaoui, M., Nafil, K., Touahni, R.: Automatic transformation of user stories into UML use case diagrams using NLP techniques. Procedia Comput. Sci. **130**, 42–49 (2018)
10. Elmasry, I., Wassif, K., Bayomi, H.: Extracting software design from text: a machine learning approach. In: 2021 Tenth International Conference on Intelligent Computing and Information Systems (ICICIS), pp. 486–492. IEEE (2021)
11. Ferrari, A., Spagnolo, G.O., Gnesi, S.: Pure: a dataset of public requirements documents. In: 2017 IEEE 25th International Requirements Engineering Conference (RE), pp. 502–505. IEEE (2017)
12. Fill, H.G., Fettke, P., Kopke, J.: Conceptual modeling and large language models: impressions from first experiments with ChatGPT. Enterp. Model. Inf. Syst. Archit. **18**(3) (2023)
13. GitHub.com: GitHub CoPilot (2022). https://copilot.github.com/
14. Guo, D., et al.: GraphCodeBERT: pre-training code representations with dataflow. In: ICLR 2021 (2021)
15. Hamza, Z.A., Hammad, M.: Generating UML use case models from software requirements using natural language processing. In: 2019 8th International Conference on Modeling Simulation and Applied Optimization (ICMSAO), pp. 1–6. IEEE (2019)
16. Hou, X., et al.: LLMs for software engineering: a systematic literature review. arXiv:2308.10620 (2023)
17. Kaggle: Kaggle software requirements dataset (2021). https://www.kaggle.com/iamsouvik/software-requirements-dataset. Accessed 2021
18. Kamarudin, N.J., Sani, N.F.M., Atan, R.: Automated transformation approach from user requirement to behavior design. J. Theor. Appl. Inf. Technol. **81**(1), 73 (2015)
19. Kolahdouz-Rahimi, S., Lano, K., Chenghua, L.: Requirement formalisation using natural language processing and machine learning: a systematic review. In: International Conference on Model-Based Software and Systems Engineering (2023)
20. Lano, K.: Requirements formalisation repository (2023). https://github.com/kevinlano/RequirementsFormalisation. Accessed 2023
21. Lano, K., Xue, Q., Haughton, H.: A concrete syntax transformation approach for software language processing. Springer (2024)
22. Lano, K., Yassipour-Tehrani, S., Umar, M.: Automated requirements formalisation for agile MDE. In: 2021 ACM/IEEE International Conference on Model Driven Engineering Languages and Systems Companion (MODELS-C), pp. 173–180. IEEE (2021)

23. Levenshtein, V.I., et al.: Binary codes capable of correcting deletions, insertions, and reversals. Soviet Physics Doklady **10**(8), 707–710 (1966)
24. Maatuk, M.A., Abdelnabi, A.E.: Generating UML use case and activity diagrams using NLP techniques and heuristics rules. In: International Conference on Data Science, E-learning and Information Systems 2021, pp. 271–277 (2021)
25. Mendeley: Mendeley user story dataset (2021). https://www.data.mendeley.com/datasets/bw9md35c29/1. Accessed 2021
26. Mikolov, T., Chen, K., Corrado, G., Dean, J.: Efficient estimation of word representations in vector space. arXiv preprint arXiv:1301.3781 (2013)
27. Narawita, C.R., et al.: UML generator-use case and class diagram generation from text requirements. Int. J. Adv. ICT Emerg. Regions **10**(1) (2017)
28. Otter, D.W., Medina, J.R., Kalita, J.K.: Requirement formalisation using natural language processing and machine learning: a systematic review. Modelsward 2023 (2023)
29. Ouyang, S., Zhang, J., Harman, M., Wang, M.: LLM is like a box of chocolates: the non-determinism of ChatGPT in code generation. arXiv **2308.02828v1** (2023)
30. Princeton University: Wordnet (2021). https://www.wordnet.princeton.edu. Accessed 2021
31. Rahimi, S.K., Lano, K., Tehrani, S.Y., Lin, C., Liu, Y., Umar, M.A.: Comparative evaluation of NLP approaches for requirements formalisation. In: Mayo, F.J.D., Pires, L.F., Seidewitz, E. (eds.) Proceedings of the 12th International Conference on Model-Based Software and Systems Engineering, MODELSWARD 2024, Rome, Italy, 21–23 February 2024, pp. 125–132. SCITEPRESS (2024)
32. Santorini, B.: Part-of-speech tagging guidelines for the penn treebank project. university of Pennsylvania, School of Engineering and Applied Science (1990)
33. Sanyal, R., Ghoshal, B., et al.: Automatic extraction of structural model from semi structured software requirement specification. In: 2018 IEEE/ACIS 17th International Conference on Computer and Information Science (ICIS), pp. 543–58. IEEE (2018)
34. Sedrakyan, G., Abdi, A., Van Den Berg, S.M., Veldkamp, B., Van Hillegersberg, J.: Text-to-model (TeToMo) transformation framework to support requirements analysis and modeling. In: 10th International Conference on Model-Driven Engineering and Software Development, MODELSWARD 2022, pp. 129–136. SCITEPRESS (2022)
35. Sharma, R., Gulia, S., Biswas, K.: Automated generation of activity and sequence diagrams from natural language requirements. In: 2014 9th International Conference on Evaluation of Novel Approaches to Software Engineering (ENASE), pp. 1–9. IEEE (2014)
36. Stanford University: Stanford NLP (2020). https://nlp.stanford.edu/software/. Accessed 2020
37. Umar, M., Lano, K.: Advances in automated support for requirements engineering: a systematic literature review. Requir. Eng., 1–31 (2024)
38. Vaswani, A., et al.: Attention is all you need (2023)
39. Xu, X., Chen, K., Cai, H.: Automating utility permitting within highway right-of-way via a generic UML/OCL model and natural language processing. J. Constr. Eng. Manag. **146**(12), 04020135 (2020)
40. Zhao, W., et al.: A survey of large language models. arXiv **2303.18223v10** (2023)

A Pluggable Type Checker for Representing Kinds of Quantities

Steve McKeever$^{(\boxtimes)}$

Department of Informatics and Media, Uppsala University, Uppsala, Sweden
steve.mckeever@im.uu.se

Abstract. A system of measurement consists of several basic units that represent observable phenomena, and a method for combining them to form compound units. Units provide context to numerical data. In science and engineering, quantities are usually expressed as values paired with units. In software systems, handling these quantities is often the responsibility of the programmer, leading to well-documented failures when not managed correctly. Although numerous tools and libraries exist for validating expressions denoting units of measurement, they do not enable the kind of quantity to be specified. Furthermore, tools that extend the underlying type system of the language limit backwards compatibility, while libraries are both cumbersome and further specialise the code base. In this paper, we address the issue of quantities that, despite having the same units, represent different kinds, such as work and torque. We propose a data type that models compound units using a tree structure instead of a tuple. This structure preserves the compound nature during arithmetic operations, facilitating more thorough static analysis and a comprehensive definition of arithmetic for different kinds of quantities. Finally, we present the system as a lightweight pluggable type checker which integrates smoothly with existing compilers and code bases.

Keywords: Kind of quantity · Dimensional analysis · Units of measurement · Pluggable types · Static checking

1 Introduction

Humans have developed systems of measurement since the early days of trade, enhanced over time to fulfil the accuracy and interoperable needs of science and technology. The Cubit was based on the length of the arm from the elbow to the tip of the middle finger, originated in Egypt about 3,000 B.C. and was used to build the pyramids. In the 19th century, James Clerk Maxwell [21] introduced the concept of a system of quantities with a corresponding system of units. This generalisation allowed scientists working with different measurement systems to communicate more easily, as unit names (such as inch or metre) are treated as numeric variables and can be interchanged through multiplication.

Dimensions are physical quantities that can be measured, while units are arbitrary labels that correspond to a given dimension to make it relative. For example a dimension is length, whereas a metre is a relative unit that describes length. Units of measurement

F. José Domínguez Mayo et al. (Eds.): MODELSWARD 2024, CCIS 2547, pp. 151–172, 2026.
https://doi.org/10.1007/978-3-031-96841-9_8

Table 1. Some SI standard base and compound units.

Name	Symbol	Quantity	Base Units in SI
metre	m	Length	m
kilogram	kg	Mass	kg
second	s	Time	s
radian	rad	PlaneAngle	$m \cdot m^{-1}$
newton	N	Force, Weight	$kg \cdot m \cdot s^{-2}$
pascal	Pa	Pressure, Stress	$kg \cdot m^{-1} \cdot s^{-2}$
joule	J	Energy, Work	$kg \cdot m^2 \cdot s^{-2}$
newton metre	$N \cdot m$	Torque	$kg \cdot m^2 \cdot s^{-2}$
watt	W	Power	$kg \cdot m^2 \cdot s^{-3}$
square metre	m^2	Area	m^2
cubic metre	m^3	Volume	m^3
metre per second	m/s	Speed, Velocity	$m \cdot s^{-1}$
metre per sec squared	m/s^2	Acceleration	$m \cdot s^{-2}$

(UoM) can be defined in the most generic form as either *base quantities* or *compound quantities*. Fundamental physical quantities are the basic quantities that require no other physical quantities to express. Physical quantities that can be derived from the combination of two or more fundamental physical quantities are called compound physical quantities. For instance, velocity (m/s or $m \cdot s^{-1}$) can be derived from the base quantities of metre and second. The International System of Units (SI) defines seven base quantities (length, mass, time, electric current, thermodynamic temperature, amount of substance, and luminous intensity) as well as a corresponding unit for each quantity [4]. Some popular examples of both base and compound units are shown in Table 1. It is common for quantities to be declared as a number (the magnitude of the quantity) with an associated UoM [28].

Two values that share the same UoM might not represent the same *kinds of quantities* (KOQ) [8, 19]. The relationship between quantities and unit names is *many-to-one*. For example, torque is a rotational force which causes an object to rotate about an axis while work is the result of a force acting over some distance. They both share the same UoM, namely $kg \cdot m^2 \cdot s^{-2}$, but torque is usually written as $N \cdot m$, while work is conventionally expressed as J. Other examples are heat capacity and entropy ($kg \cdot m^2 \cdot s^{-2} \cdot K^{-1}$), and electric current and magnetomotive force.

With digitalisation affecting most facets of our lives, the need to faithfully represent and manipulate quantities in physical systems is ever increasing [35]. Popular programming languages allow developers to describe how to evaluate numeric expressions but not how to detect inappropriate actions on quantities. Consequently there have been infamous examples, such as the Mars Climate Orbiter [33], or the Gimli Glider incident [36], where UoM conversion omissions led to dire outcomes. Developers can choose to use tools or libraries to ensure UoM are managed correctly. However, KOQ analysis has only recently been formalised [23]. Efforts are underway to include similar analyses into popular programming languages such as the Python Pint library [32] and C++ [30].

In this paper we introduce a more refined version of our system that connects both dimensional and kind of quantity analysis through an alternative representation of UoM that allows quantities in arithmetic expressions to be named and handled *safely*. Explicitly naming quantities also allows known conversions to be applied to particular values, such as a becquerel for measuring radioactivity. In doing so we can ensure separate quantities (such as torque and work) are not combined but also that dimensionless quantities (such as radians or steradians) are distinct. We demonstrate a pluggable type-checker for a simple imperative language that catches KOQ errors in the handling of quantities. A pluggable type-checker leverages simple additional syntax, usually as a comment or after a @ symbol, to strengthen a programming language's type system. Thereby allowing programmers to detect and prevent, at compile-time, defects that would otherwise have manifested at run-time.

This paper is an extended version of [25] in which we present a more complete version of the analysis on a model imperative programming language with functions. The paper is structured as follows. In Sect. 2 we discuss efforts to include UoM into conventional programming languages and modeling platforms. In Sect. 3, we introduce a simple programming language and show how expressions are defined and evaluated. In Sect. 4, we explain how traditional dimensional analysis ensures correct arithmetic operations. Section 5 introduces the concept of kinds of quantities, utilising an algebraic data type that represents the structure of compound quantities and their comparison operators. In Sect. 6, we demonstrate how this data type can identify errors that conventional unit of measure checkers miss. Lastly, in Sect. 7, we summarise our approach to quantity validation and discuss potential extensions.

2   Background

Physicists and applied mathematicians typically assume that quantities are treated like unit-independent values, allowing all arithmetic and comparison operators to be applied to them. However, it does not make sense to multiply scales of intelligence or personality traits. Stevens [34] identified four categories of scale that places limits on the type of measurement that can be used to construct valid terms: *nominal, ordinal, interval* and *ratio*. We shall focus on quantities that belong to the ratio scale as these are used to model the physical world and include all the usual arithmetic operators.

The incorporation of units of measurement into programming languages began in the 1970s [18] and continued with extensions for Fortran [10] and Pascal [7]. These early efforts primarily relied on syntax modifications to the base languages, which decreased backward compatibility and limited their adoption. The operator overloading and type parameterisation of Ada allowed for a more versatile approach [16] to labeling variables with UoM features. As realistic object oriented programming languages started to emerge in the early 90s, such as C++ and Java, developers began to implement UoM via the Quantity pattern [9]. This has led to a veritable explosion in the number of UoM libraries available for all popular programming languages [3] based on this pattern [26]. However, a survey of scientific coders [31] revealed that these libraries have significant limitations that impedes their adoption. Even C++ with a de facto UoM library based on the template meta-programming feature, that ensures efficient run-time computation, suffers from both accuracy and usability issues. The F# programming language has excellent native support for UoM but lacks popularity. An alternative compile-time approach is to define UoM through a pluggable type-checker and to build a tool that attempts to perform as much inspection as possible [17, 20, 37]. These approaches are lightweight and scalable but they need to be maintained.

It is common for software development to begin at a more abstract level using diagrams and rules that focus on the conceptual model that is to be constructed. Adding UoM to software modeling languages has been successful but unless the workflow has been created specifically, declaring quantities in a system specification language offers no guarantee that the UoM information is supported in the eventual implementation. Extensions to the Unified Modeling Language (UML) have been proposed to support quantities. SysML[1], for instance, is defined as an extension of a subset of the UML to support systems engineering activities and has extensive support for quantities. The Event-B modeling language [11] provides UoM and leverages the Rodin theorem prover to detect errors before translating to Java. Comparable techniques have been proposed for more formal notations such as Z [15] and Maude [5]. Unit checking and conversion of UML can be undertaken before code is generated, either through a compilation workflow that leverages Object Constraint Language (OCL) expressions [22] or staged computation [1].

A crucial limitation of all these systems is that, by representing only dimensions, they are unable to differentiate between types of quantities and units of measure. We lack a definite understanding of how often any form of quantity error occurs in practice: be it a naming, dimensional or unit conversion error. There are some small studies [2, 6, 29] which put the figure at roughly 10% of projects evaluated had UoM errors. These were post development studies and are not representative of a quantity adhering software discipline. However, in the current software development landscape, it would be negligent to model complex systems solely with floating point numbers and without additional clarification or annotation.

3   Evaluating Expressions

Performing calculations in relation to quantities, dimensions and units is subtle and error prone. We shall begin by looking at a very simple imperative language of declarations and statements so that we can focus on the key aspects involved in managing quantities correctly. A *Program* consists of one or more quantity variable declarations, *dec*, followed by one or more statements, *stmt*. Quantity variables, *v*, are represented as real numbers. Quantity arithmetic expressions, *exp*, impose syntactic restrictions so that their soundness can be inferred using the algebra of quantities. The language is similar to that found in undergraduate semantics text books [27].

---

[1] https://sysml.org.

$$\begin{aligned}
\mathcal{E} &: \textit{Expression} \rightarrow (\textit{Var} \rightarrow \mathbb{R}) \rightarrow \mathbb{R} \\
\mathcal{E}[\![v]\!]_\rho &= \rho\, v \\
\mathcal{E}[\![r \star exp]\!]_\rho &= r \times \mathcal{E}[\![exp]\!]_\rho \\
\mathcal{E}[\![exp_1 + exp_2]\!]_\rho &= \mathcal{E}[\![exp_1]\!]_\rho + \mathcal{E}[\![exp_2]\!]_\rho \\
\mathcal{E}[\![exp_1 - exp_2]\!]_\rho &= \mathcal{E}[\![exp_1]\!]_\rho - \mathcal{E}[\![exp_2]\!]_\rho \\
\mathcal{E}[\![exp_1 \star exp_2]\!]_\rho &= \mathcal{E}[\![exp_1]\!]_\rho \times \mathcal{E}[\![exp_2]\!]_\rho \\
\mathcal{E}[\![exp_1 / exp_2]\!]_\rho &= \mathcal{E}[\![exp_1]\!]_\rho \div \mathcal{E}[\![exp_2]\!]_\rho
\end{aligned}$$

Fig. 1. Rules for evaluating expressions.

$$\begin{aligned}
prog &::= \texttt{program}\ dec\ \texttt{begin}\ stmt\ \texttt{end} \\
dec &::= \texttt{var}\ v : \texttt{float} \mid \texttt{var}\ v : \texttt{float} = r \mid dec_1; dec_2 \\
stmt &::= v := exp \mid \texttt{if}\ bexp\ \texttt{then}\ stmt_1\ \texttt{else}\ stmt_2 \\
&\quad \mid \texttt{while}\ bexp\ \texttt{do}\ stmt \mid stmt_1; stmt_2 \\
exp &::= v \mid r \star exp \mid exp_1 + exp_2 \mid exp_1 - exp_2 \mid exp_1 \star exp_2 \mid exp_1 / exp_2 \\
bexp &::= \texttt{true} \mid \texttt{false} \mid bexp_1\ \texttt{and}\ bexp_2 \mid exp_1 >= exp_2
\end{aligned}$$

By creating a constraint syntax for unit expressions we can distinguish between scalar values, such as r, and *unitless quantities* in which all the dimensions are zero, such as moisture content. Consider a simple program to calculate Newton's second law of motion:

```
program
    var f : float;
    var m : float = 5.7;
    var a : float = 3.2
begin
    f := m * a
end
```

We can use the evaluate function $\mathcal{E}$ of Fig. 1, with an environment consisting of values for m and a, to calculate f.

4   Dimensional Analysis and Unit Conversion

As is the case in nearly all programming languages, users must assume coherent units for the assignment to be correct.

A dimensional analysis needs to ensure that (1) two physical quantities can only be equated if they have the same dimensions; (2) two physical quantities can only be added if they have the same dimensions (known as the *Principle of Dimensional Homogeneity*); (3) the dimensions of the multiplication of two quantities is given by the addition of

$$
\begin{aligned}
&\mathcal{D} \ : \ \mathit{Expression} \rightarrow (\mathit{Var} \rightarrow \mathit{Dimensions}) \rightarrow \mathit{Dimensions} \\
&\mathcal{D}[\![v]\!]_\sigma && = \sigma\ v \\
&\mathcal{D}[\![r \star \mathit{exp}]\!]_\sigma && = \mathcal{D}[\![\mathit{exp}]\!]_\sigma \\
&\mathcal{D}[\![\mathit{exp}_1 + \mathit{exp}_2]\!]_\sigma && = \mathcal{D}[\![\mathit{exp}_1]\!]_\sigma \cong \mathcal{D}[\![\mathit{exp}_2]\!]_\sigma \\
&\mathcal{D}[\![\mathit{exp}_1 - \mathit{exp}_2]\!]_\sigma && = \mathcal{D}[\![\mathit{exp}_1]\!]_\sigma \cong \mathcal{D}[\![\mathit{exp}_2]\!]_\sigma \\
&\mathcal{D}[\![\mathit{exp}_1 \star \mathit{exp}_2]\!]_\sigma && = \mathcal{D}[\![\mathit{exp}_1]\!]_\sigma \mathbin{\hat{\times}} \mathcal{D}[\![\mathit{exp}_2]\!]_\sigma \\
&\mathcal{D}[\![\mathit{exp}_1 / \mathit{exp}_2]\!]_\sigma && = \mathcal{D}[\![\mathit{exp}_1]\!]_\sigma \mathbin{\hat{\div}} \mathcal{D}[\![\mathit{exp}_2]\!]_\sigma
\end{aligned}
$$

Fig. 2. Dimensional Analysis rules for Expressions.

the dimensions of the two quantities. If we only consider the three common dimensions of *length*, *mass* and *time*, a tuple of integers can be used to represent these dimensions.

$$
\begin{aligned}
dec \ &::= \cdots \mid \texttt{var}\ v\ :\ \texttt{float @dim}\ dims \mid \texttt{var}\ v\ :\ \texttt{float @dim}\ dims\ =\ r \\
dims \ &::= (\mathbb{Z},\ \mathbb{Z},\ \mathbb{Z})
\end{aligned}
$$

Dimensional homogeneity can be used to check for equality:

$$
\begin{aligned}
(l_1, m_1, t_1) &\cong (l_2, m_2, t_2) \\
&= (l_1, m_1, t_1),\ \text{if } l_1 = l_2 \wedge m_1 = m_2 \wedge t_1 = t_2
\end{aligned}
$$

While the rules for multiplication and division on as follows:

$$
\begin{aligned}
(l_1, m_1, t_1) \mathbin{\hat{\times}} (l_2, m_2, t_2) &= (l_1 + l_2, m_1 + m_2, t_1 + t_2) \\
(l_1, m_1, t_1) \mathbin{\hat{\div}} (l_2, m_2, t_2) &= (l_1 - l_2, m_1 - m_2, t_1 - t_2)
\end{aligned}
$$

This allows us to rewrite the rules of Fig. 1 by replacing the arithmetic operators to create a dimensional checker, shown in Fig. 2. Scalar multiplication does not affect the dimensions of a quantity. The dimension of mass, m, is described as $(0, 1, 0)$, while acceleration, a, is $m \cdot s^{-2}$ or $(1, 0, -2)$ as a tuple. Our dimensional checker will compute with dimensions and *attempt* to ensure all assignments are correct. Consider our example program:

```
program
    var f : float @dim (1,1,-2);
    var m : float @dim (0,1,0)  = 5.7;
    var a : float @dim (1,0,-2) = 3.2
begin
    f := m * a
end
```

The assignment is safe as $(0, 1, 0) \mathbin{\hat{\times}} (1, 0, -2)$ yields $(1, 1, -2)$. Most UoM checkers adopt this approach, extending the checking into the statements and function calls of typical programming language constructs. For instance, all branches of conditionals must have the same dimensions, while comparison operators can only operate on quantities of the same dimension. If the dimensions of all variables are known at compile-time then this checking can be undertaken before the program is executed, incurring no run-time cost. Furthermore, if UoM annotations are used then unit conversions can be inserted into the run-time code [6,24].

5   Kinds of Quantities

Using a tuple representation of dimensions, torque and work are both encoded as $(1,2,-2)$. In order to distinguish them we need a richer datatype to represent units of measure, a table that maps quantity names onto their compound representations, and a means of equating them. Using an algebraic data type, we define named quantities as follows:

```
type quant = Name of string | Dimless
           | Qmul of (quant * quant)
           |Qdiv of (quant * quant)
```

Base quantities are represented as a unit name, for instance a length quantity can be represented as `Name "metre"`, while velocity would be described as `Qdiv (Name "metre",Name "sec")`. Dimension one quantities, `Dimless`, have no physical dimension. They are often obtained as ratios resulting from the division of quantities of the same kind.

Definition 1 (Converting KOQ into UoM). *A compound quantity can be converted into the length, mass and time form as follows:*

$$\mathcal{C} : \text{quant} \rightarrow Dimensions$$
$$\mathcal{C}\,(\texttt{Name "metre"}) = (1,0,0)$$
$$\mathcal{C}\,(\texttt{Name "kg"})\quad = (0,1,0)$$
$$\mathcal{C}\,(\texttt{Name "sec"})\quad = (0,0,1)$$
$$\mathcal{C}\,\texttt{Dimless}\qquad\quad = (0,0,0)$$
$$\mathcal{C}\,(\texttt{Qmul}\,(p,q))\quad = (\mathcal{C}\,p)\,\hat{\times}\,(\mathcal{C}\,q)$$
$$\mathcal{C}\,(\texttt{Qdiv}\,(p,q))\quad = (\mathcal{C}\,p)\,\hat{\div}\,(\mathcal{C}\,q)$$

Owing to the properties of the tuple arithmetic operators (identity, associative, distributive, commutative), shown in the simplification rules of Fig. 3 and the restructuring rules of Fig. 4, there are many ways of describing the same compound quantity using the `quant` data type.

Proposition 1 (UoM Preserving Simplification and Restructuring). *For given quantities p, q and r, the rules of Figs. 3 and 4 maintain the UoM of a given compound quantity.*

Proof. We assume p, q and r can be safely simplified, and apply the tuple conversion function $\mathcal{C}$ to both sides of the arrow, resulting in equivalent tuples for all cases, based on the properties of arithmetic.

$$
\begin{array}{ll}
\texttt{Qmul}\,(p,\texttt{Dimless}) & \Rightarrow p \\
\texttt{Qmul}\,(\texttt{Dimless},p) & \Rightarrow p \\
\texttt{Qdiv}\,(p,\texttt{Dimless}) & \Rightarrow p \\
\texttt{Qdiv}\,(\texttt{Dimless},p) & \Rightarrow p \\
\texttt{Qmul}\,(\texttt{Qdiv}\,(p,q),q) & \Rightarrow p \\
\texttt{Qmul}\,(p,\texttt{Qdiv}\,(q,p)) & \Rightarrow q \\
\texttt{Qdiv}\,(\texttt{Qmul}\,(p,q),q) & \Rightarrow p \\
\texttt{Qdiv}\,(\texttt{Qmul}\,(p,q),p) & \Rightarrow q \\
\texttt{Qdiv}\,(p,p) & \Rightarrow \texttt{Dimless}
\end{array}
$$

Fig. 3. Directional rules for Named Quantity Expression Simplification.

$$
\begin{array}{ll}
\texttt{Qmul}\,(p,q) & \Leftrightarrow \texttt{Qmul}\,(q,p) \\
\texttt{Qmul}\,(\texttt{Qmul}\,(p,q),r)) & \Leftrightarrow \texttt{Qmul}\,(p,\texttt{Qmul}\,(q,r)) \\
\texttt{Qdiv}\,(\texttt{Qdiv}\,(p,q),r) & \Leftrightarrow \texttt{Qdiv}\,(\texttt{Qdiv}\,(p,r),q) \\
\texttt{Qmul}\,(\texttt{Qdiv}\,(p,q),r) & \Leftrightarrow \texttt{Qdiv}\,(\texttt{Qmul}\,(p,r),q) \\
\texttt{Qmul}\,(\texttt{Qdiv}\,(p,q),r) & \Leftrightarrow \texttt{Qdiv}\,(p,\texttt{Qdiv}\,(q,r)) \\
\texttt{Qdiv}\,(\texttt{Qdiv}\,(p,q),r) & \Leftrightarrow \texttt{Qdiv}\,(p,\texttt{Qmul}\,(q,r)) \\
\texttt{Qdiv}\,(\texttt{Qmul}\,(p,q),r) & \Leftrightarrow \texttt{Qmul}\,(p,\texttt{Qdiv}\,(q,r))
\end{array}
$$

Fig. 4. Bidirectional rules for Named Quantity Expression Restructuring.

In order to construct *named compound quantities* we create a pair binding the name of a compound quantity to its quant form:

```
("Velocity",
    [Qdiv (Name "metre",Name "sec")])
```

The quant form is modeled as a list because some quantities have many applicable units. Consider the quantity Work that has two compound forms:

```
("Work",
    [Qmul (Name "Force",Name "metre");
     Qmul (Name "Power",Name "sec")])
```

A system of kinds of quantities can be created by building a table τ that maps names to their equivalent compound forms, resembling Table 1.

```
τ= {("Velocity", [Qdiv (Name "metre",Name "sec")]);
    ("Acc", [Qdiv (Name "metre",
             Qmul (Name "sec",Name "sec"))]);
    ("Force", [Qmul (Name "kg",Name "Acc")]);
    ("Work",
        [Qmul (Name "Force",Name "metre");
         Qmul (Name "Power",Name "sec")]);
    ("Power", [Qdiv (Name "Work",Name "sec")]);
    ("PlaneAngle", [Qdiv (Name "metre",Name "metre")]);
    ("Torque", [Qmul (Name "Force",Name "metre")]);
    ...}
```

5.1 Equality of Kinds

A named quantity can be *expanded* through repeated lookups in the table. However, the table can be cyclic so we need to be careful when accessing a name not to end up in an infinite loop. While replacing compound names one can also apply the simplification rules of Fig. 3 and restructuring rules of Fig. 4, such that there may be many more ways of representing a compound quantity than just those in the table. For instance, a named quantity of `Power` has 18 representations:

```
Name "Power"
⇒ Qdiv(Name "Work",Name "sec")
⇒ Qdiv(Qmul(Name "Force",Name "metre"),Name "sec")
⇒ Qdiv(Qmul(Name "metre",Name "Force"),Name "sec")
⇒ Qdiv(Qmul(Qmul (Name "kg",Name "metre"),
      Qdiv(Name "metre",
      Qmul(Name "sec",Name "sec"))),Name "sec")
  ⋮
```

Definition 2 (Structural Equality of Named Quantities). *Two quantities, p and q are considered structurally equal if they have the same representation in terms of the algebraic data type* `quant`. *If the two quantities are structurally equal then $p \stackrel{\triangle}{=} q$ holds:*

$$
\begin{aligned}
\texttt{Name } n &\stackrel{\triangle}{=} \texttt{Name } m & &= (n = m) \\
\texttt{Dimless} &\stackrel{\triangle}{=} \texttt{Dimless} & &= \textbf{true} \\
\texttt{Qmul}\,(p_1,q_1) &\stackrel{\triangle}{=} \texttt{Qmul}\,(p_2,q_2) & &= (p_1 \stackrel{\triangle}{=} p_2) \wedge (q_1 \stackrel{\triangle}{=} q_2) \\
\texttt{Qdiv}\,(p_1,q_1) &\stackrel{\triangle}{=} \texttt{Qdiv}\,(p_2,q_2) & &= (p_1 \stackrel{\triangle}{=} p_2) \wedge (q_1 \stackrel{\triangle}{=} q_2) \\
\_ &\stackrel{\triangle}{=} \_ & &= \textbf{false}
\end{aligned}
$$

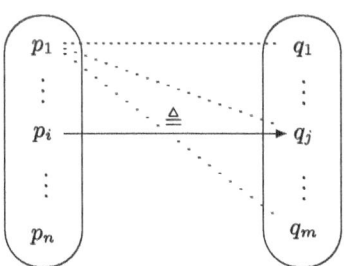

Fig. 5. Equality of named quantities p and q.

Definition 3 (Equality of Named Quantities). *Given a system of kinds τ, two quantities p and q are considered equal, if they share a representation. This is achieved by expanding and simplifying p into the set of forms $\{p_1, \ldots, p_n\}$ and q into the set of forms $\{q_1, \ldots, q_m\}$, performing the cartesian product of both sets and comparing the pairs for structural equality, $p_i \stackrel{\triangle}{=} q_j$. If there is at least one identical pair then we say that $p =_\tau q$ holds, as shown in Fig. 5.*

For example:

$$\text{Name "Force"} =_\tau \text{Qmul(Name "Acc",Name "kg")}$$

When we expand `Name "Force"`, we have the following forms:

```
Name "Force"
⇒ Qmul(Name "kg",Name "Acc")
⇒ Qmul(Name "kg",Qdiv(Name "metre",Qmul(Name "sec",Name "sec")))
⇒ Qmul(Qdiv(Name "metre",Qmul(Name "sec",Name "sec")),Name "kg")
⇒ Qmul(Name "Acc",Name "kg")
```

while expanding `Qmul(Name "Acc",Name "kg")` creates the forms:

```
Qmul(Name "Acc",Name "kg")
⇒ Qmul(Qdiv(Name "metre",Qmul(Name "sec",Name "sec")),Name "kg")
⇒ Qmul(Name "kg",Qdiv(Name "metre",Qmul(Name "sec",Name "sec")))
⇒ Qmul(Name "kg",Name "Acc")
```

The cartesian product of both simplifications has at least one identical pair, shown as underlined. Thus, the two named quantities are equal (dimensionally). This will yield the same result as expanding p to create p', expanding q to create q', and performing $\mathcal{C}\, p' \cong \mathcal{C}\, q'$.

Definition 4 (Homogeneity of Named Quantities). *Given a system of kinds τ, two quantities, p and q are considered to represent the same named quantity, $p \equiv_\tau q$, if they share the same kind name, or if they are equal. It is defined as follows:*

$$\text{Name } n \equiv_\tau \text{Name } m = (n = m)$$
$$p \qquad \equiv_\tau q \qquad = (p =_\tau q)$$

Using our previous example, the equality:

$$\text{Name "Force"} \equiv_\tau \text{Qmul(Name "Acc",Name "kg")}$$

will hold as both quantities share a common representation. However, attempting to equate work and torque will not succeed:

$$\text{Name "Work"} \not\equiv_\tau \text{Name "Torque"}$$

as even though they are dimensionally equal, they do not share the same name. Hence, addition and subtraction can only proceed if $p \equiv_\tau q$ holds.

5.2 Safe Guarding Assignment

As there are many ways of representing the same UoM, we cannot simply rely on homogeneity because that would allow us to assign a value of kind torque to one of work through a temporary variable or associativity of arithmetic expressions. We therefore need a way of capturing the representation that is closest to the conceptual description of the quantity to ensure KOQ information is maintained.

Proposition 2 (Most Abstract Named Quantity). *If we have two* quant *trees denoting the same UoM, and neither are in the* Name *form, then the one that can generate the greater number of representations denotes the most abstract quantity, which we shall write as* maq (p, q).

Proof. A named quant *entity is the most abstract as it describes explicitly what kind of quantity the entity is, and is unique. A table lookup will replace a* Name *by one or more compound quantities that are less abstract but more complex. The simplification rules of Fig. 3 will reduce the complexity while the restructuring rules of Fig. 4 will maintain the complexity of a given quant expression. These three actions create new representations of a given quantity, and will recursively explore all the allowable forms of the original quantity. If two quantities have the same dimensions, then the one that generates the larger set of possible representations will have required the greater number of lookups, and thus will be the most abstract.*

Definition 5 (Most Abstract Form of Homogeneous Named Quantities). *Given a system of kinds* τ, *two quantities,* p *and* q *are considered to represent the same named quantity if they share the same kind name, or if they are equal. The operator* $p \circledast_\tau q$ *will return the most abstract* quant *representation of two equal named quantities. It is defined as follows:*

$$\begin{aligned}
\text{Name } n \circledast_\tau \text{Name } m &= \text{Name } n, & \text{if } n = m \\
\text{Name } n \circledast_\tau q &= \text{Name } n, & \text{if Name } n =_\tau q \\
p \quad \circledast_\tau \text{Name } m &= \text{Name } m, & \text{if } p =_\tau \text{Name } m \\
p \quad \circledast_\tau q &= maq\,(p,q), & \text{if } p =_\tau q
\end{aligned}$$

To ensure the rules for arithmatic and assignment are *safe* in terms of quantity arithmetic, we need to demonstrate that the $\circledast_\tau$ operator is both commutative and associative. This is necessary to show that the KOQ of subexpressions are not subsequently overridden.

Proposition 3 (Commutativity of $\circledast_\tau$**).** *For given quantities* p *and* q *that represent equal quantities,* $p \circledast_\tau q$ *yields the same result as* $q \circledast_\tau p$.

Proof. By case analysis of the function $\circledast_\tau$, *the first case will hold as string equality is commutative, case 2 and 3 can each be reordered, while the maq function is independent on the ordering of the arguments. Hence, changing the order of the operands of the homogeneity operator does not change the result.*

Proposition 4 (Associativity of $\circledast_\tau$**).** *For given quantities* p, q *and* r *that represent equal quantities, we need to show that* $(p \circledast_\tau q) \circledast_\tau r \triangleq p \circledast_\tau (q \circledast_\tau r)$.

Proof. By structural induction on quant *entities that are either named or unnamed. We need to show the following eight cases, where* non *denotes any unnamed quantity, will result in structural equality:*

Case 1: *(Name* n $\circledast_\tau$ *Name* m*)* $\circledast_\tau$ *Name* o
   $\triangleq$ *Name* n $\circledast_\tau$ *(Name* m $\circledast_\tau$ *Name* o*)*
  $\Rightarrow$ *Name* n $\circledast_\tau$ *Name* o
   $\triangleq$ *Name* n $\circledast_\tau$ *(Name* m $\circledast_\tau$ *Name* o*), where* $n = m$
  $\Rightarrow$ *Name* n $\circledast_\tau$ *Name* o
   $\triangleq$ *Name* n $\circledast_\tau$ *Name* m*, where* $m = o$
  $\Rightarrow$ **true***, where* $n = m = o$

Case 2: $(\text{Name } n \circledast_\tau \text{Name } m) \circledast_\tau non$
　　　$\triangleq \text{Name } n \circledast_\tau (\text{Name } m \circledast_\tau non)$
　$\Rightarrow \text{Name } n \circledast_\tau non$
　　　$\triangleq \text{Name } n \circledast_\tau (\text{Name } m \circledast_\tau non), \textit{where } n = m$
　$\Rightarrow \text{Name } n \circledast_\tau non$
　　　$\triangleq \text{Name } n \circledast_\tau \text{Name } m, \textit{by rule 2 of } \circledast_\tau$
　$\Rightarrow$ **true**, *by rule 2 and* $n = m$

Case 3: $(\text{Name } n \circledast_\tau non) \circledast_\tau \text{Name } o$
　　　$\triangleq \text{Name } n \circledast_\tau (non \circledast_\tau \text{Name } o)$
　$\Rightarrow \text{Name } n \circledast_\tau \text{Name } o$
　　　$\triangleq \text{Name } n \circledast_\tau (non \circledast_\tau \text{Name } o), \textit{by rule 2}$
　$\Rightarrow \text{Name } n \circledast_\tau \text{Name } o$
　　　$\triangleq \text{Name } n \circledast_\tau \text{Name } o, \textit{by rule 3 of } \circledast_\tau$
　$\Rightarrow \text{Name } n \triangleq \text{Name } o, \textit{where } n = o$
　$\Rightarrow$ **true**

Case 4: $(\text{Name } n \circledast_\tau non) \circledast_\tau non$
　　　$\triangleq \text{Name } n \circledast_\tau (non \circledast_\tau non)$
　$\Rightarrow \text{Name } n \circledast_\tau non$
　　　$\triangleq \text{Name } n \circledast_\tau non, \textit{by rule 2 and 4}$
　$\Rightarrow \text{Name } n \triangleq \text{Name } n, \textit{by rule 2}$
　$\Rightarrow$ **true**

Case 5: $(non \circledast_\tau \text{Name } m) \circledast_\tau \text{Name } o$
　　　$\triangleq non \circledast_\tau (\text{Name } m \circledast_\tau \text{Name } o)$
　$\Rightarrow \text{Name } m \circledast_\tau \text{Name } o$
　　　$\triangleq non \circledast_\tau \text{Name } o, \textit{by rule 3 and } m = o$
　$\Rightarrow \text{Name } o \triangleq \text{Name } o, \textit{by rule 3 and } m = o$
　$\Rightarrow$ **true**

Case 6: $(non \circledast_\tau \text{Name } m) \circledast_\tau non$
　　　$\triangleq non \circledast_\tau (\text{Name } m \circledast_\tau non)$
　$\Rightarrow \text{Name } m \circledast_\tau non$
　　　$\triangleq non \circledast_\tau \text{Name } m, \textit{by rule 3 and 2}$
　$\Rightarrow \text{Name } m \triangleq \text{Name } m, \textit{by rule 2 and 3}$
　$\Rightarrow$ **true**

Case 7: $(non \circledast_\tau non) \circledast_\tau \text{Name } o$
　　　$\triangleq non \circledast_\tau (non \circledast_\tau \text{Name } o)$
　$\Rightarrow non \circledast_\tau \text{Name } o$
　　　$\triangleq non \circledast_\tau \text{Name } o, \textit{by rule 4 and rule 3}$
　$\Rightarrow \text{Name } o \triangleq \text{Name } o, \textit{by 3}$
　$\Rightarrow$ **true**

Case 8: $(non \circledast_\tau non) \circledast_\tau non$
　　　$\triangleq non \circledast_\tau (non \circledast_\tau non)$
　$\Rightarrow non \circledast_\tau non$
　　　$\triangleq non \circledast_\tau non, \textit{by rule 4}$
　$\Rightarrow non \triangleq non, \textit{by rule 4}$
　$\Rightarrow$ **true**

The proof ensures that when checking the KOQ correctness of a program where nested sub-terms are meant to represent the same quantity, the $\circledast_\tau$ operator will guaran-

tee the property that named subexpressions must represent the same entity. In essence, one always casts upwards from unnamed entities to known named ones, or unknown named ones that represent the most abstract representation of the given quantities.

5.3 Dimensionless Units and Quantity-Dependent Conversions

Units of dimension one can be divided into two types based on their dimensions. So called *dimensionless variables* are physical quantities which have no physical units. They arise when there is complete cancellation of dimension variables or unit names. For example, a plane angle in radians is the ratio of arc to the radius, dimensions of length get canceled resulting in a unit of dimension one. Whereas *dimensionless constants* are those quantities that have no dimensions and have a constant unchangeable value, such as π.

Our `quant` datatype is able to distinguish between the two. A radian can be described as `Qdiv (Name "metre", Name "metre")`. Naturally the simplification rules will derive the alternative representation `Dimless` but there may be instances where we need to match on the KOQ name. For instance, the standard name for the unit of activity is the becquerel and is expressed as s^{-1}. Using the name explicitly distinguishes it from the unit for angular frequency, which is also s^{-1}. We can perform static checks on expressions using the `@assert` comment to ensure structural equality, or the `@check` comment to ensure homogeneity as shown in Fig. 7.

Partial cancellation can also occur and affect the KOQ. Torque, for instance, is a measure of the force that can cause an object to rotate about an axis. The unit of torque is typically represented as $N \cdot m$, but it can also be represented as $(N \cdot m)/°$, or `Qdiv (Qmul (Name "Force",Name "metre"),Name "PlaneAngle")`. This is because angles do not have physical units and can be expressed as ratios of lengths. However, the magnitude of torque is independent of any angle, so both representations are correct.

6 Kinds of Quantity Analysis

We are now in a position to define the kinds of quantity checking rules for our simple programming language. We will begin with expressions and then add statements, including functions. All the rules are described using partial functions as they will only succeed if dimensional homogeneity can be shown for kinds of quantities. The rules for statements update the environment mapping variable names to their quantities.

We extend our definition of *dec* to include pluggable types for quantities, described using our `quant` datatype, rather than dimensions:

$$dec ::= \cdots \mid \texttt{var}\ v : \texttt{float @unit quant} \mid \texttt{var}\ v : \texttt{float @unit quant} = r$$

These are used to construct a quantity environment as shown in Fig. 6. The first rule binds the quantity kind to the variable, while the second rule enables one to iterate through a sequence of declarations in order to construct the complete γ environment.

$$
\begin{aligned}
&\mathcal{D} \;:\; Declaration \to (Var \to \text{quant}) \to (Var \to \text{quant}) \\
&\mathcal{D}[\![\text{var } v : \texttt{float @unit } q]\!]_\gamma = \gamma \;\oplus\; \{v \mapsto q\} \\
&\mathcal{D}[\![dec_1 ; dec_2]\!]_\gamma \qquad\qquad\quad = \mathcal{D}[\![dec_2]\!](\mathcal{D}[\![dec_1]\!]_\gamma)
\end{aligned}
$$

Fig. 6. Named Quantity rules for Declarations.

6.1   Arithmetic and Boolean Expressions

The rules of Fig. 7 calculate the quant representation of an arithmetic expression given an environment γ mapping variables to their named quantities. The rules for multiplication and division build compound quantities, while the rules for addition and subtraction will check the homogeneity of both operands. In other words, only quantities that have the same dimensions can be added or subtracted. The rules of $\mathcal{K}$ will return the most abstract quant representation for the given expression, based on the commutativity and associativity of $\circledast_\tau$. The rules for boolean expressions, $\mathcal{B}$, return a result type of OK if the expression handles units correctly. In the case of relational operators, we need to ensure that both operands share the same quantity.

$$
\begin{aligned}
&\mathcal{K} \;:\; Expression \to (Var \to \text{quant}) \rightharpoonup \text{quant} \\
&\mathcal{K}[\![v]\!]_\gamma \qquad\qquad\quad = \gamma\, v \\
&\mathcal{K}[\![r * exp]\!]_\gamma \qquad\quad = \mathcal{K}[\![exp]\!]_\gamma \\
&\mathcal{K}[\![exp_1 + exp_2]\!]_\gamma \;\; = \mathcal{K}[\![exp_1]\!]_\gamma \circledast_\tau \mathcal{K}[\![exp_2]\!]_\gamma \\
&\mathcal{K}[\![exp_1 - exp_2]\!]_\gamma \;\; = \mathcal{K}[\![exp_1]\!]_\gamma \circledast_\tau \mathcal{K}[\![exp_2]\!]_\gamma \\
&\mathcal{K}[\![exp_1 * exp_2]\!]_\gamma \;\; = \texttt{Qmul}\,(\mathcal{K}[\![exp_1]\!]_\gamma, \mathcal{K}[\![exp_2]\!]_\gamma) \\
&\mathcal{K}[\![exp_1 / exp_2]\!]_\gamma \;\; = \texttt{Qdiv}\,(\mathcal{K}[\![exp_1]\!]_\gamma, \mathcal{K}[\![exp_2]\!]_\gamma) \\
&\mathcal{K}[\![exp \text{ @assert } q]\!]_\gamma = \mathcal{K}[\![exp]\!]_\gamma, \quad \text{if } \mathcal{K}[\![exp]\!]_\gamma \triangleq q \\
&\mathcal{K}[\![exp \text{ @check } q]\!]_\gamma = \mathcal{K}[\![exp]\!]_\gamma, \quad \text{if } \mathcal{K}[\![exp]\!]_\gamma \equiv_\tau q \\[6pt]
&\mathcal{B} \;:\; BoolExpression \to (Var \to \text{quant}) \rightharpoonup \text{result} \\
&\mathcal{B}[\![\texttt{true}]\!]_\gamma \qquad\qquad = \text{OK} \\
&\mathcal{B}[\![\texttt{false}]\!]_\gamma \qquad\quad = \text{OK} \\
&\mathcal{B}[\![bexp_1 \text{ and } bexp_2]\!]_\gamma = \text{OK}, \quad \text{if } \mathcal{B}[\![bexp_1]\!]_\gamma = \text{OK} \wedge \mathcal{B}[\![bexp_2]\!]_\gamma = \text{OK} \\
&\mathcal{B}[\![exp_1 \text{ >= } exp_2]\!]_\gamma \;\; = \text{OK}, \quad \text{if } \mathcal{K}[\![exp_1]\!]_\gamma = p \wedge \mathcal{K}[\![exp_2]\!]_\gamma = q \wedge p \equiv_\tau q
\end{aligned}
$$

Fig. 7. Named Quantity rules for Expressions.

6.2   Statements

The rules for statements are given in Fig. 8 and update the environment γ according to the imperative action described. The rule for sequences updates the environment for the first statement, and then updates this new environment with the second statement. Assignment statements derive the quant of the arithmetic expression. For the analysis to be *safe*, it is not sufficient to just check for homogeneity of the quantity to that of the variable, instead we must update the variable's quantity to reflect a potentially more abstract quantity assignment. Consider the following example where we will try to force a torque value to be assigned to a work variable through a temporary variable.

$$
\begin{aligned}
&S \;:\; Statement \to (Var \to \text{quant}) \to (Var \to \text{quant}) \\
&S[\![stmt_1 \,;\, stmt_2]\!]_\gamma \quad\quad = S[\![stmt_2]\!](S[\![stmt_1]\!]_\gamma) \\
&S[\![v \,:= exp]\!]_\gamma \quad\quad\quad\; = \gamma \oplus \{v \mapsto ((\gamma\, v) \circledast_\tau \mathcal{K}[\![exp]\!]_\gamma)\} \\
&S[\![\text{while } bexp \text{ do } stmt]\!]_\gamma = S[\![stmt]\!]_\gamma, \quad \text{if } \mathcal{B}[\![bexp]\!]_\gamma = \text{OK} \\
&S[\![\text{if } bexp \text{ then } stmt_1 \text{ else } stmt_2]\!]_\gamma \\
&\quad\quad = \text{let } \gamma_t = S[\![stmt_1]\!]_\gamma \\
&\quad\quad\quad\quad\; \gamma_f = S[\![stmt_2]\!]_\gamma \\
&\quad\quad\quad\; \text{in } \forall v \in \text{dom } \gamma \cdot \gamma \oplus \{v \mapsto ((\gamma_t\, v) \circledast_\tau (\gamma_f\, v))\}, \quad \text{if } \mathcal{B}[\![bexp]\!]_\gamma = \text{OK}
\end{aligned}
$$

Fig. 8. Named Quantity rules for Statements.

```
program
    var t : float @unit Name "Torque";
    var w : float @unit Name "Work";
    var temp : float @unit Qmul(Name "metre",Name "Force")
begin
    temp := t;
    w := temp
end
```

The rules for declarations will construct the initial environment:

$$
\gamma = \{\, t \mapsto \text{Name "Torque"}, \\
\quad\quad w \mapsto \text{Name "Work"}, \\
\quad\quad temp \mapsto \text{Qmul(Name "metre",Name "Force")} \,\}
$$

We can then apply it to the sequence of two assignments:

$S[\![temp := t;\ w := temp]\!]_\gamma$
$= S[\![w := temp]\!](S[\![temp := t]\!]_\gamma)$
$= S[\![w := temp]\!](\gamma \oplus \{temp \mapsto ((\gamma\, temp) \circledast_\tau \mathcal{K}[\![t]\!]_\gamma)\})$
$= S[\![w := temp]\!](\gamma \oplus \{temp \mapsto ((\text{Qmul(Name "metre",Name "Force")}) \circledast_\tau \text{Name "Torque"})\})$
$= S[\![w := temp]\!](\gamma \oplus \{temp \mapsto \text{Name "Torque"}\})$
$= \gamma \oplus \{temp \mapsto \text{Name "Torque"}\} \oplus \{w \mapsto (\text{Name "Work"} \circledast_\tau \text{Name "Torque"})\}$

which will fail to resolve further as our temporary variable has been assigned a torque quant.

While loops require the boolean expression to manage quantities correctly before checking the statement loop body. Conditionals are choice functions, but we still need to ensure that both branches update the environment in a consistent manner. By this we mean that any new assignment in the true branch, γ_t, will not conflict with any new assignment in the false branch, γ_f. This is achieved by ensuring all variables can be re-assigned to the most abstract version of their definitions after both branches have been successfully validated. Consider the following example where we assign the temporary variable to a torque value if the condition is true or a work value if the condition is false:

```
program
    var t : float @unit Name "Torque";
    var w : float @unit Name "Work";
    var temp : float @unit Qmul(Name "metre",Name "Force")
begin
    if true
    then temp := t
    else temp := w
end
```

The initial environment will be the same as before. We step through the analysis as follows:

$$
\begin{aligned}
&\mathcal{S}[\![\texttt{if true then temp := t else temp := w}]\!]_\gamma \\
&= \texttt{let } \gamma_t = \mathcal{S}[\![\texttt{temp := t}]\!]_\gamma \\
&\qquad\quad \gamma_f = \mathcal{S}[\![\texttt{temp := w}]\!]_\gamma \\
&\qquad \texttt{in } \forall v \in \text{dom } \gamma \cdot \gamma \oplus \{v \mapsto ((\gamma_t\ v) \circledast_\tau (\gamma_f\ v))\} \\
&= \texttt{let } \gamma_t = \gamma \oplus \{\texttt{temp} \mapsto \texttt{Name "Torque"}\} \\
&\qquad\quad \gamma_f = \gamma \oplus \{\texttt{temp} \mapsto \texttt{Name "Work"}\} \\
&\qquad \texttt{in } \forall v \in \text{dom } \gamma \cdot \gamma \oplus \{v \mapsto ((\gamma_t\ v) \circledast_\tau (\gamma_f\ v))\} \\
&= \gamma \oplus \{\texttt{temp} \mapsto ((\gamma_t\ \texttt{temp}) \circledast_\tau (\gamma_f\ \texttt{temp}))\} \\
&= \gamma \oplus \{\texttt{temp} \mapsto (\texttt{Name "Torque"} \circledast_\tau \texttt{Name "Work"})\}
\end{aligned}
$$

which will also fail to complete due to conflicting, and thus *unsafe*, assignments.

6.3   Functions

Functions allow us to repeat a sequence of statements without having to write the code multiple times. They can accept named quantity arguments and return a quantity as a result. Additional constructs with pluggable types are appended to our syntactical definitions, as follows:

$$
\begin{aligned}
dec\ &::= \cdots \mid\ \texttt{fun } fn\ (v_1 : \texttt{@unit } q_1, \ldots, v_n : \texttt{@unit } q_m) : \texttt{float @unit } q_{out} \\
&\qquad\qquad \texttt{begin } stmt \texttt{ end} \\
exp\ &::= \cdots \mid\ fn\ (exp_1, \ldots, exp_n) \\
stmt\ &::= \cdots \mid\ \texttt{return } exp
\end{aligned}
$$

To ensure a function safely manages named quantities, we must not only ensure all return expressions match the defined return quantity but that we also derive the *most abstract* return quantity possible for a given function call. In order to aggregate return expressions we use the function name as a local variable such that the existing rules for statements will guarantee it is updated safely. We perform an initial source-to-source modification that transforms the various `return` statements within the function definition into variable assignments.

```
fun fn (v₁:@unit q₁,...,vₙ:@unit qₙ) : float @unit q_out
begin
   ... return e₁                    ⇒ fun fn (v₁:@unit q₁,...,vₙ:@unit qₙ) : float @unit q_out
                                      begin
   ... return eⱼ                         ...   fn := e₁
end
                                         ...   fn := eⱼ
                                      end
```

Both a definition mechanism and an invocation mechanism are provided for named quantity functions, as shown in Fig. 9. Function definitions are stored in a new environment, ν, binding function names to their input parameters, the output variable quantity, and statement body. The rules for $\mathcal{D}$ are extended to create both variable and function environments. Consequently our rules for expressions ($\mathcal{K}$ and $\mathcal{B}$) and statements ($\mathcal{S}$) will need to be extended to pass this second environment around but otherwise stay unchanged. A function can be thought of as a parameterised block in which all the arguments to the block are bound to the function's arguments and its return quantity. On invocation we retrieve the definition from ν, and then build a local named quantity variable environment, γ', which compares the evaluated arguments, exp_i, to their assigned quantities, q_i, calculating the most abstract version of the two, before binding them to their parameters, v_i, and also creating a binding for the return quantity fn. Once that local environment has been constructed, we can then check the function body with respect to the new variable environment, γ'. When validating a function call, the analysis will ensure that each return statement matches the expected return named quantity q_{out} through the use of the local variable fn. Moreover, it will derive the most abstract version of the return quantity or reveal attempts to equate quantities of different kinds.

Consider the following example where we pass a torque value into a function `double` that expects and returns a $N \cdot m$ quantity, before assigning the exposed returned value to a work quantity variable.

```
program
    t : float @unit Name "Torque";
    w : float @unit Name "Work";
    fun double (i:float @ Qmul (Name "Force",Name "metre")):float
```

$$
\begin{aligned}
&\mathcal{D}[\![\text{fun } fn \ (v_1:\text{@unit } q_1,\ldots,v_1:\text{@unit } q_n) : \text{float @unit } q_{out} \text{ begin } stmt \text{ end}]\!]_\gamma^\nu \\
&\quad = (\gamma,\nu \oplus \{fn \mapsto (\langle(v_1,q_1),\ldots,(v_n,q_n)\rangle, q_{out}, stmt)\})
\end{aligned}
$$

$$
\begin{aligned}
&\mathcal{K}[\![fn \ (exp_1,\ldots,exp_n)]\!]_\gamma^\nu \\
&\quad = \text{let } (\langle(v_1,q_1),\ldots,(v_n,q_n)\rangle, stmt) = \nu \ fn \\
&\qquad \gamma' = \{v_1 \mapsto (q_1 \circledast_\tau \mathcal{K}[\![exp_1]\!]_\gamma^\nu),\ldots,v_n \mapsto (q_n \circledast_\tau \mathcal{K}[\![exp_n]\!]_\gamma^\nu), fn \mapsto q_{out}\} \\
&\quad \text{in } (\mathcal{S}[\![stmt]\!]_{\gamma'}^\nu) \ fn
\end{aligned}
$$

Fig. 9. Quantity Checking rules for Function Declarations and Invocation.

```
                @unit Qmul (Name "Force",Name "metre")
                begin
                   return 2*i
                end
   begin
       w := double (t)
   end
```

Our analysis correctly shows that the assignment w := double (t) is unsafe, as we cannot equate a work value with one of torque:

$\mathcal{S}[\![w := \text{double (t)}]\!]_\gamma^\nu$

$= \gamma \oplus \{w \mapsto (\text{Name "Work"} \circledast_\tau \mathcal{K}[\![\text{double (t)}]\!]_\gamma^\nu)\}$

$= \gamma \oplus \{w \mapsto (\text{Name "Work"} \circledast_\tau$

     let $(\langle(\text{i}, \text{Qmul (Name "Force",Name "metre")})\rangle,$

      Qmul (Name "Force",Name "metre"),double $:= 2*\text{i}) = \nu$ double

      $\gamma' = \{ \text{i} \mapsto (\text{Qmul (Name "Force",Name "metre")} \circledast_\tau \mathcal{K}[\![\text{t}]\!]_\gamma^\nu),$

       double $\mapsto$ Qmul (Name "Force",Name "metre") $\}$

     in $(\mathcal{S}[\![\text{double} := 2*\text{i}]\!]_{\gamma'}^\nu,)$ double $)\}$

$= \gamma \oplus \{w \mapsto (\text{Name "Work"} \circledast_\tau$

     let $(\langle(\text{i}, \text{Qmul (Name "Force",Name "metre")})\rangle,$

      Qmul (Name "Force",Name "metre"),double $:= 2*\text{i}) = \nu$ double

      $\gamma' = \{ \text{i} \mapsto (\text{Qmul (Name "Force",Name "metre")} \circledast_\tau \text{Name "Torque"}),$

       double $\mapsto$ Qmul (Name "Force",Name "metre") $\}$

     in $(\gamma' \oplus \{\text{double} \mapsto (\gamma' \text{ double}) \circledast_\tau \mathcal{K}[\![2*\text{i}]\!]_{\gamma'}^\nu,\})$ double $)\}$

$= \gamma \oplus \{w \mapsto (\text{Name "Work"} \circledast_\tau$

     let $(\langle(\text{i}, \text{Qmul (Name "Force",Name "metre")})\rangle,$

      Qmul (Name "Force",Name "metre"),double $:= 2*\text{i}) = \nu$ double

      $\gamma' = \{ \text{i} \mapsto \text{Name "Torque"},$

       double $\mapsto$ Qmul (Name "Force",Name "metre") $\}$

     in $(\gamma' \oplus \{\text{double} \mapsto \text{Qmul (Name "Force",Name "metre")}$

          $\circledast_\tau \text{Name "Torque"}\})$ double $)\}$

$= \gamma \oplus \{w \mapsto (\text{Name "Work"} \circledast_\tau (\gamma' \oplus \{\text{double} \mapsto \text{Name "Torque"}\})$ double $)\}$

$= \gamma \oplus \{w \mapsto (\text{Name "Work"} \circledast_\tau \text{Name "Torque"})\}$

The real potential of quantity functions is that they can re-establish a named quantity. This is of particular interest when evaluating expressions containing multiplication or division as new unnamed quantities are generated. An example of this Type 2 KOQ error [8] is the incorrect analysis of a turbine, of moment-of-inertia I (SI unit of $\text{kg} \cdot \text{m}^2$) rotating with an angular velocity of ω_1 (s^{-1}) with a torque T ($\text{kg} \cdot \text{m}^2 \cdot \text{s}^{-2}$) applied for duration t in seconds. The initial kinetic energy E_1 is defined as $E_1 = 0.5 * I * \omega_1^2$. It is easy to code this quantity equation incorrectly as $E_1 = 0.5 * I/t^2$, where the units of both sides of the assignment ($\text{kg} \cdot \text{m}^2 \cdot \text{s}^{-2}$) are compatible, and our analysis would succeed.

```
   program
       e  : float @unit Name "Torque";
       i  : float @unit Name "MomentOfInertia";
       t  : float @unit Name "sec"
   begin
       e :=  0.5 * i / (t*t)
   end
```

However, if we demand a discipline of programming with quantities where expressions involving multiplication are promoted to functions then we can ensure that results have a known named quantity:

```
program
    e  : float @unit Name "Torque";
    i  : float @unit Name "MomentOfInertia";
    v  : float @unit Name "AngularVelocity";
    fun rot_kin_energy (i: float @unit Name "MomentOfInertia",
        w: float @unit Name "AngularVelocity"): float @unit Name "Torque"
    begin return 0.5*i*(w*w) end
begin
    e := rot_kin_energy (i,v)
end
```

In this second case, the arguments to `rot_kin_energy` have to represent moment of inertia and angular velocity kinds of quantities. On completion the function will return a torque quantity, `Name "Torque"`, so subsequent calculations can be undertaken safely. The function behaves like a contract even through we cannot ascertain the KOQ of `0.5*i*(w*w)` directly using our algebra.

7 Summary

Global and existential challenges, from infectious diseases to environmental breakdown, require high-quality data [14]. Ensuring software systems support quantities explicitly is becoming ever more important. While there are solutions that allow UoM to be specified at both the model and code level, adoption is challenging due to the annotation burden and also the lack of perceived benefits.

We have presented a simple pluggable type-checker for *kinds of quantities*, and a means of ensuring safe program evaluation, that extends the traditional dimensional analysis through the use of a recursive data type. Our model of quantities allows compound units to be constructed, and a table which enables named quantities to be mapped to one or more compound forms. We provide ways of comparing and constructing such quantities to ensure that (1) only values of the same kind can be added or subtracted; and (2) that multiplication and division create new compound forms that represent the addition or subtraction of their dimensions. As unit variables are all assigned a named quantity, our current system effectively combines dimensional analysis with the naming scheme presented in [23], and formalises the quantity calculus presented by Lodge [19]. It allows us to distinguish between quantities that share the same UoM, even if that UoM denotes a dimensionless entity, and subsequently apply conversions that only apply to that particular kind. Moreover, our system is lightweight, unobtrusive and only requires annotations on declarations.

Hall [12, 13] has developed a more comprehensive notation for modeling quantities that includes both scale and aspect. The notion of aspect is more general than our formulation of KOQ as it can be used to denote measurable properties. However, the intention of Hall is to enable effective exchange of information, where aspect and scale tables are stored in a central register, rather than the robust evaluation of numeric expressions.

Our methodology can be implemented natively or as a pluggable-type system for modeling or programming languages. It allows for a richer static analysis than dimensional analysis, and a complete definition of arithmetic on kinds of quantities. It is less suited to run-time checking due to the additional overhead of supporting the `quant` data type. Quantity annotations are initially costly for the developer but relatively stable to program evolution. Therefore scalability and maintainability within potentially safety-critical code is assured. Moreover, the syntactic cost of our KOQ annotations is equivalent to most UoM annotations as they are both written in terms of multiplication on base units and then converted into internal representations. Our naming scheme improves the scope of existing dimensional analysis.

To enhance the utility of our technique we are currently exploring two essential features: generics and unit conversion. Unit annotations need to be as unobtrusive as possible to encourage adoption [31]. The quantity datatype is being extended with generic variables so that we can write polymorphic functions over quantities. Once assigned, generic variables must remain the same, but can become more abstract, within the scope that they are defined. This requires an equivalence relation to store the bindings, and can be implemented using a union-find data structure. Our current system does not distinguish between dimensions and base quantities, such that a *Watt hour* is not equal to a *Watt second*. We need to define prefixes and alternative base quantities, such as *yard* for *metre*, with corresponding conversion tables to inject scalar values into expressions for when equality holds.

If a software system fails to maintain the algebraic attributes of a system's quantity information correctly when evaluating expressions then disastrous problems can arise. However, it is perhaps the more mundane unit mismatches and lack of interoperability that over time incurs a greater cost. Alas this cost is undocumented and hard to ascertain as it would guide both the depth and breadth of the analysis required. Nonetheless, the software engineering benefits of enforcing quantity checking and enabling automatic unit conversion are undeniable.

Acknowledgement. I would like to thank Blair Hall, Marcus Foster and Andrew Savage for their corrections, insights and guidance.

References

1. Allen, E., Chase, D., Luchangco, V., Maessen, J.W., Steele, Jr., G.L.: Object-oriented units of measurement. In: Proceedings of Object-oriented Programming, Systems, Languages, and Applications, OOPSLA 2004, pp. 384–403. ACM (2004). https://doi.org/10.1145/1028976. 1029008. http://doi.acm.org/10.1145/1028976.1029008
2. Antoniu, T., Steckler, P.A., Krishnamurthi, S., Neuwirth, E., Felleisen, M.: Validating the unit correctness of spreadsheet programs. In: Proceedings of Software Engineering, ICSE 2004, pp. 439–448. IEEE Computer Society, Washington, DC (2004). http://dl.acm.org/citation. cfm?id=998675.999448
3. Bennich-Björkman, O., McKeever, S.: The next 700 unit of measurement checkers. In: Proceedings of Software Language Engineering, SLE 2018, pp. 121–132. Association for Computing Machinery (2018). https://doi.org/10.1145/3276604.3276613

4. Bureau International des Poids et Mesures: SI Brochure: The International System of Units (SI), 9th edn., Dimensions of Quantities (2019). https://www.bipm.org/utils/common/pdf/si-brochure/SI-Brochure-9.pdf. Accessed 24 July 2024

5. Chen, F., Rosu, G., Venkatesan, R.P.: Rule-based analysis of dimensional safety. In: RTA (2003)

6. Cooper, J., McKeever, S.: A model-driven approach to automatic conversion of physical units. Softw. Pract. Exp. **38**(4), 337–359 (2008). https://doi.org/10.1002/spe.828

7. Dreiheller, A., Mohr, B., Moerschbacher, M.: Programming pascal with physical units. SIG-PLAN Notes **21**(12), 114–123 (1986). https://doi.org/10.1145/15042.15048

8. Foster, M., Tregeagle, S.: Physical-type correctness in scientific python (2018). https://doi.org/10.48550/ARXIV.1807.07643

9. Fowler, M.: Analysis Patterns: Reusable Objects Models. Addison-Wesley Longman Publishing Co. Inc, Boston (1997)

10. Gehani, N.: Units of measure as a data attribute. Comput. Lang. **2**(3), 93–111 (1977). https://doi.org/10.1016/0096-0551(77)90010-8

11. Gibson, J.P., Méry, D.: Explicit modelling of physical measures: from Event-B to Java. In: International Workshop on Handling IMPlicit and EXplicit Knowledge in Formal System Development (2017). https://hal.archives-ouvertes.fr/hal-01798224

12. Hall, B.: The problem with 'dimensionless quantities'. In: Proceedings of the 10th International Conference on Model-Driven Engineering and Software Development (MODEL-SWARD), pp. 116–125. INSTICC, SciTePress, Portugal (2022). https://doi.org/10.5220/0010960300003119

13. Hall, B.: Modelling expressions of physical quantities. In: Proceedings of the 15th International Joint Conference on Knowledge Discovery, Knowledge Engineering and Knowledge Management IC3K. INSTICC, SciTePress, Portugal (2023)

14. Hanisch., R., et al.: Stop squandering data: make units of measurement machine-readable. Nature **605**, 222–224 (2022). https://doi.org/10.1038/d41586-022-01233-w

15. Hayes, I.J., Mahony, B.P.: Using units of measurement in formal specifications. Formal Aspects Comput. **7**(3), 329–347 (1995). https://doi.org/10.1007/BF01211077

16. Hilfinger, P.N.: An Ada package for dimensional analysis. ACM Trans. Program. Lang. Syst. **10**(2), 189–203 (1988). https://doi.org/10.1145/42190.42346

17. Jiang, L., Su, Z.: Osprey: a practical type system for validating dimensional unit correctness of C programs. In: Proceedings of the 28th International Conference on Software Engineering, ICSE 2006, pp. 262–271. ACM, New York (2006). https://doi.org/10.1145/1134285.1134323

18. Karr, M., Loveman, D.B.: Incorporation of units into programming languages. Commun. ACM **21**(5), 385–391 (1978). https://doi.org/10.1145/359488.359501

19. Lodge, A.: The multiplication and division of concrete quantities. General Report (Association for the Improvement of Geometrical Teaching) **14**, 47–70 (1888). http://www.jstor.org/stable/24681261

20. Hills, M., Feng, C., Grigore, R.: A rewriting logic approach to static checking of units of measurement in C. Electron. Notes Theoret. Comput. Sci. **290**, 51–67 (2012). https://doi.org/10.1016/j.entcs.2012.11.011

21. Maxwell, J.C.: A Treatise on Electricity and Magnetism, vol. 1. Clarendon Press, Oxford (1873)

22. Mayerhofer, T., Wimmer, M., Vallecillo, A.: Adding uncertainty and units to quantity types in software models. In: Software Language Engineering, SLE 2016, pp. 118–131. ACM (2016). https://doi.org/10.1145/2997364.2997376

23. McKeever, S.: Discerning quantities from units of measurement. In: Proceedings of the 10th International Conference on Model-Driven Engineering and Software Development (MODELSWARD), pp. 105–115. INSTICC, SciTePress, Portugal (2022). https://doi.org/10.5220/0010971300003119

24. McKeever, S.: Acknowledging implementation trade-offs when developing with units of measurement. In: Pires, L.F., Hammoudi, S., Seidewitz, E. (eds.) Model-Driven Engineering and Software Development, pp. 25–47. Springer, Cham (2023)

25. McKeever, S.: Torque not work, representing kinds of quantities. In: Proceedings of the 12th International Conference on Model-Based Software and Systems Engineering (MODELSWARD), pp. 133–140. INSTICC, SciTePress, Portugal (2024). https://doi.org/10.5220/0012318900003645

26. McKeever, S., Paçaci, G., Bennich-Björkman, O.: Quantity checking through unit of measurement libraries, current status and future directions. In: International Conference on Model-Driven Engineering and Software Development (MODELSWARD) (2019). https://api.semanticscholar.org/CorpusID:174800563

27. Nielson, H.R., Nielson, F.: Semantics with Applications: A Formal Introduction. Wiley, USA (1992)

28. NIST: International System of Units (SI): Base and Derived (2015). https://physics.nist.gov/cuu/Units/units.html. Accessed 24 July 2024

29. Ore, J.P., Detweiler, C., Elbaum, S.: Lightweight detection of physical unit inconsistencies without program annotations. In: Proceedings of International Symposium on Software Testing and Analysis, ISSTA 2017, pp. 341–351. ACM (2017). https://doi.org/10.1145/3092703.3092722

30. Pusz, M., et al.: Quantities and units library. https://www.open-std.org/jtc1/sc22/wg21/docs/papers/2024/p3045r0.html#systems-of-quantities. Accessed 24 July 2024

31. Salah, O.A., McKeever, S.: Lack of adoption of units of measurement libraries: survey and anecdotes. In: Proceedings of Software Engineering in Practice, ICSE-SEIP 2020. ACM (2020). https://doi.org/10.1145/3377813.3381359

32. Savage, A.: Quantities and units library. https://github.com/hgrecco/pint/pull/1967. Accessed 24 July 2024

33. Stephenson, A., et al.: Mars Climate Orbiter Mishap Investigation Board Phase 1 Report (1999). https://llis.nasa.gov/llis_lib/pdf/1009464main1_0641-mr.pdf. Accessed 24 July 2024

34. Stevens, S.S.: On the theory of scales of measurement. Science **103**(2684), 677–680 (1946). http://www.jstor.org/stable/1671815. Accessed 24 July 2024

35. Wilkinson, M.D., et al.: The FAIR guiding principles for scientific data management and stewardship. Sci. Data **3** (2016)

36. Witkin, R.: Jet's Fuel Ran Out After Metric Conversion Errors. The New York Times (1983)

37. Xiang, T., Luo, J.Y., Dietl, W.: Precise inference of expressive units of measurement types. Proc. ACM Program. Lang. **4**(OOPSLA) (2020). https://doi.org/10.1145/3428210

Model-Driven Engineering for Data Provenance: A Graphical W3C PROV Modeling Tool

Marcos Alves Vieira[1,2(✉)] and Sergio T. Carvalho[2]

[1] Instituto Federal Goiano (IF Goiano), Campus Iporá, Iporá, GO, Brazil
marcos.vieira@ifgoiano.edu.br
[2] Instituto de Informática (INF), Universidade Federal de Goiás (UFG), Goiânia, GO, Brazil
sergiocarvalho@ufg.br

Abstract. Data provenance is crucial for capturing and tracing the origins, transformations, and movements of data, ensuring its reliability, integrity, and quality, particularly in IoT and ubiquitous computing environments. The W3C introduced the PROV standard, which includes a data model (PROV-DM) for representing provenance instances. Despite the importance of provenance modeling, there is a significant lack of tools that enable developers to graphically create provenance models. Consequently, developers often rely on textual notations like PROV-N, which necessitate cumbersome conversions to generate static graphical representations. This paper presents a graphical tool for creating data provenance models in compliance with the W3C PROV standard. The tool facilitates intuitive and interactive graphical provenance modeling, from which the corresponding PROV-N code can be easily obtained. Developed using Model-Driven Engineering (MDE) principles, the process involved converting PROV-DM into an Ecore metamodel and implementing the tool with Eclipse Sirius, along with model-to-text transformations using Eclipse Acceleo. This work addresses the absence of graphical modeling tools for provenance design, offering developers an effective solution for managing data provenance interactively.

Keywords: Data provenance · W3C PROV · Graphical modeling · Metamodel · PROV-N · Modeling tool · Model-to-text · MDE

1 Introduction

The advent of the Internet of Things (IoT) and ubiquitous computing has fundamentally transformed our interactions with the digital environment, resulting in the generation of extensive volumes of data that necessitate meticulous management and comprehension. Data provenance, which involves recording and tracking the origins, transformations, and movements of data throughout its lifecycle, is essential in this context. It encompasses capturing the entities, activities, and agents involved in data processes, thereby enabling a thorough record of modifications from the data's source to its current state [9]. The adoption of data provenance mechanisms aims to ensure the reliability, integrity, and quality of data across a wide range of applications, including data science, forensic analysis, and large-scale data management.

© The Author(s), under exclusive license to Springer Nature Switzerland AG 2026
F. José Domínguez Mayo et al. (Eds.): MODELSWARD 2024, CCIS 2547, pp. 173–197, 2026.
https://doi.org/10.1007/978-3-031-96841-9_9

To facilitate the representation, serialization, and storage of data provenance, the World Wide Web Consortium (W3C) introduced the PROV standard, which comprises the PROV-DM (Data Model) and various concrete syntaxes for describing provenance instances [25]. One such syntax is PROV-N, a notation that supports the textual representation of provenance information. Additionally, provenance data can be graphically depicted using directed graphs, adhering to the layout conventions prescribed by the PROV standard.

These diverse forms of provenance representation are underpinned by a common data model, which allows for the seamless conversion between different representations while preserving the coherence of relationships among entities. For example, a provenance record in PROV-N can be translated into its graphical representation and vice versa, ensuring consistent and comprehensive documentation of data provenance.

When integrating data provenance capabilities into software systems, developers must model the provenance information relevant to the data objects and determine appropriate points in the application flow for capturing this information. For instance, in an electronic health record (EHR) system, it may be crucial to document interactions by healthcare professionals, including consultations, diagnostic tests, medication prescriptions, and hospital admissions. Similarly, in an IoT-based security system, it may be vital to trace the conditions leading to the activation of emergency alarms by various sensors.

An alternative approach to obtaining data provenance involves mining data produced by the software, which can be implemented using the PROV-Template methodology [23]. This technique entails extracting relevant provenance data directly from databases or log files, thus bypassing the need for explicit tracking or recording of provenance information during the execution of activities.

Regardless of the approach employed for capturing data provenance, it is imperative to model the provenance data in a manner that accurately reflects the data and their interrelationships. However, to the best of the authors' knowledge, there is a notable absence of tools that enable developers to graphically create the desired provenance models to be captured by the software. Consequently, developers are often required to use one of the W3C PROV notations, such as PROV-N. If developers wish to visualize the modeled provenance graphically, they must convert the PROV-N code into a static PROV graph, which does not support interactive modifications. Any changes in the PROV-N model necessitate the regeneration of the corresponding PROV graph.

This paper presents an extended version of our work originally published in the proceedings of the 12th International Conference on Model-Based Software and Systems Engineering (MODELSWARD 2024) [31]. It introduces a graphical tool designed for the creation of data provenance models in compliance with the W3C PROV standard. The tool enables developers to engage in direct graphical provenance modeling, thereby offering a more intuitive and interactive visualization of provenance models. From the generated graphical model, the corresponding PROV-N code can be readily obtained. The development of this graphical modeling tool was guided by Model-Driven Engineering (MDE) principles. Initially, the PROV-DM was converted into an Ecore metamodel, and the modeling tool was implemented using Eclipse Sirius. To facilitate the conversion of graphical models into PROV-N code, model-to-text transformations were developed using Eclipse Acceleo.

The remainder of this paper is organized as follows: Sect. 2 elaborates on the theoretical and technological foundations underpinning this work; Sect. 3 provides an analysis of related works and delineates the unique contributions of our proposal; Sect. 4 introduces the graphical provenance modeling tool, detailing its alignment with the W3C PROV standard and the Ecore metamodel constructed to represent the PROV-DM data model; Sect. 5 demonstrates the application of the proposed tool in modeling data provenance across various domains; and finally, Sect. 6 presents the concluding remarks and outlines potential directions for future research.

2   Background

This section provides the necessary background for understanding the foundational concepts and key technologies underlying data provenance modeling and representation.

2.1   Data Provenance

In a broad context, the concept of *provenance* encompasses information that elucidates the production process of a product, whether it be a data entity or a physical object [9]. The W3C Provenance Working Group[1] defines provenance as "information about entities, activities, and people involved in producing a piece of data or thing, which can be used to form assessments about its quality, reliability or trustworthiness." The term is derived from the Latin *prōvenīre*, meaning "coming from."

Data provenance encapsulates the lineage of an object's origins, encompassing all modifications it has undergone, the components involved in its transmission or processing, and the users who have interacted with it [17]. Specifically, "data provenance" denotes the mechanisms and methodologies utilized to capture and document information concerning the origin of data and the transformations that have influenced its current state. This compilation of information is commonly referred to as "provenance data," "provenance information," or "provenance record."

According to Pérez et al. [27], through the incorporation of specialized metadata, data provenance facilitates the explicit representation of various aspects related to the data creation process. This includes identifying the individuals or entities involved in data production, such as authors, reviewers, and contributors. Furthermore, data provenance enables a comprehensive view of the revision chain, allowing users to trace the evolution and history of the data. This chronological record offers valuable insights into the data's lineage, assisting in quality assurance, error detection, and reproducibility. Moreover, when managing integrated data from diverse sources, data provenance facilitates the identification of specific origins and the processes through which different segments of the data were derived or transformed. This provenance information enhances data integration by enabling users to comprehend the origins and transformations applied to integrated data. Additionally, data provenance captures the vocabularies, ontologies, and rules utilized during the data generation process, facilitating improved comprehension and interpretation of the data, thereby enhancing its utility for meaningful analysis.

---

[1] https://www.w3.org/2011/prov/.

Data provenance serves essential purposes across various application domains [7, 27]. In open information systems, it aids in determining data origins and identifying responsible entities for its creation. In scientific applications, provenance provides insights into how research results were derived, ensuring transparency and reproducibility. In the realm of news, provenance plays a crucial role in verifying the origins and references of blogs and news items, thereby enhancing credibility and trustworthiness. In legal contexts, provenance supports document and data licensing, attribution, and privacy management. In IoT applications, data provenance spans supply chains, health monitoring systems, digital forensics, and various intelligent IoT services [10]. Across these diverse domains, provenance ensures accountability, authenticity, and supports informed decision-making [9].

2.2   W3C PROV Family of Documents

The PROV Family of Documents (W3C PROV), introduced by the W3C Provenance Working Group, comprises a comprehensive framework that includes a model, associated serializations, and supplementary definitions. This framework establishes standardized representations and interoperable mechanisms, enabling seamless sharing of provenance data across diverse platforms and systems.

As illustrated in Fig. 1, in W3C PROV, provenance can be represented as three central figures: *Entity*, *Agent*, and *Activity* [6]:

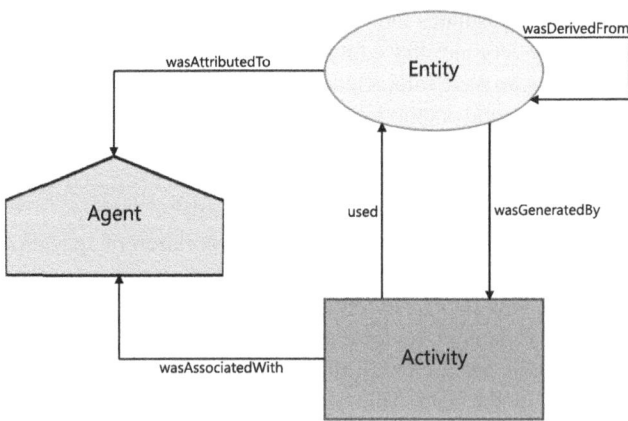

Fig. 1. Main components and their interactions within the W3C PROV Data Model. Adapted from: [6].

– *Entities* represent diverse elements that can be physical, digital, conceptual, or other types. Provenance records are essential in detailing the lineage and origin of entities, documenting their creation, modification, and sources. An entity's provenance may involve multiple other entities, establishing connections and dependencies within the broader scope of data and information.

- *Activities* are processes through which entities are created and undergo changes, resulting in the emergence of new entities. These activities often involve utilizing pre-existing entities to achieve their objectives, facilitating the transformation of attributes and characteristics. Activities encompass dynamic elements of the world, such as actions, processes, and other similar phenomena. For example, translating a document D to create document D_t constitutes an activity.
- An *Agent* can be attributed with varying degrees of responsibility for an ongoing activity. Agents can be individuals, software components, organizations, or other entities deemed accountable. For instance, in a scenario involving the creation of a statistical chart using linear regression, both the creator of the chart and the software employed can be considered agents involved in the activity.

Between these three main elements, there can be various relationships. The naming of PROV relations is specifically designed to facilitate their usage in assertions about historical events occurred in the past, as PROV primarily serves to describe processes of creation or derivation. Examples of such relations include:

- *wasGeneratedBy*: Activities *generate* new entities. For example, writing a document generates the document itself, while revising it creates a new version. Generation does not always occur at the end of an activity.
- *used*: Activities also make *use* of entities. For example, reviewing a document to correct spelling errors uses the original version and a list of corrections. The use of an entity does not always occur at the beginning of an activity.
- *wasAssociatedWith*: When an Agent has some level of responsibility in an activity, the agent is *associated with* the activity. Multiple agents can be associated with an activity and vice versa. For example, when creating a chart using specific software, the person who created the chart and the software used can be considered involved agents.
- *wasAttributedTo*: It is also possible to describe that an entity is *attributed to* an agent to express the agent's responsibility for the entity. This description can mean that the agent was accountable for the activity that generated the entity.

The PROV data model incorporates PROV Notation (PROV-N) [26], providing concise examples and serializations of PROV instances for human comprehension. PROV-N simplifies the translation of the PROV data model into concrete syntax and forms the basis for a formal semantics of PROV.

Furthermore, it is also possible to represent provenance graphically, using the layout conventions defined by W3C PROV[2]. Entities, activities and agents are represented as nodes, with yellow oval, blue rectangular, and orange "pentagon houses" shapes, respectively. Their relationships are represented as directed edges. This representation is also referred to as a *provenance graph* [24].

Figure 2 illustrates a concrete instance of a provenance record, showcasing the process of writing a journalistic article relying on a government-provided database. Both the graphical representation and the PROV-N notation code of this particular example,

---

[2] https://www.w3.org/2011/prov/wiki/Diagrams.

originally introduced by [24], was developed under the proposed graphical data provenance modeling tool, which is detailed in Sect. 4. Figure 2(a) presents the provenance
graph, while Fig. 2(b) shows the same provenance record in PROV-N notation. In this
example, journalist Bob is represented by the agent *nowpeople:Bob*, to whom the task of
writing the article specified by the entity *now:employment-article-v1.html* is attributed.
This attribution is denoted by the *wasAttributedTo* relationship. The writing of the article occurred through the activity *is:writeArticle*, as indicated by the *wasGeneratedBy*
relationship. Additionally, the *used* relationship indicates that the activity of writing the
article utilized the entity *govftp:oesm11st.zip*, representing the governmental database,
and hence the article was derived from it, as indicated by the *wasDerivedFrom* relationship.

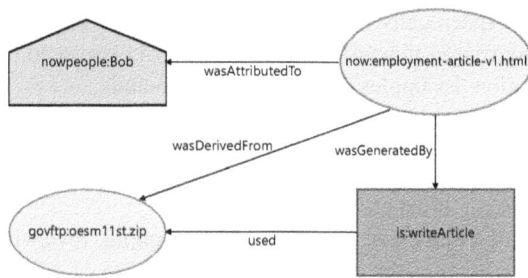

(a) Graphical representation

```
 1   document
 2      prefix is <http://www.provbook.org/nownews/is/>
 3      prefix now <http://www.provbook.org/nownews/>
 4      prefix nowpeople <http://www.provbook.org/nownews/people/>
 5      prefix govftp <ftp://ftp.bls.gov/pub/special.requests/oes/>
 6
 7      entity(now:employment-article-v1.html)
 8      entity(govftp:oesm11st.zip)
 9      activity(is:writeArticle)
10      wasGeneratedBy(now:employment-article-v1.html, is:writeArticle, -)
11      used(is:writeArticle, govftp:oesm11st.zip, -)
12      wasDerivedFrom(now:employment-article-v1.html, govftp:oesm11st.zip)
13      agent(nowpeople:Bob)
14      wasAttributedTo(now:employment-article-v1.html, nowpeople:Bob)
15   endDocument
```

(b) PROV-N notation

Fig. 2. Example of a provenance record in W3C PROV [31]. Adapted from: [24].

In the W3C PROV standard, the namespace[3] concept ensures unique identification
and avoids naming conflicts among entities, activities, agents, and other elements within
the provenance data. A namespace serves as a distinct identifier, typically represented
by a URI (Uniform Resource Identifier), that provides a globally unique name for a
particular element. By associating elements with namespaces, the W3C PROV standard enables interoperability and unambiguous referencing of provenance information
across different systems and domains. In W3C PROV, the namespaces are identified by

---

[3] https://www.w3.org/ns/prov/.

the following URIs and denoted by corresponding prefixes. For instance, in Fig. 2, *now-people:Bob* consists of a prefix and a local name, separated by a colon. From a qualified name, one can derive a URI by concatening the namespace URI denoted by the prefix and the local name. Hence, *nowpeople:Bob* denotes the URI http://www.provbook.org/nownews/people/Bob [24]. By employing namespace conventions, W3C PROV allows for the integration and exchange of provenance data while maintaining consistency and disambiguation of element names within the larger context of data provenance.

2.3 Model-Driven Engineering

Model-Driven Engineering (MDE) is a systematic software development approach that revolves around creating, manipulating, and utilizing models as foundational artifacts throughout the software lifecycle [4, 29]. It emphasizes using models to capture system aspects such as architecture, behavior, and requirements, serving as abstractions that encapsulate essential system characteristics. This facilitates analysis, reasoning, and transformation crucial for supporting the software engineering process.

Domain-Specific Modeling Languages (DSMLs) are instrumental in constructing these models and are defined by metamodels that specify their structure and semantics [18]. DSMLs provide specialized languages tailored to specific domains, enabling developers to create models that accurately represent the concepts and relationships pertinent to those domains. In this context, a metamodel serves as "a model that defines the structure of a modeling language" [28], offering a formal description encompassing syntax, semantics, and constraints [3].

Similar to natural languages, DSMLs comprise two primary components [18]: abstract syntax and concrete syntax. Abstract syntax defines the concepts and relationships within the language, while concrete syntax maps these concepts to visual representations used in modeling tools. The semantics of a DSML pertains to the meaning conveyed by its syntactic elements, ensuring clarity and precision in model interpretation and manipulation.

2.4 Eclipse Modeling Framework

The Eclipse Modeling Framework (EMF) [30] is a robust modeling framework integrated within the Eclipse Integrated Development Environment (IDE). EMF offers a comprehensive suite of tools for creating, manipulating, and validating models and metamodels. A pivotal feature of EMF is its capability to generate executable code from models, facilitating the automatic creation of Java implementations corresponding to defined metamodels. This mechanism maps each metaclass in the metamodel to a corresponding Java class, enabling developers to instantiate these classes to produce instances that precisely conform to the metamodel's specifications.

EMF comprises three main components:

– The *Ecore* meta-metamodel serves as the foundational language for defining metamodels within EMF. It supports essential features such as change notification, XML Metadata Interchange (XMI) serialization for persistence, and a reflective Application Programming Interface (API) for manipulating EMF objects.

- *EMF.Edit* provides reusable classes for constructing editors for EMF models. This includes content and label providers, support for properties, and a command framework that enables automatic undo and redo operations in JFace-based editors.
- *EMF.Codegen* offers a code generation facility for creating comprehensive editors tailored to EMF models. It includes a graphical user interface for configuring generation options and invoking generators, and integrates with Eclipse Java Development Tooling (JDT) for enhanced functionality.

Metamodels in EMF are constructed using the Ecore meta-metamodel, which itself is based on the Meta Object Facility (MOF) meta-metamodel [30]. When defining metamodels with Ecore, developers utilize class instances such as `EClass`, `EAttribute`, `EReference`, `ESuperType`, and `EDataType` to specify structure, relationships, and properties.

In conjunction with EMF, other Eclipse projects synergistically enhance its capabilities. For example, Eclipse Sirius facilitates the creation of domain-specific model editors tailored to specific metamodels, empowering users to visually manipulate instances of their models. Meanwhile, Eclipse Acceleo specializes in model-to-text (M2T) transformations, allowing for the automatic generation of textual artifacts from EMF models. The subsequent subsections provide detailed insights into these supplementary Eclipse tools, elucidating their roles and contributions within the broader context of MDE and software development.

2.5   Eclipse Sirius

Eclipse Sirius[4] is an Eclipse project designed to facilitate the creation of customized graphical modeling workbenches. It empowers architects to develop domain-specific modelers that are perfectly suited precisely to their business domains. Sirius builds upon the Eclipse Modeling Framework (EMF), allowing architects to specify modelers declaratively using a description model. This specification includes defining domain elements, visual styling, and behavioral characteristics.

Architects utilize Sirius to create these specifications, generating description models that are deployed as Eclipse plug-ins. A notable feature of Sirius is its inherent support for dynamic and incremental development, enabling architects to make real-time modifications to modeler definitions, ensuring adaptability to evolving business requirements.

On the other hand, end-users benefit from the Sirius runtime, which interprets the modeler description models to present them with interactive graphical editors within the Eclipse workbench. This runtime environment faithfully represents the specified visual and behavioral attributes of the models, allowing users to explore and manipulate their business models using predefined tools and interaction modes.

The integration of Sirius tooling and runtime components seamlessly supports the specification, deployment, and interaction with domain-specific modelers within the Eclipse environment. Sirius's capability for dynamic and incremental development empowers architects to respond quickly to changing business needs, ensuring that the

---

[4] https://eclipse.dev/sirius/.

graphical modelers remain effective tools for visualization and manipulation in dynamic business environments.

2.6 Eclipse Acceleo

Eclipse Acceleo[5] is an open-source template-based source code generation technology developed within the Eclipse Foundation. It is designed to facilitate the creation of custom code generators, offering robust integration within the Eclipse IDE environment and standalone capabilities for code generation outside of Eclipse.

Acceleo provides extensive Eclipse IDE integration, featuring syntax highlighting, real-time error detection, quick fixes, and dedicated views that streamline the design and navigation of code generators. This integration supports various code generation design patterns and enhances user productivity.

A significant feature of Acceleo is its support for incremental generation. This capability allows developers to manually modify generated code while preserving these changes across subsequent regeneration cycles. Acceleo achieves this by defining protected areas within the generated code where modifications are safeguarded from being overwritten.

Furthermore, Acceleo includes the Acceleo Query Language (AQL) [5], which facilitates navigation and querying of Ecore (meta)models. AQL offers advanced features such as robust validation and the ability to invoke methods defined through Java services, thereby improving the flexibility and functionality of code generation processes.

3 Related Work

This section reviews relevant literature, comparing existing works with the outcomes of this research. It identifies gaps in current data provenance modeling field and discusses how this study aims to address them.

3.1 PROV Python

PROV Python[6] is a Python package for managing and visualizing W3C PROV documents, focusing on data provenance and analytics. It supports in-memory classes for PROV assertions, exporting them in PROV-N notation, and offers serialization/deserialization in formats such as PROV-O, PROV-XML, and PROV-JSON, facilitating platform integration and data exchange. The package also enables exporting PROV documents to graphical formats like PDF, PNG, and SVG, and supports interaction with ProvStore, detailed in the next section.

Figure 3(a) illustrates the PROV graph of an example data provenance record, while Fig. 3(b) shows its representation in PROV Python [12]. In this example, Bob, designated as *agent* ag2, participated in *activity* a1, categorized as edit, which started

---

[5] https://eclipse.dev/acceleo/.
[6] https://pypi.org/project/prov/.

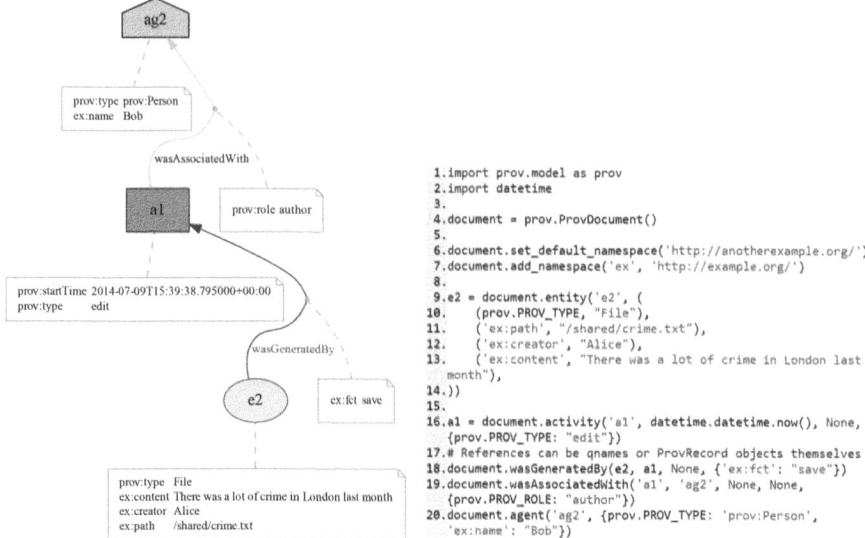

(a) PROV graph of a data provenance record   **(b)** Data provenance record in PROV Python

Fig. 3. Example of a provenance record representation in PROV graph and PROV Python. Adapted from: [12].

on July 9th, 2014, at 3:39:38 PM, the time the PROV Python code was executed. The *wasAssociatedWith* relationship denotes Bob as the author of this *activity*. Moreover, a1 resulted in the creation of *entity* e2, as indicated by the *wasGeneratedBy* relationship. Annotations for *entity* e2 classify it as a File and provide further details such as content description, original creator, and file path.

3.2   ProvStore

ProvStore[7] is a web service built on the PROV Python [11] package, utilizing the W3C PROV specification to manage provenance documents. It offers a user-friendly web interface and a RESTful API with API key-based and OAuth [8] authentication for programmatic access. The platform supports storing provenance documents with private or public access, promoting collaboration and data sharing. It accommodates multiple serialization formats, including PROV-N, PROV-JSON, PROV-XML, and RDF in Turtle [1] or TriG [2] formats.

ProvStore employs a folder-based structure for document management and provides visualization tools for graphical representation, as shown in Fig. 4. It delivers detailed metrics such as assertion counts and network metrics derived from document graphs. Additionally, it supports integration with other systems and enables real-time publication of data provenance through its RESTful API.

---

[7] https://openprovenance.org/store/.

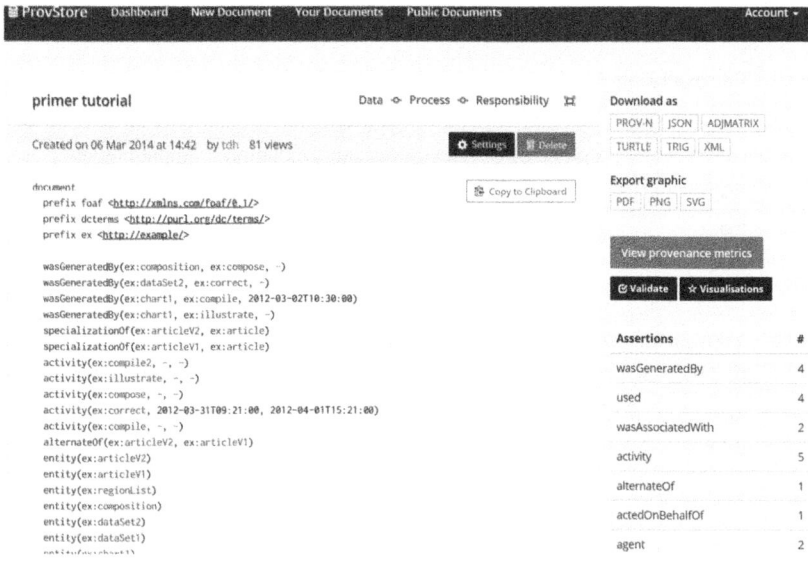

Fig. 4. The ProvStore interface for managing provenance documents [13].

3.3 ProvToolbox

ProvToolbox[8] is a Java library developed by the W3C Provenance Working Group to create Java representations of the W3C PROV Data Model (PROV-DM). It supports conversion of PROV-DM instances into formats such as RDF, PROV-XML, PROV-N, and PROV-JSON, as listed in Table 1.

ProvToolbox includes command-line utilities, Application Programming Interfaces (APIs), and graphical interfaces for various provenance-related tasks. Additional functionalities include parsing and serializing provenance documents, performing consistency checks, generating visualizations, and integrating data provenance into existing systems.

3.4 Discussion

The W3C Provenance Working Group maintains a comprehensive list[9] of implementations adhering to the W3C PROV standard. The list is regularly updated and currently includes 63 implementations such as the previously mentioned PROV Python and ProvToolbox. While these tools excel in adhering to the W3C PROV specifications, aiding in the recording, management, and transformation of data provenance across various formats, they generally lack direct support for graphical representations and conversion to formats like PROV-N. In fact, to the best of the authors' knowledge, no existing tool enables graphical modeling of provenance.

---

[8] https://lucmoreau.github.io/ProvToolbox/.

[9] https://www.w3.org/TR/prov-implementations/.

Table 1. ProvToolbox compatibility with different formats. Adapted from: [21].

File extension	File format	I/O Type
gv, dot	text/vnd.graphviz	output
prov-asn, pn, asn, provn	text/provenance-notation	input/output
rdf	application/rdf+xml	input/output
json	application/json	input/output
ttl	text/turtle	input/output
trig	application/trig	input/output
jpg, jpeg	image/jpeg	output
provx, xml	application/provenance+xml	input/output
png	image/png	output
pdf	application/pdf	output
svg	image/svg+xml	output

This paper introduces a graphical provenance modeling tool discussed in detail in the subsequent section, addressing these limitations by offering intuitive creation of graphical models compliant with the W3C PROV standard. It enables direct graphical representation and conversion of these models to PROV-N notation. These advancements provide developers with new tools to integrate provenance management into software systems, bridging theoretical rigor with practical application.

By enabling visual manipulation and export of data relationships in both graphical and textual formats, this research enhances the accessibility and usability of data provenance. It also pioneers new methods for integrating provenance into software development processes, making significant contributions that fill existing gaps in data provenance modeling.

4   Graphical Data Provenance Modeling Tool

The data provenance modeling tool presented in this work fills a gap in current tools by enabling graphical modeling of data provenance under the W3C PROV standard. Similar to modeling other software aspects, provenance modeling allows visualization of dependencies and relationships within data created, transformed, or manipulated by the software. The modeling tool's graphical interface enhances usability, offering interactive visualization of provenance models to developers. Once designed, developers can generate PROV-N codes and instrument their software to record provenance at desired levels of granularity, determining what data to capture, when, and how often.

The development of the graphical data provenance modeling tool followed a systematic approach across three stages: (1) converting the PROV-DM data model into an Ecore metamodel, named Ecore4PROV-DM; (2) constructing a graphical modeling tool based on this metamodel; and (3) developing model-to-text transformation (M2T) templates to convert the provenance models designed in the tool into PROV-N code instances. Detailed descriptions of each stage follow in subsequent subsections.

4.1 Ecore4PROV-DM Metamodel

During the initial phase of developing the graphical data provenance modeling tool, the PROV-DM data model underwent a transformation into a cohesive Ecore metamodel, serving as the foundational framework for subsequent modeling endeavors. Named Ecore4PROV-DM, this metamodel's conversion process closely adhered to the specifications outlined in the W3C PROV standard [25], as detailed comprehensively in our previous work [32]. This rigorous adherence ensured that the resulting metamodel conforms meticulously to established standards and guidelines.

Figure 5 depicts the Ecore4PROV-DM metamodel, which serves as a foundational framework for representing data provenance concepts. The metamodel's semantics are defined by the relationships between metaclasses, as indicated by edges, and their respective multiplicities, denoted numerically. Key elements of the metamodel, highlighted in blue, encompass fundamental concepts such as *Entity*, *Activity*, and *Agent*. These elements are essential for capturing and formalizing the relationships and attributes that characterize provenance instances in accordance with the W3C PROV standard.

PROV-DM is categorized into six distinct components, each grouping members according to specific purposes [25]. The Ecore4PROV-DM metamodel was developed based on this component-based approach, structured as follows:

- **Component 1 - Entities and Activities:** define relationships between an *Entity* and an *Activity*, specifically, *used* (Use), *wasGeneratedBy* (Generation), *wasStartedBy* (Start), *wasEndedBy* (End), *wasInvalidatedBy* (Invalidation), and *wasInformedBy* (Communication). This component is represented in Ecore4PROV-DM in yellow color.
- **Component 2 - Derivations:** covers the derivation of entities from other entities and their subtypes. An *Entity* may be derived (*wasDerivedFrom*) from another entity, including specific types like revision (*wasRevisionOf*), citation (*wasQuotedFrom*), or primary source (*hadPrimarySource*), each potentially related to an *Activity*. Represented in red color.
- **Component 3 - Agents, Responsibility, Influence:** addresses agents and the relationships that represent their responsibility and influence over an entity or activity. Contains the metaclasses *Entity*, *Activity*, and *Agent*, and the relationships *wasAttributedTo* (Attribution), *wasAssociatedWith* (Association), and *actedOnBehalfOf* (Delegation). Represented in green color.
- **Component 4 - Bundles:** refers to a mechanism for supporting the provenance of provenance. Contains the *Bundle* metaclass, which is defined as a specialization of the *Entity* metaclass. Represented in purple color.
- **Component 5 - Alternatives:** allows expressing alternatives or specializations of entities. Contains the *Entity* metaclass and two binary associations: *alternateOf* (Alternative) and *specializationOf* (Specialization).
- **Component 6 - Collections:** concerns the notion of collections. A collection is an entity that has members, which are themselves entities whose provenance can be expressed. Contains the metaclass *Collection*, a specialization of the *Entity* metaclass, and *EmptyCollection*, a specialization of *Collection*. Represented in orange color.

It is worth noting that there are two methods for implementing relationships between metaclasses in EMF: "element-based edges," where a metaclass acts as an intermediary between two other related metaclasses; and "relation-based edges," where metaclasses are directly connected by an edge. The former is beneficial when representing relationships as actual classes during metamodel instantiation, simplifying navigation through model components, crucial for writing templates in the AQL language for model-to-text transformations, as detailed in Subsect. 4.3. Both forms of relationships are present in Ecore4PROV-DM.

The *Attributes* and *AttributeValue* metaclasses, shown in grey in Fig. 5, are utilized to instantiate attribute-value pairs that can be associated with most of the other Ecore4PROV-DM metaclasses.

Ecore4PROV-DM Metamodel Evaluation. An evaluation was conducted by a panel of metamodeling experts to assess the completeness and correctness of Ecore4PROV-DM in relation to the PROV data model (PROV-DM). This evaluation followed the Metamodel Quality Requirements and Evaluation (MQuaRE) framework proposed by Kudo et al. [14–16], which outlines 19 Metamodel Quality Requirements (MQRs) and associated quality measures. The evaluation process encompassed five phases: (1) defining evaluation requirements, (2) specifying the evaluation, (3) designing the evaluation, (4) executing the evaluation, and (5) concluding the evaluation.

The evaluation methodology involved providing the evaluators with two comprehensive foundational documents to ensure a thorough understanding of the context and subject matter. The first document detailed fundamental concepts of data provenance and elaborated on the specifics of the PROV-DM data model. The second document offered an in-depth explanation of the implementation of Ecore4PROV-DM within the Eclipse Modeling Framework (EMF). To facilitate a clear and detailed examination, the experts were also supplied with a high-resolution image of the Ecore4PROV-DM class diagram, allowing them to visually inspect the metamodel's structure and relationships. After reviewing both documents and examining the class diagram, evaluators completed a questionnaire. This questionnaire covered personal details, including their educational background and prior knowledge of data provenance and metamodeling. It also included inquiries regarding the provided support documents and specific questions about Ecore4PROV-DM, aiming to assess its completeness and accuracy concerning alignment with the PROV-DM data model.

The evaluation questionnaire was designed to assess three of the MQRs (Metamodel Quality Requirements) proposed by the MQuaRE framework. Specifically, it targeted MQR02, which evaluates the completeness of the metamodel by assessing its coverage of the concepts specified in the PROV-DM data model. It also addressed MQR03, which examines the correctness of the metamodel, ensuring that it accurately represents PROV-DM concepts. Finally, MQR07, a usability requirement, gauged the proportion of the metamodel's concepts that are readily evident and easily identifiable to users. These MQRs were selected due to their alignment with the research objectives, enabling the evaluation of the metamodel's accuracy, comprehensiveness, and user-friendliness in terms of correctly encompassing PROV-DM concepts.

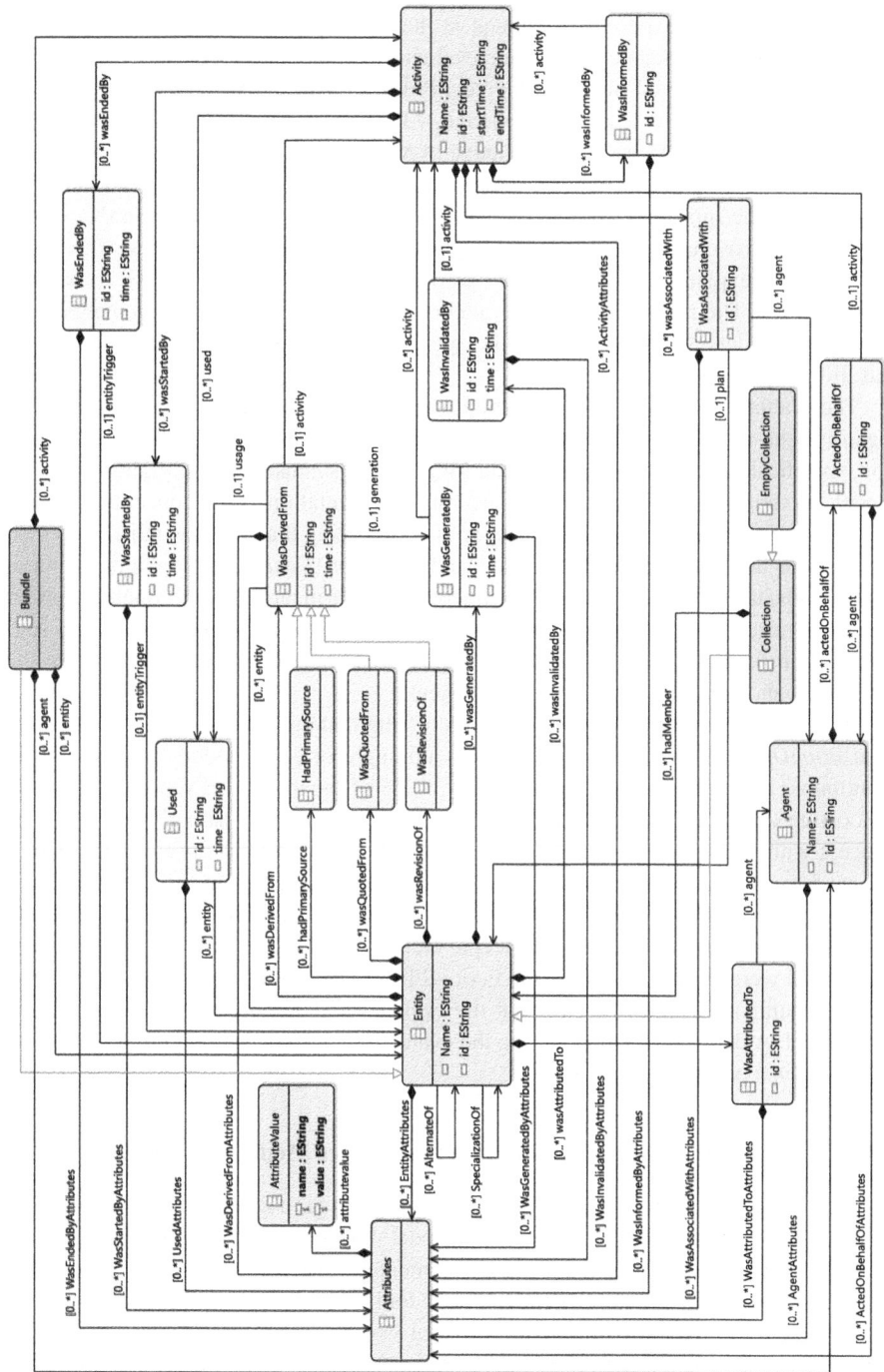

Fig. 5. Ecore4PROV-DM: An Ecore metamodel representation of the W3C PROV Data Model (PROV-DM) [31].

A total of fifteen experts participated in the evaluation process, all of whom held degrees in Computer Science. Only one evaluator had an undergraduate degree, while the others had completed master's degrees, PhDs, or were currently pursuing a PhD. In terms of the evaluators' prior knowledge, 73.3% were unfamiliar with the concept of data provenance, 20% had no knowledge of Model-Driven Engineering (MDE), and 26.7% were not acquainted with the Eclipse Modeling Framework (EMF). Concerning the clarity of the support documents provided, 93.4% of the evaluators found the document on data provenance and PROV-DM to be easily comprehensible, while 80% found the document explaining the implementation of Ecore4PROV-DM in EMF to be easy to understand. The remainder of the evaluators pointed out that both documents were sufficiently understandable. None of the specialists pointed out that either document was difficult to understand.

The evaluation results show unanimous agreement among the participating experts regarding the seamless alignment of Ecore4PROV-DM with the PROV-DM specification, specifically addressing MQR02 and MQR03. This consensus highlights the metamodel's comprehensive coverage and accurate representation of the concepts specified in the PROV-DM data model. However, it is worth noting that one specialist expressed reservations about the modeling of the "End" concept (*wasEndedBy*) within Component 1, indicating potential areas for refinement or clarification. Additionally, another specialist raised concerns about the implementation of Component 4 (*Bundles*), suggesting that further review and potential adjustments may be necessary to ensure the robustness and completeness of this component.

In the context of MQR07, the evaluators highlighted that the "Specialization" (*specializationOf*) concept within Component 5, although correctly modeled, was not easily identifiable in the metamodel. Specifically, 33.3% of the evaluators reported difficulty in locating this concept within the model. Additionally, the "Member" (*hadMember*) concept within Component 6 and the "Alternative" (*alternateOf*) concept within Component 5 were noted as less evident, with 26.6% of the evaluators indicating challenges in identifying these concepts. Despite these observations, the evaluators generally found that the majority of the forty-four concepts included within the six components of the PROV-DM were clearly evident in the Ecore4PROV-DM metamodel. Figure 6 provides a visual summary of the concepts that the evaluators identified as less evident in the metamodel. A detailed report outlining the evaluation process and its findings has been published in a previous work [32].

4.2   Development of the Graphical Data Provenance Modeling Tool

The second stage focused on the construction of the graphical modeling tool itself. Drawing upon the Ecore4PROV-DM metamodel developed in the previous stage, the concrete syntax of the metamodel was implemented using the diagram perspective of Eclipse Sirius, employing the Obeo Designer[10] tool. The selection of the Obeo Designer tool for the development of the modeling tool was based on its seamless integration with EMF, Acceleo, and Sirius, as well as its capability to switch perspectives during

---

[10] https://www.obeodesigner.com/.

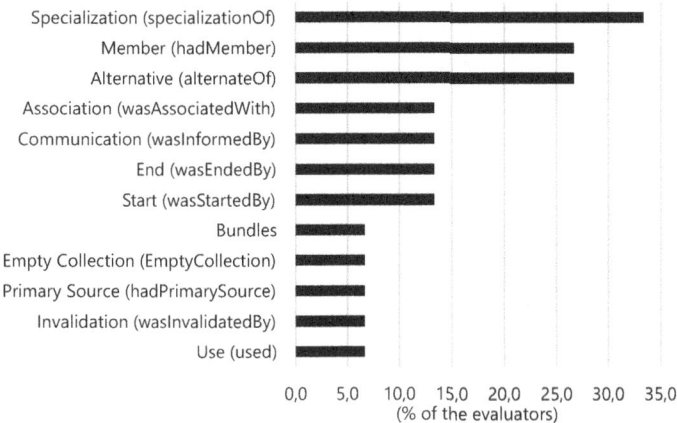

Fig. 6. PROV-DM concepts identified by evaluators as not easily identifiable in the Ecore4PROV-DM metamodel (MQR07).

the modeling process. This approach facilitated the creation of an intuitive and visually expressive modeling environment.

Incorporating style definitions compliant with the W3C PROV standard ensured that graphical models adhered to recommended visual representations and conventions. Entities are depicted as yellow oval nodes, activities as blue rectangles, and agents as orange "pentagon houses". Relationships among these elements are represented as directed edges, with labels indicating the type of relationship. Figure 7 illustrates the Sirius Specification Editor in Obeo Designer, where elements of the Ecore4PROV-DM metamodel were visually mapped to graphical elements, maintaining alignment with PROV-DM style specifications.

4.3   Model-to-Text Transformation

In the third stage of graphical data provenance modeling tool development, templates were developed within Eclipse Acceleo to encompass every element comprising the six components delineated by the data model (PROV-DM). This effort aimed to enable the conversion of the provenance model designed in the graphical modeling tool into PROV notation (PROV-N) code. Each template adhered strictly to the language syntax guidelines outlined in the PROV-DM documentation [24]. This phase was pivotal in providing a robust modeling tool, harnessing the foundational concepts of the PROV data model while harnessing the expressive capabilities inherent in the PROV-N notation.

Figure 8 presents a code snippet that exemplifies the implementation within Eclipse Acceleo, leveraging Acceleo Query Language (AQL) features to interact with the classes embedded in the Ecore metamodel. The primary objective of this code is to translate components of the W3C PROV graphical model into PROV-N code format. Specifically, it focuses on generating code that encompasses entities and their associ-

Fig. 7. Mapping Ecore4PROV-DM metamodel elements to PROV-DM specifications using the Sirius Specification Editor.

ated attribute-value pairs, as well as establishing relationships such as *alternateOf* and *specializationOf*.

An overview of the graphical provenance modeling tool is presented in Fig. 9. On the rightmost part of the editor is the Element Palette (a), where it is possible to select among the three main elements of the W3C PROV standard – Activity, Agent, and Entity – and add them to the graphical model by simply dragging them to the Diagram area (b). Once added, clicking on the element in the diagram area allows editing its Properties (d) to add or modify its relationships with other model elements. The same can be accomplished using the Tree Editor (c) of the graphical model.

Upon completion of the graphical modeling process or at any stage within it, the execution of the modeling tool can be triggered by clicking on the Execute icon (e). This action generates the corresponding PROV-N code that represents the constructed graphical model. The generated PROV-N code captures the model's relationships, attributes, and structure, providing a textual representation of the provenance information encoded within the graphical representation.

```
 5 [template public generateElement(b : Bundle)]
 6 [comment @main/]
 7 [file ('teste.provn', false, 'UTF-8')]
 8 document
 9 [comment][for (item:Entity | b.ancestors(Entity))]
10 teste: [item.Name/]
11 [/for][/comment]
12 [comment]3.1 Component 1: Entities and Activities
   [/comment]
13 [comment 3.1.1 entity /]
14 [for (e:Entity | b.eContents(Entity))]
15    [comment entity attributes/]
16    [if(e.EntityAttributes->notEmpty())]
17    entity([e.Name/], ['['/] [for (att:Attributes |
   e.EntityAttributes)][for(atts:AttributeValue |
   att.attributevalue) separator(', ')]
   [atts.name/]='[atts.value/]'[/for][/for][ ' ] )' /]
18    [else]
19    entity([e.Name/])
20    [/if]
21 [comment]3.5 Component 5: Alternate Entities
   [/comment]
22 [comment 3.5.1 entity alternateOf entity /]
23    [for (ea:Entity | e.AlternateOf)]
24    alternateOf([e.Name/], [ea.Name/])
25    [/for]
26 [comment 3.5.2 entity specializationOf entity /]
27    [for (ea:Entity | e.SpecializationOf)]
28    specializationOf([e.Name/], [ea.Name/])
29    [/for]
30 [/for]
```

Fig. 8. Code snippet in Eclipse Acceleo for transforming W3C PROV graphical model elements into PROV-N notation.

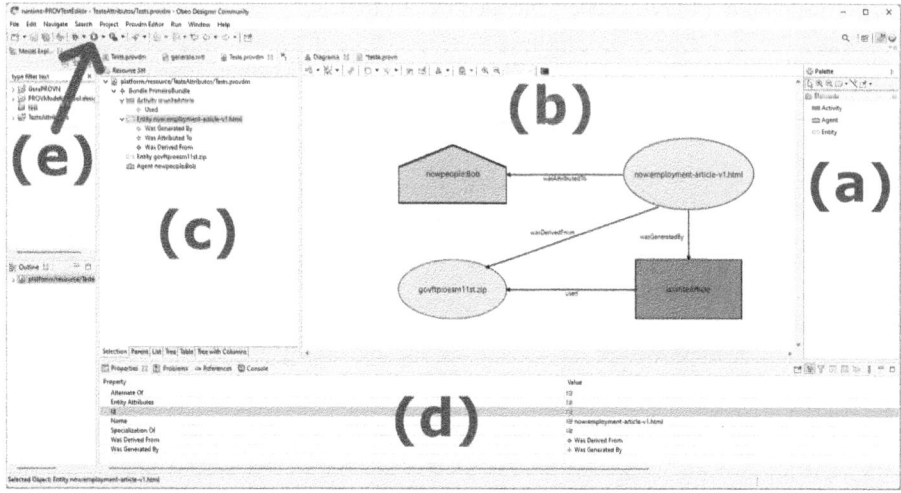

Fig. 9. MDE-based graphical tool for modeling data provenance according to the W3C PROV standard [31].

5   Modeling Data Provenance Graphically

In this section, we illustrate the practical application of the graphical data provenance modeling tool. Following the modeling of each example, the tool automatically generates corresponding PROV-N code. Subsequently, we conducted a thorough manual validation process to ensure the accuracy and validity of the generated PROV-N code. This validation was performed using the PROV document validation service hosted on the Open Provenance website[11]. This validation process confirms that the tool reliably produces PROV-N representations that adhere to the W3C PROV standard.

5.1   Image Acquisition via Sensors

The initial example showcases the graphical modeling of a provenance model sourced from ProvStore[12], a cloud-based repository for provenance data.

This model originates from the Urban Observatory project at Newcastle University in the United Kingdom, which monitors urban indicators using active sensors and CCTV cameras. Due to space limitations, only a segment of this provenance model has been modeled within our tool. Specifically, we have focused on the bundle concerning the data collected during image acquisition from sensors. This segment includes entities such as *var:sensor* and *var:image*, alongside the activity *var:acquisition*, each with its associated properties and values describing the data collection process. Figure 10 depicts the graphical representation of the provenance model, while Fig. 11 displays the corresponding PROV-N code generated by our tool.

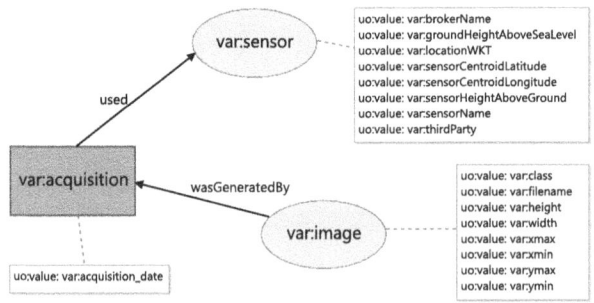

Fig. 10. Graphical provenance model depicting an image acquisition process [31].

---

[11] https://openprovenance.org/service/validator.html.
[12] https://openprovenance.org/store/documents/497.

```
1   document
2     prefix uo <http://urbanobservatory.ac.uk/uo#>
3     prefix var <http://openprovenance.org/var#>
4
5 ▾   entity(var:sensor, [ uo:value='var:brokerName',
6                          uo:value='var:groundHeightAboveSeaLevel',
7                          uo:value='var:locationWKT',
8                          uo:value='var:sensorCentroidLatitude',
9                          uo:value='var:sensorCentroidLongitude',
10                         uo:value='var:sensorHeightAboveGround',
11                         uo:value='var:sensorName',
12                         uo:value='var:thirdParty' ] )
13 ▾   entity(var:image, [ uo:value='var:class',
14                         uo:value='var:filename',
15                         uo:value='var:height',
16                         uo:value='var:width',
17                         uo:value='var:xmax',
18                         uo:value='var:xmin',
19                         uo:value='var:ymax',
20                         uo:value='var:ymin' ] )
21     activity(var:acquisition, [ uo:value='var:acquisition_date' ] )
22     wasGeneratedBy(var:image, var:acquisition, -)
23     used(var:acquisition, var:sensor, -)
24   endDocument
```

Fig. 11. PROV-N code of the graphical provenance model in Fig. 10.

5.2 Graphical Modeling of Provenance Templates

A provenance template (PROV-Template) [23] serves as a specification in the W3C PROV format, detailing the desired structure of provenance information to be generated. In this approach, variables within the template serve as placeholders for values, delineating how the intended provenance should be produced, captured, or recorded by an application. Bindings stored in an external file establish connections between variables in the template and their corresponding values. When processed using the PROV-Template expansion algorithm, this set of bindings, alongside their associated values and the provenance template itself, generates a provenance document by substituting variables with their values.

Initially, the methodology involves designing a "provenance model" that outlines the structure of the intended provenance data to be generated. Traditionally, this process involves drafting the model on paper and then translating it into PROV-N. However, this approach is outdated and prone to errors. The graphical data provenance modeling tool introduced in this paper offers a modern alternative by allowing interactive graphical design of the provenance model. Once the model is finalized, generating its corresponding PROV-N code becomes a straightforward task. This generated code, along with a "binding" file and data from the designated database, serves as input to the expansion algorithm.

Figure 12 provides a visualization of the provenance model described in [22], illustrating an arithmetic operation such as the addition of two values to produce a third value. In this model, the specific type of arithmetic operation is represented by the activity *var:operation*, which utilizes two input values identified as entities *var:consumed1* and *var:consumed2*. The result of this operation is represented by the entity *var:produced*, which is triggered by an *var:agent*. Figure 13 presents the automatically generated PROV-N code corresponding to this provenance model, generated using the graphical modeling tool.

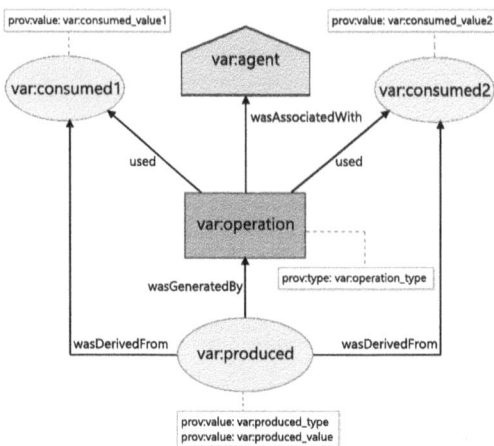

Fig. 12. Graphical provenance model depicting a PROV-Template [31].

```
 1  document
 2    prefix var <http://openprovenance.org/var#>
 3
 4    entity(var:consumed1, [ prov:value='var:consumed_value1' ] )
 5    entity(var:consumed2, [ prov:value='var:consumed_value2' ] )
 6    entity(var:produced, [ prov:value='var:produced_type',
 7                            prov:value='var:produced_value' ] )
 8    activity(var:operation, [ prov:type='var:operation_type' ] )
 9    wasGeneratedBy(var:produced, var:operation, -)
10    used(var:operation, var:consumed1, -)
11    used(var:operation, var:consumed2, -)
12    wasDerivedFrom(var:produced, var:consumed1)
13    wasDerivedFrom(var:produced, var:consumed2)
14    agent(var:agent)
15    wasAssociatedWith(var:operation, var:agent, -)
16  endDocument
```

Fig. 13. PROV-N code of the PROV-Template presented in Fig. 12.

6   Concluding Remarks

This paper has presented an extended version of our work initially published in the proceedings of the 12th International Conference on Model-Based Software and Systems Engineering (MODELSWARD 2024). It introduces a graphical tool designed for modeling data provenance according to the W3C PROV standard. The development process encompassed three key stages: firstly, the conversion of the PROV-DM data model into the Ecore metamodel, named Ecore4PROV-DM; secondly, the construction of the graphical modeling tool using Eclipse Sirius; and thirdly, the utilization of Eclipse Acceleo for model-to-text transformations to generate PROV-N code.

The Ecore4PROV-DM metamodel underwent a rigorous evaluation process by a panel of fifteen metamodeling experts, unanimously confirming its fidelity to the W3C PROV-DM. Ecore4PROV-DM served as the cornerstone for the graphical provenance modeling tool, developed using Eclipse Sirius, and further enhanced through model-to-text transformations facilitated by Eclipse Acceleo, enabling the generation of PROV-N code from graphical representations.

Validation of the graphical provenance modeling tool included modeling example scenarios, with automatic export of their PROV-N code by the tool. This exported code was subsequently validated manually by an external service to ensure its accuracy and compliance with PROV standards.

The presented graphical provenance modeling tool addresses a significant gap by providing an intuitive interface for interactively creating expressive and customizable data provenance models. This capability not only facilitates the visualization and comprehension of provenance relationships and dependencies but also supports the export of PROV-N code from the graphical model, thereby ensuring interoperability and compatibility with existing provenance representations. By empowering developers with these capabilities, the tool facilitates seamless integration of data provenance into software systems, thereby promoting the adoption of provenance-aware applications. Beyond conventional provenance capture, the tool enables users to leverage graphical data modeling for various purposes, including the extraction of provenance information from databases through the PROV-Template approach. By bridging this gap and providing efficient graphical modeling capabilities, the tool contributes to advancing and broadening the implementation of data provenance across diverse domains.

While this paper has demonstrated the tool's effectiveness in certain scenarios, further research is crucial for its comprehensive evaluation. Future studies should focus on conducting usability evaluations and gathering feedback from domain experts to enhance the tool's functionality. This includes exploring usability metrics like learnability, efficiency, and user satisfaction across diverse user groups and application domains.

Additionally, valuable research directions include integrating the graphical provenance modeling tool with existing provenance management systems to assess interoperability with different data management platforms and enhance overall provenance infrastructure capabilities. Evaluating the tool's scalability and performance in managing large-scale datasets and complex provenance graphs in real-world applications will further validate its practical utility and reliability. Further extensions could enable collaborative provenance modeling with version control mechanisms, supporting environments where multiple stakeholders contribute collaboratively. Lastly, exploring the integration of machine learning and AI techniques within the graphical modeling framework could automate aspects like pattern recognition in data flows and predictive analysis of provenance data integrity.

References

1. Beckett, D., Berners-Lee, T., Prud'hommeaux, E., Carothers, G.: RDF 1.1 Turtle - Terse RDF Triple Language (2013). https://www.w3.org/TR/turtle/
2. Bizer, C., Cyganiak, R., Carothers, G., Seaborne, A.: RDF 1.1 TriG - RDF Dataset Language (2013). https://www.w3.org/TR/trig/
3. Bruel, J.-M., et al.: Model transformation reuse across metamodels. In: Rensink, A., Sánchez Cuadrado, J. (eds.) ICMT 2018. LNCS, vol. 10888, pp. 92–109. Springer, Cham (2018). https://doi.org/10.1007/978-3-319-93317-7_4
4. Bucchiarone, A., Cabot, J., Paige, R.F., Pierantonio, A.: Grand challenges in model-driven engineering: an analysis of the state of the research. Softw. Syst. Model. **19**(1), 5–13 (2020). https://doi.org/10.1007/s10270-019-00773-6

5. Eclipse Foundation: Acceleo Query Language - Query and navigate in EMF models (2024). https://wiki.eclipse.org/Acceleo/User_Guide/
6. Gil, Y., et al.: PROV Model Primer (2013). https://www.w3.org/TR/prov-primer/
7. Glavic, B.: Data Provenance. Found. Trends® Databases **9**(3-4), 209–441 (2021). https://doi.org/10.1561/1900000068
8. Hardt, D.: The OAuth 2.0 Authorization Framework. RFC 6749 (2012). https://doi.org/10.17487/RFC6749. https://www.rfc-editor.org/info/rfc6749
9. Herschel, M., Diestelkämper, R., Ben Lahmar, H.: A survey on provenance: What for? What form? What from? VLDB J. **26**(6), 881–906 (2017). https://doi.org/10.1007/s00778-017-0486-1
10. Hu, R., Yan, Z., Ding, W., Yang, L.T.: A survey on data provenance in IoT. World Wide Web **23**(2), 1441–1463 (2019). https://doi.org/10.1007/s11280-019-00746-1
11. Huynh, T.D.: PROV Python - A library for W3C Provenance Data Model supporting PROV-JSON, PROV-XML and PROV-O (RDF) (2020). https://pypi.org/project/prov/
12. Huynh, T.D.: Prov Python package's documentation (2020). https://prov.readthedocs.io
13. Huynh, T.D., Moreau, L.: ProvStore: a public provenance repository. In: Ludäscher, B., Plale, B. (eds.) IPAW 2014. LNCS, vol. 8628, pp. 275–277. Springer, Cham (2015). https://doi.org/10.1007/978-3-319-16462-5_32
14. Kudo, T.N.: A metamodel for aligning requirements standards and testing standards and a framework for evaluating metamodels [in Portuguese]. Ph.D. thesis, Universidade Federal de São Carlos, São Carlos – SP, Brazil (2021)
15. Kudo, T.N., Bulcão-Neto, R.F., Vincenzi, A.M.R.: Metamodel quality requirements and evaluation (MQuaRE). Technical report, Departamento de Computação, UFScar, São Carlos-SP, Brazil (2020). https://doi.org/10.48550/ARXIV.2008.09459, v 2.0
16. Kudo, T.N., Bulcão Neto, R.F., Vincenzi, A.M.R.: Toward a metamodel quality evaluation framework: requirements, model, measures, and process. In: Proceedings of the XXXIV Brazilian Symposium on Software Engineering, SBES 2020, pp. 102–107. Association for Computing Machinery, New York (2020). https://doi.org/10.1145/3422392.3422461
17. Liang, X., Shetty, S., Tosh, D., Kamhoua, C., Kwiat, K., Njilla, L.: ProvChain: a blockchain-based data provenance architecture in cloud environment with enhanced privacy and availability. In: 2017 17th IEEE/ACM International Symposium on Cluster, Cloud and Grid Computing (CCGRID), pp. 468–477. IEEE (2017). https://doi.org/10.1109/CCGRID.2017.8
18. López-Fernández, J.J., Cuadrado, J.S., Guerra, E., de Lara, J.: Example-driven meta-model development. Softw. Syst. Model. **14**(4), 1323–1347 (2013). https://doi.org/10.1007/s10270-013-0392-y
19. Madiot, F., Goubet, L., Begaudeau, S., Chauvin, M., Musset, J., Pupier, A.: Eclipse Acceleo Wiki (2024). https://wiki.eclipse.org/Acceleo/
20. Madiot, F., Paganelli, M.: Eclipse sirius demonstration. P&D@ MoDELS **1554**, 9–11 (2015)
21. Moreau, L.: ProvToolbox - Java library to create and convert W3C PROV data model representations (2016). https://lucmoreau.github.io/ProvToolbox/
22. Moreau, L.: PROV-Template: A Quick Start (2017). https://lucmoreau.wordpress.com/2017/03/30/prov-template-a-quick-start
23. Moreau, L., Batlajery, B.V., Huynh, T.D., Michaelides, D., Packer, H.: A templating system to generate provenance. IEEE Trans. Software Eng. **44**(2), 103–121 (2018). https://doi.org/10.1109/TSE.2017.2659745
24. Moreau, L., Groth, P.: Provenance: An Introduction to PROV. Springer (2013). https://doi.org/10.1007/978-3-031-79450-6
25. Moreau, L., et al.: PROV-DM: The PROV Data Model (2013). https://www.w3.org/TR/prov-dm/
26. Moreau, L., Missier, P., Cheney, J., Soiland-Reyes, S.: PROV-N: The Provenance Notation (2013). https://www.w3.org/TR/prov-n/

27. Pérez, B., Rubio, J., Sáenz-Adán, C.: A systematic review of provenance systems. Knowl. Inf. Syst. **57**(3), 495–543 (2018). https://doi.org/10.1007/s10115-018-1164-3
28. Rodrigues da Silva, A.: Model-driven engineering: a survey supported by the unified conceptual model. Comput. Lang. Syst. Struct. **43**, 139–155 (2015). https://doi.org/10.1016/j.cl.2015.06.001
29. Schmidt, D.C.: Guest editor's introduction: model-driven engineering. Computer **39**(2), 0025–0031 (2006)
30. Steinberg, D., Budinsky, F., Merks, E., Paternostro, M.: EMF: Eclipse Modeling Framework. Pearson Education (2008). https://books.google.com.br/books?id=sA0zOZuDXhgC
31. Vieira, M.A., Carvalho, S.T.: MDE-based graphical tool for modeling data provenance according to the W3C PROV standard. In: Proceedings of the 12th International Conference on Model-Based Software and Systems Engineering - MODELSWARD, pp. 141–148. INSTICC, SciTePress (2024). https://doi.org/10.5220/0012354700003645
32. Vieira, M.A., Velasco, G.C., Carvalho, S.T.: An ecore metamodel for the W3C PROV provenance data model. In: Proceedings of the 20th Brazilian Symposium on Information Systems, SBSI 2024. Association for Computing Machinery, New York (2024). https://doi.org/10.1145/3658271.3658274

LLM as a Code Generator in Agile Model Driven Development

Ahmed R. Sadik(✉)⑩, Sebastian Brulin⑩, Markus Olhofer⑩, Antonello Ceravola⑩, and Frank Joublin⑩

Honda Research Institute Europe, Carl-Legien-Strasse 30, Offenbach am Main, Germany
{ahmed.sadik,sebastian.brulin,markus.olhofer}@honda-ri.de

Abstract. Leveraging Large Language Models (LLM) like GPT-4 in the auto-generation of code represents a significant advancement, yet it is not without its challenges. The ambiguity inherent in natural language descriptions of software poses substantial obstacles to generating deployable, structured artifacts. This research champions Model-Driven Development (MDD) as a viable strategy to overcome these challenges, proposing an Agile Model-Driven Development (AMDD) approach that employs GPT-4 as a code generator. This approach enhances the flexibility and scalability of the code auto-generation process and offers agility that allows seamless adaptation to changes in models or deployment environments. We illustrate this by modeling a multi-agent Unmanned Vehicle Fleet (UVF) system using the Unified Modeling Language (UML), significantly reducing model ambiguity by integrating the Object Constraint Language (OCL) for code structure meta-modeling, and the FIPA ontology language for communication semantics meta-modeling. Applying GPT-4's auto-generation capabilities yields Java and Python code that is compatible with the JADE and PADE frameworks, respectively. Our thorough evaluation of the auto-generated code verifies its alignment with expected behaviors and identifies enhancements in agent interactions. Structurally, we assessed the complexity of code derived from a model constrained solely by OCL meta-models, against that influenced by both OCL and FIPA-ontology meta-models. The results indicate that the ontology-constrained meta-model produces inherently more complex code, yet its cyclomatic complexity remains within manageable levels, suggesting that additional meta-model constraints can be incorporated without exceeding the high-risk threshold for complexity.

Keywords: Model driven development · GPT-4 code generation · Multi-agent ontology · Object constraint language · Cyclomatic complexity

1 Introduction

In the era of artificial intelligence, with Large Language Models (LLMs) trained on diverse codebases, new opportunities for innovation in Model-Driven Development (MDD) emerge. MDD seeks to enhance the efficiency and durability of software engineering practices. Accordingly, this work extends our research in [16] to augment Agile Model-Driven Development (AMDD). Our approach leverages existing LLMs, such as

© The Author(s), under exclusive license to Springer Nature Switzerland AG 2026
F. José Domínguez Mayo et al. (Eds.): MODELSWARD 2024, CCIS 2547, pp. 198–212, 2026.
https://doi.org/10.1007/978-3-031-96841-9_10

GPT-4, to auto-generate deployment-ready software artifacts [17]. Our objective is to conserve the substantial time and effort traditionally required in MDD for developing and updating a unique code generator for each deployment [10], ensuring that the auto-generated code is well-structured and meets its intended functionality and specified requirements [8].

Code generation from formal graphical languages like the Unified Modeling Language (UML), Systems Modeling Language (SysML), or Business Process Model and Notation (BPMN) diagrams has become a cornerstone of contemporary software engineering [13]. With appropriate tools, these languages can be seamlessly translated into executable code, enhancing the efficiency of the software development process [22]. By integrating static and dynamic aspects from these languages and refining the model with declarative languages such as the Object Constraint Language (OCL) [4] or FIPA meta-ontology [9], the generation of complex, well-structured code is facilitated [11, 14]. This automation ensures alignment between design and implementation, minimizes coding errors, and elevates software quality, thereby accelerating market entry [21]. A deep understanding of a system's dynamic behavior and overarching views is crucial for grasping its functionality [23].

Assessing the quality of auto-generated code is imperative in validating our proposed AMDD approach. Traditional measures of testability, maintainability, and reliability, being qualitative, were susceptible to subjective bias [12]. Our study, however, aims to apply objective, measurable standards. At the heart of our analysis is the structural integrity of the code generated from models, for which we employed cyclomatic complexity as a key measure of structural soundness. Furthermore, our evaluation encompasses a comparative analysis of the code's functionality across different programming languages, against the expected behaviors delineated in the model's design [1].

Section 2 of this article outlines the problem statement, spotlighting the inflexibilities of current MDD practices. Section 3 details the proposed AMDD approach. Section 4 introduces the UML model of a case study on an Unmanned Vehicle Fleet (UVF), and Sect. 5 integrates the case study's structure and communication meta-models using OCL and FIPA ontology language, respectively. Section 6 delves into the cyclomatic complexity of the generated code to evaluate its structure and compares the behavior of two deployments in Java and Python to assess its functionality. Section 7 wraps up with our principal findings, their implications, and directions for future research.

2   Problem Statement

Natural language's inherent ambiguity presents challenges not only for machine interpretation but also for human understanding. In leveraging GPT-4 in deployable code auto-generation, the unclear and open-ended nature of the input prompts frequently results in flawed and incomplete code. This problem is especially noticeable in scenarios where the software to be generated composed of different interconnected artifacts. Thus, rendering the software is impossible to be precisely encapsulated in natural language. MDD provides a solution to this problem by offering high-level models as the primary source for generating final code. However, designing and maintaining these models poses challenges that can detract from MDD's efficacy. First, while traditional modeling methods like UML excel at structuring data, they often fall short in providing the semantic depth and rule-based knowledge [2]. Consequently, the resulting models, though structurally sound and behaviorally accurate, lack the semantic richness required for effectively representing complex real-world situations. Second, converting these models into executable code is far from direct [15]. It necessitates manual crafting and continuous updating of the code generator to align with model modifications and evolving technology stacks, a challenge amplified when switching deployment across different programming languages [5].

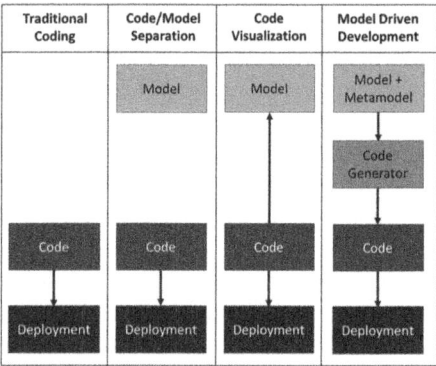

Fig. 1. Traditional coding vs MDD [16].

Addressing the challenges in code generation within the existing MDD framework necessitates a clear understanding of the distinctions between traditional coding practices and MDD code generation, as depicted in Fig. 1. Traditional coding involves directly translating software functionalities into code, which suits smaller, straightforward features. Debugging, testing, and maintenance occur at the code level. Conversely, the model-and-code separation approach uses models to abstractly grasp the system, with models often discarded post-coding due to the prohibitive cost of updates. In contrast, MDD positions models as the cornerstone of the development process, substituting source code with source models from which the target code is auto-generated. This elevates the abstraction level and simplifies complexity. Tools such as Eclipse Papyrus, MagicDraw, Enterprise Architect, and IBM Rational Rhapsody have supported this process [6]. However, any significant model updates or changes in the deployment language necessitate extensive modifications to the code generators, hindering development agility. Crafting a code generator for each programming language is both time-consuming and complex, limiting the MDD approach's adaptability and agility across different languages.

Our study explores leveraging LLM like GPT-4 as universal code generators to address these limitations. Despite MDD offering a structured approach that surpasses natural language's inadequacies for generating deployable code, the current MDD methodology hasn't fully embraced the capabilities of modern LLMs in auto-generating code. This gap renders the traditional MDD approach less effective within agile software development workflows, highlighting the need for alignment with contemporary LLM capabilities in code generation.

3 Proposed Approach

Addressing the challenges described in the problem statement, our AMDD approach uses GPT-4 as a code generator, that seamlessly interprets of the model into interconnected software artifacts that are ready for deployment. We leveraged PlantUML to translate UML diagrams into a formal text representation, to bridge the gap between GPT-4 text-based prompt and the visual UML's diagrams, therefore facilitating direct input into GPT-4. As illustrated in Fig. 2., the modeler starts by crafting the model's layers: structural, behavioral, and constraints.

The structural layer outlines the static aspects of the model, showcasing software components and their complex relationships. Class diagrams elucidate object relationships and hierarchies, package diagrams group objects to highlight dependencies, and component diagrams offer a high-level view of system functionality and inter-component links. Deployment diagrams illustrate the hardware setup and component

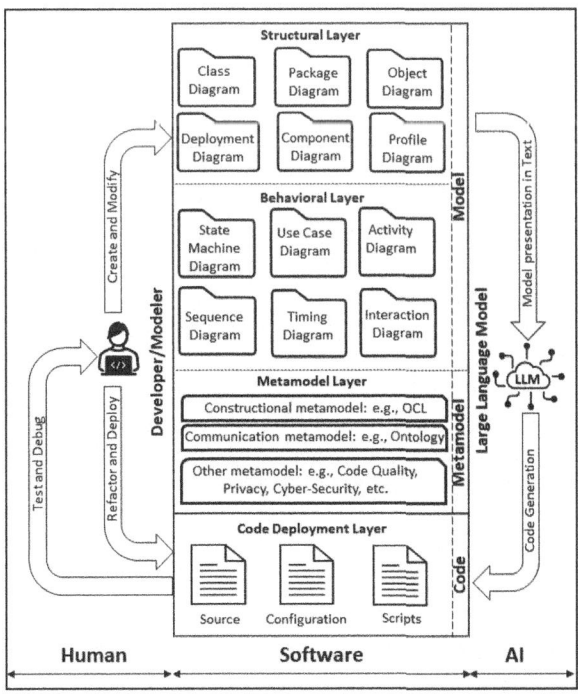

Fig. 2. Proposed AMDD approach [16].

distribution for the system's physical architecture, whereas object diagrams provide runtime snapshots of objects, and profile diagrams adapt UML models for specific platforms.

The behavioral layer depicts the system's operations and interactions through various diagrams. Sequence diagrams map out event sequences, offering a timeline of interactions, while activity diagrams provide a detailed process flow. Interaction diagrams and timing diagrams further explore component interplay and the significance of timing, respectively. Use case diagrams demonstrate interactions between external entities and the system, and state diagrams trace the lifecycle and state transitions of entities.

Despite the comprehensive view offered by structural and behavioral diagrams, they fall short in articulating the governing rules and semantics. Our research introduces a constraints layer to refine the model's architecture by incorporating explicit meta-values and rules beyond UML's scope. We employ the OCL to define detailed code construction rules for both layers, specifying class invariants, method pre- and post-conditions, and parameter value restrictions. Additionally, communication constraints are articulated using ontology languages, enhancing knowledge sharing among software artifacts.

In the deployment layer, we utilize GPT-4 for its advanced reasoning capabilities, crucial for integrating model semantics into the auto-generated code. After ChatGPT generates the code, the modeler is responsible for deploying and validating its functionality. While ChatGPT's code generation is a powerful tool, it's evolving and not without errors [7]. Anticipating and addressing potential deployment bugs, possibly with ChatGPT's assistance, is essential for ensuring the code fulfills its intended function effectively.

4 Case Study Model

The use-case selected for discussion centers around an UVF, consisting of a variety of UVs tasked with distinct missions, all orchestrated by a Mission Control Center (MCC) with human oversight. This case study has been designed as inherently distributed, making it suitable for representation and analysis through a Multi-Agent System (MAS) [3]. The case study complexity is notably high since each participating entity is modeled as an agent, which necessitates ongoing communication and information sharing among agents to fulfill a unified objective, namely the successful completion of the fleet's mission. To ensure clarity and prevent the details of the MAS from becoming overwhelming, subsequent sections will focus solely on the fundamental model, providing insights into the operational principles of the MAS without delving into its complexities.

4.1 Structure Model

Within the architecture of the model, the class diagram holds a crucial role by mapping out each participant in the case study as a distinct agent class, a relationship depicted in Fig. 3. This diagram introduces the operator agent, embodying the human operator's functions such as dispatching mission briefings and collecting performance metrics. It also details the MCC agent, defined by characteristics like its unique MCC-ID, which

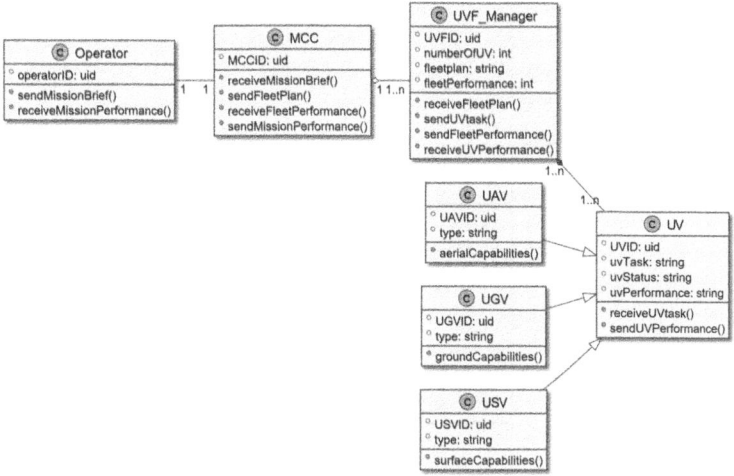

Fig. 3. Case-Study class diagram [16].

oversees mission coordination and fleet supervision. Additionally, the UVF-Manager agent is tasked with the oversight of fleet operations, encompassing the allocation of tasks and monitoring of execution outcomes. The Unmanned Vehicle (UV) agent is conceptualized as a foundational class for UVs, branching into specific subclasses for varied vehicle categories, including UAVs, UGVs, and USVs. Through this class diagram, the intricate interactions among agents are clarified, highlighting their attributes, functionalities, and the web of relationships among them, such as composition, aggregation, and inheritance, while also defining the connections' cardinality.

4.2 Behaviour Model

For conciseness and focus, the article will explore only two significant behavioral views critical for comprehending the case study model: the activity and state diagrams. These diagrams are essential for understanding the dynamic aspects of the case study. The activity diagram, detailed in Fig. 4, enriches the class diagram by thoroughly describing processes such as synchronization, parallel execution, and conditional flows, vital for the successful completion of mission objectives. Conversely, the state diagram offers a detailed exploration of the agent classes' lifecycle within the model, revealing their coordination and reactions to achieve the overarching mission goals.

The activity diagram in Fig. 4 dissects the flow of information and tasks among the agents, illustrating the orchestration of processes and the sequence of task allocation, execution, and evaluation. This diagram highlights the temporal and logical dynamics of the MAS. The interaction commences when the operator agent forwards the mission brief to the MCC agent, which then decodes the brief into a strategic plan and relays it to the UVF-manager. This manager is responsible for task distribution to the available UVs. Upon completion of these tasks, the UVF-manager gathers the performance data

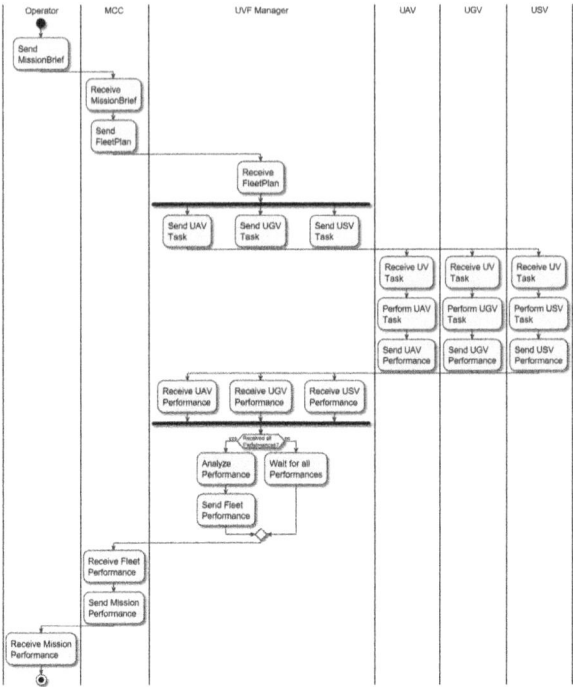

Fig. 4. Case-Study activity diagram [16].

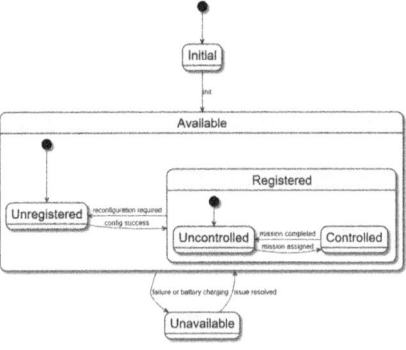

Fig. 5. Case-Study state diagram [16].

from each UV, crucial for assessing the UVF's overall performance. This comprehensive performance feedback is sent back to the MCC, where it is translated into mission performance indicators and communicated back to the operator agent.

The state diagram further uncovers the internal workings of each agent, illustrating the transitions and actions that various events can initiate. For the operator, MCC, and UVF-manager, their statuses are straightforwardly represented by either 'busy' or 'free' states. The UVs, on the other hand, demand a nuanced state machine for a precise evaluation of task performance. As shown in Fig. 5, the UV states are categorized as 'Available', indicating the UV is ready for tasks regardless of registration status; 'Unavailable', when a UV is out of service; 'Unregistered', ready for use but not yet enlisted; 'Registered', officially listed and potentially tasked, which further divides into 'Uncontrolled', listed but idle, and 'Controlled', actively assigned to a mission. This approach streamlines the understanding of each UV's current operational condition and its capacity to undertake mission-specific tasks.

5   Case Study Metamodel

In the proposed AMDD framework, the meta-model layer serves a pivotal role by encapsulating constraints that cover all facets of technical requirements not directly representable in the model layer. These constraints act as the guiding principles or rules that ensure the model adheres to specified technical standards and requirements. Upcoming sections will delve into the various types of meta-model constraints employed in the case study's modeling process, providing a comprehensive overview of how these constraints influence and shape the model's development and ensuring it aligns with the desired technical specifications and objectives

5.1   Construction Metamodel

OCL complements the UML by defining rules for classes within a model. It plays a crucial role in adding construction constraints to UML diagrams, thereby enhancing model refinement and clarity. By addressing model ambiguities, OCL ensures precise modeling, which is particularly beneficial for generating deployed code directly from UML. This precision facilitates a smoother and more accurate transition from model to code.

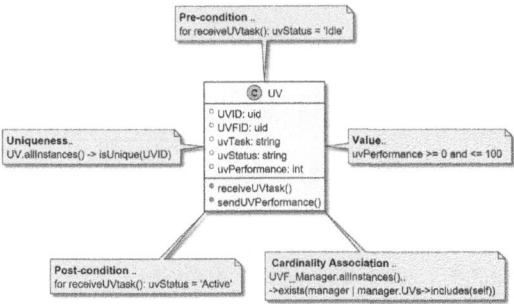

Fig. 6. UV agent construction metamodel example [16].

Our research highlights the application of OCL through the implementation of five specific types of constraints on all agent classes, as illustrated with the UV agent class example in Fig. 6. These constraints are:

- **Uniqueness.** Ensures every agent has a distinct identifier.
- **Cardinality.** Manages relationships between agents, such as a UVF-manager to multiple UVs.
- **Value.** Limits class attributes within certain ranges, like UV performance scores between 0 and 100.
- **Pre-Condition.** Verifies agents are in the correct state before transitions, for instance, a UV can only accept tasks if idle.
- **Post-Condition.** Dictates state changes after transitions, such as updating a UV's status to 'Active' after task assignment.

These constraints significantly improve model precision and reliability by strictly adhering to defined rules and conditions.

5.2   Communication Metamodel

While the OCL aims to define constraints for classes within UML models, it has limitations in facilitating inter-class communication—essential for the functionality of MAS [19,20]. To bridge this gap, technologies such as Java Agent DEvelopment (JADE) and Python Agent DEvelopment (PADE) turn to the FIPA-ontology communication language [18]. This language significantly enhances MAS by providing a rich set of interaction protocols tailored for complex agent communications, overcoming the shortcomings of OCL in this domain. Our case study specifically points out these limitations of OCL and demonstrates how FIPA-ontology language serves as a crucial tool in developing sophisticated MAS communications.

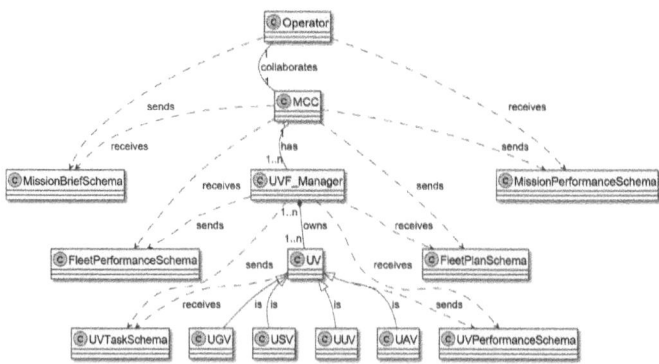

Fig. 7. UV agent construction metamodel example [16].

In our MAS communication framework, as depicted in Fig. 7, the FIPA-ontology establishes a series of structured schemas vital for facilitating complex communications within the system. These schemas are divided into key sets:

Concepts. These schemas form the backbone of mission and agent management communication, including:

- *Mission-Brief Schema:* Details such as mission-ID and status.
- *Fleet-Plan Schema:* Specifies fleet configurations.
- *UV-Task Schema:* Assigns tasks to individual unmanned vehicles (UVs).
- *UV-Performance Schema:* Records performance metrics of UVs.
- *Fleet-Performance* and *Mission-Performance* schemas, each focusing on specific performance metrics.

Predicates. These schemas define the relationships between different agent classes, covering:

- *Inheritance:* E.g., a UAV as a subtype of UV.
- *Composition:* Such as an MCC incorporating a UVF-manager.
- *Aggregation:* As seen in a UVF-manager overseeing multiple UVs.
- *Collaboration:* Demonstrated by the interaction between an operator and the MCC.

Actions. Operations that agents can execute, especially regarding message schemas, include:

- Sending and receiving data, like an operator agent sending a mission brief to the MCC or the MCC receiving it from the operator.

This structured approach, as provided by the FIPA-ontology, not only clarifies the communication protocols within the MAS but also ensures that interactions are both efficient and effective, catering to the complex needs of agent-based communication.

6   Code Evaluation

In the final stage of our AMDD approach, we employ GPT-4 for the conversion of the model and the metamodel into executable code. Our findings indicate an average occurrence of four bugs per agent class generated by GPT-4, predominantly due to the omission of necessary library imports. Nevertheless, with the correction of these bugs, the generated code becomes suitable for deployment. It is important to note that our primary interest in this study lies not in the accuracy of the auto-generated code but in its comprehensiveness. Our evaluation focuses on the examination and analysis of the structure and behavior of the auto-generated code, rather than on identifying and quantifying the bugs it may contain.

To this end, we conducted two distinct experiments. The first experiment sought to dissect the structure and complexity of the auto-generated code, providing insights into its architectural design and the intricacies of its internal mechanisms. The second experiment was designed to investigate the behavior of the auto-generated code, aiming to understand how well it performs its intended functions within a given context. These experiments collectively offer a holistic view of the auto-generated code's efficacy, highlighting areas of strength and opportunities for further refinement.

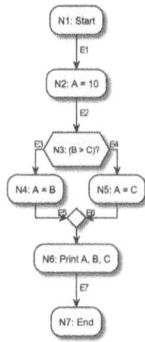

Fig. 8. UV agent construction metamodel example [16].

6.1   Structure Evaluation

In our first experiment, we concentrated on analyzing the structure and complexity of the auto-generated code using the cyclomatic complexity metric. This metric is essential for measuring code complexity, as it enumerates the number of linearly independent paths through the program's source code. The calculation relies on the code's control-flow graph, akin to the example depicted in Fig. 8. The cyclomatic complexity (M) is derived from the formula:

$$M = E - N + 2P \tag{1}$$

where E represents the number of edges in the flow graph, N is the number of nodes, and P indicates the number of disconnected parts of the graph. For instance, given the graph shown in Fig. 8, the calculated M is 3. This M value is critical for evaluating various software aspects, such as testing difficulty, maintainability, understandability, refactorability, performance, reliability, and documentation quality. Based on the M value, risk levels are categorized as follows: an M between 1 and 10 signifies low risk; an M between 11 and 20 indicates moderate risk; an M from 21 to 50 suggests high risk, potentially requiring code review or decomposition into smaller modules; and an M exceeding 50 denotes severe risk, necessitating substantial refactoring.

   In our AMDD approach, we placed particular emphasis on the impact of integrating formal constraints on the generation of deployable code. The aim of this experiment was to gauge the influence of the matemodel constraints on the complexity of the auto-generated code. Consequently, we generated two distinct deployments that varied in the degree of constraints embedded within their models. The first deployment was based on a model that implemented only OCL constraints, while the second deployment also integrated FIPA-ontology constraints into the model.

   Following the generation of these two distinct codebases, we converted the agent classes into control flow diagrams for the purpose of computing their cyclomatic complexity (M), as summarized in Table 1. A comparison of the M values from the auto-generated code indicates that complexity incrementally rises with the addition of FIPA-ontology constraints. However, it's noteworthy that the complexity levels for all classes in both deployments remained within the low-risk category. This observation suggests

Table 1. Cyclomatic Complexity Analysis of Agent Classes [16].

Class	Operator		MCC		UVF-Manager		UV	
Constraints	OCL	OCL + Ontology	OCL	OCL + Ontology	OCL	OCL + Ontology	OCL	OCL + Ontology
Edges (E)	8	12	15	22	16	23	8	12
Nodes (N)	8	11	13	19	14	19	8	11
Branches (P)	1	1	1	1	1	1	1	1
Complexity (M)	2	3	4	5	4	6	2	3

that the structure of the auto-generated code is sufficiently robust and does not require further refactoring. Importantly, the highest observed M value, which was 6, was associated with the UVF-manager class in the second deployment that included both OCL and FIPA-ontology constraints. This finding indicates a significant margin for incorporating additional constraints into our model without surpassing the low-risk threshold.

6.2 Behaviour Evaluation

In the second experiment of our study, we generated two distinct deployments: one in Java for the JADE platform, and another in Python for the PADE framework. The objective was to assess and compare the behaviors of code executed on JADE with that running on PADE, aiming to verify the system dynamics' consistency across different programming languages. This examination specifically focused on the agents' interaction behaviors within both the JADE and PADE frameworks. Observations indicated that the agents' behaviors, as captured by the JADE Sniffer tool, align with the sequence diagrams generated from PADE agent interactions, as depicted in Fig. 9.

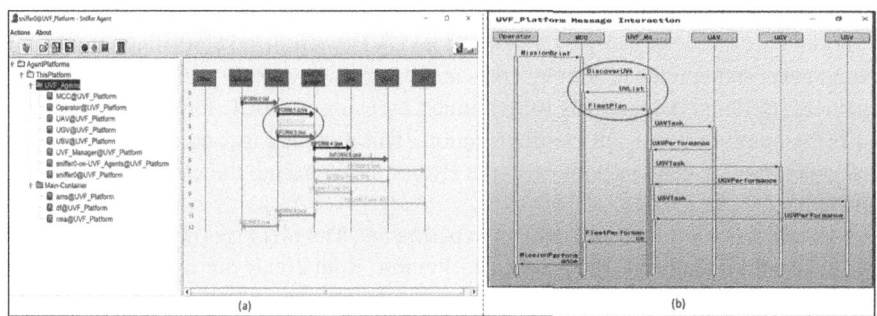

Fig. 9. UV agent construction metamodel example [16].

In the sequence diagrams presented in Fig. 9, the interaction sequence initiates with the operator sending a mission brief to the MCC. Upon receiving this message, the

MCC directs the UVF-manager to identify available UVs. With a list of accessible UVs at hand, the MCC formulates a fleet plan and relays it to the UVF-manager, who subsequently assigns specific tasks to the available UVs. Each UV, upon completing its task, transmits performance data back to the UVF-manager, who then compiles a comprehensive fleet-performance metric. This metric is forwarded to the MCC, which evaluates it in relation to the mission objectives to generate a definitive mission-performance report. This report marks the operation's culmination and is ultimately delivered to the operator.

Two notable observations emerged from the comparison of the sequence diagrams in Fig. 9 with the original case study's activity diagram in Fig. 4. Firstly, an enhancement in interaction was identified, introducing new behaviors for both the MCC and UVF-manager agents. This enhancement was particularly observed in the MCC dispatching a *DiscoverUVs* message to the UVF-Manager and awaiting the *UVList* before developing a *FleetPlan*, logically necessitating an understanding of the available UV resources prior to their mission-specific allocation. This novel interaction behavior was not explicitly detailed in the original case study's activity diagram. Secondly, variations in the timing of interactions between the MCC and UVs were noted between the JADE and PADE implementations, likely reflecting differences in the state machine of each UV instance. This variance suggests that these state machines accurately emulate the operational dynamics of the agents.

7   Discussion, Conclusion, and Future Work

Our investigation into the integration of LLMs within MDD practices has unveiled significant potential for overcoming the challenges posed by natural language ambiguities in auto-generating deployable code. By employing formal modeling languages, such as UML, and enriching them with precise metamodels' constraints, we have significantly bridged this gap. Our proposed AMDD approach, which introduces semantic depth through metamodelling, has proven to enhance the accuracy of code generation by LLMs, particularly GPT-4, which demonstrates advanced reasoning capabilities.

In our case study focusing on a MAS of an UVF, we utilized class diagrams to represent agents and employed activity and state diagrams to capture their interactions and behaviors. Detailed metamodels were defined by using the OCL for structural aspects and FIPA-ontology for agent communication. This foundational model facilitated the auto-generation of code in both Java and Python, showcasing the effectiveness of our approach.

Our evaluation through two distinct experiments. The first experiment examined the auto-generated code behavior in Java and Python. Both codes run in Java and Python showed identical behavior with the model activity diagram, however new behavior in both implementations was added by GPT-4 as shown in, to reveal the capability of LLM to interpret and then compliment the. While the second experiment assessed the structural complexity of the generated code—revealed that the addition of FIPA-ontology metamodel does not unduly increase code complexity. This suggests that our approach allows for the inclusion of further constraints without necessitating immediate code refactoring, indicating robustness and scalability.

The insights gained from integrating LLMs into MDD underscore a transformative path towards achieving the sought-after agility in current MDD practices. Future research will focus on assessing the correctness of auto-generated code, incorporating new privacy and cybersecurity metamodels, and comparing our methodology against existing MDD frameworks. Through continuous enhancement and evaluation, we aim to pave the way for more agile, efficient, and robust software development methodologies. As the domain of software development continues to evolve, the seamless interplay between structured modeling, advanced LLM reasoning, and assessments of structural complexity will be paramount. Our research represents a step forward in this direction, suggesting a future where the generation of deployable code from high-level models becomes more streamlined, precise, and reliable.

References

1. Ahmad, A., Waseem, M., Liang, P., Fehmideh, M., Aktar, M.S., Mikkonen, T.: Towards human-bot collaborative software architecting with chatgpt. arXiv preprint arXiv:2302.14600 (2023)
2. Belghiat, A., Bourahla, M.: From uml class diagrams to owl ontologies: a graph transformation based approach. In: ICWIT, pp. 330–335 (2012)
3. Brulin, S., Olhofer, M.: Bi-level network design for uam vertiport allocation using activity-based transport simulations (2023)
4. Cabot, J., Gogolla, M.: Object constraint language (OCL): a definitive guide, pp. 58–90. Springer (2012)
5. Camara, J., Troya, J., Burgueno, L., Vallecillo, A.: On the assessment of generative ai in modeling tasks: an experience report with chatgpt and uml. Softw. Syst. Model. 22(3), 781–793 (2023)
6. David, I., et al.: Blended modeling in commercial and open-source model-driven software engineering tools: a systematic study. Softw. Syst. Model. 22(1), 415–447 (2023). https://doi.org/10.1007/s10270-022-01010-3
7. Dong, Y., Jiang, X., Jin, Z., Li, G.: Self-collaboration code generation via chatgpt (2023)
8. Feltus, C., Grandry, E., Kupper, T., Colin, J.N.: Model-driven approach for privacy management in business ecosystem. In: Proceedings of the 5th International Conference on Model-Driven Engineering and Software Development, pp. 392–400 (2017)
9. FIPA, S.: Fipa ontology service specification. Technical Report, Citeseer (2000)
10. Hailpern, B., Tarr, P.: Model-driven development: the good, the bad, and the ugly. IBM Syst. J. 45(3), 451–461 (2006)
11. Kapferer, S., Zimmermann, O.: Domain-specific language and tools for strategic domain-driven design, context mapping and bounded context modeling. In: Proceedings of the 8th International Conference on Model-Driven Engineering and Software Development, pp. 299–306 (2020)
12. Liu, C., Bao, X., Zhang, N, H.H.Z.X.Y.M.: Improving chatgpt prompt for code generation. arXiv preprint arXiv:2305.08360 (2023)
13. OMG, O.M.G.: Object management group (2006)
14. Perez-Martinez, J.E., Sierra-Alonso, A.: Uml 1.4 versus uml 2.0 as languages to describe software architectures. In: Lecture Notes in Computer Science (including subseries Lecture Notes in Artificial Intelligence and Lecture Notes in Bioinformatics), vol. 3047 (2004)
15. Petrovic, N., Al-Azzoni, I.: Automated approach to model-driven engineering leveraging chatgpt and ecore (2023)

16. Sadik, A.R., Brulin, S., Olhofer, M.: Coding by design: Gpt-4 empowers agile model driven development. In: The International Conference on Model-Based Software and Systems Engineering - MODELSWARD 2024, pp. 149–156 (2024)
17. Sadik, A.R., Ceravola, A., Joublin, F., Patra, J.: Analysis of chatgpt on source code. arXiv preprint arXiv:2306.00597 (2023)
18. Sadik, A.R., Urban, B.: Cprosa-holarchy: An enhanced prosa model to enable worker–cobot agile manufacturing. Int. J. Mech. Eng. Robot. Res. 7(3), 296–304 (2018)
19. Sadik, A.R., Urban, B.: A holonic control system design for a human & industrial robot cooperative workcell. In: 2016 International Conference on Autonomous Robot Systems and Competitions (ICARSC), pp. 118–123. IEEE (2016)
20. Sadik, A.R., Urban, B.: Combining adaptive holonic control and isa-95 architectures to self-organize the interaction in a worker-industrial robot cooperative workcell. Future Internet 9(3), 35 (2017)
21. Sarkisian, A., Vasylkiv, Y., Gomez, R.: System architecture supporting crowdsourcing of contents for robot storytelling application (2022)
22. Sharaf, M., Abusair, M., Eleiwi, R., Shana'a, Y., Saleh, I., Muccini, H.: Modeling and code generation framework for iot, pp. 99–115 (2019)
23. Siricharoen, W.V.: Ontology modeling and object modeling in software engineering. Int. J. Softw. Eng. Appl. 3 (2009)

A Modeling Framework for Hardware-Software Systems with Machine Learning Components

Francesco Bedini$^{(\boxtimes)}$, Tino Jungebloud , Ralph Maschotta ,
and Armin Zimmermann

Technische Universität Ilmenau, Ilmenau 98693, Germany
{francesco.bedini,tino.jungebloud,ralph.maschotta,
armin.zimmermann}@tu-ilmenau.de
https://www.tu-ilmenau.de/sse

Abstract. Artificial intelligence is gaining prominence in diverse industrial sectors, transforming procedures and decision-making with advanced functionalities that were previously unattainable or not easily achievable with traditional software. Industries are allocating resources towards artificial intelligence-driven solutions, which have the potential to enhance operational efficiency and foster innovation within their respective domains. Regrettably, machine learning also presents novel obstacles, such as managing uncertainties arising from the decision-making process.

This paper shows the design and implementation of a framework that allows modeling and simulating time-based software and hardware systems to assess the potential impacts of uncertainties propagating across the system in various operational environments.

This is crucial as those uncertainties could result in costly system breakdowns and influence other non-functional prerequisites like system efficiency, dependability, and even security.

Our methodology involves establishing a novel domain-specific language with formal execution semantics delineated using stochastic colored Petri nets. The resultant models can subsequently undergo static analysis and simulation via an automated conversion to stochastic colored Petri nets, facilitating the computation of diverse reliability and efficiency metrics.

Keywords: DSL · SCPN · Stochastic colored petri net · EMF · Modeling · Simulation

1 Introduction

In recent years, machine learning and artificial intelligence concepts have become widespread in society as these approaches have reached consumers, enabling features that were not feasible or performant before. Companies are also looking into this trend, as by replacing traditional software with machine learning components, they may achieve better results or enable features that were out of reach before.

However, as industries must adhere to specific local legal requirements, they must ensure that their products or systems work and behave as intended. As these legislations

F. José Domínguez Mayo et al. (Eds.): MODELSWARD 2024, CCIS 2547, pp. 213–228, 2026.
https://doi.org/10.1007/978-3-031-96841-9_11

vary based on the country and fields involved, we are not referring to any particular ones in this work. The proposed solution aims to work as an analysis and simulation framework that can be extended to support the regulation of interest.

As machine learning components may deliver inaccurate results based on different factors and minimal input differences, it is fundamental to consider these uncertainties starting from the design phase of the system development.

The goal of this work is to provide practical tools that could be used by small and medium enterprises (SMEs) to design and build reliable systems containing uncertainties generated by machine learning components.

This paper is an extended version of [3], and the remainder is structured as follows: Sect. 2 discusses the background and related works. Section 3 introduces the proposed domain-specific language (DSL), describing its abstract and concrete syntaxes and semantics. The framework and its implementation are then described in Sect. 4. Section 7 summarizes this paper and discusses future works.

2   Background

While traditional systems engineering methods have been effective under the assumption of nearly deterministic processes [24], they are not always suitable for dealing with the inherently uncertain nature of machine learning (ML) techniques.

Different studies have explored the application of artificial intelligence in software engineering methodologies [38]. However, there is a limited number of research works focusing on utilizing a software engineering methodology to analyze machine learning (ML) specifically at the product or runtime application levels within the context of the AI in Software Engineering Application Levels (AI-SEAL) taxonomy [12], as demonstrated in this particular study.

Another research category involves implementing an engineering approach for developing machine learning models, exemplified in a study by [1]. This work emphasizes the significance of adopting a data-oriented engineering strategy and outlines a comprehensive 9-step workflow after examining how software teams engage with artificial intelligence (AI) at Microsoft.

Literature discussing the uncertainties introduced by ML, particularly regarding the challenges associated with distinguishing between aleatoric and epistemic uncertainties, can be identified in [15].

Models based on discrete events like Petri nets (Petri nets (PNs)) are valuable for analyzing and simulating stochastic concurrent systems and processes. However, they often lack readability for systems designers and demand a certain level of expertise for effective utilization. Hence, it is common practice to employ alternative models that can be automatically translated into a Petri net. For instance, in [14], Systems Modeling Language (SysML) activity diagrams are validated after a conversion to a Petri net.

Domain-specific language (DSLs) enables the precise expression of domain knowledge, involving domain experts directly with minimal implementation overhead [29]. Despite their advantages, there is a widespread hesitance towards adopting DSLs for various reasons, including social resistance due to perceived risks related to their maintainability and evolution, as evidenced in studies like [35]. Another challenge is the absence of a straightforward formalized method to define the execution semantics of a DSL, as discussed in research such as [8].

However, this transformational approach poses a problem after the DSL has been transformed to a Petri net, as the connection back to the source DSL elements may get lost, as discussed in [17, 18].

Considering the trade-offs in implementation as outlined in [16] and the advancements in tools, models, and languages since then, developing a DSL instead of extending generic modeling languages appears to be a viable option. Furthermore, general-purpose modeling languages like Unified Modeling Language (UML) for software and SysML for systems may not always be the most suitable choice for implementing a Model-Based Systems Engineering (MBSE) solution, as argued in studies like [7].

To the best of our knowledge, we are unaware of comparable works about proposing a DSL focused on modeling systems containing machine learning components and analyzing them holistically.

3 The Engineering for Smart Manufacturing (E4SM) DSL

The goal of our editor is to allow users to intuitively model data flows between hardware and software systems components, supporting an iterative top-down modeling approach. The models should serve as a base for computing various performance measures of interest, such as the data throughput and end-to-end delays. To simulate that, it is necessary to have a formal model with a well-defined structure and unambiguous semantics.

Petri nets are a formal mathematical model that can be used to model concurrent discrete systems that transfer data packages. Being relatively low-level (they consist of only four modeling elements: places, transitions, arcs, and tokens), it would not be feasible to model an extensive system in such a way correctly manually. Even assuming that is feasible, then these manually defined models would need to be evaluated for correctness and semantic equivalence to the real system every time.

For these reason, we propose basing our editing environment around a DSL called Engineering for Smart Manufacturing (E4SM), which enables modeling data flows between time-based hardware/software systems, with an execution semantics that was inspired by Stochastic colored Petri nets (SCPNs), as tokens of different types are required.

Hence, it is possible to see this proposed DSL as a high-level abstraction for SCPN, as there exists an injective function $f : E4SM \rightarrow SCPN$ that associates any E4SM model to a valid SCPN expressing its execution semantics.

For a DSL to be fully specified, it requires three elements:

an Abstract Syntax: which formally describes what elements are available in the language, what are the attributes that describe them, and the possible relations and constraints within them;

a Concrete Syntax: it defines how the language appears to the final users; it can be, for example, a textual language or a graphical format by defining the elements' shape and style on a diagram;

a Semantics: which defines the meaning and behavior of the different language elements.

The Engineering for Smart Manufacturing (E4SM) DSL specifies all these three elements and, moreover, supports both a textual and graphical concrete syntax, as most of the modern languages do (such as the Kernel Modeling Language (KerML) and Systems Modeling Language v2 (SysML v2) [28], for example). Graphical languages work better for specifying high-level concepts and structures and initial drafts, whereas textual language allows specifying fine details of single elements more comfortably (e.g., mathematical formulas). Graphical languages also have the advantage they can be understood and learned more effectively than textual languages. [9]

In the following sections we are going to introduce all these four building blocks.

3.1   The Abstract Syntax

The abstract syntax of a language is often described formally through the utilization of a metamodel (a model describing a model), which precisely outlines the structure and constraints governing the language components. Class diagrams formally illustrate the abstract syntax by presenting a graphical depiction of the classes, attributes, and associations present in a system [11].

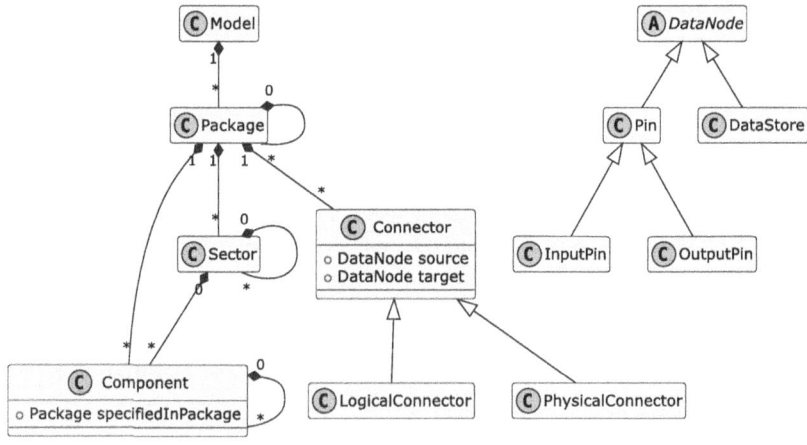

Fig. 1. Class diagram showing the main structural elements.

Figure 1 shows a small extract of the abstract syntax of the E4SM DSL. One of its root elements is the Model, which contains all model elements divided in Packages, which are the equivalent of a diagram. The main elements are components of different types, which are connected to each other via logical or physical connectors at their input and output pins. Connectors are unidirectional data flows between pins (so they always have one source and one target). DataStores allow storing data indefinitely until newer data gets received to overwrite it.

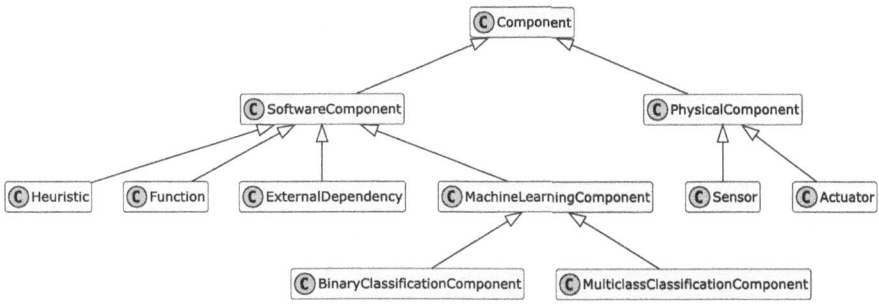

Fig. 2. Class diagram showing the inheritance between all the available component types.

Figure 2 expands on the hierarchy of all different available component types. All components can be either software or physical components. A generic `Component` type is also available (and is not abstract), as it can be used interchangeably as a place-holder for a more specific type during the design phase. The same applies to the generic type `Connector`. Physical components can either be `Sensors` or `Actuators`. In the first case, they can only produce data and, therefore, only have output pins, whereas in the latter case, they can only consume data and only have input pins. For the software components, we support different kinds based on different certainties levels, for example, in-house developed deterministic `Functions`, or `Heuristics` or `Machine Learning Components`.

3.2 Classification Components

What makes the E4SM language different from others is the possibility of providing additional information to the machine learning classification components. Thanks to this, it will be possible to estimate better the likelihood of the component delivering an incorrect outcome based on how it behaved during its test phase after learning.

Classification components generally work with a set of known `Classification Classes`. These can be specified at the `Model` level, where also an `Environment` with the probabilities of each class to appear can be defined. A model can define different environments to describe different scenarios; of course, all probabilities defined in one environment must sum to 1, which is also checked by a model constraint.

The abstract syntax of the elements related to the classification components is shown on Fig. 3. The DSL currently supports two kinds of classification components:

Binary Classification Components: given an input, it gets categorized either to a class C or to $\overline{C}$. Therefore, the outputs cover the entire universe set Ω, and out-of-distribution results are not possible.

Multiclass Classification Components: given an input, the components assign it to a class C_i out of a closed set $C = \{C_1...C_N\}$ with $|C| = N$. This means that providing an input of class $O \notin C$, out-of-distributions samples are possible.

Multi-label classification (allowing assigning multiple labels to one input) is at the moment not supported.

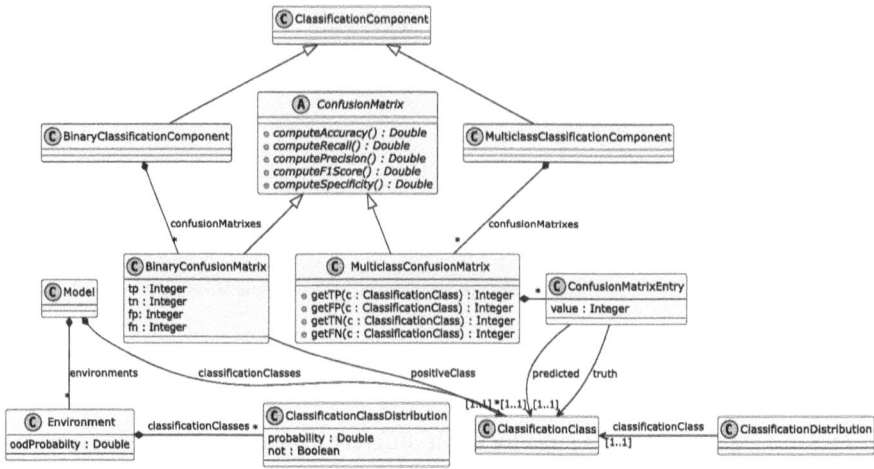

Fig. 3. Class diagram showing the abstract syntax related to the classification components.

For each of these 2 classes, it is possible to provide a confusion matrix, which describes how likely it is that the component will deliver a correct or incorrect result based on the given class. In the case of an incorrect result, it is also possible to compute the likelihood that another specific class will be chosen. All these probabilities can be computed by the methods defined in the abstract class *ConfusionMatrix*, which computes different known metrics.

For a given class i:

$$accuracy_i = \frac{TP_i + TN_i}{TP_i + FP_i + TN_i + FN_i} \tag{1}$$

$$recall_i = \frac{TP_i}{TP_i + FN_i} \tag{2}$$

$$specificity_i = \frac{TN_i}{TN_i + FP_i} \tag{3}$$

In the multiclass classification case, for N classes, where w_i describes the frequency of the class $i \in [1...N]$ and W is the sum of all weights:

$$balAccuracy = \frac{\sum_{i=1}^{N} recall_i}{N} \tag{4}$$

$$weiBalAccuracy = \frac{\sum_{i=1}^{N} \frac{TP_i}{(TP_i + FN_i) \cdot w_i}}{N \cdot W} \tag{5}$$

$$microRecall = \frac{\sum_{i=1}^{N} TP_i}{\sum_{i=1}^{N} (TP_i + FN_i)} \tag{6}$$

$$macroRecall = \frac{\sum_{i=1}^{N} recall_i}{N} \tag{7}$$

3.3 The Concrete Syntaxes

The E4SM comes with two different concrete syntaxes: a graphical one, in the form of diagrams that are inspired by the UML [23] Component and the foundational UML (fUML) [22] activity diagrams, and a textual one, which is inspired by programming languages that use curly brackets to limit blocks of codes such as Java.

The Graphical Concrete Syntax. The graphical concrete syntax consists of a diagram per package. These diagrams are called *Data Transfer Diagrams* (DTD). In DTDs, rectangles depict components, whereas pins are drawn as squares on the component edge, with the letter I or O, respectively. In case of a component connecting arc to the internal specification of a component, they become *Gateway* pins and are shown with a capital G.

When another package specifies a component, the input and output pins of the parent component being specified are depicted as white or gray rectangles with their name in the specifying package DTD.

Every component type has a different color, and the initial of its kind is displayed in bold before the component name. Similarly, physical connectors are black, logical connectors are white, and generic connectors are gray.

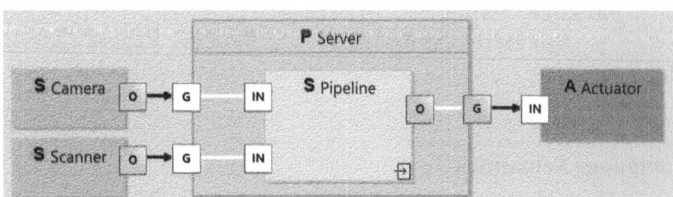

Fig. 4. A *Data Transfer Diagram* which shows an example of the graphical concrete syntax of the E4SM DSL, with two sensors, a physical component where a pipeline is running, and an actuator that receives the processed data.

Figure 4 shows an example of the graphical concrete syntax and the concepts of containment (components can contain other components) and refinement (the component *Pipeline* is further specified in another diagram, as indicated by the icon on the lower right corner).

The Textual Concrete Syntax. The textual syntax allows for the specification of fine details, such as the time distribution of the component execution time, more quickly in the form of different time functions. These functions can reference package-wide parameters or attributes of the component input pins to which they belong.

An example of the textual concrete syntax is shown in Listing 1.1. It has the same content as the diagram shown in Fig. 4, and it is also the syntax in which that diagram is persisted.

Listing 1.1. An example of the e4sm concrete syntax.

```
model "Model example" {
    import "Types"; // a model can reference other model files
    package "Package" {
        doc: "All model elements can get documente."
        sensor Camera {
            doc: "A camera shooting pictures with a fixed FPS"
            takes Det(33.3) // time function, deterministic
            out Image out_c
        }, [...]
        physicalComponent Server {
            in Image in_s_image, [...]
            components {
                softwareComponent Pipeline {
                    out Command out_p,
                    in Image in_p_image,
                    in SensorData in_p_sensor
                    specifiedInPackage "Specify Pipeline"
        }   }   }
        logicalConnector con_8b7A "Server.in_s_image" -> "Server
            .Pipeline.in_p_image", [...]
        subPackages {
            package "Specify Pipeline" {
                specifiesComponent : "Server.Pipeline" [...]
}   }   }   }
```

3.4   The Language Semantics

In order to be easily simulatable but still easily understandable, the entire execution semantics is based on a token game, similar to the fUML execution semantics [22].

As we are interested in finding problems that may also be caused by concurrency and hence we do not require the execution to be deterministic (i.e., getting the same execution flow with the same input model), the main difference with the fUML execution semantics is that when multiple arcs leave one element or elements are in the condition of execution concurrently as they are on different flows, the execution flow continues independently and concurrently on each connector, unlike in the fUML where the outgoing arcs of a fork node are executed sequentially in an order which depends on the model content itself and the execution engine implementation [4].

Whereas sensors generate data with a set deterministic or stochastic frequency, actuators consume the data they receive once they execute. All other components may have an AND or OR execution logic. In the first case, all input pins must receive data for the component to start its execution; in the latter, the component executes as soon as one input pin receives data.

In the input pins, it is possible to set the number of data packages required for the pin to deliver its data to the component. In contrast, it is possible to set a multiplier for the amount of data packages produced on the output pin.

When multiple connectors are connected to the same pin, it is possible to specify what happens in that case. For connectors leaving a pin, the possible options are *duplicate* (similar to an implicit fork node in fUML activity diagrams) or *FCFS* (default), whereas for multiple connectors leading to a pin, the options are *merge* (similar concept of the join element in fUML activity diagrams) or *FCFS* (default).

Each model element, based on its configuration (e.g., its incoming and outgoing connectors and some attribute's values), has a corresponding semantics specified as a Petri net. In particular, we use the class of Stochastic colored Petri net (SCPN) in order to support stochastic firing delays and have tokens of different types with complex data structures available. This makes it possible to see the E4SM DSL as a high-level SCPN, as it exists an injective function that transforms any E4SM model to exactly one SCPN.

3.5 Semantics Related to Classification Components

Regarding classification components, the SCPN describes its execution semantics as all other components from the execution point of view. Still, it concurrently computes stochastically, based on the measures derived from the provided element confusion matrix, what is the outcome of the current observation based on the input class, the environment, and, optionally, the probability of having out-of-distribution samples.

The input specification can be defined in the sensor components, which set with which time delay new data will be generated and which class of a given environment the data token will get.

4 The Framework

In order to be used, the DSL requires an editor. This editor will be the central element of the E4SM framework. As it was described in the previous sections, the editor needs to support both graphical and textual editing of the models, as they have 2 different concrete syntaxes. The models can then be persisted either as XML files (with the .e4sm extension) or as source files (with the .e4smcode extension).

Once a system gets modeled, the framework also allows various model transformations to be performed. For example, documentation can be generated in the form of a wiki-like website containing all elements docs and elements interface specifications through a model-to-text transformation.

The main E4SM editor application was realized around the Eclipse Modeling Framework (EMF) [30], using Eclipse [10] as the base IDE. The abstract syntax metamodel was specified using ecore. The graphical concrete syntax was implemented by specifying viewpoints describing all diagram elements' appearance, constraints, and behavior in Sirius [20]. In contrast, the textual concrete syntax was written through Xtext [34], which allows specifying a grammar based on our abstract syntax and automatically generates an editor using the approach described in [6].

Regarding model transformations, the model-to-text transformations have been written using Acceleo [19], whereas the model-to-model transformation is specified using QVTo [33]. Using such a cohesive ecosystem, it is possible to edit the models graphically and textually simultaneously, and both views are kept synchronized.

All Petri net simulations are run in an external software called TimeNET [32], an application specific for editing and simulating Petri nets [13]. Still, they can be started directly from the E4SM-Editor user interface.

4.1   Collaborative Modeling

Real-time collaboration systems   [27] allow different users to edit the same model simultaneously and see the changes from other users live as they happen to mitigate the time-consuming problems of possible conflicts when models get edited independently and need to be merged at a second time.

Being based on Eclipse Sirius, it is conceptually possible to enable collaborative modeling by using *Obeo Designer Team* [21] or by porting the diagram viewpoint specification to the web version of Sirius: *Sirius Web*, which allow users to access and edit models simultaneously. The feasibility of achieving real-time collaborative modeling using EMF and EMF.Cloud has been shown in [2].

4.2   Model Validation

Compared to a low-level formal language such as Petri net, the main advantage of the high-level approach offered by the DSL is the lower effort required to validate the modeled system, compared to a manually defined Petri net, which must be thoroughly tested for compliance.

The EMF and ecore allow for the enforcement of model constraints, invariants, and validation rules at the metamodel level but also automatically provide feedback on validation errors punctually for both the graphical and textual model editors.

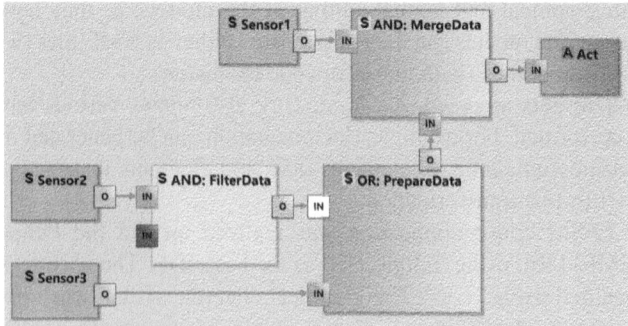

Fig. 5. A data transfer diagram with the *Check Executability* layer enabled. Now, elements with more than one input pin display their execution logic before their name. Pins and executable elements are colored in green, whereas input pins that are not executable are highlighted in red.

Moreover, it is possible to define layers on Eclipse Sirius to highlight elements with missing properties or lacking the requirements for executability. For example, according to the E4SM execution semantics, components execute with an AND or OR firing condition. To validate these and assure that actuators receive the data they need (i.e., they are executable), an ad-hoc diagram layer has been realized to show the executability of each pin or component (similar to the concept of reachability in Petri nets), demonstrated in Fig. 5. This layer allows one to locate and display at a glance what system elements will never get executed as they do not receive enough input data due to missing connections or loops with circular dependencies within components. In this example, by simulating this model, the user probably may not notice something is wrong from the simulation results, as the Actuator still receives some data. However, the model probably does not run as the user intended it to, as the component *FilterData* never executes due to the dangling input pin and its AND execution semantics.

5 Analyses and Simulations

The E4SM framework provides an *analysis* package that allows to specify different analysis methods upon the models: direct ones or indirect ones. The direct ones consist of programmatically querying the model content and computing some values of interest, such as key performance indicators (KPI), whereas the indirect one requires a transformation of the model semantics to a stochastic colored Petri net, which will be simulated to compute some performance measure.

5.1 Direct Analyses

The direct analyses approach allows for the running of standard analyses and the writing of custom ones based on specific needs. While this approach offers more flexibility, it also requires specific knowledge about the DSL execution semantics, and thoroughly testing and validating the manually written analysis algorithm is required to validate the analysis results.

Examples of possible direct analyses are:

Uncertainties Propagation: quantify how much and where uncertainties may propagate through the system;
Computation of End-to-End Delays: compute how fast data can flow from a given source to a given target element, as this may be of great interest in real-time systems that have to cope with deadlines;
Network Data Throughput: to assure that the physical connectors between the components have the required capacity for the data it flows through.

The indirect analysis shall be used to perform a more comprehensive stochastic evaluation of the system state (either for transient or steady state analyses).

5.2   Indirect Analyses

The indirect analyses approach allows the simulation to be run using the mathematical foundation of Petri nets, which better guarantees that the simulation process is correct (as the simulation algorithm remains unchanged, just the input Petri net changes, but it is automatically generated and hence less error-prone).

TimeNET supports both transient and steady-state evaluations, making it a versatile tool for modeling and analyzing complex systems with stochastic or deterministic firing delays and colored stochastic Petri nets [39]. The transient simulation allows to investigate what happens to the system from the initial marking to a specified end time. The state-state simulation allows the computation of certain average measures in the long run in a converging steady state.

The evaluation of this transformation and simulation process has been discussed in detail in [5]. The transformation's correctness was validated by assessing properties such as termination, confluence, and behavior preservation [36], also thanks to the DSL semantics being directly specified as SCPNs.

6   An Example of the Modeling and Simulation Flow

Our models can be applied to various scenarios where time-based events generate discrete data, for example, in modeling data stream processing pipelines with sensors like cameras with fixed or variable fps.

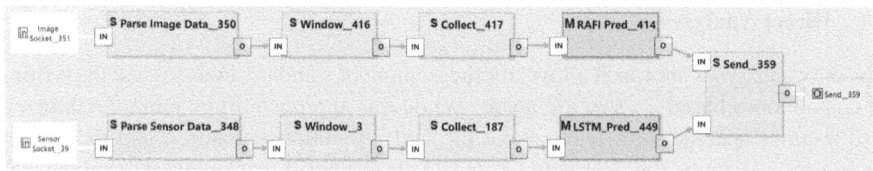

Fig. 6. An E4SM Data Transfer Diagram showing the refinement of the pipeline component shown on Fig. 4. Yellow components are software components, whereas purple ones are machine learning components.

Figure 6 shows the specification of such a pipeline, which has two input pins and sends data to one output pin after synchronizing both flows (in the *Send* component). The two parallel flows analyze the data they receive; they collect a certain number of tuples in the *Window* component and then apply a prediction algorithm in the *RAFI* [37] and *LSTM* (*Long short-term memory*) components.

The execution times of the elements of this pipeline have been approximated to stochastic functions having as variables the tokens' attributes by the method explained in [25], calibrating the components on the target hardware using the open-source software StreamVizzard [26]. The E4SM-Editor has a simple flow to export information that is useful for pipeline realization and converting and merging back pipeline models defined in StreamVizzard.

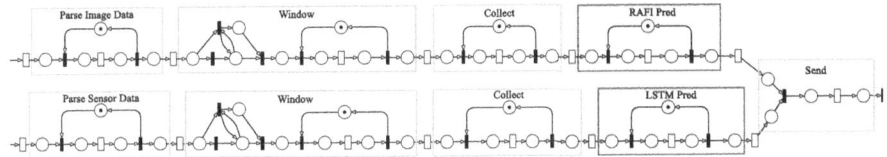

Fig. 7. The stochastic colored Petri net resulting from the automatic transformation of the pipeline shown in Fig. 6. For clarity, the single Petri net elements labels are omitted, but elements generated from the same components are grouped together.

Figure 7 shows the SCPN semantics generated by the automatic model-to-model transformation. Here, it is possible to see that some software components are single-threaded as they have been generated with a semaphore with a single token and that the *Window* components collect a certain number of tokens before executing.

Now, this Petri net can be simulated using the software TimeNET, which can be started directly from the E4SM-Editor. The transformation process automatically generated some performance measures and logging commands at the component transition in order to quantify, for example, how much data was produced by each sensor, how much data reached each actuator, and how high the component's usage rate was.

7   Conclusion

This paper presented an overview of an open-source modeling and simulation framework for time-based hardware-software systems that contain elements of uncertainties.

The framework, with its graphical drag-and-drop editor and textual editor, allows modeling such systems and running analyses either directly by querying the model elements or indirectly through a model-to-model transformation into a stochastic color Petri net, allowing analysis and simulation.

The analysis and simulation tools provide the foundation for computing performance measures of interest related, for example, to the execution times, end-to-end delays, data throughput, and quantifying the uncertainties caused by the interoperation of different non-deterministic components under different environments, such as classification components.

The methodology proposed in this study enables the examination of classification components by treating them as gray boxes, acknowledging their known confusion matrixes. By adopting a Petri net-based simulation process, it becomes feasible to replicate the behaviors of these components, leveraging the performance metrics derived from the analysis of their respective test data sets. This approach facilitates a deeper understanding of the classification process and comprehensively evaluates the components' effectiveness in real-world scenarios.

The effectiveness of the simulation process concerning the classification elements is directly linked to both the quantity and the caliber of the testing data employed in generating the confusion matrices. If a particular class was inadequately portrayed throughout the testing stage, the calculated performance metric may not accurately depict the real-world scenario. Therefore, ensuring that all classes are well-represented in the test data is crucial to obtaining reliable and meaningful simulation outcomes.

The E4SM editor is open-source, and its code is available on GitHub [31].

7.1 Future Works

The future work involves the integration of additional analysis techniques to broaden their availability as pre-made default options, as well as finalizing a more complex component specification, which shall allow for better alteration of the token content and specifying more advanced execution logics, for example, utilizing only a subset of the input or only some of the output pins and defining a more advanced token alteration semantics.

Acknowledgments. This work has received funding from the *Carl Zeiss Foundation* as part of the project Engineering for Smart Manufacturing (E4SM) under grant agreement no. P2017-01-005.

Disclosure of Interests. The authors have no competing interests to declare relevant to this article's content.

References

1. Amershi, S., et al.: Software engineering for machine learning: a case study. In: 2019 IEEE/ACM 41st International Conference on Software Engineering: Software Engineering in Practice (ICSE-SEIP), pp. 291–300. IEEE, New York, NY, May 2019. https://doi.org/10.1109/ICSE-SEIP.2019.00042

2. Aslam, K., Chen, Y., Butt, M., Malavolta, I.: Cross-platform real-time collaborative modeling: an architecture and a prototype implementation via emf.cloud. IEEE Access **11**, 49241–49260 (2023). https://doi.org/10.1109/ACCESS.2023.3276872

3. Bedini., F., Jungebloud., T., Maschotta., R., Zimmermann., A.: An analysis and simulation framework for systems with classification components. In: Proceedings of the 12th International Conference on Model-Based Software and Systems Engineering - MODELSWARD, pp. 50–61. INSTICC, SciTePress (2024). https://doi.org/10.5220/0012357000003645

4. Bedini, F., Maschotta, R., Wichmann, A., Zimmermann, A.: Towards automated fUML model verification with Petri nets. In: Proceedings of the 7th International Conference on Model-Driven Engineering and Software Development. SCITEPRESS - Science and Technology Publications (2019). https://doi.org/10.5220/0007371402980306

5. Bedini, F., Räth, T., Maschotta, R., Sattler, K.U., Zimmermann, A.: Automated transformation of a domain-specific language for system modeling to stochastic colored Petri nets. In: 2024 IEEE International Systems Conference (SysCon), pp. 1–8 (2024). https://doi.org/10.1109/SysCon61195.2024.10553543

6. Bettini, L.: Implementing Domain-Specific Languages with Xtext and Xtend. Packt Publishing Ltd, Birmingham, United Kingdom (2016)

7. Bonnet, S., Voirin, J.L., Exertier, D., Normand, V.: Not (strictly) relying on SysML for MBSE: Language, tooling and development perspectives: the Arcadia/Capella rationale. In: 2016 Annual IEEE Systems Conference (SysCon), pp. 1–6. IEEE, Orlando, FL, USA, April 2016. https://doi.org/10.1109/SYSCON.2016.7490559

8. Bucchiarone, A., Cabot, J., Paige, R.F., Pierantonio, A.: Grand challenges in model-driven engineering: an analysis of the state of the research. Softw. Syst. Model. **19**(1), 5–13 (2020). https://doi.org/10.1007/s10270-019-00773-6

9. Chen, C., Haduong, P., Brennan, K., Sonnert, G., Sadler, P.: The effects of first programming language on college students' computing attitude and achievement: a comparison of graphical and textual languages. Comput. Sci. Educ. **29**(1), 23–48 (2018). https://doi.org/10.1080/08993408.2018.1547564

10. Eclipse foundation: eclipse integrated development environment. https://eclipseide.org (2024), Accessed 25 July 2024

11. Elaasar, M., Labiche, Y.: Diagram definition: a case study with the UML class diagram. In: Whittle, J., Clark, T., Kühne, T. (eds.) MODELS 2011. LNCS, vol. 6981, pp. 364–378. Springer, Heidelberg (2011). https://doi.org/10.1007/978-3-642-24485-8_26

12. Feldt, R., de Oliveira Neto, F.G., Torkar, R.: Ways of applying artificial intelligence in software engineering (2018). https://doi.org/10.1145/3194104.3194109

13. German, R., Kelling, C., Zimmermann, A., Hommel, G.: TimeNET: a toolkit for evaluating non-markovian stochastic Petri nets. Perform. Eval. **24**(1–2), 69–87 (1995)

14. Huang, E., McGinnis, L.F., Mitchell, S.W.: Verifying SysML activity diagrams using formal transformation to Petri nets. Syst. Eng. **23**(1), 118–135 (2019). https://doi.org/10.1002/sys.21524

15. Hüllermeier, E., Waegeman, W.: Aleatoric and epistemic uncertainty in machine learning: an introduction to concepts and methods. Mach. Learn. **110**(3), 457–506 (2021). https://doi.org/10.1007/s10994-021-05946-3

16. Mernik, M., Heering, J., Sloane, A.M.: When and how to develop domain-specific languages. ACM Comput. Surv. **37**(4), 316–344 (2005). https://doi.org/10.1145/1118890.1118892

17. Möller, P., Haustermann, M., Mosteller, D., Schmitz, D.: Model synchronization and concurrent simulation of multiple formalisms based on reference nets. In: Koutny, M., Kristensen, L.M., Penczek, W. (eds.) Transactions on Petri Nets and Other Models of Concurrency XIII. LNCS, vol. 11090, pp. 93–115. Springer, Heidelberg (2018). https://doi.org/10.1007/978-3-662-58381-4_5

18. Mosteller, D., Haustermann, M., Moldt, D., Schmitz, D.: Integrated simulation of domain-specific modeling languages with Petri net-based transformational semantics. In: Koutny, M., Pomello, L., Kristensen, L.M. (eds.) Transactions on Petri Nets and Other Models of Concurrency XIV. LNCS, vol. 11790, pp. 101–125. Springer, Heidelberg (2019). https://doi.org/10.1007/978-3-662-60651-3_4

19. Obeo: Acceleo. online, https://www.eclipse.org/acceleo, Accessed 25 July 2024

20. Obeo: Eclipse sirius. https://www.eclipse.org/sirius (2024), Accessed 25 July 2024

21. Obeo: Obeo designer. https://www.obeodesigner.com (2024), Accessed 25 July 2024

22. Object management group: OMG fUML: semantics of a foundational subset for executable UML models v. 1.5, https://www.omg.org/spec/FUML/1.5

23. Object management group: OMG UML v. 2.5.1, December 2017, https://www.omg.org/spec/UML/2.5.1

24. Pennock, M.J., Wade, J.P.: The top 10 illusions of systems engineering: a research agenda. Procedia Comput. Sci. **44**, 147–154 (2015). https://doi.org/10.1016/j.procs.2015.03.033, https://www.sciencedirect.com/science/article/pii/S1877050915002690, 2015 Conference on Systems Engineering Research

25. Räth, T., Bedini, F., Sattler, K.U., Zimmermann, A.: Demo: interactive performance exploration of stream processing applications using colored Petri nets. In: Proceedings of the 17th ACM International Conference on Distributed and Event-Based Systems, DEBS 2023, pp. 191–194. ACM, New York, NY, USA (2023). https://doi.org/10.1145/3583678.3603280

26. Räth, T., Sattler, K.U.: Streamvizzard: an interactive and explorative stream processing editor. In: Proceedings of the 16th ACM International Conference on Distributed and Event-Based Systems, DEBS 2022, pp. 186–189. ACM, New York, NY, USA (2022). https://doi.org/10.1145/3524860.3543283

27. Riemer, K., Frößler, F.: Introducing real-time collaboration systems: development of a conceptual scheme and research directions. Commun. Assoc. Inf. Syst. **20**(1), 17 (2007)

28. Seidewitz, E.: Sysml v2: the new standard for model-based systems engineering. Center Model-Based Cyber-Phys. Product Dev. **31**(17), 12–12 (2023)

29. Spinellis, D.: Notable design patterns for domain-specific languages. J. Syst. Softw. **56**(1), 91–99 (2001)

30. Steinberg, D., Budinsky, F., Merks, E., Paternostro, M.: EMF: Eclipse Modeling Framework. Pearson Education, London, Great Britain (2008)

31. Technische Universität Ilmenau: the GitHub repository of the E4SM editor, July 2024, https://github.com/tuiSSE/e4sm-editor, last checked on Jul 25, 2024

32. Technische Universität Ilmenau: The official page of the TimeNET tool project, July 2024, https://timenet.tu-ilmenau.de, Accessed 25 July 2024

33. The eclipse foundation: eclipse QVT operational. https://projects.eclipse.org/projects/modeling.mmt.qvt-oml, Accessed 25 July 2024

34. The eclipse foundation: Xtext. (2024), https://www.eclipse.org/Xtext, Accessed 25 July 2024

35. Tomassetti, F., Zaytsev, V.: Reflections on the lack of adoption of domain specific languages. In: STAF Workshops, pp. 85–94 (2020)

36. Varró, D., Varró-Gyapay, S., Ehrig, H., Prange, U., Taentzer, G.: Termination analysis of model transformations by Petri nets. In: Corradini, A., Ehrig, H., Montanari, U., Ribeiro, L., Rozenberg, G. (eds.) Graph Transformations, pp. 260–274. Springer, Berlin Heidelberg, Berlin, Heidelberg (2006)

37. Walther, D., et al.: Recurrent autoencoder for weld discontinuity prediction. J. Adv. Joining Process. **9**, 100203 (2024). https://doi.org/10.1016/j.jajp.2024.100203, https://www.sciencedirect.com/science/article/pii/S2666330924000207

38. Zhang, D., Tsai, J.: Machine learning and software engineering. Software Qual. J. **11**(2), 87–119 (2003). https://doi.org/10.1023/a:1023760326768

39. Zimmermann, A.: Modeling and evaluation of stochastic Petri nets with TimeNET 4.1. In: 6th International ICST Conference on Performance Evaluation Methodologies and Tools, pp. 54–63. IEEE (2012)

Code Generation for Smart Contracts in Enterprise Application Integration

Mailson Teles-Borges[1(✉)], Rafael Z. Frantz[1], Jose Bocanegra[2], Eldair F. Dornelles[1],
Sandro Sawicki[1], Fabricia Roos-Frantz[1], Antonia M. Reina-Quintero[3],
and Carlos Molina-Jimenez[4]

[1] Unijuí University, Ijuí, RS, Brazil
mailson.borges@sou.unijui.edu.br,
{rzfrantz,eldair.dornelles,sawicki,frfrantz}@unijui.edu.br
[2] Universidad Distrital Francisco José de Caldas, Bogotá, Colombia
jjbocanegrag@udistrital.edu.co
[3] University of Seville, Seville, Spain
reinaqu@us.es
[4] University of Cambridge, Cambridge, UK
carlos.molina@cl.cam.ac.uk

Abstract. The main concern of this work is the automatic generation of executable smart contracts for enforcing constrains (policies) in application integration processes. We argue that the executable code can be generated automatically from contracts written in Domain Specific Languages. To support our argument, we have implemented a transformation engine that translates contracts written in Jabuti DSL into Golang codes that the developer can deploy and execute in Hyperledger Fabric. The paper discusses the implementation of the transformation engine and a use case study.

Keywords: Smart contract · DSL for smart contracts · Code generation · Text-to-text transformation · ANTLR · Enterprise application integration

1 Introduction

The main concern of this work is the automatic generation of executable smart contracts for enforcing constrains (policies) in application integration processes. Application integration processes are pieces of software that integrate the functionalities of two or more existing components (applications) to produce new functionalities. To appreciate the point, we can think of a shop composed of several departments such as human resources, marketing, finance, sales, delivery, customer service, and other departments. To gain in efficiency, it is advisable to integrate the functionalities of some or all the departments by means of application integration processes. As elaborated in a case study that we present in Sect. 5, the delivery department might need to interoperate with the customer service department to delegate the latter the responsibility to compensate customers affected by delayed deliveries.

The challenge is to build application integration processes from components that i) were originally implemented to operate independently and ii) have reservations to

F. José Domínguez Mayo et al. (Eds.): MODELSWARD 2024, CCIS 2547, pp. 229–246, 2026.
https://doi.org/10.1007/978-3-031-96841-9_12

interoperate unless the application integration process implements certain rules to regulate the interaction between the department and the application integration process. For example, the former might demand that the latter does not place more than a certain number of requests to prevent overloads.

In practice, application integration processes are implemented with the help of Enterprise Application Integration (EAI) platforms [23] that provide tools for modelling, implementing, and executing integration processes. In these EAI platforms, the integration process becomes a workflow composed of ports and tasks through which data messages flow. Ports are implementations of communication protocols (e.g., HTTP, FTP, SSH, JDBC, etc.). Tasks perform atomic operations (e.g., filter, merge, split, transform, copy, aggregate, route, among others) on the data flowing through the workflow [10].

In this work, we are interested in application integration processes that are able to execute operations programmatically: they are able to consume data from some components, process it, and react with the automatic execution of some operations in accordance with the results. For example, the application integration process sends notifications to other components to suggest the execution of some operations. In our view, this behaviour can be conveniently implemented by smart contracts that are deployed on blockchains to take advantage of the services that the latter provide such as immutability of the smart contract and authentication of the contractual parties and authenticity of the transactions.

A smart contract is a software artefact designed to verify and execute transactions automatically. It is normally written in a contract language such as Solidity and Golang, and is deployed on a blockchain. Usually, software engineers write a contract manually in the run-time language; however, this approach suffers from two serious drawbacks: firstly, the contract is not reusable because platforms are tightly coupled to a particular contract language, for example, Ethereum supports Serpent and Solidity while Hyperledger prefers Golang; secondly, the contract is likely to be buggy and vulnerable [7,24] because current contract languages are not easy or intuitive to use; and they include too many language details (e.g., variables, pointers, data structures) that distract the programmer from the semantics of the contract. To avoid these annoyances, it is convenient to use domain-specific languages (DSLs) that specify contracts in platform–independent languages that can be translated mechanically to a specific blockchain platform such as Ethereum or Hyperledger. DSLs have a high level of abstraction and provide constructors that are closer to the domain of interest, for example, Enterprise Application Integrations [8]. An example of a DSL for writing smart contracts for EAI is Jabuti DSL [6] which has been developed by the Applied Computing Research Group (GCA)[1] at Unijui University. Jabuti DSL incorporates both domain constructors of contracts (contract, party, condition, and types of clause) and EAI vocabulary (i.e., application, process, type of operations, and messages). It produces platform–independent contracts that can be mechanically translated to platform specific languages and executed. There are two execution alternatives. One alternative is to implement a new blockchain with an execution environment that supports a given language and convert the contract written in Jabuti DSL into this language, deploy on the new blockchain and execute.

---

[1] www.gca.unijui.edu.br.

Unfortunately, this approach demands time and resources, as such, it falls outside the scope of our current research interest. The second alternative is to translate the contracts written in Jabuti DSL into contracts written in languages supported by existing blockchains.

The demonstration of the second alternative is the main contribution of this paper. Precisely, the paper contributes the implementation of a transformation engine that translates smart contracts written in Jabuti DSL into Golang code that we deploy and execute in Hyperledger. We feel that for the time being this is a good approach to test the correctness of the transformation engine and the strengths and drawbacks of Jabuti DSL. The engine can be accessed through Jabuti CE [24], a VSCode extension to edit Jabuti DSL contracts. Alternatively, it is also available as a library from a GitHub repository[2]. Corporate environments typically deal with sensitive information. Consequently, their application integration processes normally require access controls and permissions. In the transformation engine that this paper discusses, we use the facilities offered by the Hyperledger Fabric to solve these issues. However, we clarify that Jabuti DSL is not restricted to Golang or Hyperledger; if needed, transformation engines can be implemented to target other languages and blockchain platforms.

This paper is organised as follows: Sect. 2 analyses related works; Sect. 3 introduces Jabuti DSL and Hyperledger Fabric as background; Sect. 4 details the transformation engine; Sect. 5 presents a case study to validate the execution of the transformed contract; and finally, Sect. 6 concludes and discusses future work.

2   Related Works

In this section, we evaluate works related to Model Driven Engineering (MDE) that discuss DSL languages with code generators. Transformations are classified into: *model-to-model*, *model-to-text*, *text-to-model* and *text-to-text*. *Model-to-model* transformations transform from one model to another; in *model-to-text* transformations a model is converted to a textual syntax; in *text-to-text* transformations a textual syntax is converted to another textual syntax; in text-to-model transformations a textual syntax is converted to a model. Several works are developed on the Eclipse Modelling Framework (EMF) using Xtext and Xtend [2]. Xtext is an open-source framework for the development of DSLs. Xtend is a Java dialect compatible with Xtext. Symboleo [22] is an ontology-based DSL for specifying legal contracts. The ontology separates a contract into eight concepts: Contract, Party, Obligation, Power, Asset, Event, Role, and Legal-Position. Contract is a set of obligations and powers. Party is a legal agent who owns assets; Obligations are duties that result from a prior interaction between the parties. Powers are the rights of a party to create, change, suspend, or end legal positions. Asset is an owned item of value. Event is a happening that occurs at a time instance and that cannot change. Role is a collection of obligations and powers. LegalPosition is the relationship between roles. This ontology is implemented in a JavaScript module called SymboleoJS[3]. Symboleo2SC [21] converts Symboleo smart contracts into smart contracts for Hyperledger Fabric. The authors validate the transformed contract with

---

[2] https://github.com/gca-research-group/jabuti-ce-transformation-engine.
[3] https://github.com/Smart-Contract-Modelling-uOttawa/Symboleo-JS-Core.

three legal contracts specified in Symboleo. The authors acknowledge some unresolved challenges: firstly, the lack of implementation of an authorisation and authentication mechanism. In their work any member connected to the network is allowed to execute a transaction on the contract—in our work, we address this issue. Another pending question is the cost of the execution of the transaction when public blockchains are used instead of permissioned ones. Like in our work, they avoid the issues by resorting to Hyperledger Fabric.

SPESC-Translator [3] converts SPESC [15], a DSL for legal smart contracts, into Solidity code. SPESC smart contract consists of four parts: contract name, parties, terms, and additional information (e.g. variables). The authors present four contracts in different contexts: auction contract, loan contract, house-leasing contract, and purchase contract. Such contracts are converted to Solidity through SPESC-Translator. Based on these contracts, SPESC-Translator is evaluated using two criteria: security and efficiency. Security is an issue that impacts smart contracts on public blockchains [14,17,27]. Four different tools were used to assess the vulnerabilities of the transformed SPESC contracts: Madmax [11], Mythril [4], Oyente [18] and Smartcheck [25]). Initially, three vulnerabilities were found, but they were corrected in subsequent versions of SPESC-Translator. The efficiency of SPESC-Translator is measured in Logical Lines of Codes (LLOC). They achieve approximately 85%. The missing 15% needs to be added manually. Contract Modeling Language (CML) [26,28] implements a generator that converts contracts into Solidity code. CML is a DSL for specifying smart contracts and its structure contains three main blocks: state variables, actions, and clauses. CML was evaluated with five use cases (become richest, purchase, simple auction, time lock, and voting); however, the paper does not describe the contracts. The authors mention that although the DSL provides a high degree of abstraction, this abstraction has a technical cost. As implementations become abstract, the code generated by the transformation tends to become less understandable, and the cost of execution on Ethereum tends to be higher.

iContractML [12,13] is a platform-agnostic smart contract framework for modelling and deploying smart contracts on multiple blockchains. iContractML uses Acceleo[4] to generate templates to transform smart contracts. The transformed smart contract is evaluated across multiple blockchains in different contexts: Ethereum, Hyperledger Composer and Azure blockchain. The aims of the multi-blockchain analysis is to reduce the impact of author's bias and to increase the confidence in the efficiency of the transformation. As in the previous works, the loss of readability and the increase in cost related to the code generated for Ethereum are unsolved issues. The works developed so far is mostly implemented in Eclipse-based and Java technologies. In contrast, in our work, Jabuti CE relies on Typescript. It is worth noting that in the absence of standards for evaluating the transformed smart contracts, all the works, including ours, resort to use case-based evaluation.

The exploration of related work revealed that there is a strong interest in transformations into Solidity code to be executed in Ethereum. In contrast, in our work, we aimed at Golang for Hyperledger Fabric, yet, the techniques that we discuss in our paper can be used for implementing a transformator for Solidity code to run in Ethereum. A

---

[4] https://eclipse.dev/acceleo/.

salient feature of our work is modularity. We have implemented at modular architecture where each component works independently and, as such, can be replaced by other implementations. Our architecture also provides a validation layer that we use to add semantic validations that enhance the syntactic definitions created for the Jabuti DSL.

3   Background

In this section, we present a summary of the syntax of Jabuti DSL – the DSL language for EAI that we use to write platform-independent smart contracts. Next, we present the relevant concepts of Hyperledger Fabric.

3.1   Jabuti DSL

Integration processes are programs responsible for interconnecting two or more applications, manipulating the information transmitted as necessary. Figure 1 shows the architecture of an integration process. Ports are used as communication interfaces with applications, slots, and tasks process received information. Slots enable communication between tasks, receiving messages from a given task, and delivering messages to the next task. Tasks, on the other hand, transform the transmitted data [6, 9, 19]. Communication constraints between App 1 and the Integration Process in the Entry port or the Integration Process and App 2 in the Exit port can be implemented by a Jabuti DSL contract.

Figure 2 shows the Jabuti DSL metamodel. The metamodel represents the abstract syntax of the Jabuti DSL, presenting its constructors and cardinalities. Contract is the main metaclass and represents the contract. The contract contains a validity period (beginDate and dueDate), parties (application and process) and clauses. Clauses have an operation and terms and can be of three different types: prohibition, right and obligation. Operation represents the type of interaction carried out between the application and the integration process. Terms specifies the communication restrictions and can be: TimeInterval, WeekDaysInterval, SessionInterval, Timeout, MaxNumberOf-Operations and MessageContent. TimeInterval specifies a time interval between two hour periods for which the clause must be executed. WeekDaysInterval specifies the days of the week on which the integration is valid. SessionInterval specifies a period of time in which a session is active and will expire. Timeout specifies a time in which the clause should be processed. MaxNumberOfOperation specifies the number of operations per unit of time. MessageContent allows one to extract data from the processed message. Finally, the clause may have one or more integration rules. A case study with a contract written in Jabuti DSL is discussed in Sect. 5.

3.2   Hyperledger Fabric

Hyperledger Fabric is a permissioned [1] blockchain therefore, it can only be accessed by members that have permission, after successful authentication. This contrasts with

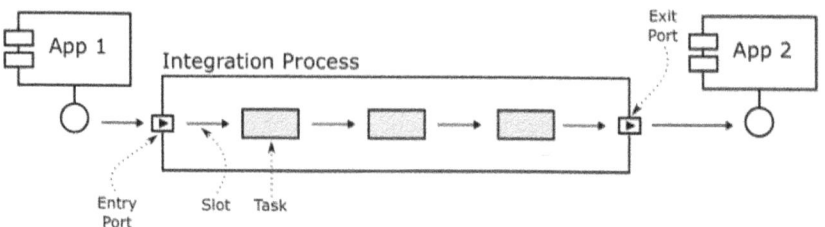

Fig. 1. Integration process architecture.

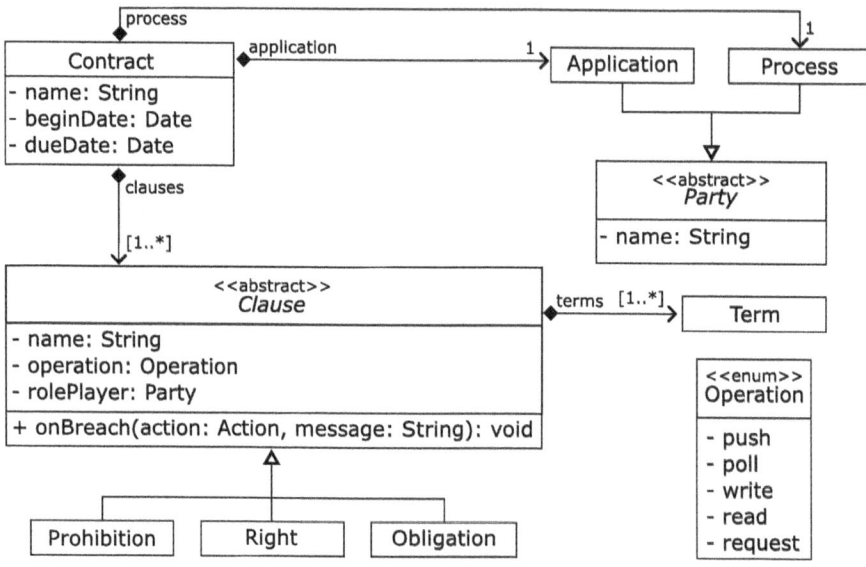

Fig. 2. Jabuti DSL metamodel.

public blockchains which require no permission [29]. Membership and authentication reduce the risk of malicious code being introduced by users [16].

Hyperledger Fabric has a set of components that can be configured to match the particularities of the applications, the main components are:

Certificate Authority (CA): members and transactions, executed on the network, are identified via digital identities. A Certificate Authority is responsible for issuing users with digital certificates, which are digital identities based on private/public key pairs. The certificate's private key is stored in a secure location by the owner and used to sign his or her transactions.

Member Service Provider (MSP): members need to prove their identity on permissioned blockchains. The CA issues the certificates. At the time of transaction the MSP validates the certificate; it checks it's validity and the public key associated to the transactions.

Peers: are hyperldger nodes that endorse transactions and execute smart contracts. There are three types of peers: Endorsing Peers, Committing Peers and Anchor Peers. Endorsing Peers simulate and endorse proposed transactions. Committing Peers validate and commit the transaction to the ledger. Anchor Peers facilitate the discovery of peers in other organisations, and the communication between channels. They are essential for maintaining the network's communication structure but do not have a direct rule on transaction processing or ledger maintenance.

Ordering Service: guarantees that all transactions are processed in a logical and consistent order across all peers.

Chaincode (smart contract): is a piece of code written in Go, Java, Node, or another language, that facilitates interaction between application and blockchain.

Figure 3 shows a sample Hyperledger Fabric network. Network Configuration is a collection of policies that has been accepted by the organisations Org 1, Org 2 and Org 3. Peers 1 and 2 are peers belonging to Orgs 1 and 2 and are part of the Channel 1. These peers maintain a copy of the channel database (Ledger). Org 3 holds the Ordering Service. App 1 and App 2 are applications used by Org 1 and Org 2 to interact with the channel. Each peer receives the same smart contract instance.

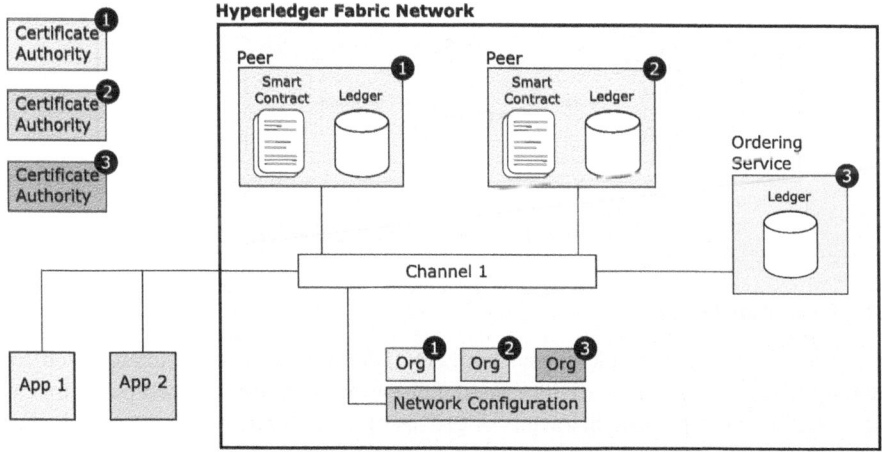

Fig. 3. Hperledger Fabric Network. Adapted from [5].

4   Transformation Engine

The transformation engine accepts a Jabuti DSL contract as input, processes it, and converts it to the requested format. It is composed of five components (see Fig. 4: Grammar Parser, Validators, Canonical Parser, Code Generator and Code Formatter. The Grammar Parser converts the Jabuti DSL contract into an Abstract Syntax Tree (AST). The Validators are a set of validators responsible for the syntactic and semantic evaluation of the contract. The Canonical Parser converts the AST generated by the Generic Parser to the structure required by the `Code Generator`. The `Code Generator` converts the data received from the previous component to the defined format of the target blockchain. Finally, the `Code Formatter` formats the resulting file according to the formatting rules of the target language of the smart contract. The following subsections detail these components.

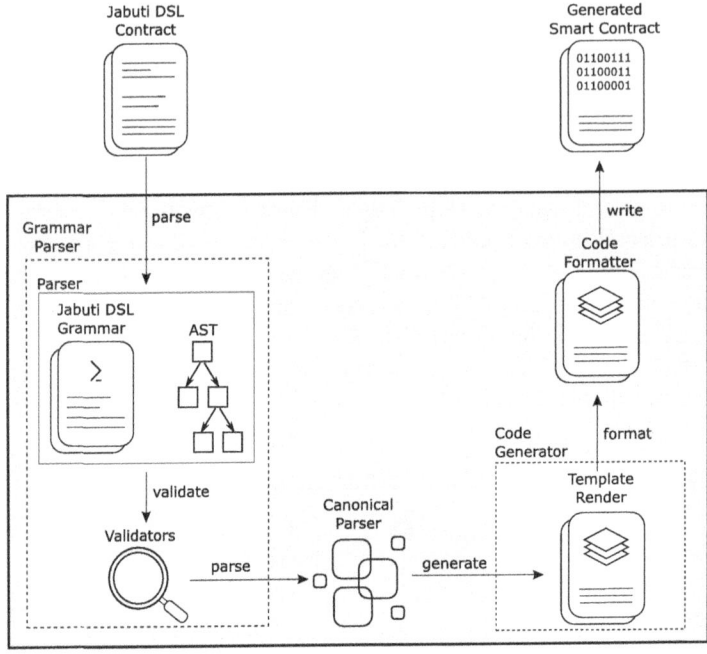

Fig. 4. Transformation engine components.

4.1 Grammar Parser

`Grammar Parser` is implemented with ANTLR [20], a parser generator used for building languages. ANTLR divides the definition of grammar into two parts: tokens and rules. Tokens represent characters or groups of them, while rules are logical combinations of these tokens. Jabuti DSL's grammar is available on Github[5]. The grammar is a formalism that do not allow us to specify richer constraints. For example, in Listing 1.1 that shows an excerpt of the Jabuti DSL grammar, the rule in line 7 specifies that a second must written as 1 or 2 digits, but we cannot specify that the maximum value of seconds is 60. As a `Digit` (line 4), can be a number between 0 and 9, the specification of the Digit rule allows a second with a value of 99, which is syntactically correct, but semantically incorrect. The `Validator` component validates these semantic constraints. The `Grammar Parser` generates an Abstract Syntax Tree (AST) from the Jabuti DSL contract. The AST is a hierarchical data structure that establishes a relationship between each token present in the DSL to facilitate separate analysis. Figure 5 shows a graphical representation of the AST generated for the extract of a contract section presented in Listing 1.2.

---
[5] https://github.com/gca-research-group/jabuti-ce-jabuti-dsl-grammar.

```
1   // Tokens
2   Minus: '-';
3   Colon:':';
4   Digit: [0-9];
5
6   // Rules
7   datetime: year Minus month Minus day time?;
8   time: hour Colon minute (Colon second)?;
9   second: Digit Digit?;
10  minute: Digit Digit?;
11  hour: Digit Digit?;
12  day: Digit Digit? ;
13  month: Digit Digit?;
14  year: Digit+;
```

Listing 1.1. Jabuti DSL grammar excerpt.

```
1   dates {
2       beginDate = 2024-01-11
3   }
```

Listing 1.2. Begin date excerpt.

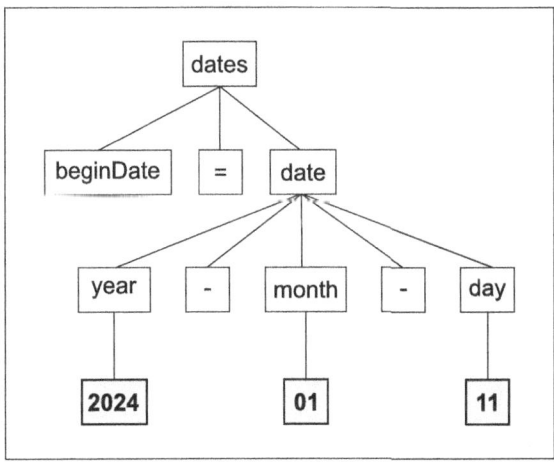

Fig. 5. Begin date AST.

4.2 Validators

The Grammar Parser component automatically runs the syntactic validations. Syntactic validations are validations of the language structure. Although the contract may be syntactically correct, it may contain semantic violations. Semantic violations are related to the information's meaning in the contract. Below are some examples:

- The grammar allows months of up to 31 days; however, February has 28 or 29 and April has 30.
- Two clauses with the same type and name are not allowed.
- Timeout is a term that should only exist in clauses whose operation is response.

```
1   export class JabutiGrammarListenerImpl implements JabutiGrammarListener {
2     enterDate(ctx: DateContext) {
3       const year = +ctx.year().text;
4       const month = +ctx.month().text;
5       const day = +ctx.day().text;
6
7       const maxDays = getDaysInMonth(year, month);
8
9       if (day > maxDays) {
10        throw new Error('The date given is invalid.');
11      }
12    }
13
14    // ...
15  }
```

Listing 1.3. Detection of invalid dates.

- The contract due date must be greater than the begin date.
- The content present in the `MessageContent` constructor must be a *jsonpath* or a *xpath*.

Semantic validations are implemented using an interface provided by the ANTLR library. This interface gives access to all the rules defined in the grammar in such a manner that custom validations can be added for each of them. Listing 1.3 shows a code excerpt responsible for date validation. Line 2, shows the definition of the `enterDate` method, which is responsible for validating a date. This method has as parameter `ctx`, that refers to the context that receives the AST for the given date. In Lines 3–5, the year, month, and day are extracted from the context. In Line 7, given a year and a month, the maximum number of days of that month and year is calculated. Finally, Lines 9–11 show a piece of code that generates an error if the day entered in the context date is greater than the maximum number of days.

4.3 Canonical Parser

The `Canonical Parser` is the component responsible for converting the grammar's AST into a standard data structure in JSON. This JSON structure is used by the `Template Generator` component. An example of a JSON structure is presented in Listing 1.4. The AST is converted to this JSON structure so that the process and aggregation of information necessary for the transformation process can be performed. For example, there are some constructors that have the attribute *name* (see Lines 2, 12, 15 and 19). This attribute contains naming variations that are used according to the transformation performed.

The `name` attribute (Line 2) receives the contract name. The `dates` and `parties` attributes (Lines 3 and 4), receive the effective dates and the respective parties of the contract. Lines 5-8 contain `timeoutTerms` which is a list of timeout terms. These terms require special treatment since, despite being executed in response-type clauses, they depend on information regarding the execution date/time of the request-type clause. The items in `timeoutTerms` contain the names of the respective terms and the clauses to which they belong. When converting request-type clauses, the clause

```
1    {
2        name: { snake, camel, pascal },
3        dates: { beginDate, dueDate },
4        parties: { application, process },
5        timeoutTerms: [{
6            clause: { snake, camel, pascal },
7            term: { snake, camel, pascal}
8        }],
9        clauses: [{
10           rolePlayer,
11           operation,
12           name: { snake, camel, pascal },
13           messages: { error, success }
14           variables: [{
15               name: { snake, camel, pascal },
16               type
17           }],
18           terms: [{
19               name: { snake, camel, pascal },
20               type
21   }]}]}
```

Listing 1.4. Structure of the Jabuti DSL JSON.

execution date/time is recorded and then used to validate whether there was *timeout* or not. `clauses` is a list containing the contract's clauses. The `rolePlayer` and `operation` attributes store the executor and operation type of the clause, respectively. The `name` attribute of a clause stores the variations for the clause names. `messages`, on line 13, stores the success and error messages for clause violations. The `variables` attribute (line 14) represents the variables that are used as arguments for executing the clause. Each `variables` has two attributes `name` and `type`, that represent name and type of the variable, respectively. The type can be one of the following values: *number*, *time*, *datetime*, *text* and *boolean*. These types are used to assign the correct type according to the target language. For example, while a variable with the value *datetime* becomes *uint32* in Solidity, it is converted to *time.Time* in Golang, because Solidity does not have a specific type for dates. Terms are stored in the attribute `terms` (line 18).

4.4   Template Generator

The `Template Generator` component generates the transformed smart contract by joining the JSON structures assembled by the `Canonical Parser` and the target blockchain template. These pre-made templates contain methods and standard variables that are necessary for any transformed smart contract. Every blockchain has its own set of operating rules that are part of its design and operating model, thus, it is important to take this into account when developing the contract template. Hyperledger Fabric, for example, treats the smart contract as an API to access and interact with the blockchain, so the same contract can be used to regulate more than one integration. The blockchain is responsible for storing the execution state of the contract between the two parties involved. For this reason, a contract must first be set up and signed by both parties after being published on the network. Only then can the other clauses be executed. In addition

```
1  [{
2     "beginDate": "2025-01-01T00:00:00Z",
3     "dueDate": "2024-12-31T00:00:00Z",
4     "parties": {
5        "application": { "name", "id": "" },
6        "process": { "name", "id": "" }
7     }
8  }]
```

Listing 1.5. Parameters for executing the *Init* method of the Jabuti DSL contract.

to the methods from the Jabuti DSL contract, another four are added by default: Init, Sign, QueryAsset and QueryClientId. They are detailed below:

Init: is the method responsible for registering the initial data of the contract (start date, end of validity and parties) generating a unique identifier that is used for subsequent interactions with the contract. In the transformation process, a comment containing execution examples of each clause is added at the beginning of the resulting smart contract. Listing 1.5 shows a concrete example of a real parameter for Init method. BeginDate and DueDate are formatted according to RFC 3339[6] which is the format supported by the smart contract in Golang. The parties receive *name* and *id*. The *name* attribute facilitates the identification of the party, while *id* attribute is the *Client Id* of the party on the blockchain.

Sign: is the method responsible for recording the signature and consent to the terms of the contract by both parties. When the contract is signed, both the consent and the date of signature are recorded.

QueryAsset: s the method used to query the smart contract.

QueryClientId: is the method used to query the Client Id.

Template rendering libraries are used to render the smart contract that was transformed from the information provided by `Canonical Parser`. There are several libraries of this kind available, such as *ejs*[7], *pug*[8], *handlebars*[9] and *mustache*[10]. These libraries work in a similar way, the main difference among them is the syntax and whether they support or not certain features. We selected *ejs* because it is more frequently used. Listing 1.6 presents an example of a template processed with *ejs*: line 1 contains the template declaration that dynamically receives two variables: *research-Group* and *university*. These variables are identified using the characters <%= =%>. In line 3, the render method of *ejs* is executed having as real parameters the previously defined template and an object containing the expected variables and their respective values. Finally, line 5 shows the final result of the transformed template.

```
1  const template = <p><%=reseachGroup=> is a research group at <%=university=>.</p>;
2
3  const output = ejs.render(template, \{ reseachGroup: 'GCA', university: 'Unijui' \});
```

---

[6] https://www.rfc-editor.org/rfc/rfc3339.

[7] https://ejs.co/.

[8] https://pugjs.org/API/getting-started.html.

[9] https://handlebarsjs.com/.

[10] https://github.com/janl/mustache.js.

```
4
5   // output: <p>GCA is a research group at Unijui.</p>
```

Listing 1.6. Transformation of a template using EJS.

Each transformation implemented has a corresponding `Template Generator`. The implemented `Template Generator` will inherit the `Generator` interface as displayed in Listing 1.7. This interface forces `Template Generator` to implement two methods: `render` and `generate`. The `render` method receives the template and the Jabuti DSL contract. Internally, this method runs a `Canonical Parser` to obtain the JSON mentioned above and then runs the `Template Rendering Library` to transform the contract as desired. `Generate` executes the render method for transformation and implements logic relevant to the desired target blockchain.

```
1   export interface Generator {
2     render: (contract: string, template?: string) => string;
3     generate: (contract: string) => string[];
4   }
```

Listing 1.7. Generator interface.

4.5 Formatter

The `Formatter` component corrects formatting errors generated in the transformation process. It is common for programming languages to have style standards such as the number of spaces for indentation (number of spaces used to organise blocks of code), use of semicolons at the end of each line, number of empty lines after each expression, among others. Each language usually has a specific tool that corrects code formatting according to these styles: Golang uses gofmt[11] while Solidity uses Prettier[12]. `Formatter` uses these tools to execute code style standardisation.

5 Case Study

This section demonstrates how the transformation engine operates. We describe a hypothetical scenario in Subsect. 5.1 and in Subsect. 5.2 we explain how the resulting smart contract is converted into Golang and executed in the Hyperledger Fabric.

5.1 Description

Imagine that a company operates the following three policies:

Policy 1. Customers who have spent $300.00 or more and affected by delayed deliveries are entitled to 5% discount vouchers to spend on subsequent purchases.

Policy 2. Customers who have spent $100.00 or more and affected by delayed deliveries are entitled to 3% discount vouchers to spend on subsequent purchases.

---

[11] https://pkg.go.dev/cmd/gofmt.
[12] https://prettier.io/.

```
1   contract DiscountCouponLateDelivery {
2       dates {
3           beginDate = 2024-06-06 00:00
4           dueDate = 2024-06-10 23:59
5       }
6
7       parties {
8           application = "Delivery App"
9           process = "Integration Process"
10      }
11
12      variables {
13          totalPurchaseAmount = MessageContent("sum($.[*].value)")
14          deliveryDate = "$.deliveryDate"
15          expectedDate = "$.expectedDate"
16      }
17
18      clauses {
19          obligation purchasesBetween100USD300USD {
20              rolePlayer = application
21              operation = response
22
23              terms {
24                  MessageContent(totalPurchaseAmount >= 100),
25                  MessageContent(totalPurchaseAmount < 300),
26                  MessageContent(deliveryDate > expectedDate)
27              }
28
29              onBreach(log("[100USD300USD] delivery date later than expected date"))
30          }
31
32          obligation purchasesGreatherThan300USD {
33              rolePlayer = application
34              operation = response
35
36              terms {
37                  MessageContent(totalPurchaseAmount > 300),
38                  MessageContent(deliveryDate > expectedDate)
39              }
40
41              onBreach(log("[300USD] delivery date later than expected date"))
42          }
43      }
44  }
```

Listing 1.8. Policies representation through Jabuti DSL.

Policy 3. Policy 1 and Policy 2 apply only from 2024-06-06 to 2024-06-10, inclusive.

Listing 1.8 encodes these policies as a Jabuti DSL contract. We assume that there is a tracking system that notifies the smart contract of deliveries. The smart contract reacts by verifying whether the policies listed above apply. If so, the corresponding discount is credited to the customer's account automatically.

```
1  const grammarParser = new GrammarParser();
2  const grammarContext = grammarParser.parse(jabutiDSLContract).contract();
3
4  const canonicalParser = new CanonicalParser();
5  const canonicalContext = canonicalParser.parse(grammarContext);
6
7  const generator = new HyperledgerFabricGolangGenerator();
8  const files = generator.generate(canonicalContext);
9
10 const formatter = new HyperledgerFabricGolangFormatter();
11
12 const golangSmartContract = formatter.format(files.content);
```

Listing 1.9. Transformation of the Jabuti DSL Smart Contract.

5.2   Execution

To monitor the policies of Subsect. 5.1, we will generate a smart contract to be executed in the Hyperledger Fabric. This implies the transformation of the Jabuti DSL contract into Golang and the configuration of Hyperledger blockchain. In pursuit of this aim, our Golang transformation engine transforms the JabutiDSL contract, introduced in Listing 1.8, into Golang. The code snippet that executes this transformation is shown in Listing 1.9. Recall that this piece of code corresponds to the components and phases shown in Fig. 4. The resulting smart contract is available on Github[13]. We configure the blockchain network using *Spydra*[14] which is an extension available from VSCode. *Spydra* automatically sets up a local blockchain network and manages the smart contract publishing process.

The contract is firstly initiated and then signed. Once signed, it is ready to validate the policies of Subsect. 5.1. Listing 1.10 shows the file used to execute the ClauseObligationPurchasesBetween100USD300USD method generated in the transformation that corresponds to the purchasesBetween100USD300USD clause of the original Jabuti DSL contract. This method consists of four parameters: assetId, totalPurchaseAmount, deliveryDate and expectedDate. AssetId is the contract code generated by the Init method. The other parameters (totalPurchaseAmount, deliveryDate and expectedDate) are the respective clause parameters in the Jabuti DSL contract. Listing 1.11 shows the result of executing this clause. As the delivery date is greater than the expected date (see Line 7 of Listing 1.10) the contract generates a failure that returns an error message that warns that the delivery date is greater than the expected date (see Line 6 of Listing 1.11). We assume that this message will be used at some point to issue the discount voucher to the affected customer.

---

[13] https://github.com/gca-research-group/jabuti-ce-transformation-engine.
[14] https://marketplace.visualstudio.com/items?itemName=Spydra.hyperledger-fabric-debugger.

```
1   {
2       "invoke": "ClauseObligationPurchasesBetween100USD300USD",
3       "args": [
4           {
5               "assetId": "17819fdd-575e-46a7-aef9-9467ac9e8ad9",
6               "totalPurchaseAmount": 250,
7               "deliveryDate": 1717758000, // 2024-06-07 12:00:00
8               "expectedDate": 1717844400 // 2024-06-08 12:00:00
9           }
10      ]
11  }
```

Listing 1.10. Arguments of clause execution.

```
1   Error: endorsement failure during invoke.
2   Response: status:500
3   Time: 664 ms
4
5   Result:
6   message:"[100USD300USD] delivery date later than expected date"
```

Listing 1.11. Clause execution response.

6   Conclusions and Future Work

We have demonstrated how to convert smart contracts written in a DSL language for EAI into codes that are ready for deployment on target blockchains. As an example, we have discussed a transformation engine that converts smart contracts written in Jabuti DSL into Golang code that can be deployed on Hyperledger Fabric. The transformation engine is composed of independent components implemented based on the grammar defined using ANLTR. This engine converts the Jabuti DSL contract to an Abstract Syntax Tree (AST), validates the syntax and semantics of the contract, and converts this AST to a data structure that is used by the `Code Generator` component. This component converts these data to the needed format. The last step formats the generated contract to match the style guidelines of the target language. We believe that the results presented in this paper are contributions in the right direction, as they facilitate the monitoring of application integration processes to detect potential violations of constrain policies and take compensation actions. We feel that our work addresses a problem that has not received enough attention, namely, monitoring of contractual constraints in application integration processes. However, there are still pending tasks. One of them is the inclusion of more comprehensive compensation (contingency) actions that are triggered when then main actions fail to execute.

Acknowledgements. This work was supported by the Co-ordination for the Brazilian Improvement of Higher Education Personnel (CAPES); and the Brazilian National Council for Scientific and Technological Development (CNPq) under the following project grants 309425/2023-9 and 402915/2023-2 to Rafael Z. Frantz and 311011/2022-5 to Fabricia Roos-Frantz. The work of Antonia M. Reina has been funded by projects AETHER-US (PID2020-112540RB-C44/AEI/10.13039/501100011033) and ALBA (TED2021-130355B-C32), in Seville, Spain. Carlos Molina was funded by the UKRI CAMB project, grant EP/X015785/1(G115169).

References

1. Androulaki, E., et al.: Hyperledger fabric: a distributed operating system for permissioned blockchains. In: Proceedings of the Thirteenth European Conference on Computer Systems (EuroSys), pp. 1–15 (2018)
2. Bettini, L.: Implementing Domain-Specific Languages with Xtext and Xtend. Packt Publishing Ltd (2016)
3. Chen, E., et al.: Spesc-translator: towards automatically smart legal contract conversion for blockchain-based auction services. IEEE Trans. Serv. Comput. 3061–3076 (2021)
4. ConsenSys: Mythril: security analysis tool for ethereum smart contracts. https://github.com/Consensys/mythril (2024), Accessed 25 July 2024
5. Documentation, H.F.: How fabric networks are structured (2024), https://hyperledger-fabric.readthedocs.io/en/latest/network/network.html, Accessed June 2024
6. Dornelles, E.F., et al.: Advances in a dsl to specify smart contracts for application integration processes. In: Anais do XXV Congresso Ibero-Americano em Engenharia de Software, pp. 46–60 (2022)
7. Durieux, T., Ferreira, J.F., Abreu, R., Cruz, P.: Empirical review of automated analysis tools on 47,587 ethereum smart contracts. In: Proceedings of the ACM/IEEE 42nd International Conference on Software Engineering, pp. 530–541 (2020)
8. Fowler, M.: Domain-Specific Languages. Pearson Education (2010)
9. Frantz, R.Z., Quintero, A.M.R., Corchuelo, R.: A domain-specific language to design enterprise application integration solutions. Int. J. Coop. Inf. Syst. 143–176 (2011)
10. Freire, D.L., Frantz, R.Z., Roos-Frantz, F., Sawicki, S.: Survey on the run-time systems of enterprise application integration platforms focusing on performance. Softw. Pract. Exp. 341–360 (2019)
11. Grech, N., Kong, M., Jurisevic, A., Brent, L., Scholz, B., Smaragdakis, Y.: Madmax: surviving out-of-gas conditions in ethereum smart contracts. In: Proceedings of the ACM on Programming Languages, pp. 1–27 (2018)
12. Hamdaqa, M., Met, L.A.P., Qasse, I.: icontractml 2.0: a domain-specific language for modeling and deploying smart contracts onto multiple blockchain platforms. Inf. Softw. Technol. 106762 (2022)
13. Hamdaqa, M., Metz, L.A.P., Qasse, I.: Icontractml: a domain-specific language for modeling and deploying smart contracts onto multiple blockchain platforms. In: Proceedings of the 12th System Analysis and Modelling Conference, pp. 34–43 (2020)
14. Han, Q., Wang, L., Zhang, H., Shi, L., Wang, D.: Ethchecker: a context-guided fuzzing for smart contracts. J. Supercomput. 1–27 (2024)
15. He, X., Qin, B., Zhu, Y., Chen, X., Liu, Y.: Spesc: a specification language for smart contracts. In: 42nd IEEE Annual Computer Software and Applications Conference (COMPSAC), pp. 132–137 (2018)
16. Khan, S.N., Loukil, F., Ghedira-Guegan, C., Benkhelifa, E., Bani-Hani, A.: Blockchain smart contracts: applications, challenges, and future trends. Peer-to-peer Networking Appl. 2901–2925 (2021)
17. Liu, Y., Wang, C., Ma, Y.: Dl4sc: a novel deep learning-based vulnerability detection framework for smart contracts. Automat. Softw. Eng. 24–65 (2024)
18. Luu, L., Chu, D.H., Olickel, H., Saxena, P., Hobor, A.: Making smart contracts smarter. In: Conference on Computer and Communications Security, pp. 254—269 (2016)
19. Parahyba, F., et al.: On the need to use smart contracts in enterprise application integration. In: XXV Ibero-American Conference on Software Engineering, pp. 203–217 (2022)
20. Parr, T.J., Quong, R.W.: Antlr: A predicated-ll (k) parser generator. Softw. Pract. Exp. 789–810 (1995)

21. Rasti, A., et al.: Symboleo2sc: from legal contract specifications to smart contracts. In: Conference on Model Driven Engineering Languages and Systems, pp. 300–310 (2022)
22. Sharifi, S., Parvizimosaed, A., Amyot, D., Logrippo, L., Mylopoulos, J.: Symboleo: towards a specification language for legal contracts. In: International Requirements Engineering Conference (RE), pp. 364–369 (2020)
23. Soomro, T.R., Awan, A.H.: Challenges and future of enterprise application integration. Int. J. Comput. Appl. 42–45 (2012)
24. Teles-Borges, M., et al.: Jabuti ce: a tool for specifying smart contracts in the domain of enterprise application integration. In: Proceedings of the 12th International Conference on Model-Based Software and Systems Engineering - Volume 1: MODELSWARD, pp. 195–202 (2024)
25. Tikhomirov, S., Voskresenskaya, E., Ivanitskiy, I., Takhaviev, R., Marchenko, E., Alexandrov, Y.: Smartcheck: static analysis of ethereum smart contracts. In: International Workshop on Emerging Trends in Software Engineering for Blockchain, pp. 9—-16 (2018)
26. Wohrer, M., Zdun, U.: From domain-specific language to code: Smart contracts and the application of design patterns. IEEE Softw. 37–42 (2020)
27. Wu, G., Wang, H., Lai, X., Wang, M., He, D., Chan, S.: A comprehensive survey of smart contract security: state of the art and research directions. J. Netw. Comput. Appl. 103882 (2024)
28. Wöhrer, M., Zdun, U.: Domain specific language for smart contract development. In: IEEE International Conference on Blockchain and Cryptocurrency (ICBC), pp. 1–9 (2020)
29. Yang, R., et al.: Public and private blockchain in construction business process and information integration. Autom. Constr. 103276 (2020)

Deploying Machine Learning for Automatic Metamodel Instance Generation

El Abbassia Deba[1]([✉]) [ID], Karima Berramla[2] [ID], and Abou EL Hassene Benyamina[1] [ID]

[1] University Oran 1, Oran 31000, Algeria
abbassia.deba@univ-oran1.dz
[2] University of Science and Technology Mohamed Boudiaf, Oran, Algeria

Abstract. Model-Driven Engineering (MDE) is an approach to software engineering in which the model is considered a central concept. Its main objective is to generate all or part of an application's code from models. Up to now, MDE is an active research topic that makes intensive use of metamodels, models, and model transformations.

In this context, the generation of models is generally done manually to ensure conformity with their metamodels. Several works have been proposed to automate this process, but none of them can ensure complete automation without starting from a set of models already defined by the user or with a good verification of all conformity constraints.

Automated generation of metamodel instances significantly reduces the time and effort required compared to manual creation, and the generated models offer several advantages in MDE and domain-specific language development, such as increasing productivity and improving model consistency. In this work, our goal is not only to automatically generate the models and verify all conformity constraints, but also to explore most machine learning techniques to solve modeling problems in the MDE context.

Keywords: Model-driven engineering · Space modeling · Models · Metamodels · Metamodel instance · Automatic generation · Machine learning technique · Multilayer perceptron network

1 Introduction

Since the emergence of Software Engineering (SE), the development of computer systems has become increasingly important in various fields. Model-Driven Engineering (MDE) has been proposed as a response to problems raised in the context of software engineering, such as optimizing the cost and development time of computer systems by automating more or less the lifecycle process of the computer application.

MDE is an active research field that makes extensive use of the foundations of metamodeling and model transformations. Its main focus is on applying the notion of automation to all MDE-related activities.

In general, the practice of metamodelling is to specify metamodels that reflect the static aspects of the models. A metamodel operates at a higher level of abstraction. It defines the rules and constraints for creating models within a domain. It is concerned

F. José Domínguez Mayo et al. (Eds.): MODELSWARD 2024, CCIS 2547, pp. 247–267, 2026.
https://doi.org/10.1007/978-3-031-96841-9_13

with the structure and relationships of concepts within the domain. Metamodel evolution is also an important aspect of MDE [25]. Models are used to model a system and to develop, maintain, and evolve the software by performing model transformations. In a broad sense, the MDE paradigm proposes to unify all aspects of the life cycle process by using the notions of system, model, metamodel, and metametamodel [32].

Model transformation is also another central concept in model-driven engineering. We can define a model transformation as a program that automatically generates and modifies models [30]. Model transformation plays a fundamental role in software development and aims at various objectives such as automatic code generation, model translation, migration, and reverse engineering.

In a broad sense, the MDE paradigm proposes to merge all aspects of the lifecycle process using the concepts of model and transformation. In this context, the use of models needs to describe its metamodel by manipulating one of the metamodeling languages such as Ecore [12] and KM3 [27]. A metamodel is then an abstract description of the system to be modelled, where its instantiations represent models with which the transformation can be performed to have executable code at the end. To facilitate Model-Driven Development (MDD), the Object Management Group (OMG) proposed an approach called Model-Driven Architecture (MDA) [38] in November 2000. This approach provides new software development strategies in which the specifications are considered more important than the implementation by concentrating on the modelling steps.

Since the advent of MDE, there has been growing interest in the automatic generation of metamodel instances, known as models, where these previous models play a crucial role in various aspects of software development and modeling. Automated generation of metamodel instances significantly reduces the time and effort required compared to manual creation [21]. This efficiency gain allows developers to focus on more complex aspects of system design and implementation.

Metamodel instances play a crucial role in various aspects of software development and modeling, and they are used as a versatile tool in different domains with varied purposes. Automatic model or metamodel instance generation offers several advantages in MDE and domain-specific language development. Here are some of them: Increased productivity, improved consistency, enhanced scalability, easier maintenance and evolution, and support for various tasks. For increased productivity, automatic generation of metamodel instances significantly reduces the time and effort required for manual creation, allowing developers to focus on higher-level design tasks [31]. Concerning improved consistency, automated generation ensures that instances conform to the metamodel specifications, reducing errors and inconsistencies that may arise from manual creation [39]. Also, automatic generation facilitates the creation of large-scale models and instances, which is crucial for complex systems and domains [2]. As metamodels evolve, automatically generated instances can be more easily updated to reflect changes, maintaining consistency across the modeling ecosystem [35]. This leads to easier maintenance and evolution of models. Automatically generated models can serve as input for various model transformation and analysis techniques, enabling more comprehensive testing and validation of metamodels [28]. Also, they can be used for rapid prototyping and testing of domain-specific languages, allowing for faster iteration and refinement of language designs [42].

These diverse uses underline the crucial importance of metamodel instances in model-driven engineering as versatile tools for validation, testing, development, and teaching. The automatic generation of metamodel instances is a complex and multi-faceted research area within MDE [45]. Based on current literature and trends, several key research areas have emerged, such as constraint satisfaction and solving [29,44], search-based techniques [4,28,37], graph-based generation [1,19], domain-specific language (DSL) integration [42], and recently machine learning-based approaches [6,23,36].

Although the transformation during the development was semi-automated using a set of tools and languages, the modeling space creation was not completely automated until now. Therefore, this paper gives another solution that complements previous works [3,4,19,22] by (i) building the models from their metamodels automatically and (ii) exploiting the use of machine learning techniques without focusing on a set of initial models. Our objective is not only the automation of space modeling creation but also to simplify and facilitate the software development process by ensuring the transformation test [5,7] and the programming phases by examples such as [8].

The rest of this paper is structured as follows: Background, Motivation, and Problem statement are presented in Sect. 2. A detailed description and evaluation of the proposed approach are defined in Sect. 3 and 4. In Sect. 5 we present related work and finally Sect. 6 concludes this paper.

2   Background and Motivation

This section gives a general description of MDA technology and its modeling requirements.

2.1   Definitions and MDA Basic Concepts

The principle key of MDA is to rely on the UML standard in order to describe separately the models of the different development phases of an application in its life cycle. In the following, we provide some definitions and information about MDA technology, which will be used in the rest of this paper.

More specifically, MDA has three types of models [10] that are used in software development. In the following, we define each one and the relationship between them (see Fig. 1):

Definition 1 (Computation Independent Model (CIM). *A CIM describes exactly what the system is supposed to do and masks all technical details related to system implementation.*

Definition 2 (Platform Independent Model (PIM). *A PIM specifies system views independently from the platform, where it can be linked to several platforms at the PSM level.*

Definition 3 (Platform Specific Model (PSM)). *A PSM refines the PIM with the technical details needed to describe how the system can utilize a specific platform. A PIM can be translated to one or more PSMs, which are for a specific implementation technology.*

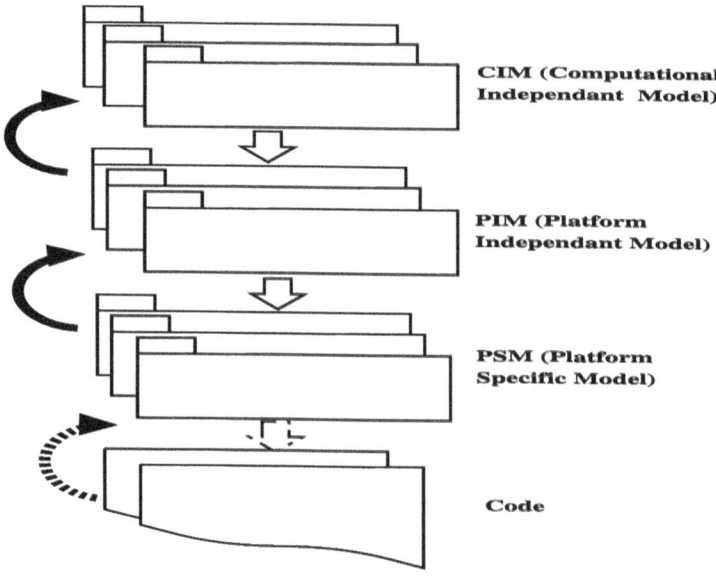

Fig. 1. An overview of MDA approach (Adapted from [10]).

Figure 1 gives an overview of the MDA approach. In this context, building a new application starts with the specification of one or more requirements model (CIM). Then, it continues with the definition of analysis and abstract-design models (PIM). These models must be partially created from the CIMs once traceability relations are established. We have seen that PIM models are perennial models that do not contain any information about the execution platforms. To create an application, it is necessary to define specific models of the execution platforms (PSMs). These models are obtained through a transformation of PIM(s) by adding technical information about the execution platforms. Their main function is to simplify code generation, which is considered as a translation into a textual formalism [10].

> **Finding 1:** Through the separation between the dependent models on the platform and the abstract independent models of application, MDA approach offers the following objectives: portability, reusability, and interoperability.

Figure 2 borrowed from [22] presents a general description of space modeling and its limits. This space has two model types: the first one describes the well-formed models, and the second defines the ill-formed models (see Fig. 2). When we generate the

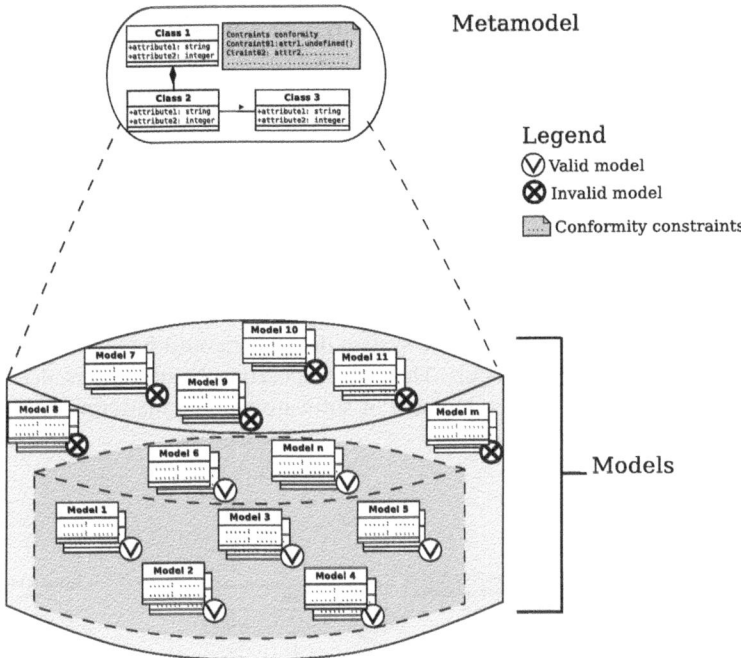

Fig. 2. Modeling space and its limit (Adapted from [22]).

models from their metamodels, we receive one of these two types: if the model is well instantiated and it verifies the defined constraints, we obtain a well-formed model; otherwise, we receive an ill-formed model. These results depend on the instantiation process, which is done manually or automatically. In the following, we present modeling requirements to provide models automatically.

2.2 Modeling Requirements

In the following, we define the modeling requirements as questions to provide a simple way of comprehension for readers. Also, we present these requirements schematically in Fig. 3.

RQ1: How can we generate the models from their metamodels automatically or semi-automatically?

In the MDE field, the generation of models from their metamodels and their conformity verification are done manually. This process requires the efforts and time of the system developers so as not to make mistakes. Thus, the automation of this process is considered the challenge of several studies, such as [22]. The goal of this paper is to solve this problem in a different way compared with the previous work [3,4,20].

RQ2: Can we verify the conformity of models automatically or semi-automatically?

In general, the conformity verification of models to their metamodels is done semi-automatically by defining the constraints in OCL language. At this time, no proposed approach automates the model creation and the conformity verification in parallel to facilitate the development in MDE context.

RQ3: Can we find a technique to simplify the system modeling process?

Recent software development, such as MDA, revolves around the use of models to separate the concerns between application logic and implementation techniques in order to increase productivity. Therefore, the system developers must have solid experience in modeling by manipulating models. Then, no proposed technique is considered as the best solution to simplify the development of software without mastering one or more tools or languages.

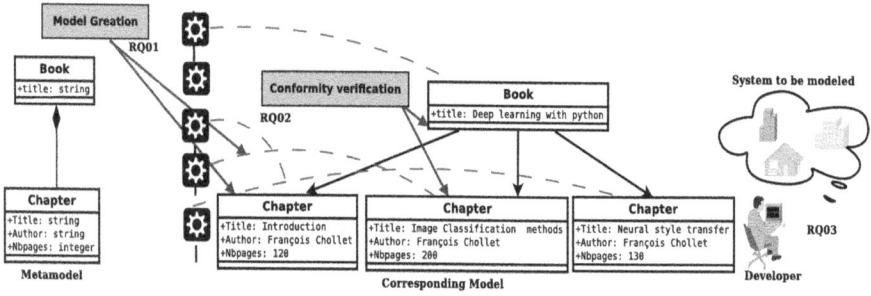

Fig. 3. Modeling requirements.

This question set describes the crucial challenges in the modeling process with which software development productivity is increasing. In the following section, we discuss our proposed approach to answering the previous questions in order to solve the principal problems of modeling steps in the MDE context.

3   Proposed Approach

Currently, machine learning is considered a solution for any problem in different areas such as signal, image, speech, natural language processing, Internet of Things and software development, since it simplifies the programming phase. Consequently, we propose to exploit its advantages in the context of MDE precisely in the modelling step.

Figure 4 shows the basic idea of our proposed approach, where machine learning was used to automatically generate models from their metamodels. Although this idea may seem very difficult, breaking down the complex problem into simple sub-problems reduces its complexity. We have divided this approach into three main steps: the first describes the data preparation, the second deals with the definition of our "Multilayer Perceptron Network" (MLP) architecture and its training functions, and the third step provides a detailed description of model generation from the MLP output. Note that each step is also divided into two sub-steps. The following subsections describe the approach in detail.

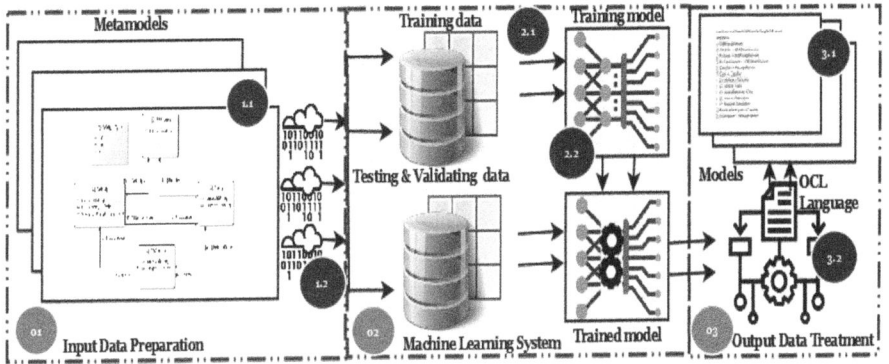

Fig. 4. Proposed approach Steps.

3.1 Input Data Preparation

In this subsection, we describe our proposed data preparation process, which defines all the example information used in our machine learning system. This process is divided into two sub-steps, which are explained below.

A. Segment Extraction Process. This process is considered the heart of our approach, as it performs the extraction of the dataset from which the metamodel instances are created. In this step, we generate all the segments from each metamodel based on the following basic definition to obtain the well models.

Definition 4 (Segment). *In MDE modeling context, A segment is a set of selected meta-model elements that will be used in the following to create models. It is defined as one relationship with its target class or a root class.*

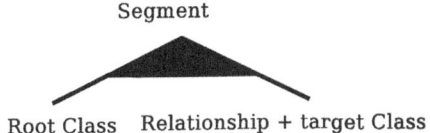

Fig. 5. Segment Basic Information.

According to the Definition 4 and the Fig. 5, we divide the metamodel into a set of segments that will later be used to define the semantics of the metamodel in order to instantiate it.

B. Digital Information Extraction Process. Once all the segments are extracted, we test a set of properties for each segment in order to compute digital information about the metamodel in use.

Table 1 describes these properties, which will be used to compute the segment semantics to generate models in the next steps.

Table 1. Description of properties.

Property Number	Property title
Property "1"	Root-class property.
Property "2"	Heritage property.
Property "3"	Composition property.
Property "4"	Association property.
Property "5"	Class-association property.
Property "6"	1..1 Cardinality.
Property "7"	0..n Cardinality.
Property "8"	1..n Cardinality.

Definition 5 (Comparison Predicate). *A comparison predicate is used to define the semantics of each segment as digital information. If one of the properties is verified, this predicate becomes true; otherwise, it becomes false.*

Based on the Definition 5, we get the results of the Table 2, where true values are translated to one and false values to zero. The table shows the extracted information from the family metamodel (Fig. 6) as an example of the data that will be used as input for the training, testing, and validation steps.

Table 2. Extracted information from Family metamodel.

	Property-1	Property-2	Property-3	Property-4	Property-5	Property-6	Property-7	Property-8
S1	1	0	0	0	0	0	0	0
S2	0	0	1	0	0	1	0	0
S3	0	0	1	0	0	1	0	0
S4	0	0	1	0	0	0	1	0
S5	0	0	1	0	0	0	1	0

Figure 6 shows the basic structure of each segment and the digitally extracted information. In this case, we consider a segment as one or two metamodel elements, and each element can be either a root class or a relationship and its target class (see Fig. 5 exactly right). From these segments and a set of basic properties defined

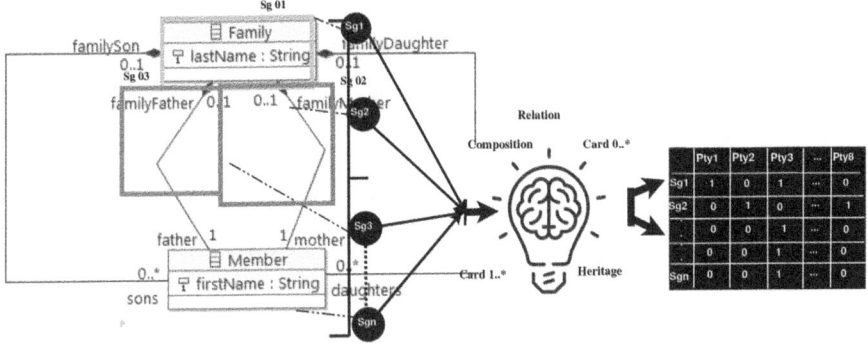

Fig. 6. Segment Structure and Extracted information.

in the previous table, we compute the digital metamodel information (see Fig. 6 exactly left).

For example, the root class in Fig. 6 is defined as the segment number "**1**" and its digital information is shown in the first column of the table defined in the same figure. The binary information reflects the properties of each segment. In our case, Fig. 6 describes the family metamodel, which contains a father, a mother, zero or more sons, and zero or more daughters. Each of them has a first name. The segment number "**1**" is defined by the root class **Family**. The segment number "**2**" is represented by the class **Member** and the relationship **Mother**. The same principle is applied to other elements to extract the rest of the segments. Once this process is done, the comparison of extracted segments with a set of properties can be computed by inserting one if the segment verifies the property and zero otherwise.

3.2 Machine Learning System

The Artificial Neural Network (ANN) is one of the most popular machine learning systems created to solve different problems in different fields. Its description was inspired by neural circuits by integrating mathematical implementations, where its first perceptron was made by the psychologist Frank Rosenblatt in the 1957 s.

A. Architecture. A basic neuron model with R inputs is described in Fig. 7, where each input model is weighted with an appropriate w. The sum of the weighted inputs and the bias defines the transfer function input f. The neuron model can use any transfer function f to compute its output. In our case we have height values that form the R^1 and only two output values.

Our proposed system is based on multilayer networks, where these networks generally use the tan-sigmoid transfer function, which is alternatively used for output computation. There is another transfer function called purelin, which is shown below. These two

---

[1] These values were computed from comparison predicates of each model segment.

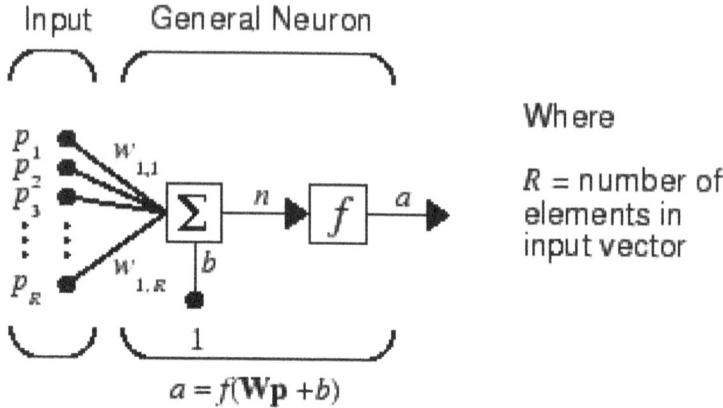

Fig. 7. Neuron Model Architecture from [41].

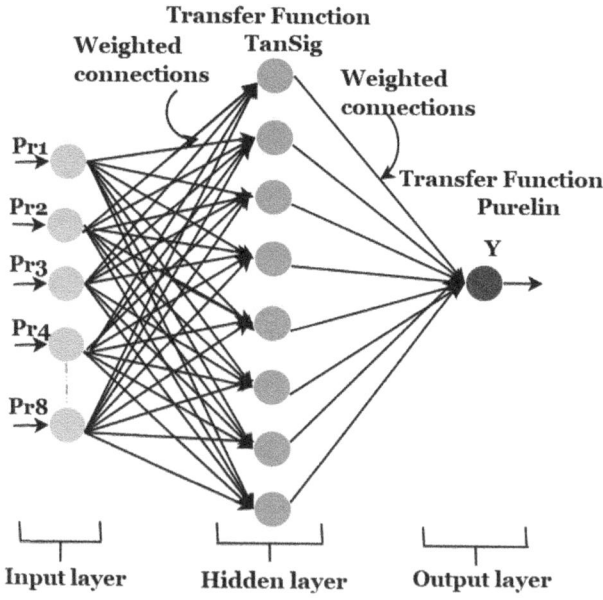

Fig. 8. Our MLP architecture (Adapted from [41]).

transfer functions, shown in Fig. 8, are the most commonly used transfer functions for multilayer networks.

Figure 8 shows our MLP architecture, where the input data are Pr_i and i was varied from 1 to 8 according to the used properties. These input data are defined by the binary values of each segment, while the output data $\hat{y}$ gives binary information about whether each input segment will be instantiated or not.

B. Training Functions. To demonstrate how training is applied, consider the simplest optimization algorithm: gradient descent. It adjusts the weights and biases of the network in the dimension where the performance function decreases fastest. An iteration of this training algorithm can be written as follows:

$$X_k + 1 = X_k - \alpha_k g_k. \tag{1}$$

In Eq. 1, X_k is a vector(or matrix) of current weights and biases, g_k is the current gradient and α_k is the rate of gain. This equation is repeated until the network converges. In our case, we use the following learning algorithms: Scaled Conjugate Gradient, Levenberg-Marquardt(trainlm) and Bayesian Regularization(trainbr) that are available in the Deep Learning Toolbox [41]. The speediest learning function is typically trainlm, and this is the default learning function feedforward neural network. As well, trainlm performs well on feature fitting problems rather than pattern recognition problems. For training big networks and pattern recognition networks, we choose trainscg [41].

3.3 Output Data Treatment

This subsection focuses on creating models from MLP output using the Algorithm 1.

A. Model Instantiating. This step is concerned with creating models from the MLP output. The following algorithm is used.

Algorithm 1. From MLP outputs To models.

Require: MLP Output;
Ensure: Creation of Models;
    Compute number of MLP outputs $N = size(Classes)$;
    Create set $C1 = outputs\ of\ Class1$;
    Create set $C2 = outputs\ of\ Class2$;
    for $i = 1\ to\ N$ **do**
        while $Ci <> \emptyset$ **do**
            $C = dequeue(Ci)$;
            Let $X = Corresponding\ Segment(C)$;
            Compute number of Segments $K = size(X)$;
            for $J = 1\ to\ K$ **do**
                Execute From Metamodel & Segment To instantiated_Segment (Xj);
                if AttrCont(Xj) $<> \emptyset$ **then**
                    Execute Verify_contraint(AttrCont(Xj));
                end if
            end for
        end while
    end for

Input Data. Input data of Algorithm 1 is our neural network outputs that describe if the segment will be instantiated or not. In our case, we have two classes (In Algorithm 1, N equals two); the first one regroups the segments that will be instantiated, and the second class presents the segments that will not be instantiated.

Output Data. The output of the Algorithm 1 is models. From this Algorithm 1 we create models and check some OCL constraints [15] in order to have well-formed models. This creation process is also based on the use of ***instantiating data***, which aims to increase the rate of well-formed model creation. For example, if we have the family metamodel as input data in this case, we instantiate the name of the person using the stored information from ***instantiating data***.

Algorithm 2 explains the process of segment instantiation, which extracts from the metamodel and segments a part of the model computed according to the metamodel structure. First, we find the segment position and its elements, and then we instantiate these elements using instantiation data. Then we run the Algorithm 3 to check the conformity constraints.

Algorithm 2. From Metamodel & Segment To Instantiated Segment.

Require: Metamodel;
Require: Segment;
Ensure: Instantiated Segment;
  1: Compute number of segment elements $N = size(Elt - Segment)$;
  2: **for** $i = 1$ *to* N **do**
  3:     Xi= Elt-Segment_i;
  4:     **while** Xi not instantiated **do**
  5:         Find its position in its metamodel.
  6:         create its definition in the output model by using Instantiating Data;
  7:         Verify its indexation in its metamodel;
  8:     **end while**
  9: **end for**

B. Constraint Verification. The following Algorithm 3 expresses the verification of conformity constraints by translating OCL constraints into instructions written in Java language. The conformity verification algorithm requires many steps, starting with reading and extracting OCL constraints, finding their elements, and ending with translating them into a programming language.

Algorithm 3. Conformity constraint Verification.

Require: Instantiated Segment;
Ensure: Well-Instantiated Segment;
  1: Compute number of segment elements $N = size(Elt - Segment)$;
  2: **for** $i = 1$ *to* N **do**
  3:     Xi= Elt-Segment_i;
  4:     **while** Xi not Verified **do**
  5:         Find its constraints in its metamodel.
  6:         Verify its constraints defintion in its Instantiated Elt-Segment;
  7:     **end while**
  8: **end for**

Code Implementation: We use the Java language to implement our approach. The meta-models are defined by Ecore language and their models are encoded in XML Metadata Interchange (XMI) using Eclipse Modeling Framework (EMF). In this case, we manipulate Matlab to use and evaluate the MLP classifier.

4 Experimentation and Evaluation

This section presents a preliminary discussion of the results of our proposed approach in order to evaluate it in relation to other work.

4.1 Results and Interpretation

Now we discuss the basic information for each training, testing and validation example mentioned in the Table 3.

Table 3. Basic Information about Training, Testing & Validating Data.

$Metamodel$	$N_{Classes}$	$N_{Segments}$	$Metamodel$	$N_{Classes}$	$N_{Segments}$
Book [17]	02	02	Family [18]	02	05
UML-CD	07	14	RS	05	05
Publication [17]	01	01	RS-Simp [13]	03	03
Person [18]	03	02	ERShema [13]	05	07
Petri-net [9]	03	05	Sate-machine [9]	13	24

These information descriptions associate to an overview of the class and the segment numbers with which the example complexity is given. For instance, the metamodel Family has two classes and fives segments that reflect its simplicity.

To evaluate the computed outputs of our system, we're interested in using the Mean Square Error defined below.

Definition 6 (Mean Square Error (MSE)). *Is a key metric for evaluating the performance of predictive models. It evaluates the mean square difference between predicted and target values in a dataset. The main objective of the MSE is to evaluate the quality of a model's predictions by carefully studying the model's alignment with the ground truth. This metric is computed by the following formula [34]:*

$$MSE = \frac{1}{D} \sum_{i=1}^{D} (y_i - y_i')^2 \qquad (2)$$

Where y_i and y_i' are observed and predicted values and D is the number of the used dataset. In general, where the MSE is lower, this means that model predictions are more closely aligned with actual values, which explains the better global performance.

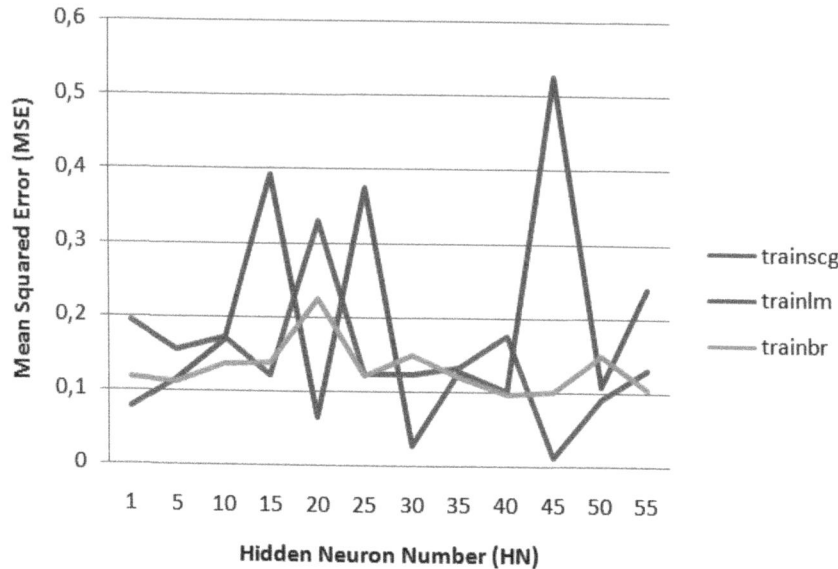

Fig. 9. MSE values of the three training functions.

Figure 9 shows the MSE of training, validation, and testing data for our system with the following training algorithms: Scaled Conjugate Gradient, Levenberg-Marquardt, and Bayesian Regularization. From this result, we conclude that the Levenberg-Marquardt training function gives the best obtained value of MSE is 0.0263 with the forty-five hidden neurons and after three epochs. As illustrated in Fig. 9, the results of the other two training functions provide the best values in their entirety, but not like the previous algorithm.

Now, we discuss on the mean-square error of the training, validation, and testing data for Scaled Conjugate Gradient function. Figure 10 illustrates that the training MSE decreases and reaches its best value after four epochs, but can stagnate over the entire training dataset after also four epochs.

In the following, we presents the MSE of the training Levenberg-Marquardt function. Figure 11 shows this MSE, where it reaches its best value after one thousand epochs, but can stagnate over the entire training dataset after one hundred epochs.

Next, we discuss the MSE of the training Levenberg-Marquardt function, where the Fig. 12 shows its results, where it reaches its best value after four epochs, but can stagnate over the entire training dataset after five epochs.

4.2   Threads to Validity

This paper describes a generic approach where the models are generated using only metamodels, a machine learning system, and other proposed algorithms. This approach gives globally high quality results without creating an initiative set of models, which generally requires a lot of time to get good knowledge about the system to be modeled.

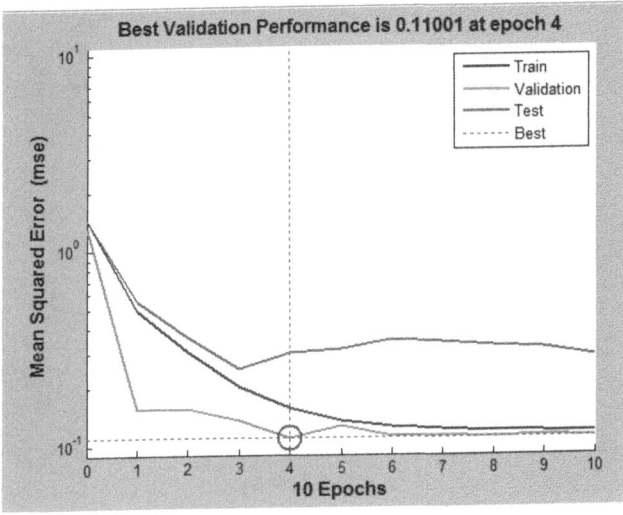

Fig. 10. The Best Performance of Training-scg Function.

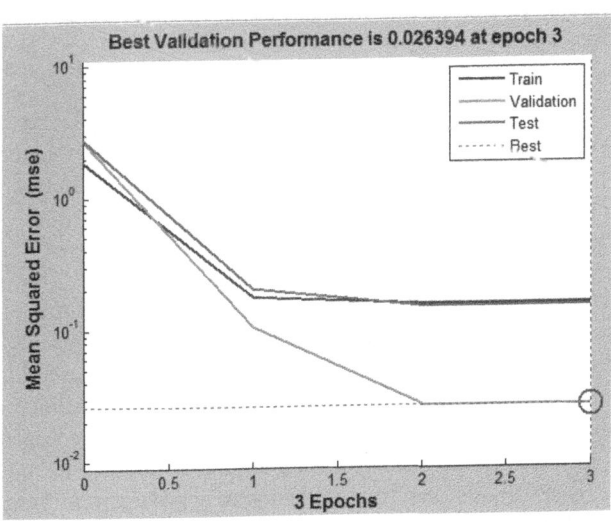

Fig. 11. The Best Performance of Training-lm Function.

In contrast to other solutions such as [3,4,20,22], our paper gives a new idea to automate the modeling steps by using the machine learning technique called "multi-layer perceptron neural networks" and answering *RQ1*, *RQ2*, and *RQ3* mentioned in the Sect. 2. For example, *RQ1* and *RQ3* are solved by using the "MLP" technique and our proposed Algorithm 1, which automatically generates the models without using an initial set of models, and also by checking some levels of conformity without the intervention of the modellers, where we also answer *RQ2*.

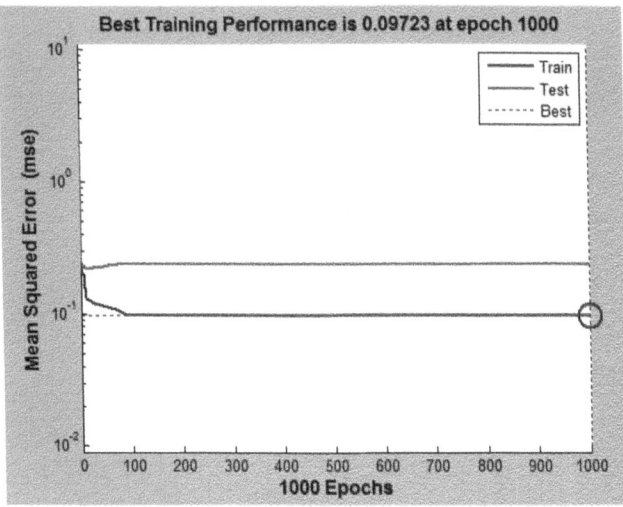

Fig. 12. The Best Performance of Training-br Function.

5   Related Work

The automatic generation of metamodel instances is a complex and multifaceted research area within MDE. Several studies have focused on the problem of automatic generation of metamodel instances. Some of them are described below, depending on the mechanism used. Table 4 summarizes some of the mentioned works by presenting some characteristics for each one.

1) Optimization Techniques. The most important approaches for modeling space are based on metaheuristic techniques. For instance, this paper [22] presents a metaheuristic approach for automatic generation of more precise models using Simulated Annealing (SA) in conformity with a set of criteria defined in [20]. Another work [4] processes this problem using another heuristic method called Genetic Algorithm (GA) to compute from an initial model set other well-structured models in order to increase modeling space. Batot [3] has also proposed another approach to solving the modeling space problem that allows using a non-dominated genetic algorithm (NSGA-II) using a metamodel and a set of models. Kessentini et al. [28] apply genetic algorithms to model transformation testing, which includes the generation of test models. They show how evolutionary algorithms can be used to generate diverse and relevant model instances for testing purposes. The focus is primarily on testing rather than general-purpose instance generation.

2) Graph Grammar. Graph grammars offer a natural way to describe the derivation process and, therefore, have an advantage for generating metamodel instances.

Karsten et al. [19] propose to use graph grammar for creating model instances of metamodels in an automatic way without using an initial set of models. This approach requires good-basic knowledge of graph grammar methodology, which takes a lot of time and effort.

Hoffmann & Minas [24] use graph grammars called adaptive star grammars. Their approach introduces a set of adaptive star grammar rules is introduced to deal with relationships defined in the metamodel, such as unique, non-unique, and composition associations. However, OCL constraints defined over the class diagram cannot be handled by this approach.

3) Formal Methods. In this context, the use of formal methods [16] is not supported due to their difficulties; nevertheless, there are only some proposed works [26]. One of the of the best-known of them is [26], which focused on instance generation by using Alloy [40]. This instance generation is based on the translation of a class diagram to an Alloy representation. After that, SAT solvers are used to create their instances by enumerating them.

Cabot et al. [14] propose a procedure that can transform a UML class diagram with OCL constraints into a Constraint Satisfaction Problem (CSP) according to a set of rules. If the CSP has a solution (instance), the user can conclude that a model satisfies the properties.

4) Machine Learning Methods. This emerging area explores the use of various machine learning techniques to learn patterns from existing model repositories and generate new, plausible instances. Recent advancements in machine learning have led to its application in metamodel instance generation. Techniques such as deep learning and generative adversarial networks (GANs) can be trained on existing model repositories to learn patterns and generate new, plausible instances [23,36]. This approach is particularly promising for domains with large, complex metamodels where manual specification of generation rules is challenging.

In [6], the authors propose an approach to automate the generation of models, focusing only on their metamodels, using the "Multilayer Perceptron Network" to obtain good and verified models in order to reduce the cost and time of software development.

5) Others. More generally, there are also other generic approaches that aim to specify or verify modeling space automatically, either to increase the size of test data for model transformations with well-structured models or even to be used as input data for example-based model transformation. This paper [20] describes one of the most genetic approaches by proposing a set of rules used to evaluate the correctness of input models.

In the area of model transformation testing, some techniques have been developed for the automatic generation of model instances. Brottier et al. [11] propose an algorithm to automatically generate a set of model instances for testing a model transformation.

Mougenot et al. [33] use an approach that is based on the Boltzmann method to generate metamodel instances. In their approach, a metamodel is first transformed into a Boltzmann tree specification, and the final instances are derived from the generated trees.

Table 4. Overview of automatic model generation approaches.

Paper	Input Elements	Prog.Language	Used Method	Output Elements
[3]	MM & Models	Java	NSGA-II	Models
[22]	MM & Models	Java	SA[a]	Models
[19]	Meta-Model	AGG	Graph Grammars	Models
[24]	UML-CD	–	Graph Grammars	Graph instances
[26]	Meta-Model	Alloy	SAT Solvers	Models
[36]	MM & Model	Python	NetGAN	Models
[6]	MM[b] & BiTable[c]	Java & Matlab	MLP & Algo	Models
[43]	MM & STM[d]	–	Genetic Algorithm	Models
[11]	Metamodel	–	Algorithm	Test models
[33]	Metamodel	Java	Boltzmann method	Models as Trees

[a] Simulated-Annealing.
[b] Meta-Model.
[c] Binary information table was defined in Sect. 3.
[d] Structural metrics.

The analysis conducted by [45] on metamodel instance generation has identified a knowledge gap between metamodel instance generation and metamodeling techniques in that there is no direct way to generate metamodel instances from a metamodel, as all techniques require preprocessing or additional knowledge of an intermediate language to achieve instance generation.

6   Conclusion

In MDE, one of the major challenges faced by developers is how to simplify or facilitate the model generation process in the software development system. In the last few years, several studies have been proposed to solve the current situation, but in general, they generate models in a random way or without verifying all conformity constraints. In this work, we propose an approach to automate the generation of models, focusing only on their metamodels by using "Multilayer Perceptron Network" to obtain good and verified models in order to reduce the cost and time of software development.

Our work has been conducted to address the challenge of model generation within the MDE research field by leveraging recent advances in machine learning, and we have explored a novel approach for inferring metamodel instances based on neural networks and metamodels. Our results show the potential of this approach, which addresses a very important issue in the MDE context.

By using the Multilayer Perceptron Network, the research demonstrates the potential of deep learning techniques in model generation and contributes to the advancement of automatic model generation methods in MDE.

In this study, we propose as a perspective work to increase efforts to solve the verification of OCL complex constraints using machine learning techniques. In addition, we propose to apply formal methods to verify all projects, step by step, in metamodel instantiation to eliminate errors.

References

1. Arendt, T., Biermann, E., Jurack, S., Krause, C., Taentzer, G.: Henshin: advanced concepts and tools for in-place EMF model transformations. In: Petriu, D.C., Rouquette, N., Haugen, Ø. (eds.) MODELS 2010. LNCS, vol. 6394, pp. 121–135. Springer, Heidelberg (2010). https://doi.org/10.1007/978-3-642-16145-2_9
2. Babur, Ö., Cleophas, L., van den Brand, M.: Hierarchical clustering of metamodels for comparative analysis and visualization. In: European Conference on Modelling Foundations and Applications, pp. 3–18. Springer (2016)
3. Batot, E.: Generating examples for knowledge abstraction in MDE: a multi-objective framework. In: SRC@ MoDELS, pp. 1–6 (2015)
4. Ben Fadhel, A., Kessentini, M., Langer, P., Wimmer, M.: Search-based detection of high-level model changes. In: 2012 28th IEEE International Conference on Software Maintenance (ICSM), pp. 212–221. IEEE (2012)
5. Berramla, K., Deba, E.A., Benhamamouch, D.: Model transformation generation a survey of the state-of-the-art. In: 2016 International Conference on Information Technology for Organizations Development (IT4OD), pp. 1- 6. IEEE (2016)
6. Berramla, K., Deba, E.A., Benyamina, A.E.H.: Automatic generation of models from their metamodels using multilayer perceptron network. In: Mayo, F.J.D., Pires, L.F., Seidewitz, E. (eds.) Proceedings of the 12th International Conference on Model-Based Software and Systems Engineering, MODELSWARD 2024, Rome, Italy, 21-23 February 2024, pp. 272–279. SCITEPRESS (2024)
7. Berramla, K., Deba, E.A., Benyamina, A., Touam, R., Brahimi, Y., Benhamamouch, D.: Formal concept analysis for specification of model transformations. In: 2017 First International Conference on Embedded & Distributed Systems (EDiS), pp. 1–6. IEEE (2017)
8. Berramla, K., Deba, E.A., Jiechen, W., Sahraoui, H.A., Benyamina, A.E.H.: Model transformation by example with statistical machine translation. In: MODELSWARD, pp. 76–83 (2020)
9. Berramla, K., Deba, E.A., Senouci, M.: Formal validation of model transformation with coq proof assistant. In: New Technologies of Information and Communication (NTIC), 2015 First International Conference on, pp. 1–6. IEEE (2015)
10. Blanc, X., Salvatori, O.: MDA en action: Ingénierie logicielle guidée par les modèles. Editions Eyrolles (2011)
11. Brottier, E., Fleurey, F., Steel, J., Baudry, B., Le Traon, Y.: Metamodel-based test generation for model transformations: an algorithm and a tool. In: 2006 17th International Symposium on Software Reliability Engineering, pp. 85–94. IEEE (2006)
12. Budinsky, F., Brodsky, S.A., Merks, E.: Eclipse Modeling Framework. Pearson Education (2003)
13. Büttner, F., Cabot, J., Gogolla, M.: On validation of atl transformation rules by transformation models. In: Proceedings of the 8th International Workshop on Model-Driven Engineering, Verification and Validation, p. 9. ACM (2011)
14. Cabot, J., Claris, R., Riera, D., et al.: Verification of UML/OCL class diagrams using constraint programming. In: 2008 IEEE International Conference on Software Testing Verification and Validation Workshop, pp. 73–80. IEEE (2008)

15. Cabot, J., Gogolla, M.: Object constraint language (OCL): a definitive guide. In: International School on Formal Methods for the Design of Computer, Communication and Software Systems, pp. 58–90. Springer (2012)
16. Clarke, E.M., Wing, J.M.: Formal methods: state of the art and future directions. ACM Computi. Surv. (CSUR) **28**(4), 626–643 (1996)
17. Eclipse: ATL use case book to publication. https://www.eclipse.org/atl/atlTransformations/Book2Publication/ExampleBook2Publication[v00.02].pdf (2005)
18. Eclipse: ATL use case families to persons. https://www.eclipse.org/atl/documentation/basicExamples_Patterns/ (2007)
19. Ehrig, K., Küster, J.M., Taentzer, G.: Generating instance models from meta-models. Softw. Syst. Model. **8**(4), 479–500 (2009)
20. Fleurey, F., Baudry, B., Muller, P.A., Le Traon, Y.: Qualifying input test data for model transformations. Softw. Syst. Model. **8**(2), 185–203 (2009)
21. Gogolla, M., Büttner, F., Cabot, J.: Initiating a benchmark for UML and OCL analysis tools. In: International Conference on Tests and Proofs, pp. 115–132. Springer (2013)
22. Gómez, J.J.C., Baudry, B., Sahraoui, H.: Searching the boundaries of a modeling space to test metamodels. In: 2012 IEEE Fifth International Conference on Software Testing, Verification and Validation, pp. 131–140. IEEE (2012)
23. Hartmann, T., Moawad, A., Fouquet, F., Le Traon, Y.: The next evolution of MDE: a seamless integration of machine learning into domain modeling. Softw. Syst. Model. **18**, 1285–1304 (2019)
24. Hoffmann, B., Minas, M.: Generating instance graphs from class diagrams with adaptive star grammars. GCM **2010**, 49 (2010)
25. Iovino, L., Pierantonio, A., Malavolta, I.: On the impact significance of metamodel evolution in MDE. J. Object Technol. **11**(3), 1–3 (2012)
26. Jackson, D.: Alloy: a lightweight object modelling notation. ACM Trans. Softw. Eng. Method. (TOSEM) **11**(2), 256–290 (2002)
27. Jouault, F., Bézivin, J.: KM3: A DSL for metamodel specification. In: Gorrieri, R., Wehrheim, H. (eds.) FMOODS 2006. LNCS, vol. 4037, pp. 171–185. Springer, Heidelberg (2006). https://doi.org/10.1007/11768869_14
28. Kessentini, M., Sahraoui, H., Boukadoum, M.: Example-based model-transformation testing. Autom. Softw. Eng. **18**, 199–224 (2011)
29. Kleiner, M., Del Fabro, M.D., Albert, P.: Model search: formalizing and automating constraint solving in MDE platforms. In: European Conference on Modelling Foundations and Applications, pp. 173–188. Springer (2010)
30. Kleppe, A.G., Warmer, J., Warmer, J.B., Bast, W.: MDA Explained: the Model Driven Architecture: Practice and Promise. Addison-Wesley Professional (2003)
31. Kolovos, D.S., et al.: A research roadmap towards achieving scalability in model driven engineering. In: Proceedings of the Workshop on Scalability in Model Driven Engineering, pp. 1–10 (2013)
32. Marcos, D.D.F., Jean, B., Frédéric, J., Erwan, B., Guillaume, G.: AMW: a generic model weaver. In: Proceedings of the 1eres Journées sur l'Ingénierie Dirigée par les Modèles, vol. 200 (2005)
33. Mougenot, A., Darrasse, A., Blanc, X., Soria, M.: Uniform random generation of huge metamodel instances. In: European Conference on Model Driven Architecture-Foundations and Applications, pp. 130–145. Springer (2009)
34. Murphy, A.H.: Skill scores based on the mean square error and their relationships to the correlation coefficient. Mon. Weather Rev. **116**(12), 2417–2424 (1988)
35. Paige, R.F., Matragkas, N., Rose, L.M.: Evolving models in model-driven engineering: state-of-the-art and future challenges. J. Syst. Softw. **111**, 272–280 (2016)

36. Rahimi, A., Tisi, M., Rahimi, S.K., Berardinelli, L.: Towards generating structurally realistic models by generative adversarial networks. In: 2023 ACM/IEEE International Conference on Model Driven Engineering Languages and Systems Companion (MODELS-C), pp. 597–604. IEEE (2023)
37. Sen, S., Baudry, B., Mottu, J.M.: Automatic model generation strategies for model transformation testing. In: International Conference on Theory and Practice of Model Transformations, pp. 148–164. Springer (2009)
38. Soley, R., et al.: Model driven architecture. OMG White Paper **308**(308), 5 (2000)
39. Stephan, M., Cordy, J.R.: A survey of model comparison approaches and applications. In: International Conference on Model-Driven Engineering and Software Development, vol. 2, pp. 265–277. SciTePress (2013)
40. The alloy analyzer-3.0 beta: http://alloy.mit.edu/index.php (2005)
41. The MathWorks, I.: Multilayer shallow neural network architecture (2024), https://www.mathworks.com/help/deeplearning/ug/multilayer-neural-network-architecture.html Accessed June 2024
42. Voelter, M., et al.: DSL engineering-designing, implementing and using domain-specific languages. M Volter/DSLBook. org (2013)
43. Wang, W., Kessentini, M., Jiang, W.: Test cases generation for model transformations from structural information. MDEBE@ MoDELS **1104**, 42–51 (2013)
44. Wu, H.: Generating metamodel instances satisfying coverage criteria via SMT solving. In: 2016 4th International Conference on Model-Driven Engineering and Software Development (MODELSWARD), pp. 40–51. IEEE (2016)
45. Wu, H., Monahan, R., Power, J.F.: Metamodel instance generation: a systematic literature review. arXiv (2012)

Author Index

A

Asal, Egehan   107

B

Bala, Saimir   23
Bastarrica, María Cecilia   88
Bedini, Francesco   213
Benyamina, Abou EL Hassene   247
Berramla, Karima   247
Bocanegra, Jose   229
Brulin, Sebastian   198

C

Carvalho, Sergio T.   173
Ceravola, Antonello   198

D

Deba, El Abbassia   247
Dornelles, Eldair F.   229

F

Fatemi, Bahareh   3
Frantz, Rafael Z.   229

G

González, Daniel   88

H

Harel, David   43

J

Joublin, Frank   198
Jungebloud, Tino   213

K

Katz, Guy   43
Kolahdouz Rahimi, Shekoufeh   132
Kose, Mehmet Alp   107

L

Lamo, Yngve   3
Lano, Kevin   132
Lin, Chenghua   132
Liu, Yiqi   132

M

Marron, Assaf   43
Maschotta, Ralph   213
McKeever, Steve   151
Mendling, Jan   23
Molina-Jimenez, Carlos   229

N

Nguyen, Thanh   23

O

Olhofer, Markus   198
Opdahl, Andreas L.   3
Ozkaya, Mert   107

R

Rabbi, Fazle   3
Ramsin, Raman   69
Reina-Quintero, Antonia M.   229
Roos-Frantz, Fabricia   229

S

Sadik, Ahmed R.   198
Sawicki, Sandro   229
Silvestre, Luis   88
Szekely, Smadar   43

© The Editor(s) (if applicable) and The Author(s), under exclusive license
to Springer Nature Switzerland AG 2026
F. José Domínguez Mayo et al. (Eds.): MODELSWARD 2024, CCIS 2547, pp. 269–270, 2026.
https://doi.org/10.1007/978-3-031-96841-9

T
Teles-Borges, Mailson   229

U
Umar, Muhammad Aminu   132

V
Vahdati, Adel   69
Vieira, Marcos Alves   173

W
Wallberg, Andrés   88

Y
Yassipour Tehrani, Sobhan   132

Z
Zimmermann, Armin   213

The manufacturer's authorised representative in the EU is Springer
Nature Customer Service Centre GmbH, Europaplatz 3, 69115 Heidelberg,
Germany. If you have any concerns regarding our products, please
contact ProductSafety@springernature.com

Printed and bound by CPI Group (UK) Ltd, Croydon, CR0 4YY
28/04/2026
02098524-0003